"In no uncertain terms, *Crossroads* opens our eyes to our responsibility to the adolescents who are now growing up without sacred rituals and hence without knowledge of spiritual roots in their culture. Many of the writers have first-hand experience and first-rate ideas of how to transform this cultural crisis. *Crossroads* also challenges us to integrate our own inner adolescent. Piercing insight with realistic hope!"

MARION WOODMAN
Jungian analyst and author of *The Ravaged Bridegroom*

"This visionary work provides basic insight into the social and psychological need for rites of passage and establishes a new dynamic frame for the re-interpretation of the full range of issues facing the American body politic regarding adolescence. I hope that *Crossroads* will indeed achieve its goals of re-introducing rites of passage as a progressive crucible for change."

BUD MAHONEY
Museum of New Zealand, Te Papa Tanperewa
Formerly Counsel to Asst. Speaker Edward Griffith
New York State Assembly, Albany

"*Crossroads* guides us in applying the wisdom of ancient cultures and the enduring patterns of human experience to the most pressing dilemmas of modern youth and arenas of social turmoil. *Crossroads* offers a pioneering vision that restores rites of passage to its essential role in contemporary psychological and social healing. It simultaneously serves as an indispensable handbook for instituting such transformational programs to all the necessary recipients, individuals, institutions, and our entire culture."

EDWARD TICK, PH.D.
Psychotherapist and author
Executive Director, Sanctuary International, Albany

"As cultures de-generate, there are always voices heralding paths for re-generation. This important book, *Crossroads,* contains those voices which integrate the wisdom of the past with the needs for the future."

JOHN ALLAN, PH.D.
Jungian analyst and author of *Inscapes of the Child's World*

"There is a theme of 'spiritual hunger' that draws together and resonates through the writings of the *Crossroads* contributors: the seemingly universal desire for psychological wholeness as well as a more palpable connection to the 'larger issues' of personal meaning and cultural significance. The writings also supply some interesting answers to the question of 'how do we get there from here?'"

RALPH E. PHILLIPS, M.S.
Marital and family therapist

"In *Crossroads,* a veritable, remarkably wide-ranging chorus of writers address how initiation and rites of passage for our youth and youth's energies is an absolute necessity—for us, for the world our ancestors have bequeathed us, and for the generations to come. In James Baldwin's words, 'If this country does not find a way to use that energy, it will be destroyed by that energy."

· RICK SIMONSON
Co-editor of *Multicultural Literacy*

"This powerful and important book penetrates the dreary materialism of our culture and recovers the essence of what it means to be a human being. The contributors offer many fresh insights into the alienation, despair, and violence that characterize modern life."

DR. RON MILLER
Author of *What Are Schools For? Holistic Education in American Culture*

CROSSROADS

CROSSROADS

THE QUEST FOR CONTEMPORARY RITES OF PASSAGE

Edited by Louise Carus Mahdi,
Nancy Geyer Christopher, and Michael Meade

OPEN COURT
Chicago and La Salle, Illinois

To order books from Open Court, call toll-free 1-800-815-2280.

Cover illustration: "Men Exist for the Sake of One Another, Teach Them Then or Bear with Them" (Great Ideas of Western Man series), 1958. Oil on prepared fiberboard, 20 3/4 x 16 3/4 in. Jacob Lawrence. National Museum of American Art, Washington DC/Art Resource, NY.

The line drawings of the basket designs used for the part openers and chapter openers are based on illustrations in *The Pima and His Basket* by J. F. Breazeale (Tucson: Arizona Archaeological and Historical Society, 1923).

Open Court Publishing Company is a division of Carus Publishing Company.

Copyright © 1996 by Carus Publishing Company

First printing 1996

Second printing 1998

Printed and bound in the United States of America.

Library of Congress Cataloging-in-Publication Data

Crossroads: the quest for contemporary rites of passage/edited by
Louise Carus Mahdi, Nancy Geyer Christopher, and Michael Meade.
p. cm.
Includes bibliographical references and index.
ISBN 0-8126-9190-3 (pbk.: alk. paper)
1. Initiation rites.   2. Rites and ceremonies.   3. Adolescence.
4. Developmental psychology.   5. Maturation (Psychology)   I. Mahdi,
Louise Carus.   II. Christopher, Nancy Geyer.   III. Meade, Michael,
1944-   .
GN473.C76   1996
392'. 14--dc20
                                                                96-41432
                                                                CIP

This book has been reproduced in a print-on-demand format from the 1998 Open Court printing.

CONTENTS

Where there is no vision, the people perish.

—PROVERBS 29:18

ACKNOWLEDGMENTS

Collaboration with coeditors Nancy Geyer Christopher and Michael Meade has been a "call to adventure" because each of us is committed to this vast subject of rites of passage from a different perspective. Each of us has devoted many years to the actual practice as well as the study of the background of rites of passage as a potentially creative approach to prepuberty, puberty, adolescence, and later years. There is so much more to be said. At least this is a beginning, building on the book *Betwixt and Between*, first published in 1987.

We want to give special thanks to Assemblyman Edward Griffith of the New York State Legislature in Albany who helped sponsor the Rites of Passage Symposium in mid-February, 1992, which launched this project. Bud Mahoney, Assemblyman Griffith's assistant, deserves special mention for his great support. Very special thanks and appreciation to all of the presenters at that Symposium—both those whose papers appear here as well as those whose original transcripts never found their way into this book.

We are grateful to many people for assistance in creating this anthology. It is not possible to mention all of these helpful people by name. On the home front we are particularly indebted to Susan M. Rublaitus, editorial assistant, who has kept the many threads of *Crossroads* from getting knotted. In weaving this book together we have had a large correspondence and direct contact with many authors and publishers to whom we want to express special thanks. Susan kept us on track throughout, particularly at the end phase. We would like to thank Susan for compiling the very comprehensive index.

We are very grateful to Carus Publishing Company and to Blouke Carus and Paul Carus for supporting this anthology and the effort needed in bringing this book out. Kerri Mommer and David Ramsay Steele, editors of Open Court Trade and Academic Books, Jennifer Asmuth and Jeanne Kerl in the marketing department, and Jaci Hydock in charge of production, have done wonders in helping *Crossroads* into print. We would like to thank Kathleen League for her extremely careful and thorough copyediting. I am especially grateful for the editorial assistance of Sharron Dorr. Betty Lou Willand, Cynthia Funfsinn, Jennifer Zinke, Ruth Morrison Hakeem, and Helen Martin also made it possible for us to meet deadlines.

Father Gabriel Bullock, Lee Roloff, Chris and Dennis Merritt, Barry Williams, Renata Ritzman, Gary Sparks, Jennette Jones, Marion Woodman, David Blumenkrantz, Miriam and George Seltzer, Amy Hart, Edith Sullwold, and Kennan McKee offered their valued opinions and counsel.

My most heartfelt thanks go to each and every author whose chapters are presented here. Their combined efforts have produced a colorful, kaleido-scopic sourcebook on rites of passage for young people. We have focused on adolescents but we need to help the adult leaders in this work, too.

There is no end to rites of passage. Just as we fold up our manuscript we hear about a boy's return from a white water river passage to Hudson's Bay. "I never want to forget this moment. I never felt so alive before. I saw my whole life in a perspective I hadn't seen before."

There are many other rites-of-passage programs sponsored by the YMCA, the Scouts, Outward Bound, and the Institute of Cultural Affairs as well as African American groups, different denominations, and schools and colleges around our country. We want to honor each of these constructive pro-grams although many of these programs are not discussed here. Some of them have their own publications.

We sense there is a growing awareness of the importance of the commu-nity, churches, schools, and parents coming forth with a new spirit and new energy to take care of our youth in a new way, including concepts and wis-dom from our rich heritage of rites of passage. We need our elders and men-tors, as well as our ancestors who have so much to teach us, particularly in the rites-of-passage field. We thank you all.

Louise Carus Mahdi
Peru, Illinois
May 1996

BIOGRAPHIES OF EDITORS

Louise Carus Mahdi worked with the American Friends Service Committee (AFSC) in her mid-20s in international voluntary camps, a rite-of-passage experience for her. While working for her diploma at the C. G. Jung Institute, Zurich, she taught in both Swiss and American secondary schools. Her first re-search camp in rites of passage for adolescents took place in 1970, and further camps have continued until the present. She and David Knudsen, with Tom Kapacinskas, started the Vision Quest at Temagami, Ontario in 1979. The present camps that take place at Lake Temagami continue to provide a transformative wilderness setting for both adolescents and adults.

Louise Mahdi was editor with Steven Foster and Meredith Little of *Betwixt and Between: Patterns of Masculine and Feminine Initiation* (Open Court, 1987), on rites of passage at the major stages of life. *Betwixt and Between* continues to be used in workshops and classrooms, as well as by individual parents and professionals as a guidebook offering general information about rites of passage.

Besides working as an editor for Open Court Trade and Academic Books, Louise has a private psychological practice in northern Illinois.

Nancy Geyer Christopher, Ph.D., a former teacher of high school, college, and adult education, has served as a VISTA (Volunteers In Service To America) volunteer in its Washington, D.C. literacy program and continues as a literacy tutor and tutor-trainer in adult literacy. She is presently a board member of the Literacy Volunteers of America—National Capital Area. Her background in anthropology, psychology, sociology, and theology has enriched her life as teacher, writer, and mother of three children who moved through their own heroic journeys to adulthood.

Nancy is the author of two books: *The North Shore Country Day School: Seventy Years of a Community of Learning* and *Right of Passage: Heroic Journey to Adulthood.*

Michael Meade, critically acclaimed author of *Men and the Water of Life,* and founder/director of Mosaic Multicultural Foundation, is a storyteller, drummer, festival-maker, and accomplished scholar of mythology and ritual. With Robert Bly and James Hillman, he coedited *Rag and Bone Shop of the Heart,* an anthology of great poetry from many ages and cultures. Meade lectures widely on ritual and expressive art as an antidote to violence, and is currently writing on mentors and elders, and the rediscovery of ritual.

Mosaic Multicultural Foundation (MOSAIC) is a network of writers, artists, community organizers, and teachers from diverse backgrounds who share a commitment to cultural healing. MOSAIC seeks ways to weave new social fabrics from existing ethnic, spiritual, psychological, and political threads. Current projects focus on youth and elders, rites of passage, and rituals of community conflict resolution.

MOSAIC events draw inspiration from the traditions of many cultures and incorporate knowledge earned in the trenches of contemporary community work. The intention is to create new alliances and social bridges built upon personal trust and commitment to cultural healing.

MOSAIC projects take the form of cross-cultural community dialogues, art projects and traditional art presentations, and extended retreats for youth and elders. Events often include public ceremonies that strengthen aspects of positive cultural heritage while incorporating social change. The intensity of these events produces active alliances and bonds like those formed through youthful adventures, struggles for justice, and spiritual ordeals. Since 1991, MOSAIC has received support from many individuals and organizations to continue this work.

P·R·E·F·A·C·E

Louise Carus Mahdi

It is increasingly clear that our cultural values have been undermined, so that even among the masses, and especially among today's youth, there are individuals who are seeking, not so much the destruction of the old, as something new on which to build. And because the destruction has been so widespread and has gone so deep, this new foundation must be located in the depths in the most natural, the most primordial, most universally human core of existence.

—MARIE-LOUISE VON FRANZ[1]

I have just left my fellow counselors and elders at our base camp at Lake Temagami, Ontario. We have just completed "Northern Lights," a camp using a new approach with a group of girls ages twelve and thirteen. The girls participating in the Northern Lights program were accompanied on a nine-day wilderness canoe-camping trip that was more than a trip: for them it was a real heroic journey. It was strenuous, the black flies and mosquitoes were the worst in thirty years, it rained every day, the portages were a challenge. The beginning and final days were at the base camp, making a total of fourteen days.

I find myself reflecting on our teamwork over the last twenty-five years, through which we have learned more each year and created a new type of camp with a new approach for boys and girls at puberty and adolescence. A primary component is better-trained counselors. We started with a small experimental group in 1970, re-searching and building camps as a constructive practical rite of passage and transition. We continue to learn from each other.

Some of this work is documented in our earlier book, *Betwixt and Between: Patterns of Masculine and Feminine Initiation.*[2] This sequel, *Crossroads: The Quest for Contemporary Rites of Passage* is a collection of multidisciplinary chapters focusing on practical and appropriate ways to try to understand and apply rites of passage concepts at the time of adolescence appropriate to our times.

This summer of 1995, the girls' experiences were reassuring, as we had hoped. In reviewing their time at camp, the girls spontaneously expressed their sense that "Now I will be able to do whatever I feel is important for me in my life. After all, we have weathered nine days in the wilderness. Feel my muscle. I have never felt so alive before." They felt it was an experience they "will never forget." At this age, at the threshold of adolescence, it is possible to take great steps, as if one were wearing "seven league boots" with which one can take giant strides. I have adult friends who remember camp experiences at this age which they feel changed their lives forever. The history of centuries of traditional rites of passage would suggest that this time of life around puberty and early adolescence is opportune for major learning, a situation not yet adequately appreciated or understood by our culture.

In terms of distance, this recent girls' trip was modest, just over thirty miles from base camp and back again, with overnights at different sites each night. Yet in terms of moving to a new place in the girls' lives, the canoe trip could be a turning point. The lively sparkle in their eyes, the joy in their smiles, their radiating of new self-confidence and self-respect when they returned, made all the effort worthwhile.

Was this a rite of passage? For these girls it was a passage to a new place, a move to new ways of growing up, with new inner strength, new friends, a new community of support, a new spirit, and, we believe, a new understanding of deep universal human values. It was an experience of what one might call "intensification," guided by the counselors who accompanied the girls on their journey in the wilderness. All the counselors on the trail were young but experienced wilderness canoe-camp leaders, familiar with Lake Temagami and the surrounding forests and lakes of Ontario.

The base-camp counselors included older women, so the community elders were also represented, including Native American women. All of the women were committed to the camp as a meaningful rite of passage experience, intentionally offering skills and learning which could help the young people find their way in becoming teenagers and young adults with greater confidence and a clearer sense of who they are. Appropriate stories were told. Discussions attended to the importance of a sense of direction and the significance of being given a new name with symbolic meaning.

A "passage" is, of course, a journey, a way of passing to a new place, as well as a new position in the community. The term "rite of passage" was first introduced into English in 1960 when a book on *Les Rites de Passage* was first translated from the French edition (1908). The author, Arnold van Gennep, was interested in finding basic universal patterns of cultural life in what he calls rites of passage. His book is still a classic on this subject, namely, the study of initiation and rites of passage at significant times of transition in the life of individuals. It is still a new field, offering a new approach to the learning process and to growing up in the early teen years. A large order![3]

Van Gennep points out that the basic patterns of rites of passage have been essentially the same in stable traditional cultures around the world. Are they applicable today? The difficulty is that modern culture itself seems to be moving and is in passage to a new place in what is called a "paradigm shift."[4]

In traditional societies of the past, the elders knew what they had to

teach their young. Our elders today are often going through passages themselves, which may be one reason why there are so few elders, parents, and
mentors available to help our young people. While contemporary culture
itself is going through a passage, some individual adults experience it as an
"urgent yearning" or a "call." One top "Executive in Passage" writes in his
recent book of the same title:

> As I moved forward, I entered a period of confusion, disorientation, and
> chaos. But some inner sense of rightness kept pulling me on. Finally, after a tor-
> turously difficult time, I was delivered into a new way of life—one filled with
> inner quiet, joy, and renewed success—an experience I can only describe as
> "uncommon fulfillment." This is . . . a remarkable journey. The story is mine, but
> the passage is universal.[5]

We need the elders who have experienced their passages. At puberty, the
girls need to be with older girls, women elders, while men elders can be
present in the background. The women are the ones who help the girls in the
core experience.[6] Boys' rites of passage at puberty traditionally involve an
experience of separation from the mother; boys stay with an all-male group in
the "men's house" where there are no women at all in the core experience.

Let us start with the girls, where the biological changes provide a significant transition time for each individual girl. At this major threshold, the
menarche, a girl's mother is an important part of the event. In some cultures,
this is more than a private occasion; it is a time of celebration and remembering for the community, for the village, certainly for the extended family. The
girl-becoming-young-woman also needs a bridge to the greater feminine
beyond the personal mother as we have learned from Edith and Victor
Turner.[7]

The Navajo girls' *Kinaalda*, their ritual passage, consisted of an
extended-family puberty ceremony. In preparation for this ceremony, each
traditional Navajo family with a daughter approaching puberty needs a large
supply of cornmeal on hand. The cornmeal was used to make the feast cake to
be shared at the final day of the ritual celebration. If possible, the girls'
puberty ceremony was enacted at the time of the girl's first period. Traditionally, timing was important, for the occasion was for new insights and learning
in an experiential way.

Such rites of passage are not only meaningful for the girl but also offer
renewal and regeneration for the larger community. They provide an opportunity to celebrate community, one's culture, feminine values, and wisdom. The
individual girl can better connect with values and traditions of her family and
culture through the support of these rituals. There is an interweaving of biological change, the family, and cultural heritage which provides a structure
that unites and strengthens the individual girl, her family, her culture, and
their future. In the Navajo tradition, each girl is given a sense of her own
worth as a young woman and future mother of her tribe. In the puberty ritual

she is strengthened in preparation for the time when she will, in turn, strengthen her growing family and her community.

In many cultures, the puberty rites of passage are the most important of all transitions, providing the background, and often the patterns, for all later passages.[8] These basic patterns are established at puberty and are often repeated again and again at later transitions. The young woman is taught how, symbolically, she becomes a carrier of culture. That is why this tremendous time of becoming a young woman is so important. A rite of passage can be one of the major moments in the transmission of culture, if celebrated in a constructive way with mentors and elders.

Our goal is to build on what is natural for the young person coming of age. Even when there are no girls' puberty rituals, most adult women remember the time of their first period, where they were and what happened, positive or negative. No wonder that puberty is an important time for girls. We are not offering a blueprint, a formula, or a quick fix. We want to present different approaches for this turning point in a young person's life. Ideally, this time should be an event with positive, life-enhancing, nourishing significance—at puberty, if possible. And that is why we need mentors and elders who are prepared. At this time we need wise men and women ready to provide positive perspectives and meaning for the responsibilities ahead.

It is true that many young people are informed about their biological and sexual development today. But there are other issues at stake, of *self, self-esteem,* and *self-confidence* (see the chapter on teen pregnancy by Sharron Brown Dorr). There are questions about oneself: Who am I? How do I become the individual I am meant to be? There are *stories* (see the chapter by Erica Meade) about individual people, about being a man or woman, about what the issues are. There are *songs* to be sung. There are *skills* to be learned (see the chapter by McKernan), and *reflections* to be made. There are *spiritual* questions. (See the chapters by Christina Grof, Sarah Kilmer, and J. G. Kohl.)

It all begins with awareness.

First and foremost, at puberty, there is a natural and needed loosening of the bond to the individual parents. The chances of coping with loosening these bonds are good where there has been adequate parenting.

Where there has been inadequate parenting, there is what Anthony Stevens calls "parent hunger," a hunger that seems almost insatiable.[9] This can lead to joining a gang. It can lead to a lifelong quest to still this "parent hunger" in an attempt to redeem oneself from a bitter fate. Unparented people keep searching, moving from one dependent relationship to another, hoping to find someone who can make good what their parents did not. Potentially, rites of passage today could help re-parent persons at this sensitive time of transition.

Second, some balance is needed between the two opposing systems of the younger and the older generation—between the youthful revolutionaries and the older generation who carry on the traditions. Over the years and generations, one sees how culture and community are important for human societies at puberty. A balance is needed between the forces of youth and change on the one hand and the traditional, conservative forces on the other. Youth, with its shot of testosterone, wants to be free of the restraints of tradition and longs to pursue new causes and new goals. Experience, with its wounds worn like trophies, longs to pass on its hard-won wisdom.

About twenty-five hundred years ago Plato must have been fully aware of this problem when he wrote:

> You are young my son, and, as the years go by, time will change and even reverse many of your present opinions. Refrain therefore a while from setting yourself up as a judge of the highest matters.[10]

Third, the young person receives his or her call to adventure and to leave home. He or she goes through ordeals. The heroic myths require leaving the home and crossing the threshold to adulthood. (See David Oldfield's chapter in *Crossroads,* a practical application of *The Hero with a Thousand Faces* by Joseph Campbell.) The young people must undergo a second birth, must be born of their culture, their community, their elders. The young woman needs to find a relationship to the greater feminine roots beyond the personal mother. Both boys and girls need their community and their elders to help cope with the chaos of this major transition. The boys need the older men. The girls need the older women.

One reason for the great demand for psychiatric services for adolescents today may be the absence of socially sanctioned rites of passage. Throughout human history these rites have served humanity well. The desire for some rites and rituals at puberty as well as at the end of the teen years is natural, even today. Young people seem to want the real thing, an authentic initiation. There is truly a "hunger for initiation" as Anthony Stevens observes.[11] Together with the culture, the community, and the individual elders offering nurturing guidance and support, whole villages are needed to help raise our children, to help them survive. (Nouk Bassomb starts us with his experience of the ancient Bassa rite of passsage in "Baskets at the Crossroads" on p. xxvii.)

As I end this introduction I am sitting outside, near the Illinois River, at dusk. The wild canaries have been here most of the day feeding on the fresh sunflowers the birds themselves had planted. Now in the twilight, nature is roaring with the crickets and cicadas. It is getting dark. An individual star is out. The fireflies are offering reassuring lights before nightfall. I believe that nature speaks to the importance of anchoring rhythms in the cycle of life. I am convinced that serious rites of passage, particularly around puberty and during adolescence, offer healing potentials that are as yet inadequately explored. In their absence, the "litima" (see the chapter with this title by Michael Meade)—the natural and potentially explosive energy of adolescence—tends to become even more destructive and dangerous. This book is an attempt to call forth what is most constructive and most natural in human puberty and adolescence, with the loving help of mentors and elders. These rites of passage can become "crucibles of change."[12]

> As their flesh once labored to bring forth flesh,
> so the minds of the elders labor,
> with like passion,
> to bring forth a mind.
> By rites of initiation
> they would accomplish
> the metamorphosis of matter into man,
> the evolution of a mind for meaning in the animal
> which is the issue of their flesh.
> By this
> they would insure that the race endure
> as a race of men.
> The rites of this second birth
> into the metaphysical cosmos,
> everywhere mime the conditions of
> the first physical birth.
> The novice is
> purified of the past,
> relieved of possessions,
> made innocent,
> placed nascent in the womb solitude . . .
> The matter,
> which is man himself,
> and the myth of a race
> are joined.
> His solitary meditation
> is a gestation
> and, in the end,
> a man emerges by ordeal,
> to be newly named, newly rejoiced in.

—Maya Deren[13]

NOTES

1. Marie-Louise von Franz, *C.G. Jung: His Myth in Our Time* (New York: G. P. Putnam's Sons, 1975).

2. This anthology, *Crossroads,* is the sequel to *Betwixt and Between: Patterns of Masculine and Feminine Initiation* (Peru, Ill.: Open Court, 1987). *Crossroads* includes some presentations of the Albany State Legislature Conference (mid-February 1992), initiated by Edward Griffith, Assemblyman from Brooklyn.

3. See Joseph Campbell, *The Hero with a Thousand Faces,* Bollingen Series 17 (Princeton University Press, 1976). We have included Michael Meade's new foreword to the latest edition of the classic, *Rites and Symbols of Initiation: The Mysteries of Birth and Rebirth,* by Mircea Eliade.

4. See Willis Harman, "What *Is* This 'New Paradigm'?" in a report by the World Business Academy (WBA). Willis Harman is a founder of the World Business Academy and President of the Institute of Noetic Sciences, the world's largest membership organization researching the human mind. This article represents some thoughts after the September 1993 WBA International Retreat with the theme "A Search for the *Real* New Paradigm in Business."

5. From the jacket, Donald Marrs, *Executive in Passage: Career in Crisis—The Door to Uncommon Fulfillment* (Los Angeles: Barrington Sky Publishing, 1990).

6. See the chapter by Claire Farrer in *Betwixt and Between.*

7. V. W. Turner, *The Drums of Affliction: A Study of Religious Processes among the Ndembu of Zambia* (Oxford: Clarendon Press and The International African Institute, 1968). Also see *For She Is the Tree of Life: Grandmothers through the Eyes of Women Writers,* ed. Valerie Kack-Brice (Berkeley, Calif.: Conari Press, 1994).

8. Kaspar Kiepenheuer, in his *Crossing the Bridge: A Jungian Approach to Adolescence,* provides a fine discussion of adolescent rites of passage in the section entitled "Death and Rebirth in Adolescence" (LaSalle, Ill.: Open Court, 1990).

9. Anthony Stevens, *On Jung* (New York: Penguin Books, 1990), p. 121.

10. Plato, *Laws* 888: A124. Quoted by Anthony Stevens in *On Jung.*

11. Anthony Stevens, *Archetypes: A Natural History of the Self* (New York: Quill, 1983). (See ch. 10, "Personal Identity and the Stages of Life.")

12. To quote Linda McCullough in her article on rites of passage (*Common Boundary* [January 1996]).

13. M. Deren, *Divine Horsemen: The Living Gods of Haiti* (New York: Book Collectors Society, 1953), p. 23.

INTRODUCTION

Michael Meade

There exists a fragment of story from the lost culture of Borneo, a shred of the little that remains of a culture lost somewhere in time. In the story Half-boy is born, a boy with only the right half of his body. Of course, he is unhappy and feels desperately incomplete. He becomes a constant source of irritation, embarrassment, and confusion for his family and the entire village. Nevertheless, he grows. That is to say, the half of him that can be seen grows. Eventually, he reaches the age of adolescence and puberty. His halfness and incompleteness become unbearable to him. His pain grows more evident and more troublesome to everyone around him.

One day he leaves the village, dragging himself along, the way a half a person drags himself through life. He drags along until he reaches a place where the road crosses a river. At that crossroad, he meets another youth who exists as only the left half, the other half of a person. Immediately, they move towards each other as if fated to join together. Surprisingly, when they reach each other, they begin to fight and roll in the dust. Eventually, they fall into the river. After a time, from the river there arises an entire youth with the sides put together. Because he has been in the river and in a great struggle, he feels disoriented and doesn't know where he stands. Then, the new youth begins to walk towards a village that he sees before him.

As he enters the village, he sees an old man and asks: "Can you tell me where I am? I have been struggling and don't know where I have arrived at." The old man says: "You have arrived home. You are back in the village where you were born. Now that you have returned whole, everyone can begin the dance and celebration ." A great dance and feast begins. Everyone in the village joins the dance, especially the Half-boy become whole.

Though it's a small story, it carries the full sense of a rite of passage and the inevitable struggle of youth seeking wholeness and a place in the heart of the village. Beside the youthful quest for identity, the story shows how the village finds its completion through the arrival of its youth as full community members. Though at first the youth feel unseen, misunderstood, and rejected; eventually, the village must wait for its youth or else lose the ability to survive and celebrate life.

The bare bones of the story don't describe what the elder does while waiting for the youth to arrive, or what the village does while waiting to learn the fate of its youth. However, the details can be gleaned from reviewing other stories of initiation and from the study of rites of passage past and present. It was a human fact, understood by most cultures, that when youth go through their transition, everyone is affected and involved. All celebrations must wait; usually, all other conflicts must wait. In the meantime, everyone prays or offers assistance, support, or guidance. The youth must cross from innocence to self-knowledge, from simple dependence to the challenges of independence on one hand and community involvement on the other.

The story reveals an underlying condition of all who move from child to adult: feeling torn in half and desperate to complete the sense of self. Inevitably, a turning point, a crossroads appears in the life of each young person.

Characteristically, a great struggle occurs, internally, if not externally. For the one living through it, the change always feels like a life and death struggle. The situation reflects how life and death commune at the threshold of birth. Everyone questions: "How is the child? How is the mother?", because we know that death is also present when life begins and when a life begins again. For youth, events at the crossroads activate all the questions about living and dying. In a sense, they are giving birth to themselves and they could get stuck, never reaching the celebration, never living life fully. Worse yet, in trying to find a way into life, they could lose the struggle and literally fall into death. It must be noted that in ancient cultures, just as in contemporary life, some slip into the river of change and are never seen again. Formal rites of passage included an education about life and death, about growth and the inevitability of funerals. There is a mysterious connection that links initiation, celebrations of life as renewable and funeral rites. A culture that forgets its rites of passage also loses its sense of funeral and eventually loses the capacity to celebrate joy and unity.

The loss and avoidance of rites of passage have created an increasing gap between young and old. As the gap widens, the fear of crossing it grows. Meanwhile, more and more youth are lost in violent or apathetic behaviors. Increasingly, communities become armed camps living in fear of their own lost children. Schools require metal detectors to keep violence out, while inside uncertainty and apathy grows. The vacuum created by the loss of serious rites of transition will be filled with something. Because youth is a stage of extremes, the vacuums that society leaves will be filled with extremes of destruction if they can't be filled with excesses of creation. The details and circumstances may differ for each generation and for each individual, but everyone shares the experience of passage from child to adult. Only through denial and forgetfulness can adults ignore the confusions and existential struggles of youth.

Meanwhile, current generations face an increasing sense of chaos because modern life has reached its own crossroads. The end of the era is attended by rapid changes, a crash of endings and challenges to every institution and cultural system. Turning points and crossroads abound and many paths cross as the past demands attention before giving way to the future. Culture itself becomes like the Half-boy. Collectively, we must drag ourselves to the river, submit to the struggles, losses and renewals that attend an epochal change and hope that we reach the next village. The chaos, violence, reluctance and apathy of modern youth are symptomatic of similar troubles in the heart and soul of culture. Rejecting them for carrying the symptoms means condemning more and young people to sink with the burdens that belong to the whole village. In rejecting or condemning our youth, we reject our own struggling selves and our own needs and desires for completion. It is more honest and just to enter the crossroads with the youth, admit that half the joy of life has been lost and join the struggle to change and to survive. The elder waiting at the entrance to the village knows where to look for change, he knows that the community finds its unity through its youth and learns its future at the crossroads.

A crossroad is a point of intersection, a place of meetings and partings, a juncture where different worlds exchange meanings. Reaching a crossroads implies that a journey has been under way and the course of life has reached a significant point where choices must be made. It is a place of change and exchange, of lost and found, of discovery and revelation. It is a space for invention and for sacrifice. Crossroads are also for burial, for life can only grow when an old or completed phase has been released and left behind. As a place of principal awareness, crossroads stand as symbols of possible change of direction and as points where the potentials of a life can be renewed. The word 'cross-roads' has intersections within as if a cross stands where roads intersect. While the sense of journey is carried in the roads, the cross indicates attention, importance, even danger. There is often a cross to bear at a crossroads. Crosses also represent the world tree which marks the intersection of the horizontal flow of life with the vertical dimension of spirit. Because possibilities and potentials, endings and beginnings become activated at crossroads, deities, spirits, and ancestors congregate there.

In times past, marketplaces were located at the crossroads because of the obvious opportunities to trade and exchange information. But, people were also aware of a complicated spiritual presence and of exchanges between the mundane world and the spiritual realm. People invoke the entire symbolic resonance of the crossroads when they make the 'signs of the cross' at the threshold of a church. In some cultures, funeral processions led to a crossroads where the soul of the dead was given over to the ancestral realm.

When standing at a crossroads, a person can look back and see the journey they have been on even when they thought they were only standing still. A person can catch a glimpse of the purpose in their life and grasp the meaning of the next step they take. As in stories, time can be suspended at a crossroad, years can pass while a necessary step is forestalled. The desire to change and the fear of the unknown can be closely matched in a person and the struggle to change can stretch over time. A full life requires many passages and accomplishing one serves to qualify the seeker for the next. The feelings of arrival and completion are always temporary, as any wholeness achieved gets worn away by the vicissitudes of life. Again and again, we each become as the Half-boy dragged to another turning point, facing another stage of life. It is as if the blows and disappointments of life wear away half of who we are and we must seek fulfillment again. Despite worldly success, we find ourselves with a new challenge or else facing old demons and entering the river once again.

In the story of the Half-boy, the village secretly waits to embrace the wholeness of the youth. The appearance of the child of the village, ordeals completed, in a state of renewed potential, brings a taste of wholeness to the entire community. When the 'new' youth consciously enter their next stage of life, they introduce the future into the village symbolically and actually. It wasn't clear that the village was even aware of the pain and suffering of the Half-boy, just as it seems that modern societies can't understand the conditions of their own youth. Yet, something within the village knew enough to prepare for his arrival. Some sense persisted, at least with the elders, that the youth was essential to the spirit of celebration and the capacity to renew the potentials of life.

In modern societies, many youth feel lost or 'out of it,' while the genuine sense of community is also missing. Although it has become easy for people to turn away from the conflicts of youth, it was common knowledge in old cultures that the future can only be born from the past struggling with the potentials in the psyches of youth. Youth unknowingly carry the burdens and unhealed wounds of the past; but, they also carry the enlivening seeds of the future. Meanwhile, there are no youth other than those each society produces and they are always half of who they want to be. They are the willing and reluctant adventurers, the discoverers and the co-creators of their own rites of change. Perhaps even now, inside cultural confusion something waits like a patient elder keeping an eye on the struggles of youth and remembering the necessity of marking life's passages. A universal sense of ritual-making and initiation remains in the crossroads of human memory. It speaks through people's dreams and can be reawakened. It may be capable of rediscovering and remaking rites appropriate to the circumstances of contemporary youth. We may be able to reimagine genuine roles for elders and relocate the unity lost from community.

Because rites of passage are essentially about change, there can be no exact way or absolute method for creating them. Rather, opportunities exist for embracing that which is locally true and for healing that which has been torn individually and collectively. The troubles of an individual or a generation don't simply dissolve or disappear. Rather, the completion of a conscious transition creates points and moments of wholeness and mutual acceptance.

In the 'ritual moment' the community accepts its youth completely. That gesture allows the youth to accept themselves as they are and creates their place in the society. Without a penetrating demonstration of belonging how can anyone be sure there is a place for them? Before anyone can contribute meaningfully to a group, it must be seen and shown that they belong. On the other hand, the community can't manifest a genuine sense of welcome unless conflicts within the group are temporarily resolved. The village must be ready to celebrate life in its fullness or the spirits of the youth won't fully enter community life.

A contemporary rite of passage may have to tolerate great confusion and chaos as both youth and community struggle for moments of connection and completion. Given half a chance, the youth will take their steps and trust the river of life. The bigger question may be whether a village can be created that can truly accept and receive them. If the second village acts like the first one they experienced, the youth may be more damaged, disillusioned, and alienated. Those who wish to work as mentors and elders have to keep one eye on the youth and another on conditions in the village. Both youth and community experience a reorientation when the two meet. Because elders and mentors help make bridges between young people and the general culture, they have to remember times of halfness and draw on times of wholeness. Elders have a foot on the side of youth, remembering that they were once and again torn in half by life, able to recall the desperate feelings of not belonging that can cause violence and alienation. The other foot must rest on ground where completion was found. Elders and mentors must be able to recall times of wholeness and acceptance, or they will be torn and disoriented themselves. The dance of the elders includes both feet, one keeping time with suffering and loss; the other remembering ordeals survived and finding a sense of being at home in the world. If elders and mentors cannot hold the doors of community acceptance open, how can youth trust any authority or deeply value their lives and the lives of others? Why should young people suffer the ordeals of self-knowledge if there's no one waiting to welcome them home?

BASKETS AT THE CROSSROADS

Nouk Bassomb

Nouk Bassomb was born in Cameroon, Central Africa. When he was twenty, he was incarcerated for four years without trial for distributing leaflets in support of a workers' strike. He holds a Ph.D. in archaeology, with anthropology, ethnology, and prehistory as areas of specialization, from the Sorbonne in Paris. In 1992 he started doing field work in New York City homeless shelters and was so moved by the desperate situation he found that he set up the Homeless Self-Help Program to assist and support the men he met there.

He has published a memoir telling of his experience in the concentration camp in Cameroon, and two volumes of plays on the political situation in his native land. He is a storyteller and writes on various subjects, including myth, tradition, and rites of passage. He is currently working on his account of his own rite of passage which lasted ninety days when he was thirteen years of age.

In "Baskets at the Crossroads," Bassomb, who is Bassa himself, shows us how his people ensure that their young ones will grow up wanting to "keep the flame alive."

Soon after a boy has been initiated, that is, soon after he has been allowed into the society of adults, African Bassa people put him to a test. Seven to nine elders materialize one morning, at around five o'clock, outside his father's compound.

"Step outside, boy!" they shout.

The boy comes out. The elders place themselves between him and the door.

"It's time for you to depart, boy. Go! Now!"

The morning this happened to me, I had only a little piece of cloth called *sarja* around my waist. I turned my back and left.

My mom ran after me, but the elders, who were behind me to make sure that I would cross the boundaries of our village, kept her from hugging me.

"Go away, woman!" I heard the elders say. "For the next eighteen moons minimum, this boy has nothing, and we mean nothing, to do with the people of this village. That's the law. Let him go."

I did not even have the right to look back. I kept going. I had to show that I was a man, a little man, who one day would be a man, a grown man, an adult. A firm, upright support for the entire village. I was thirteen.

"Be humble and compassionate." I heard Mom shout, "and praise the Father each and every day!"

"Yes, Mom. I will not miss a day," I said to myself.

"Don't forget to put your baskets at the crossroads. And check them often," she added.

Those were the last words I heard from her.

This was not the first time I heard about crossroads. Three months prior to my departure, during my initiation, I heard the word almost every day.

Dad called me one morning: "Come on, boy, wake up! The time has come for you to follow the path of men."

He meant that I had to be initiated.

To undergo the transition from being a boy to becoming a man, male children spend ninety days in the deep forest. It is required. They must learn to survive in a dangerous and hostile environment, to find their food, cook it, and share it with fellow comrades. There are no females around. In my age group, there were twenty-seven of us.

Samnik Mapuna was our initiator. I can never thank this man enough for all he taught me. Before handing me over to him, Dad hugged me. He put my head against his chest and told me to listen.

"Do you hear something?" he asked.

"Yes," I said.

"What?"

"Your heartbeat!"

He nodded, and whispered. "Go now."

I went my way, crossing the river. Samnik Mapuna was waiting for me on the other side. He, too, hugged me, and put my ear to his chest to listen to his heartbeat.

"Do you hear something?" he asked me.

"Yes."

"What?"

"Your heartbeat."

He sighed. "Let's go, now," he said simply.

That very morning he told me about crossroads: "When you walk on a path going north, you will only meet people coming from the north. At the crossroads, you'll meet people coming from the east, from the west . . . Do you understand?"

"Yes," I replied. That was my first lesson. But, to be honest, I paid it no mind.

Another day, he asked me to look at him. I did. "You and I," he started, "are from different age groups, but our coming together creates crossroads between generations. Do you understand?"

That day, and the following night, I learned that crossroads are not only where people coming from south, north, east, and west meet, but there also come together the old and the new, the traditional and the modern, the archaic and the contemporary, the young and the aged, the visible and the invisible, the world of the living and the world of the dead.

Crossroads.

Three months later, when the time to say goodbye came, Sam Mapuna asked me to hug him. I did. He put my ear against his chest. "Do you hear something?"

"Yes," I replied.

"What?"

"Father's voice."

"What says he?"

"It's a long song, a very long song."

"Tell me the first words," he said.

"Keep the flame burning in the Father's house, the voice says. And there will always be someone to feel the warmth of the legacy. Keep the flame alive," I answered.

"Aha!" He shouted, smiling. "Go now, boy. Go!"

I crossed the river. Dad was waiting for me, to take me home. He hugged me and put my ear against his chest. "What do you hear?" he asked.

"Father's voice."

"And what is He saying?"

"Keep the legacy! That's what He's saying. Increase the vital force. Keep the flame burning, the voice says. Even when there is no one to feel the warmth of Father's house, the fire must be kept burning."

Dad smiled. I read pride and affection in his eyes. It was important for his son to know the myth of origins. The son was on his way to becoming a man. And so we went home. The boy was ready to enter the society of adults.

Nine days later, I was accepted into our clan's High Order of the Hunters.

"One thing, boy," interjected the eldest of the *Mbog-Mbog* (patriarchs), during the rites of passage: "You must learn to keep the fire burning in Father's house and you must experience the crossroads."

"Absolutely," the audience replied with one voice.

They meant that we, the neophytes, had to become wanderers, to learn how to sustain our culture and traditions, to learn to open the third eye, the one that enables us to see clearly.

At one point during the ceremony, the patriarch said these words: "If you come back, we'll celebrate your return to your native land; but if you don't, it will mean that you weren't meant for us."

The Ibibio of Nigeria, who live next to the ocean, say these same words to their newborn. They throw the infant with an overhand, pushing motion into the water. If he emerges, he was meant to stay. If not, they let him go, without a wince.

It is at the crossroads that we learn kindness, love, respect for the elders, protection of children, compassion for the weak and the meek. Being generous, compassionate, humble, hospitable, all help to fill our baskets.

"Check the baskets often," Mom said. She is the one who taught me to pray, which is to say to put my basket at the crossroads, an empty basket.

I do check the baskets, Mom, I do. Today I understand the source of all wealth and personal growth. My baskets are filled with stories, teachings, experiences, wisdom. There will be a lot to talk about when I get home.

How have I made my choices? Why do I go north instead of south? Why do I go west instead of east? I always have good reasons for acting boldly. The best way to keep alive the flame in the Father's house is to think of the children—and their children. We can't change the past, can't do much to affect the present, but we can do something to improve the future. Our future, as Bassa people, but also as humans. So what do I do? I fill my baskets, not with gold and silver, but with stories and experiences. One day I'll return to my native land and, as a grandfather, I'll spark the imagination of children with my stories.

Children need to be put in a position to wander freely when their time comes. Each story, each exotic landscape, magnifies their idea of the world, and their vision of themselves-in-the-world. It's in everyone's reach to tell stories, to describe places and share experiences. Everyone can go out and meet the likes of the African wanderer. And everyone can place their baskets at the crossroads.

Reprinted from *Parabola: The Magazine of Myth and Tradition* 28, no. 3 (fall 1993). © 1993 by Nouk Bassomb.

PART ONE   AN ANCIENT PRACTICE: MODERN PERSPECTIVES

RITES OF PASSAGE: A NECESSARY STEP TOWARD WHOLENESS

Christina Grof

Christina Grof is an author, teacher, artist, founder and advisor to the board of the Spiritual Emergence Network, and co-creator of Holotropic Breathwork. She is president of Grof Transpersonal Training, Inc., and former vice-president and current board member of the International Transpersonal Association. At Sarah Lawrence College, she studied with mythologist Joseph Campbell. Ms. Grof has given workshops and lectures and coordinated international conferences. Her particular areas of interest are the issues of child abuse and the spiritual aspects of addiction and recovery.

Christina Grof is the author of *The Thirst for Wholeness: Attachment, Addiction, and the Spiritual Path* (1993). Her other books, written with Stanislav Grof, M.D., are *Beyond Death* (1980), *Spiritual Emergency: When Personal Transformation Becomes a Crisis* (1989), and *The Stormy Search for the Self* (1990). Each of her books has been translated into several languages.

In her paper, Christina Grof emphasizes drug or alcohol addiction as evidence of a spiritual longing to connect with our inner or spiritual core. Her extensive experience with Holotropic Breathwork has shown the importance of a safe and supportive environment which encourages the expression of unconscious aspects of the psyche. This work concerns an aspect of rites of passage.

The practice of rites of passage has interested me for many years and for many reasons. In my professional life, I am a former teacher of art and creative writing in elementary school. I have also worked with adults who are exploring issues such as addictions, emotional and psychosomatic problems, and spiritual concerns. As a writer and speaker, I am actively involved in the field of transpersonal psychology, a branch of psychology which emerged out of humanistic psychology and addresses the physical, emotional, mental, and spiritual aspects of the human psyche. With my husband, Stanislav Grof, M.D., I developed Holotropic Breathwork, a form of experiential self-exploration. Without our intending it at the outset, Holotropic Breathwork replicates many of the qualities that are present in group rituals. I am also a mother of two young adults, both of whom lived through their adolescence. I myself survived a painful adolescence and later, when I was an adult, went through my own rite of passage as an alcoholic who hit bottom and entered recovery early in 1986. I am also someone who has been a spiritual seeker since childhood, and have participated in various Christian, Buddhist, East Indian, and Native American rituals and ceremonies.

Drawing on all of these areas, I will do the following: I will discuss the *function and the qualities of rites of passage* and the idea that if we do not have sanctioned situations in which to deal with the important transitions in our lives, we will create our own substitutes which are often destructive and self-destructive. I will describe *the image of the human being* that emerges out of the addictions field, transpersonal psychology, and various spiritual traditions, and I will relate that image to the phenomenon of rites of passage. In addition, I will offer some *practical suggestions for implementing rites of passage* for adolescents, as well as mention some of the challenges involved.

THE DYNAMICS OF ADOLESCENCE

Let us begin by identifying some of the complex dynamics of adolescence, and as we do so, let us remember our own teenage years. Individuals in adolescence are engaged in an important transition from childhood to adulthood. Their bodies are changing rapidly as they mature physically, experience the fluctuations of hormonal levels, and feel the stirrings of their sexuality. They often do not know where they fit: they feel like children and at the same time, they begin to taste their identities as adults. Families and the culture at large are often confused about how to define adolescents, both categorizing them as children who need to be protected, disciplined, and controlled, and as adults, who have increased social, legal, and family responsibilities.

Adolescence is a time when we are confused, self-conscious, eager to explore new possibilities, and wanting desperately to find our niche. We need nurturing, but want independence; we need to belong to some kind of identified community, but we often lack discrimination; we need direction and love, but our families, our schools, or our society are not always able to give them to us.

Adolescence contains all of these components: a need for independence, excitement, keen interest, physical changes, sexuality, self-esteem questions, childlike responses, new responsibilities, a desire to be socially accepted, and much more. There is also another element, a fundamental one: a deep spiritual longing that underlies these other aspects and adds power to them. I remember it well from my adolescence, observed it in other teenagers, and I see it all the time in the adults with whom I work. Many adults tell me that this craving to know their deeper self was largely ignored until their lives became problematic in their twenties, thirties, forties, or fifties and beyond through marital difficulties, emotional, psychosomatic, or addiction problems, or a general crisis of living. I will refer to this spiritual longing throughout this paper.

Spirituality in this context does not refer to some vague or exotic or New Age phenomenon. Nor is it the dogma, the politics, and the hierarchies that are present in many religious arenas. I am discussing spirituality as a simple, but powerful aspect of human nature which is available to each individual. It involves a direct, personal, intimate experience of realities beyond our limited, everyday identity and gives meaning to our lives by adding a sacred dimension.

Throughout history, in every culture, the development of a relationship with the divine, whatever name it is given, has been an essential part of human experience. Musicians and artists often say that this force is their source of inspiration. Sports figures give it credit for their extraordinary performances. People who spend time in nature might refer to it as the power behind creation, Mother Nature, or the mystery of life. Some define it as the compassion and nurturing that comes from another person or a group of people who care. Still others say that it represents our potential, the unlimited possibilities and gifts that may be concealed from us much of the time.

WHAT ARE RITES OF PASSAGE?

The Encyclopedia of Religion, edited by historian of religion Mircea Eliade, defines rites of passage as follows:

> Rites of passage are a category of rituals that mark the passage of a person through the life cycle, from one stage to another over time, from one role or social position to another, integrating the human and cultural experiences with biological destiny: birth, reproduction, and death. These ceremonies make the basic distinctions, observed in all groups, between young and old, male and female, living and dead.

Within these rituals, individuals are given the opportunity to face their emotional and experiential limitations and to move beyond them. They often experience a "second birth," "dying" to one phase of their lives and the roles associated with that period, leaving it behind, and entering a new stage with a new identity. Mythologist Joseph Campbell says that in this process, "the attitudes, attachments, and life patterns of the stage [are] left behind." The initiates are honored by their community, and given support and guidance by those who have gone before them. Through the ceremonial form, those in transition are not only accorded a designated position within their community, but also a firm and clear definition of their identity, their social roles, and their personal boundaries. They know where they fit.

Initiates also have the opportunity to experience their own creativity, the source of inner strength, love, or spiritual power, through the evocative transformative techniques within the ritualistic event. These include such practices as trance dancing, rhythmic drumming, fasting, physical or sensory isolation, forceful breathing rhythms, a realistic confrontation with death, and other techniques to alter consciousness. All of these approaches lead to nonordinary states of consciousness which serve to propel the initiates beyond their mortal limitations. Often, they experience a symbolic confrontation with death and rebirth, and an awareness of the mystical or spiritual domains that provide guidance, inspiration, and an expanded sense of self. These positive nonordinary states are also necessary in order for healing to take place.

Many rites of passage include the following common components. For instance, they involve the completion of one cycle and the beginning of another. They define the individual as having a new social status and respect. Initiates often wear ritual dress and often share an ordeal. The ordeal might require initiates to face danger, confront fear or limitations, prove their new status, or compete with one another. Ceremonies take place outside of the framework of their ordinary family or social life; initiates are often physically removed and then psychologically, emotionally, and spiritually separated from their everyday activities and interactions through nonordinary states of consciousness. Rites of passage often involve community members who are designated as leaders, sacred technicians, or men and women of wisdom.

The ritual is always infused with a spiritual atmosphere and is often introspective. When it is complete, the initiates return to their original existence. Not only do they feel different, but they are also treated in a new way by the community. Boys become men or girls become women, and are recognized as such by their families, their peers, and their society. They are given a clearly defined set of new rights and new responsibilities. And having passed through what is often an experience of symbolic death and renewal, they have acknowledged and become familiar with the cycles that will occur within their lifetimes. The initiates have acquired experiential maps which will help them to proceed through other times of transition.

THE NEED FOR RITES OF PASSAGE IN CONTEMPORARY CULTURE

A number of teachers, researchers, and scholars have recognized that our culture is one of the few in history that does not incorporate rites of passage, and that this has severe consequences. This is confirmed by therapists and others who work with the emotional, psychological, and spiritual demands of their clients that, in other societies, are addressed through sanctioned rituals. Joseph Campbell believed that the psyche of each human being contains a rich array of mythological symbols, archetypal impulses, and initiatory images which must be expressed and affirmed within a ritualistic context. Otherwise, these essential energies remain locked within us or are acted out in inappropriate ways: "there is something in these initiatory images so necessary to the psyche that if they are not supplied from without, through myth and ritual, they will have to be announced again . . . from within." Campbell further states,

> It has always been the prime function of mythology and rite to supply the symbols that carry the human spirit forward. . . . In fact, it may well be that the very high incidence of neuroticism among ourselves follows from the decline

among us of such effective spiritual aid. (*The Hero with a Thousand Faces*, p. 11)

The well-known anthropologist Margaret Mead believed that the fact that modern society has lost sanctioned rites of passage is a critical contributing factor to the increase of various forms of social pathology. Based on her cross-cultural studies, she concluded that we carry intense emotions and impulses in our personality structure that, if they are not dealt with internally, are projected into our everyday life. Mead considered this issue to be of such importance that in 1973, she organized a special symposium sponsored by the Wenner-Gren Foundation where representatives from different fields explored the possibility of creating rites of passage and restoring them to Western culture.

Similar observations have emerged from many forms of therapeutic work, including Holotropic Breathwork. Since I am most familiar with Holotropic Breathwork, I will discuss its implications, although these ideas apply to other approaches, particularly those with a broad understanding of the human psyche. This approach to self-exploration provides a safe and supportive setting in which participants discover the rich spectrum of experiences that exist within each person. Individuals in Holotropic Breathwork sessions regularly confront memories, experiences, emotions, and physical sensations from their biography, from the circumstances before, during, and after their biological birth (this involves a confrontation with death and rebirth), and from the extensive realms that are referred to as *transpersonal*. Transpersonal experiences include realistic archetypal or mythological sequences, psychic phenomena, episodes from other cultures and historical periods, and mystical and spiritual states.

Within our workshops and training seminars, we have used an expanded, inclusive model of the human psyche which emerged from the reports of individuals involved in deep experiential work and which shares much in common with the observations of Carl Gustav Jung, Roberto Assagioli, Joseph Campbell, and the inner cartographies of various spiritual traditions, among others. Holotropic Breathwork is usually done in a group. We combine animated breathing, effective music, and focused bodywork, to evoke a nonordinary state of consciousness which is necessary to access the deep levels within the unconscious. We encourage participants to turn inward and, with the support of trained facilitators, to go wherever their inner journeys take them, without editing. In this way, this approach uses principles similar to those of Jung's active imagination, Fritz Perls' Gestalt practice, and other methods that allow the full expression of the unconscious realms.

Repeatedly, participants in Holotropic Breathwork sessions have reported that, after confronting some of the problematic areas of their unconscious, they realize how much of their lives have been dominated or motivated by them. These individuals are usually ordinary, functioning people, many of whom are professionals. They say that the problems in their lives, such as marital stress, psychosomatic illness, emotional tension, addictive tendencies, or depression, are rooted in unexpressed emotions, unrecognized experiences from the past, and unacknowledged archetypal or spiritual yearnings. And they describe the importance of a safe and supportive environment where they can confront these aspects of themselves, of a sympathetic and supportive community of like-minded individuals, and of the expanded understanding of the human being which encourages the expression of the psyche's riches.

The addiction-recovery community has something to teach us about the need for rites of passage. In 1961, the famous Swiss psychiatrist, Dr. Carl Gustav Jung, corresponded with Bill Wilson, the cofounder of Alcoholics Anonymous. Referring to one of his former patients, Jung wrote: "His craving for alcohol was the equivalent on a low level of the spiritual thirst of our being for wholeness, expressed in medieval language: the union with God."

Although Jung made his observation specifically in relation to the use of alcohol, I believe that he was describing something that many people know very well. A great number of individuals feel a nonspecific hunger for a missing piece in their lives. They describe a prevailing emptiness inside of them that is never satisfied, an insistent stirring from within to look for something more. This is what Jung was referring to: a deep thirst to discover our essential spiritual nature, which is often hidden from view.

The "thirst of our being for wholeness," as Jung called it, has great power in our lives and expresses itself in various forms. For someone who is not compromised by emotional, psychological, or social limitations, it manifests in creative and positive ways. But this powerful craving also can be distorted, acted out in a destructive and self-destructive manner. For example, I believe that this thirst for wholeness is the underlying impulse behind addictions of all kinds. It is beyond the very real physiological craving of those of us who become hooked into the cycle of chemical dependency and it is different than our desire to escape our pain through addictive behavior. We do not know how to respond to this driving inner force, and instead of turning within and utilizing it in a creative way, we act it out, attempting to satisfy it through various internal or external activities or material substances.

The point of view that emerges from all of these examples—from Campbell, Mead, Jung, from the lessons of transpersonal psychotherapy, and from the world of addiction recovery—is that we each carry with us a vast array of emotions and experiences, both positive and negative. If these forces are unacknowledged or denied, they will penetrate into our daily lives and into our culture, often in harmful ways. We need a structured environment in which to confront and express the difficult areas of our psyche and in which to discover and accept our creative, inspirational, compassionate possibilities.

We also need a caring community of people who share a common understanding and experience and can offer us safety and support.

If we have the courage to face both the dark and light aspects of ourselves, we are no longer unconsciously motivated to turn them against ourselves or project them onto others and onto our environment in harmful ways. Instead, we have the opportunity to transform ourselves and to contribute to the world around us without the influence of disturbing unconscious material. Unfortunately, our culture has lost a major tool through which this kind of transformation can take place: this tool is the age-old form of rites of passage, which has been used cross-culturally throughout history to provide an accepted context for individuals to confront and integrate their inner impulses and emotions.

PSEUDO RITES OF PASSAGE

If it is true that as human beings we are engaged in ongoing life cycles that have profound impact on our lives, how do we survive in a culture that does not recognize and acknowledge the importance of these transitions? And if it is true that we each contain profound physical, emotional, mental, and spiritual forces which demand recognition, often in relation to these transitions, how do we respond in an environment that neither appreciates the significance of these impulses nor provides a sanctioned framework for their expression? I believe that we create our own pseudo rites of passage, usually without knowing it.

The night before my son's high school graduation, I dreamed that he died. In the dream, I saw his death, held his body in my arms, and wept uncontrollably as I grieved the loss of my child. When I awoke, I was afraid that perhaps I had had one of those intuitive dreams that parents have, that something terrible was about to happen to my son. Upon further reflection, however, I realized that, as superficial as the graduation ceremony was (at least, in contrast to traditional rites of passage), it marked the transition of my son from life as a boy to existence as a man. His role as a child was dying on the way to adulthood. I realized that, somewhere deep within me, my unconscious understood the significance of this transition and provided me with its own context for facing this important passage.

These same impulses within the psyche, like those in my dream, become externalized as we create substitutes to mark these times of transition. These substitutes are often either superficial, not particularly significant or transformative, or they are destructive and self-destructive. Such surrogate activities are usually projected outward, so there is little or no awareness of their possible positive effect. They occur within the society without conscious social support or recognition. And yet, they often contain many of the same elements of true rites of passage. Let us look at some of these substitute forms.

In our innate need to mark the important transition during the adolescent years, we have created such events as sweet sixteen parties, debutante cotillions, and summer camps, in which children are removed from familiar daily life and, with their peers, introduced to various group activities. Athletics also contain ritualistic elements, such as intense physical training, competition, bonding of the players, group support, the music and drumming of the band, and the rhythmic movement of the cheerleaders. And rock concerts, with the elemental sound, large crowds, unabashed dancing, and heroic band members, are as close as we come to mass-scale rites of passage in our society today.

And then, of course, there is the adolescent gang activity that is sweeping American cities. An article from the *New York Times* described ritualistic activity in a gang which included, as part of its initiation, the demand that potential members shoot someone in order to prove their worth. This has an obvious and horrifying similarity to the young African who must kill his first lion or the Eskimo boy who shoots his first seal as a way of demonstrating his manhood. Other similarities between gang activity and rites of passage include the wearing of certain symbolic clothes, hairdos, or other accouterments, danger, competition, confrontation of fear and other limitations, encounter with death, the separation from the daily life of the culture, and the involvement of nonordinary states of conscious.

A major component of gang activity is the use of drugs and alcohol. It is also a pervasive pastime in the entire adolescent population, as well as in our society at large.

In his book, *The Natural Mind,* Dr. Andrew Weil speaks about the human need to alter consciousness. He says, "It is my belief that the desire to alter consciousness periodically is an innate, normal drive analogous to hunger or the sexual drive" (p. 19). He goes on to describe the activities of children who experiment with nonordinary states by whirling around until they fall down in a stupor, hyperventilating and having a playmate squeeze them around the chest until they faint, or by holding their breath until they feel dizzy or lose consciousness. It is important to note that this deep need to change consciousness is an impulse toward the healing potential of these states.

It is easy to see that it is not far from spinning around on the playground to change consciousness to the use of mind-altering chemicals. In February 1991, Antonia Novello, the Surgeon-General of the United States, issued a report on "Alcohol Practices, Policies, and Potentials of American Colleges and Universities." According to this report, the average college student consumes over 34 gallons of alcohol a year, or 430 million gallons total. This is enough to fill 3,500 Olympic-sized swimming pools, roughly one for each college or university in the country. Most of the alcohol intake comes from beer: just short of 4 billion cans per year. College students pay $5.5 billion out of pocket money a year on alcohol, which is more than they spend on textbooks and far exceeds the operating costs of running college and university libraries. The report goes on to discuss the growing trend toward drinking with the intent to get drunk, increased alcohol-related violence and crime on campus, and states that, "More of our current college students in America will die of cirrhosis of the liver than will ever get doctorates in Business, Management, and Communications combined."

These statistics represent one way in which a positive inner impulse can be misdirected. I believe that, rather than describing the degeneration of the college-aged population, these statistics reflect a group of human beings who are hurting and who are intensely searching for a connection with something beyond their ordinary, limited scope of existence. And those who attend college represent only a fraction of their age-group; many young people share the same addictive problems. Largely because we do not have sanctioned frameworks in which to deeply experience the thirst for wholeness, this craving is often misdirected and distorted into addictions of all kinds. By my definition, addictions involve not only the use of chemicals, but also eating disorders, sexual addictions, gambling, addiction to power, money, or relationships, and a myriad of other addictive activities.

I believe that good addictions treatment centers are some of the few sanctioned frameworks in this culture in which true rites of passage take place. There, in a loving and supportive atmosphere, an individual in the dying phase of a profound, life-transforming death and rebirth process is allowed to hit bottom and move into regeneration and healing. Many of the therapists have been introduced to their roles through their own initiation into recovery. Consequently, they are extremely able to support and guide others.

"JUST SAY NO" IS NOT ENOUGH

Now that we have identified some aspects of the problem that we are addressing and have tried to make a case for the necessity of rites of passage, I would like to offer some constructive suggestions. In order to alleviate the current crisis within the adolescent community, any attempt to implement some kind of sanctioned rites of passage must be directed at the roots of the issues. Such projects must include well-grounded, solid approaches that address the deepest levels of the problem. They cannot be band-aid measures; *"Just Say No"* is not enough, nor is fighting violence with violence. Slapping teenage addicts into jail will not quench their spiritual thirst. If we as concerned community members aim at the deep sources of the conflicts, I feel that we have an excellent chance of curtailing or even preventing much of the destructive acting-out during the teenage years. We can offer the adolescent population a chance to heal and evolve into aware and productive members of their communities and of our world.

For such a project to be truly effective, there must be some essential ingredients present. First, for some people, implementing rites of passage will necessitate *an essential shift in attitude* about the individuals with whom they are working. Early psychological approaches incorporated the idea that the deeper we go within ourselves, the worse it gets—the more we discover the instinctual forces of aggression, fear, and deviant sexual impulses, as well as the dark fantasies that we all carry. Unfortunately, this picture of human beings as scarred and defective has leaked into many of our cultural attitudes.

·The image of human beings that emerges from addictions recovery, Jungian psychology, transpersonal psychology, mythology, and various spiritual traditions is that we each exist simultaneously as limited individuals who are strongly identified with our bodies, our lives, and the material world, and as spiritual entities who have unlimited potential. We live with a paradox: we are at once human and divine, limited and eternal, the part and the whole. We are both the small self and the deeper Self. And we can directly experience these two aspects of our nature.

According to these approaches, the barriers that keep us from contacting the wisdom and healing capacity of the deeper Self are, in part, the unaddressed emotions and experiences from our past. Transformation, healing, or spiritual progress takes place through turning inward and systematically facing and removing the screens between us and our potential. This image of ourselves, as material beings who have unlimited potential, is a very different attitude from the one that seems to prevail in some of our culture. Approaching adolescents with the attitude that each one contains all of his or her own answers is a much more useful and hopeful one than seeing them as bundles of problems.

Second, if rites of passage are to be implemented, they *must address the spiritual needs of those going through them.* Otherwise they will not have much impact. In the past decades, there has been a great deal of focus on the physical, emotional, mental, educational, and social dynamics of the adolescent years. All of these areas are extremely important parts of the picture. However, one critical piece has been largely ignored or denied: the spiritual aspect. I am not talking about hierarchies and dogma, nor am I discussing the church vs. the state. I am talking about the deep pool of creativity, inspiration, and love that exists within each of us.

Third, in order to reach the spiritual potential that often lies hidden, *some work with nonordinary states of consciousness is essential.* I am aware that this is a loaded phrase, evoking for many people images of the sixties, drug abuse, and ineffective participation in the world. However, if Andrew Weil is right, human beings have a tremendous urge toward nonordinary states. I recently spent some time at Disney World in Orlando, Florida, where millions of people annually spend millions of dollars to have unusual experiences, become scared on the Space Mountain, or travel into other time periods and mythological realms. To some extent, we alter our consciousness each time we attend a powerful movie. Many adolescents already know that territory well; they alter their consciousness all the time, through music, dance, sex, excitement, drugs and alcohol, and other means. History tells us that certain forms of nonordinary states can be extremely productive, healing, and transformative, and are essential to our well-being.

Fourth, I feel that any rites of passage need to *incorporate some component of the psychological death and rebirth process.* This theme, leaving behind the old and entry into the new, is a common denominator of all traditional rites of passage. The death and regeneration cycle reflects the constant transitions in our lives, and if it is consciously recognized and experienced, it can open one to his or her larger potential, as well as provide a useful map for the life process.

HOW DO WE IMPLEMENT RITES OF PASSAGE?

What are some of the ways in which rites of passage might be implemented? Rather than reinvent the wheel, perhaps we can utilize some of the resources that are already present. Already, programs such as peer counseling, Outward Bound, vision quests, and accelerated learning camps which incorporate the ropes courses and other team-building approaches, have had great success with adolescents. My daughter Sarah, now in her mid-twenties, became involved in peer counseling and the ropes course camps as a freshman in high school. She got so much out of them that she participated all four years, ended up as the camp coordinator as a senior, and now works with corporations and teens using the ropes course and team-building methods. When she talked about the experiences at camp, she lit up in a very different way than when she told me about other school and social activities. Repeatedly, she spoke very movingly about the barriers of fear and self-consciousness that she and others passed through and of the deep sense of confidence and strength that began to emerge. She told me about the essential and enthusiastic support of the group, the social restrictions that melted away, and the sense of community that developed among the participants.

Joseph Campbell's explication of the hero's journey was used by film maker George Lucas as a basis of the *Star Wars* trilogy, which captured the imagination of millions of people, including adolescents, who identified with Luke Skywalker. Campbell's model reflects the three phases—*separation, initiation,* and *return*—which are present in many rites of passage. The heroine's or hero's journey, as well as other maps that have been defined by cross-cultural anthropology, mythology, and modern consciousness research, are reflections of the archetypal levels of the human psyche and are something to which everyone can respond. I would like to see such models used in the formulation of present-day rites of passage.

A key element in traditional ceremonies is the participation of those who are revered by the community. Perhaps heroic or inspirational figures in the immediate community, the city, state, or country could be involved. Look at the effect that basketball star, Magic Johnson, with his courage and grace, has had on AIDS awareness. If rock music and athletics already contain some of the elements of rites of passage, perhaps some aspects of these activities could be utilized, along with the participation of some of their leaders.

In addition, we exist in a time during which our culture has demonstrated a renewed interest in time-tested forms such as shamanism, African-American and Native American culture, Christian and Eastern mysticism, meditation, and group ritual. Consequently, a number of individuals have responded by developing some sound and creative work which respectfully incorporates lessons from ancient approaches and combines them with various therapeutic techniques.

For example, Angeles Arrien, an anthropologist and author who was raised and initiated in the Basque culture, is writing and teaching others about the importance of ritual in supporting life transitions. Gabrielle Roth, a dancer living in New York City, has devised an approach to movement which incorporates ceremonial components, group dynamics, and elemental music. Psychologist and actor, Paul Rebillot created an experiential version of "The Hero's or Heroine's Journey," which combines movement, theater, music, and Gestalt therapy. A number of people who are trained in Holotropic Breathwork have been using it successfully in adolescent addiction treatment, schools, group therapy, and private practice. In addition, other experiential therapies, such as Gestalt practice, psychodrama, and psychosynthesis, can serve as valuable tools. More research in this area would be valuable.

The resources for implementing rites of passage within an educational or community context are plentiful. There are also many challenges to the introduction of such a project. It will be necessary to generate family and community support in the face of an often-polarized and fragmented society. One might have to face reluctant school boards, teachers, or administrators who are strongly tied to traditional ways of approaching educational and social issues. And there may be confusion about or resistance to an approach that is experientially based. A lot can be done by presenting projects such as this in understandable language. With some effort, almost anything can be translated into terms and metaphors that make sense to those who might be otherwise resistant.

The challenges before children and adolescents in today's world can sometimes appear overwhelming. I am someone who has always cared deeply about the problems of the world; in the past, whenever I allowed myself to think too hard about the scope of the challenges, I would feel discouraged. Then, several years ago, I had a chance to meet Mother Teresa and see her do her work in India. Since that day, she has remained an inspiration to me. If Mother Teresa had walked into Calcutta and had allowed herself to be overwhelmed by the tremendous suffering there, she would never have accomplished what she has. Instead, she simply did what was in front of her. She picked up the first person from the street. And look what happened.

REFERENCES

Arrien, Angeles. 1993. *The four-fold way: Walking the paths of the warrior, healer, teacher, and visionary.* San Francisco: HarperCollins.
———. 1992. *Signs of life.* Sonoma, Calif.: Arcus Publishing Company.
Campbell, Joseph. 1949. *The hero with a thousand faces.* Princeton: Princeton University Press.
———. 1972. *Myths to live by.* New York: The Viking Press.
Cohen, David, ed. 1991. *The circle of life: Rituals from the human family album.* San Francisco: Harper.
Eliade, Mircea. 1987. *The encyclopedia of religion.* New York: Macmillan Publishing Company.
Gennep, Arnold van. 1909. *Les rites de passage.* Paris. (Translated by Monika B. Visedom and Gabrielle L. Caffee as *The Rites of Passage,* University of Chicago Press, 1990.)
Grof, Christina. 1993. *The thirst for wholeness: Attachment, addiction, and the spiritual path.* San Francisco: HarperCollins.
Grof, Christina, and Stanislav Grof. 1990. *The stormy search for the self.* Los Angeles: Jeremy P. Tarcher, Inc.
Grof, Stanislav. 1988. *The adventure of self-discovery.* Albany: State University of New York Press.
Grof, Stanislav, ed. 1988. *Human survival and consciousness evolution.* Albany: State University of New York Press.
Grof, Stanislav, and Christina Grof. 1980. *Beyond death: The gates of consciousness.* London: Thames and Hudson.
———. 1989. *Spiritual emergency: When personal transformation becomes a crisis.* Los Angeles: Jeremy P. Tarcher, Inc.
Harner, Michael. 1980. *The way of the shaman.* New York: Harper and Row.
Keen, Sam. 1986. *Faces of the enemy: Reflections of the hostile imagination.* San Francisco: Harper.
Mead, Margaret. 1973. Ritual: Reconciliation in change. Paper given at a symposium at Burg Wartenstein, Austria, Wenner-Gren Foundation, New York City.
Mettrick, Sidney, and Renee Beck. 1990. *The art of ritual.* Berkeley, Calif.: Celestial Arts.
Novello, Antonia. 1991. *See* U.S. Department of Health and Human Services. Alcohol, Drug Abuse, and Mental Health Administration. 1991.
Rebillot, Paul. Forthcoming. *Entering the mystery: Following the path of the hero.* San Francisco: HarperCollins.
Roth, Gabrielle. 1989. *Maps to ecstasy: Teachings of an urban shaman.* San Rafael, Calif.: New World Library.
U.S. Department of Health and Human Services. Alcohol, Drug Abuse, and Mental Health Administration. 1991. *Alcohol practices, policies, and potentials of American colleges and universities.* Washington, D.C.
Weil, Andrew. 1972. *The natural mind.* Boston: Houghton Mifflin Company.

TWO

RITUAL, THE SACRED, AND COMMUNITY

Malidoma Somé

Malidoma Somé offers a new perspective on modern America from his background among the Dagara people of West Africa. He challenges us to awaken our own inner indigenous aspects. This is a recurrent image coming from deep layers within modern people and closely connected to the instincts and the soul. He writes: "A different set of priorities dwells there, a set of priorities long forgotten in higher cultures. People in touch with that archetype are in search of caring. . . . these are the kind of people in need of ritual."

Malidoma, whose name means "be friends with the stranger/enemy," was born under the shadow of French colonial rule in Upper Volta (now Burkina Faso), West Africa. When he was four years old, he was taken by a Jesuit Father and "imprisoned" in a seminary built for training a new generation of black Catholic priests. This was the beginning of fifteen years of isolation from his family, during which Malidoma's keepers abused him and attempted to intimidate him into forgetting everything "tribal" and indoctrinate him into seeing the world through the lens of French language, culture, and white man's religion.

With the help of the spirit of his grandfather Bakhye, his teacher, guide, and constant companion in childhood, Malidoma resisted the daily brainwashing which he and his fellow students experienced. Malidoma stubbornly refused to forget where he had come from or who he was.

Finally, a decade and a half later, Malidoma escaped from the seminary and walked 125 miles through the jungle, back to his own people, the Dagara. Once home, however, he received a mixed welcome. He could not remember enough Dagara to speak to his own mother and father. Many people in the tribe regarded him as a "white black," a person to be looked upon with suspicion and fear because he had been contaminated by the "sickness" of the colonial world. Malidoma had become an outsider, a man of two worlds, at home in neither.

Over the next year, he came to realize that his only hope of reconnecting with his people was to undergo the traditional Dagara initiation ritual, even though that meant risking death. During this month-long initiation in a wilderness camp, Malidoma experienced a dramatic meeting with the forces of the supernatural, and his own personal power.

Today, Malidoma is a medicine man, diviner, author, and teacher. He lives as a man of two worlds, flying the jetways and writing on his laptop computer, sharing ancient wisdom of the Dagara with thousands of people, and bringing an understanding of the Western perspective back to his village. Malidoma holds three master's degrees, as well as Ph.D.'s from the Sorbonne and Brandeis. For three years he taught literature at the University of

Michigan. A popular speaker at Men's Movement gatherings, he discusses tribal customs, daily life, and spiritual beliefs, the world of the ancestors, and—most importantly—the life-giving process of initiation. He lives with his wife, Sobonfu, in Oakland, California.

Malidoma Somé is author of *Ritual: Power, Healing, and Community* (Newberg, Oregon: Swan Raven & Company, 1993) from which this chapter is adapted, and also *Of Water and the Spirit: Ritual, Magic, and Initiation in the Life of an African Shaman* (New York: Tarcher/Putnam, 1994).

Just as some Westerners can't conceive of life without running water, electricity, commodities, and MTV, indigenous people in tribal Africa can't conceive life without ritual. People's lives on both sides are defined by their attachment to these things, and the attachments on each side are equally strong. But although ritual is an old ingredient in the rhythm of indigenous life, it has been replaced in the modern world with a number of things including those mentioned above, and it seems as if its absence in the West is being felt at great cost, namely in the general impoverishment of the psyche and the spirit. The inability of material accumulation to replace the craving for spirit, the loss of viable forms of community, and the all-out epidemics of isolation and individualism, are symptomatic of the crushing effects of the abandonment of rituals. Where ritual is absent, the young ones are restless or violent, there are no real elders, and the grown-ups are bewildered. The future is dim. Consequently, we must stress that ritual is an inevitable and necessary component of human life. It will not suffer any substitution or deletion from memory.

A people that lives as a community takes ritual as the soil upon which its future grows. Ritual is therefore something fundamental to look at if modern society wants to make the effort to reconnect with its own sense of wholeness, with spirit, and with a durable sense of community. It establishes the inescapable tie with the Otherworld, namely the ancestors, and is one of the things that young people respond to the most. In every society, the young ones are the future of the old ones. To allow this future to happen, the old ones must work with the Otherworld. For the old ones to do this work, they must be acknowledged and empowered. When an elder fails to perform his work with respect to the spiritual, the future of this elder, the youth, is threatened.

For the Dagara people of West Africa, ritual is above all else that by which the entire community is genuinely connected. In a way, they think of themselves as coming from the spirit world that is composed of the world of the ancestors—the place where the dead go to rest—and the world of spirits where nonhuman entities in charge of the order of nature dwell.

In such a tribal community, there are several types of ritual. There are *communal rituals,* which every grown-up member of the village is obliged to attend. These gatherings take care of the village's need to reaffirm its unity under one spirit. There are also *family rituals,* which are done by a subcommunity to honor certain spirits in the name of family unity or for other more personalized reasons. It is the community ritual that allows these isolated semiprivate family rituals to work effectively. Family rituals are performed under the guidance of the family head and in the presence of every responsible family member. Any initiated or married person is considered responsible and must attend family rituals.

From these family rituals and, in a way, from community rituals too, there are derived *individual rituals.* A father who fails to perform certain kinds of rituals designed to ensure the steady growth of his children puts them at a high risk of being snatched away by sudden violent accidents including death. Violent death does not only affect the families in which it occurs, but also affects the community as a whole because it constitutes a troubling reminder of the high cost associated with the abandonment of rituals.

Individual rituals are just as important as family rituals and community rituals. This means that these rituals are interdependent even though they look separate. Likewise, a ritual performed by a community liberates a certain energy that makes it possible for other rites to happen on a family, clan, and individual level.

These ritualistic hierarchies are not designed at random. Among certain tribal communities in Africa, including the Dagara, when the customary village rituals are not performed, other rituals suffer in effectiveness. Ten years ago, my village suffered drought because the priest of the Earth Shrine had passed away, leaving his first son to carry on the priestly tradition. But his son either forgot or refused to perform this fundamental rite. It should be noted that the priest of the Earth Shrine is usually seen as a collective person. Whatever he does, alone or in the presence of the village, is considered communal. So if he fails to do anything, the community suffers.

Families gathered to carry on with their family rituals and individuals complied with their individual rituals, but disaster resulted anyway. Many died in the drought including the new priest of the Earth Shrine. Individual duties in ritual cannot take the place of communal duties and vice versa. We all owe to the cosmic order, and it is impossible, at this level, to do for the others what the others are expected to do for themselves. We owe to the cosmic order because we are individually and communally responsible for its maintenance, not its domination and control.

Social decay creeps in when everyday living displaces ritual as the focus. The fading and disappearance of ritual in modern culture is, from the viewpoint of Dagara people, expressed in several ways: the dangerous weakening of links with the spirit world, the general alienation of people from themselves and each other, the frightening violence spreading like a gangrene from the middle of cities, and the militaristic approach to its resolution. In a context like this there are no elders to help anyone remember through rites of passage his or her important role in community and in life. Those who seek to remember have an attraction toward violence. They live their life constantly upset or angry, or in a life-threatening high, and those responsible for them are at a loss as to what to do. To be able to face our fears, we must remember how to perform rituals. To remember how to perform rituals, we must slow down.

I believe that one of the differences between the modern industrial world and the indigenous world has mostly to do with speed—and not with whether one world needs to have ritual and the other doesn't. Speed takes a toll on our attention by weakening our vigilance. By doing so it endangers the person in speed. On the contrary a life in the slow lane, however boring it may look to the person speeding away, affords the traveler many scenic details to enjoy and saves him the upsetting surprises that result from oversight.

Indigenous people are indigenous not because they don't look and act like everybody else, but mainly because there are no machines between them and their gods. There are no machines to bar the doors to the spirit world: one can enter, listen to what is going on within at a deep level, and participate in the vibration of Nature. Where machines speak in place of gods, people are hard put to listen, even more hard put to vibrate with the realm of Nature.

Thus the two worlds of the traditional and the industrial seem to be oddly opposed. The indigenous world, in trying to emulate Nature, espouses a walk in life which is slow and quiet. The modern world, on the other hand, steams through life like a locomotive, controlled by an intimidating sense of power, carelessness, waste, and destruction. Such life eats at the psyche; as it moves its victims faster and faster along, they are progressively emptied of their spiritual and psychic fuel. It is here, consequently, where one's Spirit is in crisis, and speed is the yardstick by which the crisis itself is expressed.

In other words, the indigenous archetype within the modern soul is in serious need of acknowledgment. There is a starvation of the soul within the person. A different set of priorities dwells there, a set of priorities long forgotten in higher cultures. People in touch with that archetype are in search of caring, for their spirits seek to transcend the stress placed on the body and the mind by the rapid motion of everyday life around them. Such people would not be ashamed to express their hunger for transcendence—these are the kind of people who are in need of ritual.

The modern seeker of ritual primarily acknowledges that she or he is wounded, or hollowed out, or emptied of his or her vital spiritual substance, and lured into the fast lane of life in an attempt to cover up. Yet, these wounds are evidence of the need to enter into a special creative process. They are the language with which entry into the realm of ritual is possible. As long as one does not deploy special energy to repress and deny these wounds, but rather contains them creatively, that is, in ritual, then one is working on oneself as a potential survivor of the hurt that one feels in the midst of modern culture.

This is so because human senses are devices of communication. Sight is a language, as are touch, smell, taste, pain, and sound. The most powerful among them is the feeling of pain. For the Dagara elder, pain is the result of a resistance to something new—something toward which an old dispensation is at odds. We are made of layers of situations and experiences. Each one of them likes to use a specific part of ourselves in which to lodge. It's like a territory. A new experience that does not have a space to sit in within us will have to kick an old one out. The old one that does not want to leave will resist the new one, and the result is registered by us as pain. This is why elders call it Tuo. It means invasion, hunting, meeting with a violent edge. It also means boundary. Pain, therefore, is our body complaining about an intruder. Body complaint is understood as the soul's need for some communication with its spiritual counterpart.

More often than not, the fast pace of life, made worse by so many drug substitutes, does not allow us to work through our pain. Instead, we think that pain is a signal that we must stop, rather than follow it up to its source. Yet, our souls do not like stagnation. Our souls aspire toward growth, that is, toward remembering all that we have forgotten in the course of our trip to this earth. In this context, a body in pain is a soul in longing. To shut down the pain is to override the call of the soul to change. When this happens it is a repressive measure taken against oneself, which has somber consequences.

Is it possible then to say that pain is good, primarily because it is a call to growth? The Dagara elders would say yes. They believe that a person who has suffered is a person who has heard pain (Won Tuo). The person hears pain as a creative action, and this connects that person with his or her highest self. This connection is in itself a ritual experience awaiting acknowledgment. It pulls the person into the neighborhood of mystery and spirituality. So pain at least teaches us something. It is commotion, emotion, and a call for a rebirth. It teaches that one must return to a code of living that begins with life itself. It draws from nature and seeks to align with what ancient tribal communities have valued for thousands of years: a code of living that allows room for the entire person to exist. In this context ritual means a return to the ancients with a plea for help directed to the world of the spirit. It is therefore evident that, in order for the modern world to heal, it must return to the past, to exactly the point where it began to forget rituals.

Village life revolves around subsistence activities (farming and hunting) and the practice of ritual. In a way, subsistence work links humans together while ritual links humans to the gods or God. If one lives in a context in which everything that is done is first ritualized, the sense of wholeness and belonging is greatly enhanced. Living with my people during my university years, I had the sense that the dead were not really dead. At least once a day there was something to say to the ancestors. At least once a day a word was addressed to the shrine of Nature, be it at home before undertaking a journey to the farm or to another village, or in the farm before working at it. The overall impression was that there is a constant need to involve the divine in our activities, because we believe that human output is only possible through the intervention of spirit. More importantly, an output that excludes spirit becomes dangerous to the person to whom this output is credited, and in the long run human achievements become dangerous to anything that lives.

Consequently, each time we enter a ritual space we do so because we are involved with a creative process which requires spirit's sponsorship in order for its output to benefit us properly. We also enter into ritual space because something in the physical world has warned us of possible deterioration at hand. This presupposes that one does not enter into a ritual without a purpose, a goal. Ritual is called for because our soul communicates things to us that the body translates as need, or want, or absence. So we enter into ritual in order to respond to the call of the soul. So illness, perhaps, is the sign language of the soul in need of attention. This means that our soul is the part of us that picks up on situations well ahead of our conscious awareness of them. Purpose is the driving force that contributes to the effectiveness of ritual.

In the village, there are rituals that can backfire on the person performing them. These rituals do not have a purpose and thereby turn against the performer. This is tricky, because one would assume that any ritual done to heal must be good. Elders say that ritual is like an arrow shot at something. When the intended target is not there, it seems that the arrow invents one. In such cases, the target may be a positive manifestation, but it could also be a negative manifestation. Take, for example, a case in which someone sacrifices a chicken prior to a journey instead of pouring libation. The chicken sacrifice has the power, say, of righting a wrongdoing. In this journey, no wrongdoing existed. Because of that, the person would meet trouble along the way because that person had set himself up for it. It is like taking pills for a headache when you are fine, and ending up with a stomach ache because of it. So, in such a case, the ritual is just misdirected.

Ritual is also imposed on us by our souls even though we can still prevail on our souls for rituals. In other words, ritual can happen without someone feeling pain. It can happen just because someone is about to do something creative. In this case it is either a preventive ritual or a celebration ritual. Among the Dagara, a good harvest must be celebrated with the gods. The whole village chooses one day in the course of which samples of harvest are brought to the gods along with sacrifices of chickens or goats. This ritual offering is followed by a feast that translates the human expression of oneness with the divine. Consequently, the purpose of this ritual is to avoid having to face a later ritual having to do with pain. This means that when one cruises with the world of the spirits, rituals are less and less a matter of stopping commotions than they are a matter of maintaining a healthy balance. Yet to arrive at that level of harmony, one must stay in the practice of ritual for a lengthy period of time.

The success of a ritual depends on the purpose of the individuals involved with it. Any ritual designed to satisfy an ego is a ritual for show, and therefore is a spiritual farce. But when the persons involved invite the spirits to come and help in something that humans are not capable of handling by themselves, or when humans honor gift giving from the divine, there is likelihood of the ritual working.

So ritual draws from this area of human existence where the spirit plays a life-giving role. We do not make miracles; rather, we speak the kind of language that is interpreted by the supernatural world as a call to intervene in a stabilizing way in a particular life. Consequently, our role in ritual is to be human. We take the initiative to spark the process, knowing that its success is not in our hands but in the hands of the kind of forces that we invoke into our lives. So the force field we create within a ritual is something coming from the spirit, not something coming from us. We are only instruments in this kind of interaction between dimensions, between realms.

Consequently, there is ritual each time a spirit is called to intervene in human affairs. The structure of the ritual is what I would like to call ceremonial because it can vary from time to time and from place to place. So a ceremony, perhaps, is the anatomy of a ritual. It shows what actually is taking place in the visible world, on the surface. The invisible part of the ritual, that which actually happens as a result of the spirit being there, is what carries the ritual quality within itself.

In the ritual, one has to have participants who are invisible and can actually produce the result that is expected. And because we take the risk or the initiative of putting a request to spirits to intervene in our affairs, their coming turns our activity (ceremony) into a ritual. It still means that we, as individuals, play a central role in making a ritual happen. The gods themselves will not enact a ritual without us. What actually makes a ritual a requirement is far beyond what the world, as it is, can handle. In the surface world our ability to make things happen is very limited. This limitation is a reflection of the incompleteness of a world without the spirit realm. So spirit is our channel through which every gap in life can be filled. But the spirit realm will not take care of these gaps without our conscious participation. Thus our collaboration and surrendering make us central to the actual happening of a ritual.

Initiation is the longest ritual one gets involved in within the village. In it there are things that can be talked about by initiates and things that can be revealed to noninitiates. But there are several specifics about certain rites or secrets that can never be disclosed. To do so is not just forbidden; it can be deadly to the discloser. One reason is found in the sacred, hidden, and silent space of ritual itself. Things native to that space have no intention of being brought into the surface world, lest they lose their power or lose their ability to act the way they are expected or needed to act. It would be like taking a fish out of water and expecting the fish to demonstrate its ability to swim. For the elder who is usually officiating, hiding the nature of his relationship with a spiritual force is the way to keep this relationship alive. The relationship draws more strength, more power, and even gets more momentum within its hiddenness.

We call spirits into a crowd of people in order to help achieve goals that cannot be achieved in any other way. This calling needs to remain in safe containment, the way a baby remains hidden prior to being born. Safe containment means keeping the space away from any impurities, any unwanted intrusions. This is why the space in which we do ritual must be clearly delineated, made to look beautiful, and command our respect. A society that is accustomed to sacred space will have no problem noticing it elsewhere. Conversely, a society that can't tell the difference between a sacred space and a profane space is showing the symptoms of spiritual erosion. It wants everything to be barren, clear in a predefined way, and ultimately controllable.

Disclosure or exhibition threatens the relationship between us and the spirit we invoke within ritual. Consequently, an outsider cannot be invited into a ritual already in progress unless that person is already in a ritual space of his own. This presupposes that every person you meet on the road has had a little ash and water ritual at home and has spoken to his own ancestors before starting the journey. This is common in traditional Dagara world. So when not sure, better to avoid taking risks. Intrusion into a ritual space is a profaning of that ritual space and the spirits invoked. The spirit will become agitated and will react as though the intruder intends to rip it open. Spirits care about our having called them in without telling them that there are intruders who intend to rip them open. The profane is the allergy of spirit. Within a ritual space, anything that is not sacred threatens to desecrate the hallowedness of what is happening. Consequently, if ritual space is the ideal place of community, the profane is the place where community breaks apart.

Community is formed whenever more than one person meets for a purpose, in the sense required for ritual. Any group of people meeting with the intention of connecting to the power within is a community. Each member is like a cell in a body that feels an indivisible sense of unity. But a community is also a place of self-definition.

It is therefore evident that if the modern world has shrunk the sacred and pushed it away into some buildings, it has done so to fragment the much needed sense of community. So every time someone craves for the sacred, that person also craves for community and vice-versa. The sacred does not compete with whatever else is, but endows genuine functionality to existence.

Without a community you cannot be yourself. The community is where we draw the strength needed to effect changes inside of us. What one acknowledges in the formation of the community is the possibility of doing together what is impossible to do alone. This means that individual problems quickly become community problems. Being open to each other depends on trust. What we want is to create a community that meets the intrinsic needs of every individual. The individual can finally discover within the community something to relate to, because deep down inside each of us is a craving to be honored and be seen for who we are. Finding a home is what people in community try to accomplish. In community it is possible to restore a supportive presence for one another. The others in community are the reason that one feels the way one feels. The elder cannot be an elder if there is no community to make him an elder. The young boy cannot feel secure if there is no elder whose silent presence gives him hope in life. The adult cannot be who he is unless there is a strong sense of presence of the other people around. This interdependency is what I call supportive presence.

We need ritual because it is an expression of the fact that we recognize the difficulty of creating and remaining in community. A community that does not have a ritual cannot exist. A corporate community is not a community. It is a conglomeration of individuals in the service of an insatiable soulless entity. What we need is the ability to come together with a constantly increasing mindset of wanting to do the right thing, even though we know very well that we don't know how nor where to start. This seemingly frightening position is amusing to the spirit that watches over you. Your desire alone is strong enough to guide you along the path. But, of course, it is useful to know certain elemental steps such as invoking the Spirit of the Ancestors, or Nature, or the Earth. Knowing what spirit to invoke and what to do with that spirit depends on your ability to stay focused on your purpose. You must be willing to speak of your inabilities, your clumsiness. And for this to happen, ritual must be the principal ingredient of one's operating dynamics. Ritual must be constantly invoked as an opportunity for the weak to become strong and the strong to get even stronger.

THREE

RITES OF PASSAGE AT THE END OF THE MILLENNIUM

Michael Meade

Michael Meade writes: "There may be no time more suited to the study of rites of passage than the threshold between the end of modernity and the uncertain future of humanity." This threshold involves all of us as we return to the roots of knowledge, the roots of consciousness, and the seeds of meaning hidden in each person.

(The biography of Michael Meade appears at the beginning of this book.)

The close of the twentieth century can be looked at simply, even fundamentally, as "The End," or else can be seen as a time of thorough change, a period of radical alteration, a rush of endings and beginnings. The distinctions between the ways we view change and death become more important at the end of eras, at funeral rites, and at births. The attitudes of mourners have a crucial effect on a funeral, and the manner of the attendants at a birth can help or harm the new life. Midwives once assisted the newborn into this world and helped the newly dead on to the "other world." Willingly, or not, we are all attendants at the funeral of the last era and the birth of the next. We are all midwives placing the shroud on a body soon to disappear and anointing the next birth with our prayers, fears, denials, and hopes.

The radical dismantling of institutions, boundaries, beliefs, and ecosystems that characterizes the end of the era is an extended funeral that we can consciously attend or try to deny. At some level we each know that huge shifts in nature and culture are affecting us daily. But, without some spiritual vision and ritual structure we lose the capacity to handle death and embrace life fully. Instead, we build walls of denial to hold off terror and confusion and try to cover our helplessness with displays of force and greed. Denial arises as a primary symptom of the age because of the scope of changes already under way and as a defense against the flood of losses and endings. The cost of mass denial can be found in the increase of random violence, increased abuse of drugs, the collapse of medicine, and the confusion in personal, gender, and national identities. And the momentum of loss increases because a death unmourned becomes a lingering ghost that haunts the living until it receives its allotment of attention and tears. Meanwhile, each birth unprepared and uncared for invites the reckless spirits of chaos to feed on the next generation.

At the end of the millennium, underlying patterns of initiatory death and rebirth erupt through the surface of cultures and disrupt cycles of nature. There may be no time more suited to the study of rites of passage than the threshold between the end of modernity and the uncertain future of humanity.

As old proverbs remind: "We can only see as far forward as we remember back." The future is contained in the past; and the past is carried within us like seeds of memory waiting for the waters of attention.

In this light, a study of initiation rites becomes a tracing of the lines of "spiritual history." When rites of passage disappear in the storm of modern, materialistic cultures, we can track the survival of the rites and symbols in the realms of dreams, anthropology, literature, and psychotherapy.

Initiation is a universal rite, an archetypal form that surfaces and influences life wherever events have the spirit of beginning or the weight of an end. As an elemental pattern or archetypal style, initiation is a "whole way" of seeing into the world, one that sees death as part of the fabric of life. On the ground of initiation, death is the opposite of birth, not the opposite of life. Life includes both, and the spirit of life regenerates in the land of death. Archaic rites of initiation show the basic pattern for genuine change. For any transformation to be meaningful it must be thorough, and to be thorough requires both the ache of loss and a spirit of regeneration.

Mircea Eliade writes that "it is only in initiation that death is given a positive value." More than an empty tomb, death becomes also the womb of change. In dreams and dramas of initiation, death represents change for the entire psyche and life of a person. It means change inside and out, not a simple adaptation or switch in "lifestyle." Initiation includes death and rebirth, a radical altering of a person's "mode of being"; a shattering and shaking all the way to the ground of the soul. The initiate becomes as another person: more fully in life emotionally and more spiritually aware. Loss of identity and even feeling betrayal of one's self are essential to rites of passage. In that sense, every initiation causes a funeral and a birth; a mourning appropriate to death and a joyous celebration for the restoration of full life. Without conscious rituals of loss and renewal, individuals and societies lose the capacity to experience the sorrows and joy that are essential for feeling fully human. Without them life flattens out, and meaning drains from both living and dying. Soon there is a death of meaning and an increase in meaningless deaths.

Traditional rites of passage were based in the hard knowledge that the sanctity of life and the making of a meaningful death must be struggled for by each person and that the entire drama must be recast for each generation. Participating in "ordeals of finding meaning" was both an inheritance and a requirement that made each child a central figure in his or her own dream and in the life of the tribe. In contrast to our practice of criticizing young people for unnecessarily drawing attention to themselves, an awareness of initiation draws everyone to the young people to see the future emerging from them. Youth naturally feel drawn to thresholds of the "unconscious" and the unfinished; they are both knowing and unknowing. If our first birth is a fall into life, this "second birth" falls toward death and the underworld. It requires a return to the roots of knowledge, the roots of consciousness, and the seeds of meaning hidden in each person. Only by a descent and a series of adventures along the dark roads of the unconscious can the inner life fully awaken. Rites of initiation are intended to make the inevitable descent a direct opening of the spirit and soul in the life of each youth. Through that opening the woman comes out of the girl, and the man separates from the boy. Childhood ends and the next drama begins.

Initiation means beginning the revelation of one's true self. It includes the opening up of the inner life of the spirit and releasing the potentials and possibilities within the individual. Beyond that, the initiations of youth always imply an opportunity for the cleansing and restoration of the life force of the community and the society. The initiation of youths into full life also represents a critical opportunity for a society to sustain meaning and teach life-affirming values. As Eliade says, "this meaning is always religious." Or as we now might say, the meaning is always spiritual, elementally spiritual, before becoming religious. During initiation the individual becomes bound through spiritual experience to the future of the society as well as open to the origins and ancestral beginnings of the group in the past. For a time, the initiate steps out of being simply himself or herself and becomes an ancestral, dream-time hero or heroine reentering the origin stories of the culture. By shedding the skin of their limited sense of self, marked by the time they were born into and the family they were born amongst, the initiates encounter the sacred. Temporarily, they walk in the footsteps of heroes and heroines engaged in elemental struggles, touched by mystery, learning to sustain life and face death.

When rites of passage disappear from conscious presentation, they nonetheless appear in unconscious and semi-conscious guises. They surface as misguided and misinformed attempts to change one's own life. They become miscarriages of meaning, tragic acts or empty forms, and ghostly shapes. For, underlying the surface structures of schools, fraternities, sororities, maternity groups, military organizations, street gangs, rap bands, crack houses, meditation centers, and prisons lie the bones and sinews of initiatory rites and symbols. Whenever life gets stuck or reaches a dead end, where people are caught in rites of addiction, possessed by destructive images, compelled to violent acts, or pulled apart by grief and loss, the process of initiation presses to break through. The most important reason to study rites of passage may be to see, in the events erupting in the streets and at the borders and crossroads of our post-historic era, the archaic energies of life renewing itself. As old walls fall and institutions rattle, even older forces of change and renewal gather to pour through the cracks.

Learning the language of initiation, as Eliade points out, means finding in the inevitable struggles of our own lives "certain types of real ordeals . . . the spiritual crises, the solitude and despair through which every human being must pass in order to attain to a responsible, genuine, and creative life. Even if the initiatory character of these ordeals is not apprehended as such, it remains true nonetheless that man becomes *himself* [and woman herself] only after having solved a series of desperately difficult and even dangerous situations; that is, after having undergone 'tortures' and 'death,' followed by an awakening to another life. . . . If we look closely, we see that every human life is made up of a series of ordeals, of 'deaths,' and of 'resurrections.'"

Seen with an eye for initiation and mystery, addictions are rites of substitution, where "tortures and death" occur on a "junk" level that can't quite create a breakthrough. The ritual revolves around a "cracked quest" for spiritual relief, but keeps repeating the same alchemical mistake and moves toward actual death when real change was the desire. In descriptions of shamanic dismemberment and dazed/crazed out-of-body wanderings can be seen the "spirit afflictions" of the hordes of homeless psyches and homeless people that increasingly haunt the cracking streets of modern cities. Like scenes from initiatory rituals, the unconscious breaks through, the psyche turns inside-out, and inner sufferings become outer dramas. But, unlike the conscious efforts of rites of passage, the sacrifice doesn't work; a spiritual home in the heart of the tribe is not found. Rebirth does not happen.

Without a ritual to contain and inform the wounds of life, pain and suffering increase, yet meaningful change doesn't occur. Where drops of blood once symbolized life trying to change, pools of blood stain street after street without renewing the spirit of life. Instead of ritual descent and emotional resurrection, complete death occurs; actual corpses pile up. Instead of the startling hum of bullroarers twirled by unpredictable elders, the wail of sirens, the crack of bullets, and the whirl of flashing lights bring the "underworld" to life each night. Instead of participating in a prepared rite for leaving childhood games through ordeals of emotional struggle and spiritual alertness, gangs of blindly wounded youth hurl their woundedness at the darkness and spit angry bullets at groups that are their mirror image, attacking masks of themselves. The sacrificial blood once offered by those trying to glimpse mysteries at the thresholds of the stages of life has become bloody "street sacrifices" of entire generations. An unconscious, chaotic amassing of death gathers where the terms of passage instead required some honest suffering, a scar to mark the event, and a community to accept and acknowledge the change. Denying that each individual must struggle at the thresholds of spiritual and emotional self-discovery eventually destroys any shared awareness of the sanctity of life.

In the symbolic mind and in the ritual imagination of most peoples, a small amount of blood exposed to the outside world represents the immediate, mutual presence of life and death. The metaphor of showing blood to make a change brings the death of what was contained and the birth of something that was hidden. In the history of initiation, woundings, beatings, scarifications, and hair-cutting represent dying by losing some part of the living world to the "other world" of death. In order to gain an increase of life for the individual evolving and for the community involved with that individual, something must be sacrificed or "made sacred." When a culture loses its ability to make real changes and new meaning out of individual suffering, the quantity of violence, blood spilling, and meaningless death increases for everyone.

Behind all involvements of young people with danger hides the desire to find full life through a symbolic death that reveals a core of meaning and purpose in their lives. The beatings administered to prospective members of modern street gangs are semi-conscious reflections of ancient rites of separation. The foolish dramas of fraternity and military hazings increasingly miss and obscure the actual need to experience "spiritual hazards." Unguided by ritual elders and genuine spiritual aims, all groups become simple "gangs." In contrast are the many examples of complete rituals of separation, ordeals, and return of the "twice-born." In one pattern, the ritual beating of the initiate is followed by a fall into narcotic sleep and a funeral service. Family and friends mourn the death of their loved one, who undergoes partial burial in a grave. During the burial time he receives specific spiritual and psychological instruction, has time to reflect on the past, and an opportunity to view the future from the grave. Eventually, there follows the resurrection of the new person, more fully in life by feeling a "little death."

Now, it seems that we increasingly live only the first half of these rites, unconsciously enacting the wounding, narcotic sleep, and spiritual death. Living becomes profane, a "half-life," a modern tragedy of pointless suffering, abuse or addiction, loss of identity, and death-like isolation. Descents and ordeals occur randomly, without a ritual surrounding, without the benefit of the love and instruction necessary to guide a person toward the chance of a second birth. When the inner purpose and spirit of a person do not get revealed, revalued, and acknowledged by an appropriate community, people increasingly feel like victims and act like outcasts. When the rites of change are incomplete, there is an increasing sense of chaos and loss of the possibility of restoring the community through the shared joy over the return of "the dead." When the death-side of life is denied, the birth-side becomes obscured and some of the importance of each life is lost right at birth, at the beginning. In this process of loss, women's rites and mysteries get diminished as well and the womb seems to lose its place at the center of life.

Puberty rites often begin the psychological and spiritual division of rights and powers between the genders, and rites of separation often distinguish different paths for each. Boys often get called to initiatory events as part of a group that forms when there happen to be enough eligible age-mates. By contrast, a girl often begins her rite of passage individually when the mystery of her menses breaks the seal of her inner world and indicates that the spirit of a woman wants to come out. When rites of coming out are lost, the girl loses touch with her place in the community. What has been lost over time is the sense that each daughter represents the psychic as well as genetic womb of the village. Each represents the well of ancestral memories and the creative crucible from which the future will come. During initiation the womb manifests as symbol of renewal and generativity showing the body to be a spiritual vessel, necessary for understanding the body of nature and for carrying knowledge of the tribe.

When the daughter of the tribe temporarily separates from the village, she becomes as a fetus in the womb of Mother Nature. She enters a time of segregation and isolation in darkness that represents a return to the womb. Dwelling in the dark may occur in a cave, a hut with no windows, or within the hollow enclosure of a sacred tree. Each daughter must find a mysterious and unique connection to the darkness from which all life originates. The hollow tree stands symbolically as a tomb in which the daughter disappears and as a womb of the tree of life from which the woman will step. During isolation, the female initiate may not be allowed to feed or care for herself. Rather, she retreats into a still meditation on the origins of life while she is being nourished and sustained by older women. These spiritual and psychological mothers hold her in a fetal crucible prior to the second birth.

What begins as an individual and very personal break in the world of childhood typically ends as a unifying public celebration upon the return of the initiated woman. The one who disappeared into Mother Nature returns adorned with new clothes, wrapped in the knowledge of the old women of the tribe and acknowledged as a carrier of life and deep creative will. At the return, all of the village is present to recognize, admire, and acknowledge the birth of a woman from the blood and trials of a girl.

When rites of this kind are not enacted, or if they lose genuine spiritual elements, reverence for the feminine is lost and brutality toward women and girls increases. Other losses can be seen in the lack of understanding and respect for body, nature, and the mysteries of birth. Hidden behind many current afflictions of the feminine—anorexia, bulimia, and obsession with surface beauty—is a ritual emptiness, a lack of being seen, a spiritual omission. The woundings that occur during initiations can be rejected as brutal, but I would argue that greater brutality results where there are no "ordeals of meaning" and no rites of acceptance into the adult community.

In *Rites and Symbols of Initiation,* Eliade writes, "It does not fall to us to determine to what extent traditional initiations fulfilled their promises. The important fact is that they proclaimed their intention, and professed to possess the means, of transmuting human life." The intention of keeping alive the symbols and rites of passage becomes necessary for renewing life and surviving the onslaught of changes at the end of an age. Being alive at the end of this millennium means getting caught in fundamental crises that call into question every aspect of life and death. Amongst the sadness, loss, and litter at the end of the age, it becomes essential to have an eye for the symbolic and a feel for ritual as radical changes affect both time and place, both culture and nature.

© 1994 by Michael Meade. Adapted from the introduction to Mircea Eliade's new edition of *Rites and Symbols of Initiation: Mysteries of Birth and Rebirth* (Woodstock, Conn.: Spring Publications, 1994).

FOUR

THE INITIATION OF TELEMACHUS[1]

Jean Houston

"Mentor" is the name of Telemachus' tutor in the *Odyssey* of Homer. A mentor is a close, trusted, experienced counselor and guide. Mentor was called to assist in the education of Telemachus because Telemachus' father was absent. It was not known whether Odysseus, the father, was dead or alive. This story of the single-parent home and what to do about the missing father is almost three thousand years old.

Other elements of initiation are worth including in any discussion of the *Odyssey* as the great, ancient story of rites of passage. These would include purification, ritual bathing and sleep, and the wisdom of the unconscious (see Homer's *Odyssey*, translated and edited by Albert Cook [New York: W. W. Norton & Co., Inc., 1974]).

The following selection is adapted from Dr. Jean Houston's chapter about Telemachus in her book, *The Hero and the Goddess: The Odyssey as Mystery and Initiation* (New York: Ballantine Books, 1992). An internationally known author, psychologist, scientist, philosopher, and teacher, Dr. Houston has presented seminars and worked in human development in over forty countries, helping local and international developmental agencies in their quest for cultural growth and social transition. She directs the Foundation for Mind Research in New York and guides two schools, a graduate school in human capacities training and a school of cross-cultural mythic and spiritual studies, based on the ancient mystery schools.

After a decade of war in the siege of Troy described in Homer's *Iliad*, Odysseus turns toward home in Ithaca, his island kingdom west of mainland Greece, where his faithful wife, Penelope, and his young son, Telemachus, are struggling to keep alive some hope of his return. In other words, Telemachus grew up in a one-parent home.

Despite distractions, dangers, and detours along the way, Odysseus is helped by the goddess Athena who appears to him in many disguises as his guide and friend. She also decides to help Telemachus, who has been fatherless for more than ten years of childhood and adolescence, and presents herself to Odysseus' son as Mentor, whom Odysseus had asked to assist his son in his absence. This is the origin of the word "mentor," meaning counselor.

There stood up among them
Mentor, who was a companion of excellent Odysseus;
When he went on the ships he turned over his whole home to him,
To obey the old man[2] and steadfastly to protect all.

. . . .
Athena came close to him,
Likening herself to Mentor in form and in voice.
And speaking out to him, she uttered winged words:
"Telemachos, hereafter you will not be a coward or senseless.
If there is really instilled in you the good might of your father
And you are as he was to achieve both word and deed,
Then the journey will not be fruitless or unachieved."[3]

Athena/Mentor convinces Telemachus to sail from his home on the island of Ithaca to the Greek mainland on a journey of initiation. He is changed by his experience into a young man full of confidence in his heritage and potential; he previously had been a fearful adolescent, lacking in confidence. Almost one-third of the *Odyssey* is devoted to Telemachus' rite of passage.

The *Odyssey* is above all a book of initiations, the first being the initiation of Odysseus; but there is another equally important initiation, the rite of passage of Odysseus' son, Telemachus, out of boyhood into manhood. Indeed, some scholars feel that the story of the education of Telemachus, whose name means "Far Fighter," is complete in itself.

Telemachus must be "educated" to become the true heir of Odysseus, capable of assuming heroic stature. Let us now observe how this initiation process occurs for the son of Odysseus.

We first meet Telemachus in a state of utter inadequacy and living in outmoded conditions. Telemachus has ceased longing for anything. He sits passively in the background, amiably weak, and with none of the yearning we have come to expect of adolescence. He whines and complains but does nothing to oppose the men who are ruining his estate. He seems incapable of making any decisions or taking any action.

Clearly, he is deeply wounded—his wounding taking the form of disempowerment, for no one has given him the attention and acknowledgment usually shown a young prince. Instead, he is mocked and mortified, and his powerlessness is constantly thrown up in his face by his mother's suitors. Because his father was absent since he was a baby and his mother was in a constant state of grief, he has become limp and dispirited, the antithesis of his father. But all along, the gods have been paying attention: Athena pleads before Zeus and the other gods on Telemachus' behalf and announces that she herself will attend to his needed education and training.

His education begins when Athena arrives in the form of an old family friend, Mentes. Mentes-Athena finds that while Telemachus possesses a fine natural character, he is so depressed and frustrated that he is unable to do anything to prevent the wasting of his inheritance. He sits daydreaming about his father returning out of the blue and putting the wastrel-suitors to rout.

Athena proceeds to educate Telemachus in the Socratic mode, by question and answer. She inquires into his situation. Is he really Odysseus' son? He certainly looks like him. With the wise Penelope as his mother, his future will surely be a glorious one. But why is all this riotous banqueting going on? Are not these rude feasters making free with his house in a most improper way?

With only a few questions, Athena has reminded him of his potent heritage and the contrast between it and the present conditions in the house. It is a brilliant psychological maneuver to draw him out and begin his true education.

Telemachus tells his visitor of the wasteland created by the suitors. As for his father, Odysseus has ceased to exist for Telemachus, having left a legacy of only sorrow and tears. Indeed, he is even uncertain about his paternity.

Mentes-Athena responds with sympathy: Yes, indeed, it would be just the thing if Odysseus could show up right away and lead the suitors to a bitter wedding with death. But in case that doesn't happen, would it be possible for Telemachus to start to grow up and stop acting like an infant? Instead of dreaming heroic fantasies, consider how they may be put into action.

The goddess then gives advice: take a ship and go in quest of your father. But first, stop at Sandy Pylos to see King Nestor, and then at Sparta to see Menelaus. Ask these men if they have any news of Odysseus.

Telemachus is filled with courage and confidence. He knows that a god has come to inspire him and get him moving on the path to manhood. In typical adolescent fashion, he immediately asserts his newfound belief in himself before his mother, by reprimanding her for making a remark he considers inappropriate. She returns to her rooms in a state of wonder: Her depressed adolescent boy is asserting himself for the first time in his life!

Telemachus then turns to his mother's suitors and tells them to stop brawling, to stop eating up his provisions, and to stop destroying his estate. "I will be master of my own house!" he announces, to their astonishment; "I am old enough to learn from others what has happened and to feel my own strength at last."

Athena is there to lend her godly power to assure this happening; this time she turns up as another old family friend, Mentor, whose name means "teacher." What happens next in this journey of education follows the first phase of the classical form of a boy's initiation into manhood: the initiatory night journey or night theft of the boy away from his home.

In examples found the world over, an older man takes, or even sometimes steals, a boy away from his home and mother at night in order to begin his initiation into adulthood. Thus, Telemachus leaves under the cover of darkness and without his mother's knowledge. Telemachus has Athena-Mentor accompanying and advising him. Athena serves as guide and initiator to a deeper life.

The traditional initiation next demands that the young initiate travel to some sacred ground. The sacred ground for Telemachus was the region around the original site of Mycenean civilization, now governed by Nestor and Menelaus, two of the surviving royal victors of the Trojan war. Telemachus must leave his life of limited possibilities and childhood expectations and go to his sacred ground to learn more of his father and family background, and to receive the education required to make him a man.

A second phase of initiation requires the initiate to be hidden in fearful seclusion. This allows the boy to die to his inadequacy and be reborn as a man capable of taking on the challenges of the adult state. As part of this ritual, the boy is given secret tribal knowledge—myths of creation and creators, stories of the early struggles of the godlike founders of this culture with primal destructive power. These stories introduce the young initiate into the great tradition. He hears the stories too—the latest about the long line of heroes and preservers of his society's deepest purposes and morality.

On his dangerous night journey, Telemachus accomplishes these initiatory requirements. And the sacred knowledge imparted to him by the older men, Nestor and Menelaus, contains the quintessential myth of his society.

During his visit with Nestor, a banquet is given in Telemachus' honor, before which he is given a bath by Nestor's own daughter. This signals the beginning of his rebirth.

Telemachus and his new friend, Nestor's son Peisistratus, arrive in Sparta in the midst of the double wedding of Menelaus' son and daughter. Telemachus is awed by Menelaus' magnificent wealth and compares his court to that of Zeus.

The gracious Menelaus puts him at his ease by contrasting his treasures with his sorrows. Too many terrible things occurred in the acquisition of these rich things—the murder of his brother Agamemnon by his treacherous wife Clytemnestra, the ruin of one previous house, the untold misery and death of so many of his friends in war. Incredible sorrows prey upon his conscience and ruin whatever pleasure he might have enjoyed in his present rich life.

Having been enchanted with the heroic world of Nestor and with his tales of brave deeds and noble codes of honor, Telemachus is now being exposed to disappointment or disenchantment with the "ideal" world. This phenomenon of disenchantment is found in many cultures, for it serves to further the awakening of the young person from belief in the appearance of things to pursuit of their reality. Among the Hopi, for instance, children grow up regarding the kachinas as the "real" gods who come to their village at intervals to perform awesome acts and marvelous dances. Wearing the heads of birds and storms and clouds, carrying the power of cosmic forces, they bear the stories of origins and contain the secret knowledge of the tribe. They are the tribal myths incarnate. Then, one day, when children reach a certain age, they are taken down into the sacred *kiva*, or meeting place, to await a kachina dance. They listen with mounting excitement as the drums play the rhythm of the dance and the kachinas begin to enter the *kiva*. But they are without their masks. And, worst of all, they are their own fathers and uncles! This is a wrenching and traumatic experience.

In all of these rites of disenchantment, the initiate is moved from naive belief through the crisis of disbelief to the active pursuit of the deeper meaning behind the events.

Telemachus' education in Sparta complete, he now desires to return home. Our boy has now become a self-possessed young man of action, schooled in the forms and the emotions of the noble life, but also properly disenchanted with it at the same time. Now he is ready for phase three of his rite of passage.

The third phase of initiation generally has to do with some scarring—the creation of a "conspicuous mark of adult male status." This phase then leads into a fourth—the revelation of certain sacred objects and/or sacred beings.

These last stages in the classical process of initiation are generally embedded in long, difficult, and dangerous journeys. Often, as in the walking of the Australian aboriginal's Songlines, the initiate retraces the paths taken by the mythical ancestral beings. And this is precisely what Telemachus does.

Phase four of his initiation occurs almost immediately after his escape, when he experiences the revelation of his father's living presence in his disguise as an old beggar. There is also the revelation of the presence and guardianship of Athena, who, for all practical purposes, is the totemic deity of his tribe.

There are other initiatory details as well. Athena accompanies Odysseus and Telemachus with a blazing light as they advance against the suitors who have invaded their home. She encourages Odysseus to treat his son as an equal in this defense of home and hearth.

The required ritual scarring occurs when Athena controls the spears that are thrown by the suitors and allows Telemachus to be cut near the wrists. She then terrorizes the suitors with her shield, revealing her presence, and sends them flying. This emphasizes the fearful power of the guardian, which contains both glory and terror.

The ancient sacred psychologies spoke to a wider range of the human experience than we are accustomed to today. These ancient psychologies, with their rituals, initiations, rites of passage, and profound sense of protection and protectors—both individually and communally—involved participants in a far more complex movement of the soul than our present limited, nonritualized therapies. Perhaps that is why there is such a strong drive to understand the nature and practice of rituals of renewal and transition through a study of remaining aboriginal societies.

'With the story of Telemachus we are given a tremendous and absolutely classical rite of boys' initiation. And that is one of the reasons why fully one-third of the *Odyssey* is devoted to his rite of passage: first maturity must be achieved before the depth of second maturity can be known.

When Telemachus returned from his journey of initiation with Athena/Mentor, he knew that his rightful place was beside his father, defending all they held sacred in family and home. His rite of passage through new experiences, to learn his tribal history, to pass from enchantment to reality, to understand the heritage worthy of his loyalty, helped Telemachus find within himself new courage and power, to the delight of his mentor. And therein lies a pattern that is valid for the ages.

NOTES

1. The following is adapted from Jean Houston, "The Initiation of Telemachus," chap. 11 of *The Hero and the Goddess: The Odyssey as Mystery and Initiation* (New York: Ballantine Books, 1992).

2. The "old man" probably refers to Laertes (father of Odysseus), though some take it as meaning that the household shall obey Mentor.

3. From Homer, *Odyssey,* translated and edited by Albert Cook (New York: W. W. Norton & Co., Inc., 1974), pp. 22–23.

FIVE

BUDDHIST MONASTIC INITIATION

Jack Kornfield

Jack Kornfield tells of his experience of Buddhist monastic initiation in the oldest existing monastic order. Most young men and some young women in Southeast Asia, until recently, went through this training to find a freedom in themselves, "something greater than that which they knew to be true."

Jack Kornfield was trained as a Buddhist monk in Thailand, Burma, and India and has taught meditation worldwide since 1974. He is one of the key teachers to introduce Theravada Buddhist practice to the West. For many years his work has been focused on integrating and bringing alive the great Eastern spiritual teachings in an accessible way for Western students and Western society. A wonderful storyteller and a great teacher, Jack also holds a Ph.D. in clinical psychology. He is a husband, father, psychotherapist, and founding teacher of the Insight Meditation Society and the Spirit Rock Center. His books include *Seeking the Heart of Wisdom, A Still Forest Pool, Stories of the Spirit, Stories of the Heart,* and *A Path With Heart.*

In this chapter I would like to describe the centuries-old traditional initiation of entering a Buddhist monastery, a rite of passage that until recently was required of most young men and some young women in Southeast Asia society. As a Buddhist teacher and a former Buddhist monk, I had the privilege of participating in this training in the 1960s, beginning when I was twenty-two years old, after graduating from Dartmouth College, having majored in Asian Studies.

Part of what drew me to enter several of the strictest ascetic forest monasteries was a longing for traditional Buddhist training. When I first visited these temples I met a number of truly wise elders who seemed to "know," to hold in their bones a wisdom about life and death that I sought. Somehow I realized I would have to undergo a difficult and potentially painful training to begin to discover what they knew.

Let me first speak about initiation in a general way. To awaken a spiritual authority, an inner sense of knowing, always involves a shift of identity, a rebirth, a recovering of the spirit. In the Buddhist tradition we speak of this as finding our True Nature. When we go through times of great difficulty, it is this alone that carries us through.

To find such authority requires a shift from our limited or small sense of self, what's called "the body of fear," to a deeper knowing within us. There are two speeds to this process. At times this shift may happen in an abrupt radical way through intensive meditation, ritual, initiation, or ceremony. At other times this shift happens slowly through repetitive practice. The Buddha

likened this gradual process to the great oceans which descend little by little
to the floor of the sea; similarly, the heart gradually deepens in knowing,
compassion, and trust.

Recently, a Japanese Zen Master was asked by a student about the beautiful faith and warmth he radiated. "This is what I want to learn from you.
How do I learn that?" Katagiri Roshi answered, "When people see me today,
they don't see the years I spent just being with my teacher!" He described
how he practiced year after year, living simply, hearing the same dharma
teachings over and over, sitting every morning no matter what, doing the rituals of the temple.

This is the slow way of initiation, putting yourself into the rituals of
attention and respect, baking yourself in the oven, until your whole being is
cooked, matured, transformed.

The second common form of initiation is more intense and rapid. Most
spiritual life calls for times of sudden radical transformation brought about by
powerful initiation and rites of passage. For modern young men and women
this is a desperate need. If nothing is offered in the way of initiation to prove
one's entry into the world of men and women, it will be done unguided in the
road or the street, with cars at high speed, with drugs, with weapons.

Even those not seeking rites of passage will find initiations arising unin-
tentionally, by loss, by accident, or through a near-death experience. Sometimes initiation comes in travel, bringing an abrupt maturing when one
encounters danger, disease, and difficulty in India or other Third World countries. A rite of passage is described as a forced journey through a rocky
canyon so hard and narrow that you can't take your baggage with you. Initiation usually involves a brush with death in order to find what one truly knows.
In the Buddhist tradition our initiation is intended to awaken our Buddha
Nature, the great fearless heart of a Buddha within us. This is one reason one
bows when we meet a master or spiritual teacher. We bow not only to that
person, but to the lineage of fearlessness that is carried in their presence.

In the process of initiation, if you wish to enter a Buddhist monastery,
you must seek a mentor, someone who will be your preceptor, your guide.
You may begin by visiting a forest monastery to meet with the master, listening to see if this is someone you would entrust yourself to. When you decide
to take them as your mentor, you bow to them, you agree to be with them, to
listen to their teachings, to follow their teachings, and to serve them. So that
when they come back from collecting alms food, you make their seat, you
bring them water, you do the kind of service to a teacher that offers them
respect and sets your heart in line with theirs. In this you demonstrate an
openness to listen and follow what they have to offer you.

Once you have entrusted yourself to a certain master and the community
of elders who practice with him, you must truly surrender. Yet your surrender
is not blind. You both know that it has a conscious value. My teacher Achaan

Chah always said, "I'm always asking my students to do difficult things. The food is unpredictable and poor; we sit up all night; it's freezing cold and you only have these simple cotton robes; it's boring here; it's demanding, it's lonely; and you do things that are fearful, like sitting alone all night in the forest. Yet all of it has the purpose of leading you to a freedom in yourself, to something greater than that which you knew to be true."

The Buddhist ordination practices, which Achaan Chah offered, are held by a community that has carried this universal message of wisdom and freedom for twenty-five hundred years. They are the oldest existing monastic order on the face of the earth.

In Thailand or Laos or Cambodia, young men, and in some cases women, generally enter a monastery when they reach the age of nineteen or twenty. Without entering a monastery and going through the training of a monk or a nun, one is considered an unripe person, not ready to live in that society, you don't know yourself, your spirit is not mature. Until recently, each young man, and certain young women, would go into a monastery for a year. Modern life has shortened this considerably, but hundreds of thousands still enter the monastic order.

The form of ordination and initiation repeats the ancient account of the life of the Buddha. In preparation for the ordination of a man or woman, the family and village hold a ritualized celebration. It begins with feasts and banquets for all to join. Various priests and Brahmins attend to officiate with blessings and offerings. The person to be ordained takes off their ordinary clothes and is dressed as a prince or princess, as a noble person, in white silk and beautiful jewelry. If they come from a family that can afford it, they may go in procession to the monastery riding on the back of an elephant.

The procession, whether by elephant, ox cart, or even bicycle, then arrives at the gates of the temple and reenacts the leave-taking of Sakyamuni Buddha, the prince of a great kingdom who renounced all the pleasures and possibilities of his worldly life to seek inner freedom and awakening, the sure heart's release. When you arrive at the gate, your head is shaved, all your jewelry and silken clothes are left behind. The gate marks the boundary of a great forest where the monks live. Here you are met by the elders of that forest, the abbot and the senior monks.

Sometimes the temple gates will have guardian demons. These demons symbolize the powerful forces one must pass through to enter the realm of the spirit. In the Zen tradition, when a young man or woman comes to enter a monastery, the encounter with the demons at the gate is formalized in a ritual called Tangario. The postulants must sit unwaveringly outside the gates of the monastery for two or three or more days, even in the winter, to show their sincerity in wanting to receive the teachings and undertake the training. After one sits for three or more days, finally the gates are opened and the monks say, "Come in. What brings you here?"

In the forest monasteries, having left clothing, jewelry, and all of the things of the world at the gate, and wearing only a simple white sarong, you are received by a group of twenty elders. They take you from your family and lead you into the forest. You realize that this is a place unlike other places in the world, a place of wonder and peace and a sacred connection with nature. The elders lead you to a place deep in the forest which is a consecrated ground called a Sima. Sometimes the Sima includes a small temple building, sometimes it is just a circle of rocks in the forest, sometimes it is surrounded by water. To properly consecrate the ground of a Sima, one of the elders must sit in every spot of it. Every square yard is marked off and sat in, and a series of blessings, prayers, and ceremonies are done in each square. When this ground is consecrated the only ones who are allowed to enter during ceremonies are the fully ordained members of the monastic order. In a traditional forest monastery, the consecrated ground is a place of peace, refuge, forgiveness, and truth. You can feel it.

Once you are led to the consecrated ground, the elders sit and chant together. After you bow to them, they address you respectfully. The Buddha spoke of ordination as an invitation to the sons and daughters of noble families. You are received respectfully as if you were nobly-born. Traditionally, the nobility which was so important in ancient India was determined by what caste or class or race you were born into. The Buddha turned this upside down and said, "Nobility has nothing to do with being born into any caste or class or race, whether the priestly class, warrior class, lower class, or untouchables." He was adamantly opposed to class-structured society and racism, and spoke of those things as madness. He said, "On this earth the only true nobility is the nobility of heart and spirit that a human being brings to their life. The absence of greed, the absence of hatred, the absence of delusion, and a wise and loving heart, this is what makes a noble being."

So when you arrive, you are greeted by the elders who address that intention in you which is noble. Then you take refuge in the path of the elders by making three bows. The first constitutes a vow to follow the way of the Buddha, and to see the possibility of awakening Buddha Nature in every being. The second bow is to the Dharma, the truth, the law, expressed by the path of practice. The third bow is to the Sangha, the lineage of the elders who for generations have carried the awakened heart and offered practices to renew it in each generation.

They don't just accept you automatically. After receiving your bows and refuge, the elders ask you some questions: "Are you free from debt? Are you free from disease? Are you free from obligation? You're not running away? Are you coming of your own volition? Why do you come? What brings you to practice in this sacred forest?"

When you answer and demonstrate your own sincerity, you are given vows and practices which speak of the great cycles of birth and death and the possibility of discovering Nirvana, a freedom which is timeless and deathless in the midst of all things. You are also given to understand that this task will not be easy.

I remember when I first arrived at my teacher Achaan Chah's monastery, he looked at me and said, "I hope you're not afraid of suffering." I replied, "What do you mean? I came here to meditate and find inner peace and happiness." He explained, "There are two kinds of suffering, the suffering that we repeat over and over because we are unwilling to face the truth of life, and the suffering that comes when we're willing to stop running from the sorrows and difficulties of the world. The second kind of suffering can lead you to freedom."

In bowing you commit yourself in body, speech, heart, and mind to join the elders. You bow again and again in different parts of the ceremony. You are asked in joining this community to devote your life to awakening compassion, truthfulness, and freedom. Then, after your commitment is made, you are given a new name. It's as if you are born anew as you enter into this community. In respect for your inner nobility and Buddha Nature, your new name given in Pali, the ancient language of the elders, might be "Luminous Virtue," "Aspires to Peace," "The Birth of Patience," or "Guardian of Wisdom."

Then, still among the trees in the deep forest, the first meditation instruction is given. This meditation is based on the mystery of birth and death itself. You are asked to meditate on the question "Who Am I?" To do this you are instructed how to examine your own body to see that it is made up of earth, water, fire, and air, and how these form into these disparate body parts: skin, hair, nails, teeth, fluid, blood, heart, lungs, and kidneys. You are asked to examine deeply the makeup of your human body to see its true nature.

Then the elders begin a series of teachings on how to live as a monk. The first is the teaching of dignity. You are shown how to treat everything in your life with respect and dignity. It is beautiful. You're given a patchwork robe and a bowl. You're shown how to fold your robe and how to carry your bowl. For each item of use you are given chants to recite several times daily to remember your true purpose. "I carry this bowl with great respect for what is offered. I receive this food with great sincerity. I wear this robe out of respect for a life devoted to awakening." Everything you do serves the purpose of mindfulness, awareness, and compassion.

Following these offerings, the elders give you further teachings to calm your heart, because if you want to investigate "Who Am I?" there must be an inner silence that allows such a question to drop to the depths of your being. You are given breath practices to deepen your concentration and walking practices to stabilize mindfulness throughout the day. From this day on, you are enjoined to live according to the principles of mindfulness. Your outer life is one of respect and your inner life is one of attention. In this way you enter the community.

After the ordination ceremony you take up the daily meditations of a monk. You are reminded to regularly reflect on the truth of impermanence and death. You are to begin a process of meditation on change by sitting and walking, examining the nature of all perceptions as they come and go, being mindful without being entangled with them. You learn to notice the movement of thoughts and feelings, to see impermanence, to study the changing flow of body and mind, in order to find an equanimity in the midst of it all. It is explained that you never possess anything for very long. You can love and care for people and things in your life but you do not own them. Your children, the things around you, your ideas, even your own body, are not yours. You are instructed to find freedom and compassion in renunciation. "'Look how he abused me, how he threw me down and robbed me.' Live with such thoughts and you continue the cycle of hatred. You too shall pass away. Knowing this, how can you quarrel?"

Along with the practices of dignity, respect, and renunciation, the monks undertake a series of practices of surrender. You wear one set of robes patched together from discarded cloth. You must eat one meal a day, only what is given. Through these practices of surrender there grows a ripening of faith as the heart learns to face the mystery of life with patience, trust, and compassion.

Monks must go out each morning with a bowl for alms rounds. This is not like street-corner begging. To me, it was one of the most beautiful experiences of my life. Just as the sun rises you walk across the green rice paddies into small villages with packed earthen lanes. Those who wish to offer alms wait for the monks to come and often bow before they offer their food. Even the poorest villages will offer part of their food as if to say, "Even though we are poor, we so value what you represent that we give of what little we have so that your spirit may be here in our village, in our community, and in our society."

Alms rounds are done completely in silence. When you receive the food you can't say, "Thank you; I love the mango you gave me," or "Thanks for the fish this morning; it looks really good." The only response you can make is the sincerity of your heart. After you receive this food you take it back to support and inspire your practice. If the villagers so value the monk's life to give the little they have, you must take that. The extraordinary generosity of the village brings a powerful motivation in a monastery.

The rule about alms food that governs monastic life is that monks or nuns are not allowed to keep food overnight or eat anything that's not put *into their hands* each morning by a lay person. This means that monks can't live as hermits up in the mountains far from the world. They must live where people can feed them. This immediately establishes a powerful relationship. You have to do something of enough value that they want to feed you. Your presence, your meditation, your dignity, has to be vivid enough so that when you bring your bowl, people want to offer food because that's the only way you can eat! This creates an ongoing dynamic of offering that goes both ways, from those who are in the process of being initiated in the monastery, and those of the community whom it benefits.

The process of surrender builds as you live in the community. You may chant from 3:30 in the morning for hours and hours, both morning and night. You may hear the same dharma talk over and over again. You must sit in meditation all night long at least one night a week. Young monks do long alms rounds barefoot in the morning before the sun comes up, walking five, ten, or more miles before they eat anything.

When your practice becomes more deeply established, the elders will give you ways to more directly face death. You will have already done regular contemplations on the brevity of life and the certainty of death. You will have done days of visualization of the decomposition of your body, and have meditated on the movement of consciousness in the process of death and rebirth. You may then be instructed, as I was, to sit all night in the charnel grounds in the forest. There villagers will bring in a procession the body of one who has died, and the monks recite the funeral prayers. The body is placed on the burning grounds, and you sit with it through the night while you meditate on your own body and the inevitable death that will come to everyone you know.

In Achaan Chah's monastery where I practiced, the traditional funeral meditation led to one further practice. When any of the monks died, rather than burn his body, it was set on a platform in the Buddha Hall for the monks to contemplate. The body was left out for ten days to bloat and decompose as would happen to any meat left out in the sun for this period of time. We sat, meditated, and chanted in front of the body. It brought a vividness to our meditations on death.

Initially the training requires long periods of communal walking and sitting practice, and frequent all-night sittings in the Buddha Hall. After training together with the collective of monks, you may then be directed to a period of practice in solitude for some months. For this part of the training, monks live in isolated caves or in more distant parts of jungles and mountains, a long morning's walk from the last remote village. Or, in certain retreat centers, small huts are provided for solitary intensive meditation. My own training included a solitary retreat for one year and two months. I didn't leave my room, just meditated fifteen to eighteen hours a day, sitting for an hour, walking for an hour, then sitting again. I'd see my teacher every two days for a fifteen-minute interview. You don't have to be in solitude very long before any pride you have goes away. It is quite humbling. Your mind will do anything. Every past thing you've ever done or imagined comes back. Every mood, every fear, every longing, your loneliness, your pain, your love, creativity, and boredom appear with great intensity.

Gradually these are followed by many visionary states, and by powerful releases of the energy system that dissolve the body into light. Then there are ecstatic states, samadhi states, and techniques for entering profound states of emptiness and silence. Throughout this meditative process, your teacher gives instructions on how to understand or skillfully transform each of these forces, and yourself as well. As you sit, you are taught how to rest in the archetype of a Buddha, with great compassion and emptiness, containing all things, yet not limited by them.

Your wisdom and spiritual maturity deepens in these many forms of practice, augmented by the communal life of the monks. The life of the community includes regular council meetings, practices for conflict resolution, vow renewals, and practices of mutual respect. The repetition and surrender of this life is guided by a community of elders consciously intended to bring a deep trust of ourselves and the ground of our being.

Throughout the whole duration of the monastic training, you are guided to hold all experiences in a great heart of loving kindness for yourself and all beings. Formal instructions for developing practices of loving kindness, compassion, and forgiveness are offered to all members of the community. These include visualizations and recitations which are first directed toward yourself through repeated phrases such as "May I be well, may I have ease of body and mind, may I be filled with compassion and forgiveness." You are taught to direct the phrases of loving kindness and forgiveness to yourself over and over because loving kindness is the basis of true respect. Then you gradually extend it to others, to the members of your community, the villagers nearby, the beings of the forest, the whole of the world. As you repeat these practices a thousand times, you notice the barriers of the heart that interfere with your openness. In the spirit of this practice you're given the traditional story of Angulimala, a mass murderer who went through a profound process of forgiveness and healing as a monk. You are asked to study in your own heart how each of us contains the source of all suffering and the source of all freedom. You are directed to see how conflict, fear, hatred, and attachment, all of the afflictions of the heart, are cured by true generosity and respect.

Finally, like the Buddha, you are invited to sit and find an unshakable knowing in yourself. In your meditation you become a yogi sitting like the Buddha in the unmovable spot under the bodhi tree seeking the knowledge of the deathless. Sometimes your teacher will pose a question: "What is your true self?" "What was your true nature before you were born?" To discover your true nature, you meditate on sights and sounds, smells and tastes, thoughts and feelings, until you see how ephemeral all sense perceptions are. Relinquishing the senses, you are directed to meditate and enter a deep stillness. From this silence you must find that which is beyond your usual "small self," your ordinary identity. Your task is to awaken within to "the one who knows" and come to rest in the timeless, unconditional, or eternal.

Achaan Chah, the elder of our forest monastery, put it this way: "When you can rest in the original heart and mind, it shines like pure clear water.

This is the Buddha. But what is the Buddha? When we see with the eyes of wisdom, we know that the Buddha is timeless, unborn, unrelated to any body or history of image. Buddha is the ground of all beings, the truth of the unmoving mind. So the Buddha was not enlightened in India. In fact, he was never enlightened, he was never born and never died. When we take refuge in the Buddha, the Dharma, the Sangha, all things in the world are free for us; they become our teacher moment after moment, proclaiming the one true nature of life."

Over the months and years you continue to practice, combining periods in community with periods of solitude, cultivating wisdom, fearlessness, and compassion, studying death, and surrendering to the rhythms of nature, always guided in these rhythms by the elders. After a suitable period of practice, when you have integrated and stabilized these teachings, you may choose to remain in the monastery to teach others or you may find that you are called to return to the world to integrate and manifest your new-found maturity there. When you have completed your initiation, the Zen description is of a joyful reentry: "I enter the marketplace with my wine bottle and my staff and all whom I look upon become enlightened."

As monks prepare to leave, they gather for a last time with the elders in the sacred grove. They remove their vows of renunciation, return their robes, and are given a set of new clothing. They bow three times and retake the refuges, adding the five precepts of nonharming that are the ground of practice for all Buddhist lay people.

After their time in the monastery, most young men and young women will return to their villages, having completed their training with the elders. They are now accepted as "ripe," as initiated men and women, respected in their community. Outwardly what they will have been taught in the monastery will be the religious forms and sacred rituals of the Buddhist community. What these ancient forms aim to awaken is unshakable virtue and inner respect, fearlessness in the face of death, self-reliance, wisdom, and profound compassion. These qualities give one who leaves the monastery the hallmark of a mature man or woman.

Perhaps as you read about this ordination process, its beauty will strike a chord in you that intuitively knows about the need for initiation. That doesn't mean that you have to go to Asia and enter a monastery to seek this remarkable and wonderful training. By describing this tradition, we simply touch that place in each of us that longs for wholeness and integrity because the awakening that comes through initiation is a universal story. In our time we again need to reclaim rites of passage, we need to honor elders, we need to find ways to remind our young people and the whole of our communities of the sacredness of life, of who we really are.

Remember, too, that initiation comes in many forms. I have a friend who has three children under the age of five. This is a retreat as intensive as any other, including the charnel grounds, the sitting up all night. Marriage and family are a kind of initiation. As Gary Snyder says:

> All of us are apprentices to the same teacher that all masters have worked with—reality. Reality says: Master the twenty-four hours. Do it well without self-pity. It is as hard to get the children herded into the car pool and down the road to the bus as it is to chant sutras in the Buddha Hall on a cold morning. One is not better than the other. Each can be quite boring. They both have the virtuous quality of repetition. Repetition and ritual and their good results come in many forms: changing the filters, wiping noses, going to meetings, sitting in meditation, picking up around the house, washing dishes, changing the dipstick. Don't let yourself think that one or more of these distracts you from the serious pursuits. Such a round of chores is not a set of difficulties to escape so that we may do our practice that will put us on the path. It IS our path.

What gives a spiritual initiation or a rite of passage its great blessing, whether it is marriage or child rearing or entering the monastery, is that it is held in a sacred context. The difficulties one goes through are conscious and purposefully used to find freedom. Otherwise, it will be an incomplete initiation where you don't know what you have learned; you have simply suffered. True initiation is done purposely and consciously. In traditional Buddhist societies it is repeated again and again as a system of prayer, discipline, meditation, surrender, ritual of life-long practices that are held by the elders. The elders are there to teach the practices that generations have gone through before you. They offer a way to step outside of your small sense of self, your worries and past, and awaken the "one who knows," the elder within.

To awaken this understanding in yourself is the blessing of spiritual life. To offer the energy of wisdom, fearlessness, and compassion to the society around us is the gift that your spiritual life brings to this world.

THE AGE OF ENDARKENMENT

Michael Ventura

"The Age of Endarkenment" comments on the missing enlightenment from the elders. Surely rites of passage would not have been necessary in the past unless the young were as extreme as ours, Ventura writes. He points out that the collective community has not taken care of the youth who are part of its genetic coding, and who are crying out for initiation in their own way.

Michael Ventura is a columnist for the *Los Angeles Weekly.* He has coauthored the book, *We've Had A Hundred Years of Therapy And The World Is Getting Worse* with James Hillman.

Mr. Ventura resides in Austin, Texas and Los Angeles, California.

"**A**dolescence" is a cruel word. Its cruelty hides behind its vaguely official, diagnostic air. To say someone is "adolescent," going through adolescence" or, worse, "being adolescent" is to dismiss their feelings, minimize their troubles, and (if you're their parent) protect yourself from their uncompromising rage. The words "teenager" and "teen" are worse. They reek of cuteness. But we all know that being a "teen" doesn't feel cute.

People that age hardly ever use those words. They tend to call themselves "kids" when pushed, as in, "What makes you think you know so much about kids—you sure don't know much about *me*!" Or they dress up and act out and give themselves better words: "punk," "gothic," "rapper," "gangbanger," "low-rider," "freak"—words to remind us just how volatile, how dangerous, how "freaked out," "radical," "awesome," "bummed," "bitchen," "groovy," "wasted," and "bad" those years really are.

When we don't have apt words for something it's because of an unspoken collective demand to avoid thinking about it. *That's* how scary "adolescence" is. Which is also to say: that's how scary our very own unspeakable adolescence was. And when we finally are past it (which often doesn't happen till we near forty), then we turn around and see the young and pretend that they are foreign to us, that we don't know what they're going through, that we don't get their music, their fashions, their words. James Baldwin said, "One can only face in others what one can face in oneself." What we cannot face when we cannot face the young is, plainly, ourselves. (And this is the song of families.) Our secrets, our compromises, our needs, our lacks, our failures, and our fear that we're going to fail again—all this stirs and starts to growl somewhere deep inside when the young look hard into our grown-up eyes. It's as though, in some dark way, they are privy to our secrets, even to what we don't know or want to know about ourselves, and when they so much as glance toward those parts of us, oh, our old panics resurrect, those demons we thought we'd dealt with, grown out of, transcended, escaped—it only takes this goddamn kid, and the beasts awake. As a parent, you may measure your fears by the extent of your distance from that kid.

But perhaps, when we love them, our greatest fear is: that we cannot help them, cannot protect them, and that we have nothing real to give them. And their greatest rage is: that we cannot help, cannot protect them, and that we have nothing to give.

When something is true of virtually everyone, it's unlikely that the fault is individual, but we feel and fear this mess as individuals—kids and grown-ups both. Individually, kids can't help but judge us for this state of affairs, just as we can't help but flee their judgment. All that we share with them, then, is a scream: THIS ISN'T FAIR! We *do* have useful things to give, if they would only take them, but they can't seem to. Again, individually, their refusal to take what we try to give seems pernicious and willful, but when you look at them collectively, you see that they're obviously not in control of their refusal; they *have* to refuse us, no one knows why. They must, even when that refusal makes them secretly ashamed, which in turn makes them worse, which makes us worse. It seems that no matter what, the very act of raising kids will, at the onset of adolescence, throw kids and parents both into nega-tive extremes.

It's as though kids have a fundamental craving for negatives in their dealings with their parents and with adults in general, and will stop at practi-cally nothing to invoke that negativity. We've come (unofficially) to accept this. "How old is your kid?" "Fifteen." *"Oh my god."* And everyone knows what that means.

Our models for dealing with these issues are psychological. Which is absurd. You can't reduce a collective phenomenon, a phenomenon that cuts across every class and culture, a phenomenon with fundamentally the same elements in Harlem and Beverly Hills, at Woodstock and Tian An Men Square, in English soccer matches and Palestinian villages—you can't reduce a phenomenon like that to individual or family causes. To do so ignores and dismisses *the* most important piece of data we have: the fact that, despite dif-ferent histories, cultures, technologies, and economies, the same basic thing is happening everywhere to everyone—often in waves of simultaneity.

Two writers have described "adolescence" most tellingly for me. The first is Los Angeles educator Mike Rose, in his crucial book *Lives on the Boundary* (Free Press/Macmillan, 1989): "Kids have no choice but to talk in extremes; they're being wrenched and buffeted, rabbit-punched from the inside by systemic thugs." Rose's thought gets elaborated by rock critic Michael Corcoran in *The Austin Chronicle:*

> Rap and its polar opposite but sometimes bedfellow, heavy metal, are the [present] counterpart to '50s rock & roll and '70s punk. It's rebel music, soul music, kids' music. It understands what parents and teachers don't, that puberty is not about hair or pimples or cracking voices; it's a beast, a demon. It's a

beautiful rage that wants to belong and sometimes only can through dumb, simple, angry music. Rap doesn't incite violence, nor does metal. It stirs deep emotions that sometimes get out of hand. It ignites the same spirit that makes us fall in love, have children and believe in God.

We tend to think of this extremism in the young as something new, peculiar to our times, caused by pop or television or the collapse of values. The history of our race doesn't bear this out, however. Robert Bly and Michael Meade, among others, remind us that for tens of thousands of years tribal people everywhere have greeted the onset of puberty, especially in males, with elaborate and excruciating initiations—*a practice that plainly wouldn't have been necessary unless their young were as extreme as ours.* This is terribly important. It means that when conservatives talk of rock culture subverting the young, when others talk about that same culture liberating the young, or when postmodern technologists talk of our electronic environment "rewiring the software" of new generations—they are all making the same mistake. They fail to understand that a psychic structure that has remained constant for one-hundred thousand years is not likely to be altered in a generation by stimuli that play upon its surfaces. What's really going on is very different: the same raw, ancient *content* is surging through youths' psyches, but adult culture over the last few centuries has forgotten how to meet, guide, and be replenished by its force.

Unlike us, tribal people met the extremism of their young (and I'm using "extremism" as a catchall word for the intense psychic cacophony of adolescence) with an equal but focused extremism from adults. Tribal adults didn't run from this moment in their children as we do: they celebrated it. They would assault their adolescents with, quite literally, holy terror: rituals that had been kept secret from the young till that moment—rituals that focused upon the young all the light and darkness of their tribe's collective psyche, all its sense of mystery, all its questions, and all the stories told both to contain and answer those questions.

The crucial word here is "focus." The adults had something to teach: stories, skills, magic, dances, visions, rituals. In fact, if these things were not learned well, the tribe could not survive. But the adults did not splatter this material all over the young from the time of their birth, as we do. They focused, and were as selective as possible about, what they told and taught, and when. They waited until their children reached the intensity of adolescence, and then they used that very intensity's capacity for absorption, its hunger, its need to act out, its craving for dark things, dark knowledge, dark acts, all the qualities we fear most in our kids—the ancients used these very qualities as teaching tools.

Through what the kids craved, they were given what they needed. Kids of that age crave extremes of experience—they crave this suddenly and utterly, and are possessed by their craving. They can't be talked out of it, or conditioned out of it. It's in our genetic coding, if you like, to crave extremes at that age. (So they must certainly feel rage if, as in our culture, adults tell them that these cravings are wrong.) At the same time, these kids *need* the cosmology and skills appropriate for survival in their world. The kids can create the extremes for themselves—they're quite good at that—but not the cosmology, not the skills. And without those elements, given at the proper time through the dark-energy channels that have suddenly opened in the young and go clear down to their souls, the need for extremes is never really satisfied in its *purpose,* and hence it goes on and on (creating what we call "modern culture," which, looked at this way, is little more than a side effect). Our ancestors satisfied the craving for dark energy while meeting the need for cosmology and knowledge, and we call that "initiation." This practice was so effective that usually by the age of fifteen a tribal youth was able to take his or her place as a fully responsible adult.

Because our culture denies the craving, we can't possibly meet the need—so most of us never truly grow up or feel, in our hearts, adult. How, then, have we responded? For about forty years now, the young have generated forms—music, fashion, behaviors—that prolong the initiatory moment. In other words, we cherish and elongate adolescence (or "initiatory receptivity") as though hoping to be somehow initiated by chance somewhere along the way. For tribal people, the initiatory moment was by far the most intense period of life, lasting no more than weeks, at most about a year. For us, it now lasts decades. And it's as though the pressure to make it last decades increases its chaotic violence. This very extension of the initiatory moment is helping to drive everyone mad.

PART TWO YOUTH CRISIS: PROBLEMS AND SOLUTIONS

SEVEN

LITIMA: THE INNER HEAT

Michael Meade

"Litima"* is an ancient term for adolescent energy. It can refer to the urge for independence as well as high ideals or it can be the source of ruthlessness and brutality. How can we best approach this vital energy? Michael Meade presents various alternatives from different cultures.

(The biography of Michael Meade appears at the beginning of this book.)

Societies that attend to the initiation of youth provide rituals that require everything else come to a halt. Questions hang in the air: Will this generation of youth find a connection to spiritual meaning and beauty that will keep the light at the center of the tribe burning? Or, will they be a generation of possessive, power-driven people?

If the elders of the society do not seriously consider these questions, if they forget about or ignore the matter of initiating their youth, sooner or later there is bound to be a spontaneous eruption of inner forces among the youth themselves: a move toward physical violence, possessiveness, and brutality.

The Gisu people in Uganda have a name for it—*Litima*. To them, Litima is the violent emotion peculiar to the masculine part of things that is the source of quarrels, ruthless competition, possessiveness, power-drivenness, and brutality. It is also the source of independence, courage, upstandingness, and meaningful ideals. Litima names and describes the willful emotional force that fuels the process of becoming an individual. Struggles with this ambiguous, fiery force characterize the period between childhood and maturity.

Young men and women need help in order to open themselves to adulthood. The raw passions and ideals of youth need expression and attention if they are to grow toward the skills and wisdom of elders. Although radical change can occur at any time in a person's life, the focus and desire for it necessarily occur in youth. Cultures that provide initiations offer a ritual for awakening the spirit of each initiate and letting his or her emotions flow; they give the Litima a channel through which it can be expressed. These cultures know that the fire in each youth, the emotional body of each, must be seen, tested, and educated.

To educate means to lead out, to educe, to elicit, or even to extract something. Litima is that something—both the capacity to erupt in violence and the capacity to courageously defend others, both the aggression that breaks things and the force that builds and protects.

Litima names a spirit characteristic of youth as well as periods of dramatic change. It is volatile, asocial, and mobile. It disrupts, makes friction, throws sparks, blows smoke. Litima intensifies everything, and the fires of Litima light up the hidden, shadow areas of the individual, family, and society.

THE COLORS OF LITIMA

Red and black are colors often worn during initiations. These colors express the fiery explosive energy that is about to erupt. They are immanently fitting, for they warn us that the road of initiation is made of flames and shadows, fire and ashes, tears and smoke.

This warning might as well have been inscribed on the care-instruction tags inside our gang jackets when we were kids in New York. My first jacket had to have the perfect combination of brightness and darkness, and I went from store to store looking for a coat that would display what my friends and I felt. We were ten to twelve years old. We had stripped-down bikes made from the used parts of other people's bicycles. We swooped through the neighborhood day and night, arms extended like wings, feet pedaling like mad, trying to catch up to our own spirits. If we had the same jackets, we would be part of the same spirit even when we were apart.

As soon as I saw the jacket, I knew I had found what we were looking for. One side was orange-red satin, smooth and shiny; it reflected light like fire. The other side was completely black, a dense fabric that absorbed light and reflected nothing. Even its black buttons were dull. You could disappear into that darkness. It was perfect. We each struggled to buy one. We wrapped ourselves in them and flew through the neighborhood day and night, sometimes red and sometimes black.

Later, we learned to walk slowly up to the corner, as if there was nothing going on within us. On the corner, Litima would accumulate around us like an atmosphere. The amount of Litima in the air would increase noticeably when specific guys or certain combinations of guys showed up. If the group was large, the amount of Litima would multiply rapidly. The feel of it, the direction it would take, the intention that would form could be dictated by the heat of one member, by an accidental occurrence, or even by a single word.

If there was "nothin' doin'," or only a few of us showed up, our Litima might turn us into an *a cappella* singing group, and we would look for a subway or hallway to serve as a resonating chamber. We would get lost then in the harmonies and dissonances of the songs and the little dreams they evoked, singing our way through the images and emotions in one song after another. Love songs expressed our interest in union as well as the loss and longing we already felt. The early songs of rock and roll and bluesy jazz allowed us to sing out our inner conflicts and rebellion. We made harmonies of our conflicts, and we made conflicts where there were dull, predictable harmonies.

We wanted to be seen by the people passing by: We were posing, we were singing in public, we were dressed to draw attention. But we also felt very separate from the mundane march of life through the subway and the streets. We were outside it, at the crossroads, on the edge. We became heated and volatile if questioned, yet we needed to get something out of us and into the air. Hanging out on the corner was like being on the edge of the village; singing in the subway was a way to visit the underworld; and roaming the streets was an internal as well as external experiment with Litima.

If we had worn red cloth, or had painted intricate, black patterns on our limbs and woven feathers into our hair, if we had been half-leaning on tall spears, half-standing on one leg like the Gisu initiates in Uganda, we would have looked even more like we felt. The feathers and painted designs would have expressed our affinity with the song and flight of the mythical firebird. Leaning on the spears would have shown our willingness to defend or fight: One hand was committed to the song; one was ready to protect the longing of the singers or accept any challenge that came along.

Without knowing it, we stood like the youthful warriors of the Red Branch in Ireland, who set themselves up along the borders of a province. When a stranger came along, they would offer him a choice: Would you have a poem or a battle? For youth, it can go either way—burst into song or burst into battle.

The corner on which we stood was the crossroads of song and battle. The dark stairs leading to the underground train were also irresistible, for there, between the ear-tearing, mind-wrenching passage of subway trains, we sang harmonies, bringing a kind of light to that underworld. Without knowing why, we found and made ambiguous asocial places in which to display ourselves. We were finding the edges of our culture, finding the marginal areas within the landscape of the city. This is the inevitable task of youth as they stand on the border of adulthood.

Our other job was to be ready for anything; readiness and edginess were all we had. We were strangely dependent on a surprise, an accident, or a sudden inspiration in order to move. If nothing moved us, we simply hung out, like a crew on a becalmed ship waiting for a wind to rise. It was as though we were waiting for instructions from some hidden source we couldn't name.

Then, into the gathering at the corner would come a member who was angry at a parent, a cop, a store owner, or some rival, and this would ignite everyone's anger. The corner would turn red with activity. Boasting, cursing, threatening would erupt. We would push each other physically and emotionally like a football team before a game. The corner would heat up; lethargy would turn to frenetic dance. The outcome might be a simple dance of anger that overthrew garbage cans or broke some windows, or it could become a fight within the group or a battle with outsiders.

Our outer cool was a covering for an ongoing inner dance of constantly changing emotions and sudden crises of the spirit. In our case, eruption into dance, song, challenges, and fights were random events that overtook us.

Cultures with active rites of passage prepare the ground for crises of the spirit and develop dances that display the emotions and spirits moving through the youths. The steps from childhood to adulthood are danced; the motions, emotions, and spirits of the youth are indulged, encouraged, exposed, and educated.

What modern society tries to dismiss as a stage out of which youth will grow automatically is actually a crucible in which the future of the culture gets forged. Take away the nourishment of a community, which sees beauty and value in the extreme dances of the initiates, and youth appear to be wasting time. Replace a sense of experimentation, in which youth learn about human nature and the unifying images of spirit and myth, with fear of change, and the corner becomes simply dangerous.

On "our corner" everything in life got dealt with in some fashion. But the edges of legality, morality, sexuality, and spirituality were approached and crossed randomly. Life-altering events and attitudes were neither focused through ritual nor guided by those who had consciously crossed the same borders. Where the accidental knowledge of the group ended, fear and ignorance took over. Our displays of loyalty to each other could be proven by attacking anyone different: anyone too gay or even too straight, people who talked differently or had different colored skin or just different colored jackets. Our internal conflicts were pushed out onto other people and attacked out there. We had to act out and emote or we became depressed, but our actions lacked the focus brought by the intentions and shapes of rituals.

Looking back at those days on the corner, I can see that the conflicts we were acting out were in the culture as well. If you hang on the corner long enough, you can see every conflict in a culture go by. If you stay there too long, angers and resentments get out of control. The marginal period can easily become a marginal life.

In tribal cultures, these "marginal ones" would be in the bush or in the wilderness, like the Maasai and Samburu initiates in Africa, or like the Fianna, who used to roam the wilds of Ireland for half the year, or like Australian aborigines, who went on "walkabout," wandering out, crossing borders, seeking the edges of consciousness. Each feature of nature was also part of a mythic story, so that they walked in nature and myth at once. In these cultures, the separation from ordinary activities, from families, and from the previous stage of life was literal and mythical. It was lived out, carried out, worn on the body, made evident to everyone.

The instinct and inspiration to separate, decorate, and be seen in the extremes and margins of life occurs to all modern youth, but the shaping containers of nature, myth, and elders usually do not. Displays of long hair or baldness, earrings, tattoos, strange clothing, or nakedness are typical initiatory styles that arise spontaneously in youth. Although the roots of the displays are in ancient symbols and universal emotions, they often become random codes or even fashion statements in modern societies. What occurs randomly among modern youth was often turned toward art within ritual cultures.

The initiation of groups of youth, called Morani amongst the Maasai in eastern Africa, provides an excellent example of complicated and elaborate initiation rituals. The ritual camps are set up for several months each year, and the rites of passage take many years to reach completion. Similar to rites in ancient Europe and the Americas, many of the displays focus on the heads of the initiates. They cut their hair and enter a period of darkness and loss. When the new hair grows, it is colored red and covered with feathers. As the initiates heat up within, they take on the image of fire and birds. Eventually, they become moving works of art, dancing symbols of the spirit of the tribe. They move from loss through fire toward beauty, and eventually to a coolness that prepares the way to becoming elders.

The Morani wear the colors red and black throughout their initiation rites. Cloths of these colors are worn as emblems of the heating and cooling of the psyche, the flights and falls, the heights of hope and depths of despair. Psychologically, the period of youth is naturally manic and naturally depressive. Because their lives are being remade, they are being pulled to the extremes. One extreme is the heat of battle where life can be made and destroyed; the other is the emptiness and endless reach of solitude. Both require courage to face. On his own, a youth can easily soar into an excess of flight or fall into inertia. In modern societies, it is only when a youth displays an excess of one or the other that his or her predicament will finally draw the attention and concern of adults.

Among the Maasai, Litima intensifies as initiates enter a decade or more in which they will "redden" their psyches. Red becomes the dominant color. The hair is braided, plaited into dreadlocks, and turned red. Many rituals are worked up for these initiates, and the youths perform leaping dances that grow longer and longer in duration. During the dances, they spend more and more time in the air; in a sense, they are flying. And they are heating up; they are growing toward red. The message to any onlooker is that this psyche is on fire.

As the reddening increases, quarrels and displays of competition occur. Fights break out among the initiates, often in front of the unititiated girls of the tribe. Actually, the girls encourage the fighting; they egg it on. This series of spontaneous fights exposes the aggressions and even brutalities of the youth. Older initiates, confirmed warriors, monitor the goings-on so that the initiates don't seriously injure others or themselves.

In these old traditions the eruptive, aggressive behavior of the young males is carefully observed for its brutal and artful qualities, just as modern people observe sports heroes. The ritual attention we give to a specialized group of performers is, among the Maasai, given to the entire group of youthful initiates in order to learn the strengths and faults of their individual characters and of their generation. Eventually, they will be the tribal elders. Since they are writing the story of the tribe's future, everyone wants to read it and see who the authors are.

In contemporary societies, we pretend that this behavior should not happen, in spite of overwhelming evidence that it is happening, has always happened, and will happen again. Often, adults repress their memories of those disturbances, and the youth rebel, or hide their own turmoil. Instead of rituals of connectedness on deeper levels, there is increasing alienation.

The borders and limits of everyday culture need to be broken so that the individual finds himself in some deeper place beyond childhood. Too strong a restriction on the extreme aggressions of youth restricts their imagination and spiritual capacities. Not allowing the outbreak of the fires of youth narrows their ambitions. In fact, when the aggressions, even the brutality, of the young men of a culture are not accepted and reshaped, then those aggressions are eventually directed outward toward another group. Aggressions that are not educated, led out, and directed can only erupt inappropriately or burn internally under layers of suppression or doses of numbing.

In contemporary cultures, the capacity of youth and men to erupt in aggression, rage, and violence is in daily evidence. The concept of Litima indicates that in order to release the part of the flame that burns with beauty and idealism, the part of the flame that has the capacity for brutality and rage must be risked as well.

Rites of passage have always had to engage the fiery elements in individuals and address the ambiguous forces that drive youths to extremes of creation and destruction. Any reimagining or reinvention of rites of passage for modern youth will have to negotiate territories where the psyche turns red and black, where roads are marked by the intensity of fire and ashes and the cleansing caused by tears and smoke finally reveals the way home.

---

*See J. S. La Fontaine, *Initiation* (New York: Harper Torch Books, 1958).
Based on excerpts from *Men and the Water of Life: Initiation and the Tempering of Men*, chapter 16, "Litima: The Inner Heat." Reprinted by permission of Harper Collins.

EIGHT

TEEN MOTHERHOOD AND ABORTING THE SEARCH FOR SELF-IDENTITY: A REVIEW OF THE WORK OF JUDITH S. MUSICK AND MARION HOWARD

Sharron Brown Dorr

The legislators of our country need some of the information in Sharron Dorr's essay on "Teen Motherhood." Why is it that approximately half a million births in the United States each year are to teenage mothers, many of whom are destined to grow up in poverty? There is, of course, no simple answer. Most of these teenage mothers have their own developmental needs that are not met. Many have not had adequate parenting and have not been guided to make the best choices. How can girls who badly need a mother become good mothers themselves? What makes teen moms different from other teen girls?

Sharron Brown Dorr, editorial assistant, has been a professional storyteller since 1987, and also leads workshops on storytelling and related topics. With her background in arts therapies, film, and literature, Sharron now specializes in the use of myths and folktales to enliven our sense of communion with nature, to empower women, and to facilitate the spiritual development of adolescent girls. She is one of the founders of the Fox Valley Storytelling Guild in Illinois.

A DREAM COME TRUE

grass so green
with flowers in bloom
grass so green
growing in my room

house so white
watch them stare
with a white picket fence
and a porch swinging chair

every day
people passing by
wishing their family
as happy as mine
not a care in the world
not a frown in sight
I would watch them play
by day, by night

beautiful and happy
my husband would be

their shining like the sun
eyes sparkling like the sea

my fantasy of the future
Is the same as you
people wishing for happiness
a dream come true. . . .
—Sarah Jane[1]

. . . But here's the reality. As developmental psychologist Judith Musick tells us in *Young, Poor, and Pregnant: The Psychology of Teenage Motherhood,* "Eighteen and pregnant with her third child, Sarah Jane has an extremely volatile relationship with her boyfriend, the father of two of her children. They have no money and chronic housing problems. Steven moves out and moves back in. He drinks and they fight. Sometimes he hits her. Their parenting difficulties are periodically serious enough to require the intervention of child protective services. The children already have some developmental problems" (29–30).

So much for the dream.

CHILDREN HAVING CHILDREN

The Carnegie Corporation calls it the "Quiet Crisis." Sarah Jane is only one of about half a million teenagers now giving birth every year in the United States—at the rate of about one every minute (Carnegie Task Force 1994, 4)—a number giving the nation "the dubious honor of the highest teen birth rate in the developed world" (Hymowitz 1994, 19). By the late 1980s, one in four fifteen-year-olds was having sex, five times as many as were active in the 1970s (Howard 1992, 181). Even some eleven- and twelve-year-olds are doing it (Hymowitz 1994, 22).

Over the past few decades, the numbers of unwed births have risen dramatically (Carnegie Task Force 1994, 4) and may now be as high as *30 percent* (Rodrigue 1995). And while in the past adolescent mothers were or would soon be married, today most will remain single, considering marriage out of fashion (Hymowitz 1994, 23). In addition, they face more dangerous neighborhoods, access to fewer social services, and fewer opportunities for employment. Further, as Musick points out, "they are more likely to lack both a family to instill high expectations and a community environment to provide a vision of a productive future, two time-honored pathways for getting up and out of poverty" (8). And so the majority will remain poor, perpetrating the cycle in the next generation. The *Chicago Tribune* reports that eighty percent of the children born to unwed high school dropouts grow up in poverty (Rodrigue 1995).

> . . . there were about ten of us. . . . It seems you know like when a new style comes in and everybody tries to get it? That's what it was. Everybody got pregnant. . . . As soon as one got out of the hospital, another one went in. It was just like a train. (138–39)

What are we to make of this costly surge of children having children in some self-created rite of passage? Not that there haven't been sixteen-year-old mothers throughout human history. But these days we mature biologically much faster than we do socially. Generally, girls begin menses at about twelve, while to "succeed" in our technological society requires delaying parenthood until at least one's early twenties. And teenage childbearing presents other ironies that would be funny if lives weren't at stake.

> [When I have my baby] I'll be more independent, more smarter . . . I'll have to sometimes make my own decisions.

> I got my mom and dad to realize that I'm not a baby anymore, and they know I'm grown up. (122)

They dream of independence, but most teen moms are high school dropouts who have to remain dependent on mom and dad or on government welfare programs for support. Then there is the obvious irony that having a baby does not automatically transform the mother into an adult. Nurses say that in the labor room, younger teens suck their thumbs and clutch their teddy bears between contractions (Hymowitz 1994, 22).

Also, there are medical risks: Studies show that teenagers often give birth prematurely, delivering early almost twice as often as older mothers (Associated Press 1995). The phenomenon isn't fully understood but may have to do with the fact that the adolescent body is still growing and so competes with its fetus for nutrients. Considering that prematurity is the leading cause of death among newborns (Associated Press 1995), teen moms whose first baby is premature need special instruction not only on pregnancy-prevention but also on early prenatal care.

INTERVENTION STRATEGISTS: THE STATE OF THE ART

For perspective and strategies for change, we turn to two concerned pioneers in this field, Dr. Marion Howard, clinical director of the Teen Services Program at Grady Memorial Hospital in Atlanta, Georgia; and Dr. Judith Musick, vice chairman of the Ounce of Prevention Fund, created in Illinois in 1981 to help disadvantaged youth and their families and now a statewide system of research, training, and technical assistance working with community-based organizations. This review limits discussion to Howard's work to delay teen sex and Musick's work to help girls cope with motherhood once it is a reality, although Musick's fund provides prevention programs as well.

PEER COUNSELING TO POSTPONE SEXUAL INVOLVEMENT

Marion Howard explains the rise in teen sexual activity in terms of a great cultural shift that has occurred over the past few decades: we are seeing soaring divorce rates, more absent fathers and single working mothers, fewer grandparents in the home, and ambivalent sexual mores following the "free love" revolution of the 1960s. Nowadays, in the absence of clear parental guidelines, peer pressure and the sex-heavy media hold the power of influence. Models with Barbie-doll figures sell everything from rubber tires to beer. Popular teen magazines concentrate on appearance and attracting the boys instead of developing personal interests.[2] Such a cultural milieu joins with lack of supervision to put many girls at risk for becoming teen moms.

Howard appeals to education to fill the gap, suggesting a reform of schools instead of welfare. Through Atlanta's Grady Memorial Hospital, since 1985 she has run an outreach program in the public schools for eighth graders called Postponing Sexual Involvement for Young Teens—an effort she began because an earlier traditional program teaching birth control alone proved ineffective. Now state-wide, the program consists of two equal parts taught in ten classroom periods: the first teaches about anatomy and contraception; the second concentrates on keeping kids from exploring these subjects in real life. More than four thousand eighth-grade students participate annually.

And now the program *is* effective. Recently it has been recognized as *the* most successful program for preventing teen pregnancy in the country (Rodrigue 1995). Surveys show that class participants are four times less likely than their counterparts to have sex in the eighth grade, with the delay lasting to some extent throughout high school (Howard 1992, 187). Here are some of the program's key elements:

- Capitalizing on the power of peer pressure, sexually abstinent and popular eleventh- and twelfth-grade students lead the classes. As Howard remarks, "Older youth who demonstrate being successful teens without being sexually involved provide needed role models in a climate in which many youth assume 'everybody's doing it'" (Howard 1992, 184).

- These older teens teach through dramatic skits in which the younger students also take part. People sixteen and younger, Howard observes, are often unable to anticipate the consequences of their actions in abstract terms. Participating in dramatizations in which these consequences are played out is a form of experiential learning which seems better suited to most teens (Howard and McCabe 1990, 21).

- Survey results show that the main concern of teen mothers is how to say "No" without hurting the boy's feelings. Accordingly, in the dramatic skits the older teens model that it's "cool" to say "No" by acting out the dialogue of sexual pressure:

Boy: "If you love me, you'll have sex with me."

Girl: "If you love me, you won't pressure me to do something I don't want to do"; or, "If I had sex with anyone, it would be with you. But I'm not going to do it now." (Rodrigue 1995)

Significantly, Howard's program changes the perspective of the teen teachers as well as the younger students. "At first, I wondered if I had a right to say no," said one teen leader. "Afterwards, I knew that I could and that they should respect my feelings" (Rodrigue 1995).

Howard is encouraged by her program's positive results:

The Grady Hospital study suggests that abstinence programs given at young ages can "buy some time" for young people, allowing them to mature physically and socially for a few years before they begin sexual intercourse. It may be that the added maturity combined with early exposure to family planning information can reduce teenage pregnancy. Whether "booster" programs given at later grades can sustain initial early gains in abstinence behavior is unknown. Such efforts seem to be indicated as a next step (Howard 1992, 193).

ADOLESCENCE: THE CRISIS OF IDENTITY

Who am I? Where did I come from and where am I going? What is my reason for being? Judith Musick reminds us that one of Erik Erikson's great contributions to psychology was his insight that the formation of identity is the primary task of adolescence. Erikson recognized that although identity newly becomes an issue at every major transition, never is it more critical than during the teen years. Adolescence is the identity crisis *par excellence,* the time when it is not only appropriate but absolutely necessary for a youth to forge the sense of self that will eventually empower him or her to leave the family and begin functioning as an adult in the larger community (64).

Following Erikson, Judith Musick's great contribution in *Young, Poor, and Pregnant* is her insight that *the resolution of this crisis of identity for some teens is motherhood.*[3] Although Musick's focus is girls growing up in poverty, her insights apply as well to those in dysfunctional families of any class. For such young women, Musick says,

the dream (and sometimes the reality) of parenthood answers the unanswerable question of what to do about the future. It fits best with . . . her internal representations of who she is and what she can safely do with her life. (139)

For a girl to form a strong sense of identity in adolescence, Musick stresses, she must have had a "good enough" developmental foundation in childhood.[4] By "good enough" she means an environment providing affection, security, stimulation, structure, and a sense of limits. Children need adults who can be trusted to provide a safe, nurturing place, but impoverished and dysfunctional families are often unable to create and maintain such an environment. As a result, an adolescent girl, lacking the psychological tools, confidence, and motivation to give birth to *herself,* will tend to resolve the issue of identity by giving birth to a *baby* instead. In essence, premature motherhood aborts or at best delays the young mother's true task because it saps the time, money, and energy she needs for self-development. The mother (and her children) become trapped in a life of ever-shrinking horizons.

Approaching the problem psychologically promises to solve a puzzle that has long baffled interventionists—that is, why these girls resist other alternatives. Listen to this frustrated counselor:

> Just as Carrie was on the brink of making some positive changes in her personal and educational life, she seemed to *deliberately* stop herself from succeeding by getting pregnant *again.* . . . Maria accomplished much the same thing by dropping out of her teen-parent support group—right after we told her that she had been accepted to a really good job-training program. Lisa just happened to "forget" to register for the junior college program she had been planning to attend for months, and Ginny took her twin sons out of the day care program that was enabling her to finish high school. And after going round and round with us about how bad he was for her, Dina went back to the boyfriend who tyrannizes her and practically keeps her a prisoner in the house. (9–10)

Why don't such girls leap at the chance to get up and out? Why do they resist all attempts to help them? *Why do they just keep on having babies? Because it's the best or the only way they know to become somebody and find the love they need.* Musick emphasizes that it's not enough to approach the problem at the outer level of education and jobs because such girls just keep sabotaging themselves. In order to truly help them change their lives and the lives of their children, we must understand adolescent childbearing as a psychological problem as well as a societal one.

Opportunities that are *objectively* available may not be *subjectively* available to such girls, so they can't even *see* them, let alone take advantage of them. The reason most intervention efforts have failed is because they have concentrated almost exclusively on social factors (14–15). What most policy makers don't understand, Musick says, is that early pregnancy is the only way these girls have of meeting fundamental needs and moving forward, given their developmental backgrounds. However self-destructive and illogical it may appear, they are doing the best they can, given who they are. If they could meet these needs in more positive ways, they would.

> In order for a program or policy to have an impact on the factors that lead an adolescent to become a mother, it must in some way alter her identity. . . . To be so motivating, interventions must reach and touch the girl at the level of the self, the deepest and most strongly felt sense of who she is. (66–67)

THE NATURE OF THE PROBLEM: DEVELOPMENTAL FACTORS

What, then, *are* the inner realities pushing a girl toward early motherhood and affecting her ability to change? Here is one young mother's story:

> I grew up with two alcoholic parents. . . . I had my first boyfriend at 11; he was 22. I guess I needed a father figure. . . . I never knew how to say "no." . . . When my parents got a divorce Mom got worse if that's possible. I got crazy. I got into a gang when I was 12. I got drunk with friends, tried a joint, and came home at 1 A.M. At 13 I was getting bad grades. . . . Soph year I met Bob, the father of my son. I fell in love and wasted my virginity on him. I got pregnant and was lost alone and confused. (Louisa, age 16 [35])

Stories like Louisa's inspire Musick's point that identity problems arise in homes that do not provide a "good enough" foundation in early childhood. In families compromised by poverty, divorce, alcoholism, sexual abuse, violence, or simply the absence of enough parental attention, basic developmental needs are likely to go unmet. Poor schools, bad neighborhoods, and weak community support compound the problem. These kids often have no adults they can trust or they learn to trust the wrong people. They lack positive role models to inspire them and appropriate challenges to help them build skills and competencies; they have inadequate cognitive and spiritual tools for developing a vision for their future; and they typically suffer low self-esteem. All such factors inhibit a girl's ability to develop the sense of self she will need at adolescence and put her at risk for managing that task by getting pregnant instead.

> Well Diary, I'm scared. A scared little girl on the inside, and an immature adult on the outside. I don't want to grow up. Gees, I never thought—17 years old and two kinds of lives. A mother in one life and a teenager in the other and put it together and you got a Teen Mom. As a little girl I was deprived of a father—as Courtney is now. I never did want that for my child—any child. A single mother is hard. *Very hard.* It is hard finding yourself. Who am I, Diary? Really, I don't know. (Nina [64])

Musick observes that when a girl from the mainstream with a "good enough" upbringing asks "Who am I?" the question means something like:

> Do my parents understand me? . . . What do they know? . . . How do I feel about sex? . . . Will I go to college? If so, where? . . . Will I have a career, or marry and raise children, or both? (59)

But when disadvantaged girls like Nina ask "Who am I?" the question comes from a much earlier stage of development: It's not "Who am I becoming and what will I do?" but rather,

> Who cares about me? Whom can I trust. . . . Where and how can I find
> security?. . . What do I need to do, and who do I need to be, to find a man who
> won't abandon me, as the men in my life and my mother's life have done? (60)

Girls without a strong developmental foundation are likely to try to find
their identity not within their own being, but in their relationships instead.

> If an adolescent's psychological energies are too strongly focused on defen-
> sive and security measures, much of her time and effort will be focused on trying
> to resolve her unmet dependency needs, searching for and trying to maintain
> attachments. When this occurs, her attention and energies are diverted from the
> critical development tasks that undergird adolescent and, later, adult competence
> in our society. Girls for whom basic acceptance and love are the primary moti-
> vating forces have little interest or emotional energy to invest in school or work-
> related activities unless they are exceptionally bright or talented. Even then, the
> pull of unmet . . . dependency needs may be more powerful than anything the
> worlds of school or work have to offer. . . . (60)

RESPONSE TO LOW SELF-ESTEEM: SEEKING IDENTITY IN RELATIONSHIPS

RELATIONSHIP WITH A MAN

A girl who lacks a strong, loving father in the home is especially at risk for
seeking her identity through a man. Listen to this story:

> All my life has been hurt. My stepdad started it. I went through so much
> mental abuse. . . . [The counselor] . . . is worried about me being around Alex
> cause he has beat me up. But I am hoping that him having the responsibilities of
> a child will change him. Maybe I am only dreaming, I don't know. I feel that I
> don't make good choices for friendships.
> I think I might be pregnant again . . . 18 and three children—I don't know if
> I can handle it. . . . How did I get caught in this mess? Am I ever going to be
> loved by a real man? Will I be a great mother? (15–16)

Lacking the inner strength to slay her own dragons in a competitive
world, such a girl will dream instead of the knight on the white horse charg-
ing to the rescue. And this is a dream that dies hard. Still unconsciously trying to fulfill her relationship with her father, she will cling to a man—or man
after man—even when he repeatedly abuses or abandons her. Even when
experience has shown her it doesn't work, often the only way she can think of
to hold on to a man is to have his baby. And this is why she will continue to
sabotage her future in favor of motherhood.

RELATIONSHIP WITH THE MOTHER

Another powerful, if unconscious, adolescent motive for motherhood is to
expect love from the baby to make up for the love one missed as a child from
one's own mother. As Musick puts it, "Through pregnancy and parenthood,
an adolescent girl can . . . recreate a close mother-child bond to heal the pain

provoked by conflict with her own parents . . . [and] extend her dependent bond with her mother through identification with her baby . . . whom she fervently hopes her mother will love and care for" (111).

> Interviewer: What will it be like when the baby is first born?
> Pregnant teen: My mom holding it all the time [tone is almost cooing with love]. (133)

As this girl's fantasy suggests, teen motherhood usually intensifies rather than distances the mother-daughter relationship. Here is another reason why girls sabotage themselves. Musick says a girl is often afraid to risk change precisely because it would mean separating from the mother and other emotionally significant women in her life who validate her sense of who she is. Often such a girl is enmeshed in a family history of poverty, dysfunction, and early childbearing that has lasted for generations. For her to "do it better" than the women around her would feel like a betrayal of all the people she needs most (111).

RELATIONSHIP WITH THE BABY

A third way a girl might try to strengthen her sense of self through relationship is in terms of her baby:

> Dear Kimmie, I lov you. You make me feel special and needed. With out you my life was boring and almost meaningless. (110)

The dream is that the baby will fulfill the unmet need for affection and a sense of self-worth missed in early childhood. But the reality, as we know, is that babies don't give, they take; and what they eventually can give back as adults depends largely on the quality of what they've been given. In teen mothering, Musick says, conflict is unavoidable because the adolescent process is naturally selfish, focused on nurturing the self, whereas the parenting process is—or should be—self*less,* focused on nurturing another. If the mother's own needs get in the way of her giving, then often the cycle will repeat itself in another generation of too-needy people. And there is yet another danger for the adolescent who has a baby to satisfy her longing for love: When her adorable infant becomes a demanding toddler, she won't be able to project her need for intimacy onto him any longer, and so is likely—to have another baby! There are such girls, Musick says, "virtually addicted to childbearing" (225).

TIME TO EXPLORE

How, then, to help adolescent girls form the sense of identity that will enable them to avoid the pitfall of early parenthood or, once in it, empower them to climb out?

One thing that seems to be essential to adolescent identity formation is the *time to explore* alternatives before having to assume adult responsibilities.

Again, Musick refers to the work of Erik Erikson:

> For Erikson, identity is not something given to the individual . . . Rather, it
> is something that is acquired through sustained personal effort. For this to tran-
> spire, adolescents require a moratorium—a period of time in which they are pro-
> vided with and take advantage of—opportunities to widen their experience, to
> increase the breadth of their exposure to diverse aspects of life, to explore alter-
> natives, and to experiment with various roles. The adolescent selects, sorts
> through, tries on, discards, reshapes, and eventually fashions a unique sense of
> self by integrating the values, beliefs, and goals that feel most personally expres-
> sive and appropriate—the ones that feel right for him or her. (64–65)

The wild clothes and weird hairdos teens insist on are colorful signs of this
impulse to experiment, as are gangs, daredevil activities, and teen pregnancy.

Although our culture has lost sight of how to provide a time out for
forming identity, the process was well understood in antiquity, and we can
find clues in myths. The Greek goddess Artemis, for instance, takes her initiates away with her to the rugged mountains of a wild country (Graves 1989,
121). There she inspires her girls with a sense of adventure, a sense of personal calling, and an elemental sense of joy in being alive.

Significantly, during this threshold time Artemis covers her girl adepts
with bearskins to scare away the boys. Such formidable protection is necessary for a girl to develop the mature identity she will need in order to form
healthy relationships with men later on. Bears hibernate, symbolic here of the
girls' need to take time out to dream of what they might become in the future.
The bearskin is like a cocoon, sheltering the miraculous change taking place
within so that the emerging young woman is not exposed to adult relationships and responsibilities before she is ready.

STRATEGIES FOR CHANGE

In a sense, Marion Howard's program, in helping girls postpone sex, is like
the bearskin that protects and gives them time before assuming the adult
responsibility of motherhood. Judith Musick's programs also help teens to
focus on the inner growth and vision they will need to construct a positive
future for themselves *and* their children. All such strategies provide the initiatory time out for developing identity that our youth so desperately need.

Here are some further suggestions about what parents and teachers can
do:

1) Follow Marion Howard's lead in convincing middle-schoolers to
   postpone sexual activity by

   —taking advantage of the power of peer pressure by using peer
   counseling; and

—showing girls how to say "No" experientially through drama. Teaching girls how to say "No" is key to the work of identity formation, for a well-developed sense of identity depends upon being able to set meaningful boundaries.

2) Beyond sex-education classes, make changes in the schools to correct what Mary Pipher in *Reviving Ophelia: Saving the Selves of Adolescent Girls* (1994) sees as a gender bias. She mentions a 1992 report prepared at Wellesley College for the American Association of University Women, *How Schools Shortchange Girls: A Study of Major Findings on Girls and Education,* which claims that teachers give five times more attention to boys than to girls and are more likely to ask boys the more complex, thought-provoking questions. Textbook illustrations, stories, and biographies more often feature men. Boys are more likely to be praised for academic work and girls, for appearance and nice behavior. Teachers attribute boys' successes to ability and their failures, to external factors. For girls, it is the opposite. Somewhere in the crowded halls of middle school girls lose their confidence and their dreams of being an astronaut or a zoologist (Pipher 1994, 62–63).[5]

This research suggests two further strategies for change:

3) Separate some middle and high school classes by gender, a practice possible even in coed, public schools. Myra Sadker, Dean of the School of Education at American University, says that away from the boys, girls "stop being the audience and become players" (Belitski 1994, 1). All-girl classes in math and science might be particularly helpful, given the 1992 National Assessment of Educational Progress Test results showing that, among seventeen-year-olds, boys outperformed girls by four points in math and ten points in science (Sommers 1994).

4) Raise the consciousness of well-intended teachers who may not be aware of the subtle ways they perpetuate gender bias. Pipher knows one elementary teacher who routinely changes the sex of the powerful male characters in animal stories so the girls will have strong role models (Pipher 1994, 62).

5) Shift general emphasis in middle school from the biology of sex to broader concepts of the masculine and the feminine. John F. Gardner, now retired twenty-five-year faculty chairman of a New York Waldorf School, argues for such a shift and speaks of the masculine and feminine as great cultural values and energies. As he eloquently states:

The main problem for young people today is that they have no conception of what is possible in the way of human development. They imagine that the purpose of life is to use their inherited or acquired powers to accomplish something in the outer world, not in themselves. It never occurs to them that their greatest task is to conceive and bring themselves to birth as creative, self-directing human beings. . . .

If only the young boy could imagine what it means ideally to be a man: the high daring, the humble service; the instant decision, the patient endurance . . . the gentle succor—the fearless championing, the compassionate shielding! If only the young girl could imagine what it means to be a woman: the eternal feminine that draws mankind ever forward toward beauty and romance, toward enlightenment and love, toward creativeness and salvation! Yet neither the truly masculine nor the truly feminine is an attribute of birth—neither is given, both must be attained, and that is what the years between 12 and 24 or so are primarily for. (Gardner 1995, 18)

6) At intervention agencies, model a healthy family structure by providing a stable, predictable environment where behavior leads to appropriate consequences—unlike in the dysfunctional or disadvantaged home. Good programs are like good families, Musick says. "They set high standards and reinforce positive values. . . . they link expectations and goals with the tangible means to achieve them, providing realistic opportunities to grow" (227). In such settings, "girls are made to feel special and protected and worthy of such care" (233). Musick also emphasizes the importance of beauty in the environment—fresh paint, flowers, comfortable furniture—for communicating the promise of positive growth: "The setting communicates a message about how we see these young women and what we believe they deserve for themselves. An aesthetically pleasing setting . . . says we think they are beautiful. Never underestimate how meaningful this is" (233).

7) Give teen mothers a sense of joy and adventure by exposing them to life outside the mundane boundaries of poverty. As Musick observes, "Adolescent mothers will not be inspired—let alone equipped—to move into the wider world if they have no knowledge of it beyond what they see on television" (233). That such excursions can be empowering as well as fun—and let us never underestimate the therapeutic value of fun!—is evident in this girl's report:

We all went to see the ballet, and a play downtown. We had field trips by ourselves and with our kids to the zoo and museums. This summer we're going camping. . . . We raised some of the money for camp ourselves. (232)

8) Help teens create a vision for their future. Many adolescents lack information about positive options. More unfortunately, survivors of trauma and abuse may lack the trust in life necessary to plan ahead.

These young women are often especially vulnerable to sexual impulses of the moment. Musick speaks of the useful process of *scaffolding,* by which mentors serve as competent parents in helping adolescents take one manageable step at a time toward a long-range goal initially beyond reach—e.g., to get a college degree, first you have to ask for an enrollment application (227).

9) Take advantage of the enormous power of adolescent peer pressure by providing a safe place for girls to share concerns and build a supportive "community" of their own. Musick speaks of the healing and transformative process that begins when girls have a chance to express themselves without fear of criticism, retaliation, or estrangement from family and friends (231). Learning that peers have had similar experiences allows them to feel more normal and less alone. Sometimes younger adolescents have questions that need to be answered very directly:

Is it totally wrong to have sex with your uncle if he's not really a relative? (231)

10) Encourage journal writing. Personal writing, Musick says, "can provide an authentic means of self-expression, a new and different route to self-awareness. For an adolescent at risk, it can also provide a certain distance between feeling and doing, a way to help her think before she acts" (20–21). Putting one's thoughts and feelings in words lets the writer express memories and feelings too painful to share otherwise:

Dear Diary, . . . things that had happened, that even though they happened a long time ago, they had left profound scars in me. I had never been able to have enough courage to tell that to anybody. Nobody but my dear diary. (22–23)
I like writing in my journal because . . . I can write about things I can't talk about in person. Writing in my journal has helped me understand things more clearly and better. (23)

Diary writing can also bring to light less conscious reasons for having a baby. Consider this entry:

You've never been truly loved until you've been loved by a child. (122)

11) Provide opportunities to tell one's story. As participants in twelve-step programs know, telling our personal story raises consciousness about destructive patterns of behavior so that we are less likely to repeat them; this increased understanding permits us to assume authorship over our lives and gives us a sense of freedom about future choices. Although we can't alter past hurtful events, telling

about them can break their hold on us so we can move on. Musick says that when a young victim of abuse tells her story,

> Speaking the unspeakable shifts the sense of control from others to the self . . . the past becomes a series of events that she can objectify. When she tells her story, she acts, and in acting she stops protecting . . . those who have done her harm. For many, this process is a first step away from victimhood. (230)

One girl said after telling her story,

> My heart feels so clean. (I am not kidding. It feels like I washed it out with soap and water.) (230)

12) Provide ceremonies and awards to recognize achievement. Especially for adolescents, Musick observes, change requires rituals to mark accomplishment and growth. She mentions graduation ceremonies at Family Focus programs[6] where teens are elevated in status from participant to big sister—an important volunteer role that capitalizes on a girl's natural desire to be a heroine. Newsletters recognizing achievement serve the same purpose (232).

13) Mentor the mentors and heal the healers. Musick stresses that the efficacy of all the above strategies depends on the ability of the people carrying them out. A recurring problem is that many of the women working with teen moms don't have the professional knowledge or experience to lead the girls into appropriate career paths. How can they be effective guides into what is also for them unknown territory?

More problematically, many of these workers have the same psychological issues as the girls themselves—such as a family history of violence, unhealthy relationships to men, and poor childrearing practices or trouble with sexuality, trust, autonomy, and assertiveness. Squeamish about discussing sex, for instance, a leader might skirt the subject until forced to confront it when one of the teens in her group gets pregnant again. It is imperative that helpers do their own inner work if they are to be effective in helping the girls (202).

14) Create a *caring community,* which is essentially what Musick's social service agencies strive to provide:

> Such communities widen the world of possibilities for us, transforming our sense of who we are and what we can do. As a nation we have yet to really understand, let alone create, such caring communities and institutions for the increasing numbers of young people who will surely be lost without them. (234)

The last teenager she quotes testifies to the difference such care can make:

I was going through some emotional changes and so the times that I could-
n't make it they would visit and talk with me and comfort me in some way. . . .
they stayed with me and on me about finishing school. . . . I could have been out
on the streets, young girl pregnant you know, just at home on welfare you know,
but they showed me I could be more than that, I could be a lot more than
that. . . . I see that I can be anything I want to be and still take care of my baby.
. . . Life is not that bad and it's not that hard, just give it a chance. . . . Confidence, don't talk about confidence, I didn't have any. My confidence was gone.
They picked up my pieces, even put them back together. They showed me I'm a
person. (234)

We can add to Musick's work two other important ways to engender
change:

15) Support storytelling. Beyond the therapeutic value of telling and
hearing personal stories is the value of storytelling *per se*—stories of
healing, of self-empowerment, of coming of age. Thematically
appropriate folktales, fairytales, and myths—stories of collective
wisdom—are a powerful medium for nurturing the self. We know
stories are a particularly effective way of teaching in that leaders of
all the great religions have always used them. Through imagery,
character, and plot, stories mirror our own struggles and free the
mind to imagine options for creative change. Stories seem to go
directly into long-term memory and so become part of the fabric of
our being, a spiritual handbook of information to draw on. A healing
story has the power to guide and inspire for a lifetime.[7]

16) Lastly, nurture the creativity of children. Jungian analyst Louise
Mahdi remarks that perhaps girls are now unconsciously driven to
produce baby after baby because they don't have the foundation by
which to give birth inwardly through creative work and care for
themselves. People make the same mistake over and over again until
the true lesson is learned. To do creative work necessarily sounds
one's depths and draws on inner resources, and so frequently leads
to greater self-understanding. Almost by definition, it helps us discover more about who we are—and who we may become. When we
open the imagination, images and symbols spontaneously arise from
a deep place in the psyche; the very process of selection seems to
activate an inner artist. One can become one's own good companion
in this activity and so be less dependent on others for a sense of personal worth.

I believe the same would be true for most fields of artistic endeavor. But
in our high-tech culture, the arts are neglected and the life of the imagination
is not generally honored or developed. The writer Robert Bly observed at a
workshop a few years ago that Russians characteristically flock to poetry

readings the way we do to football games. In Bali, we are told, a word for "art" does not even exist, so fundamental is artistic expression to every industry. In India, Louise Mahdi says, a sense of joy in ritual—the enactment of a mythology nurturing the symbolic life of the self—flowers still, even as it did, according to Riane Eisler, in matriarchal Crete, where the life of the imagination was expressed communally in "mythically meaningful ritual and artistic play" (1987, 32).

But that was four thousand years ago. What about here and now? There is another "quiet crisis" besides pregnancy plaguing our youth—that of growing up in a declining materialistic culture devoid of a living mythology.[8]

In this context, the identity issues inherent in teen pregnancy can arise for any woman. Even mature women faced with an existential crisis calling for personal creativity—getting a higher degree, going back to work, taking on a major project—often choose to create a child instead. Teenagers have an abundance of role models for how to defeat themselves. The theme of women's struggle to find their authentic voice is surfacing even in popular films, but too often the woman's character is still defined mainly in relationship to a man. In spite of the woman's movement, young Sarah Jane's ideal of the swing in the backyard and she in the kitchen watching her children play is still very much alive. Motherhood is still a prevailing dream, and that means being contained within the family.

On one hand, staying at home with the kids is critically important— Musick's whole thrust is that teen pregnancy is largely due to the failure of absentee parents to meet their children's dependency needs. But without the inner certainty that one *can* be independent, one always lives in fear. Relationships can't be equal: the man, by default, will have the upper hand. Women have to seek personal fulfillment and their unique places in the world, if only so that their relationships can be truly a matter of choice and not a perceived necessity born of dependency. Until they become willing to do that, girls are going to be in danger of aborting their own journeys of self-discovery by having babies too soon.

NOTES

1. Sarah Jane's poem is taken from Judith S. Musick's *Young, Poor, and Pregnant: The Psychology of Teenage Motherhood* (New Haven and London: Yale University Press, 1993), p. 29. (© 1993 Yale University.) All such quotes of girls' material retain original spelling. Further references to this book are incorporated into the text by page number only.

2. One such magazine carries a coupon advertisement by Johnson and Collins, Inc. of Minneapolis reading "Yes! I want to be noticed and loved and get a gorgeous guy of my own! *RUSH me the bestselling Get Him System Now!* . . . I am enclosing $12.00 for the complete system plus $3 for postage and handling."

3. Her data includes interviews with junior high school girls living in a high-risk

environment; findings from a pioneer study of 445 pregnant and parenting teens correlating childhood sexual abuse and adolescent childbearing; conversations with parents whose children are growing up in conditions of extreme urban poverty; group interviews funded by the Woods Charitable Trust to determine how intervention did (or did not) prevent additional childbearing; clinical case material covering parent-child relationships; and diaries and journals of adolescent mothers (17–19).

4. Musick, like Erikson, is a developmental psychologist, meaning that she focuses on normal human growth and maturation (in contrast to the field of *ab*normal psychology, which focuses on deviations); that is, she considers how young people resolve the challenges of maturing presented naturally within the context of their specific environment, and how that environment does or does not help them meet those challenges.

5. The AAUW report is the subject of some controversy—for instance, the top career aspiration among girls was lawyer, which hardly indicates lack of self-esteem (Sommers 1994).

6. Family Focus was founded by president Bernice Weissbourd in 1976 in Evanston, Illinois as a resource center for helping teens cope with parenthood and is now being imitated nationally. See separate chapter on this organization.

7. For particular stories for girls, see Clarissa Pinkola Estes's best-selling work, *Women Who Run with the Wolves: Myths and Stories of the Wild Woman Archetype* (New York: Ballantine Books, 1992).

8. A pioneer in redressing this lack is the Beacon Street Gallery and Performance Company, a multi-cultural, multi-arts organization founded by visual artist Patricia Murphy in 1982 and now codirected by poet and teacher Susan Field to serve underclass youth at Uptown Hull House in a Chicago area where over sixty languages are spoken in the schools. Offering hope in a sometimes unquiet neighborhood, the organization has provided cultural heritage classes taught by mentoring artists for the past twelve years: Native American youth, for instance, learn painting from nationally known Chippewa/Winnebago artist Eugene Pine; Guatemalan youth learn to play the marimba from a master musician; black youth learn dance and poetry from South African artists Ndikho and Nomusa Xaba.

Such programs give these adolescents a sense of pride and identity in their own culture at the same time they teach them a self-enhancing art form. Master artists also guide youth in junior curating to produce exhibitions, a craft that can later lead to employment. Increased self-esteem, broadening horizons, new skills, exciting and successful artists as role models, the joy of creative expression, increased sense of community—these are some of the advantages. Significantly, Murphy recalls that there were three young women in the arts program who were unable to make any creative connection—and they were the ones who all got pregnant, one of them twice (1995).

REFERENCES

Associated Press. 1995. Study: Teen-age moms face double risk of early births, 27 April.

Belitski, Pam. 1994. All-girl math class. *New Moon Parenting* 2, no. 2 (November/December): 1.

Blankson, Mary L., M. D., Cliver, SP, Goldenberg, RL, Hickey, CA, Jin, J, Dubbard, MB, et. al. 1993. Health behavior and outcome in sequential pregnancies of black and white adolescents. *Journal of the American Medical Association* 269, no. 11 (17 March): 1401–3.

Carnegie Task Force. 1994. *Starting points: Meeting the needs of our youngest children.* New York: Carnegie Foundation of New York.

Eisler, Riane. 1987. *The chalice and the blade: Our history, our future.* Cambridge: Harper and Row.

Gabriel, Ayala and Elizabeth R. McAnarney, M.D. 1983. Parenthood in two subcultures: White, middle-class couples and black, low-income adolescents in Rochester, New York. *Adolescence* 18, no. 71 (fall): 594–608.

Gardner, John F. 1995. The opportunity of adolescence. *Holistic Education Review* (March): 15–21.

Gliatto, Tom, Tom Cunnett, Lyndon Stambler, Kristina Johnson, Danelle Morton, Kurt Pitzer, and Joyce Wagner. Paradise lost. 1995. *People Magazine* (1 May): 70–75.

Graves, Robert. 1989. Introduction to *New larousse encyclopedia of mythology.* Translated by Richard Aldington and Delano Ames. New York: Crescent Books.

Howard, Marion. 1992. Delaying the start of intercourse among adolescents. *Adolescent Medicine: State of the Art Reviews* 3, no. 2 (June): 181–93.

Howard, Marion and Judith Blarney McCabe. 1990. Helping teenagers postpone sexual involvement. *Family Planning Perspectives* 22, no. 1 (January/February): 21–26.

Hymowitz, Kay S. 1994. The teen mommy track. *City Journal* (autumn): 19–29.

McMahon, Colin. 1994. Babies born into peril. *Chicago Tribune,* 22 May.

Musick, Judith S. 1993. *Young, poor, and pregnant: The psychology of teenage motherhood.* New Haven and London: Yale University Press.

Pipher, Mary. 1994. *Reviving Ophelia: Saving the selves of adolescent girls.* New York: Ballantine Books.

Rodrigue, George. 1995. Saying "no" to sex. *Chicago Tribune Womanews,* 26 February.

Sommers, Christina Hoff. 1994. The myth of schoolgirls' low self-esteem. *The Wall Street Journal,* 3 October.

Woodman, Marion. 1985. *The pregnant virgin: A process of psychological transformation.* Toronto: Inner City Books.

NINE

FAMILY FOCUS: COMMUNITY-BASED SOLUTIONS

Sharron Brown Dorr

Family Focus, a midwest service organization, is described in some detail since it is a program which nurtures the community's own children without federal funding. Part of the article is directly from our interviews with the founder and director of Family Focus. Some of the staff are trained in Rites of Passage programs and processes. (See Sharron Dorr's chapter, "Teen Motherhood and Aborting the Search for Identity: A Review of the Work of Judith S. Musick and Marion Howard.")

For more information, the administrative offices of Family Focus, Inc. are located at 310 South Peoria Street, Suite 510, Chicago, Illinois 60607-3534.

I felt like I wanted to drop out of school. . . . And I thought my kid couldn't grow up with love and care," remembers Yvonne Heard of Chicago's West Side about the time she was pregnant at the age of seventeen. Then Yvonne found out about Family Focus, a locally funded social service agency, and began attending prenatal classes taught by a nurse at the agency's closest center. She also joined a discussion group with other pregnant teens. For three years after her baby was born, she attended Family Focus classes to gain parenting skills. Family Focus enabled her to stay in school and graduate.

Later on, Yvonne completed an associate degree in child development and began working for Family Focus part time as a "home visitor," someone who visits new mothers in their homes and then reports to a social worker. In time, she was promoted to the position of "home educator," teaching new mothers about nutrition, child care, and parenting (Little 1989).

Charrisse Fairman was a single mother of three living on public aid. "The head on my shoulders now, I don't believe I'd have . . . if it wasn't for Family Focus," she says. At that time Charrisse might have easily slipped into a pattern of child abuse. When she first came to Family Focus at age nineteen, the staff helped her form a healthier emotional relationship with her children. A decade later, Fairman was bringing her youngest to Family Focus three times a week and had the wisdom to warn her eleven- and thirteen-year-old girls against the unglamorous drudgery of teen parenthood (Lev 1994).

Yvonne, Charrisse, and their children are only two of thousands of families receiving ongoing help from Family Focus. This nonprofit agency was founded in Evanston, Illinois in 1976 by Bernice Weissbourd, early childhood educator and lecturer at the University of Chicago School of Social Work, and her partners—husband and real estate developer, Bernard Weissbourd and businessman/philanthropist, Irving B. Harris.[1] When the first Family Focus center opened in an Evanston school, the group expected to serve 50 people; 250 families came the first year (Pesman 1985). By the early 1990s that figure had jumped to 1,300 (Family Focus, Inc. 1992, 1). A program especially for teen parents opened in 1979, named by the teens, "Our Place," was located in a storefront.

Originally intended to help teen moms cope with responsibilities of parenthood, the program soon also reduced the likelihood of those moms having subsequent babies and increased the number of those who stayed in school or went on to college. Moreover, fewer of the babies born suffered from low birth weight—one of the main hazards of teen pregnancies—because the agency had tutored the moms in nutrition and prenatal care (Pesman 1985).

Now, Family Focus operates in several locations throughout the Chicago area and has become a national model for how to prevent teenage pregnancy or, once pregnancy is a fact, how to help teens have healthy babies and assume the responsibilities of parenthood.[2]

"To promote the well-being of children by supporting and strengthening their families" is its simple mission statement (Family Focus, Inc. 1994, 2) which might sound unremarkable until we remember that until a few decades ago, the large extended family of grandparents, aunts, and uncles could be counted on to provide struggling young parents with the support and wisdom they needed to bring children to a healthy maturity. Today, increasing mobility, divorce, unemployment, and a host of other social ills have fragmented families, leaving young people isolated and floundering. Weissbourd, in a recent interview with *Crossroads* editors Louise Mahdi and Nancy Christopher, said that she wanted to establish an agency that would function in much the same way as the extended family support system of the past.

> Our program is very focused on giving the young people we serve a sense of self because they don't feel valued, and a sense of a future, rather than feeling hopeless. We do it by building relationships between the children and the staff. When a teen knows that somebody "cares about me", lots of things start happening. (1994)

Also central to Weissbourd's vision is the concept of involving the whole community. Families become strongest when there is a social network made up of church, school, recreational, business, and health professionals all joining hands to help with the responsibilities of child-rearing so that single teen moms aren't left to do it all alone. If we as communities support young parents and guide them in their child-rearing, everyone will win: as parents become more competent, their children will be healthier, and so the community itself will be strengthened.

For Weissbourd, this is no armchair philosophy. At six locations in Evanston, Chicago, and Aurora, social workers and counselors work very closely with trained volunteers and community institutions to promote the well-being of children in a variety of ways. For instance, family "drop-in" centers offer child-rearing and self-development programs and parent-child group activities, and provide child care while the parent is on the premises. They offer job training and internship programs that enable teen parents to become self-supporting. Partnerships with local civic organizations, churches, schools, and businesses strengthen the family's sense of belonging to a community and foster the concept of community service as a natural part of day-to-day life.

At Our Place, Family Focus staff works with the local health department, school district teachers, and volunteer peer supporters in *Step-by-Step,* a program for fourth through eighth graders designed to prevent early sex and pregnancy, gang involvement, drug use, delinquency, and school dropout (Family Focus, Inc. 1992, 2).

Two elements of the Step-by-Step program are particularly creative: *Working Wonders* is a six-week summer day camp that introduces fourth through eighth graders to the world of work to build self-esteem and help break the cycle of unemployment for children who do not have a role model of a working parent. For six hours a day, participants attend classes stressing work skills and job readiness and perform duties in the areas for which they are being trained. On the fifth day of the week, they are rewarded with special events and field trips. They receive a $25-a-week stipend for participating. They're required to get a social security card and to open a bank account (Family Focus, Inc. 1992, 3).

Another esteem-booster is performing in a gospel choir at concerts sponsored by Family Focus. The choir gives the children the opportunity, usually for the first time, to be artistically disciplined and to sing in harmony. And it gives them a chance to be part of a social process of give and take: "The community gives a lot to Family Focus," says director Geneve Wade. "The choir is a way in which the children can give something back to the community" (Claessens 1993).

Another aspect of Step-by-Step's primary prevention program, *No Deposit, No Return,* is designed to help high-school athletes make a successful transition into adulthood. The idea is that without a deposit made in academics, there truly will be no return later in life. Weekly meetings at Our Place include a meal, tutoring in science and math, and rap sessions where the boys can relax their macho image and share difficult feelings.

Avoiding teen pregnancy is a main topic in these sessions: high-profile athletes, of course, are at high risk for becoming fathers too soon. The staff stresses that the boys are just as responsible as the girls for preventing pregnancy and teach them to protect themselves from adoring advances like, "I love you so much, you don't have to wear a condom."

For teens who *have* become parents, Our Place offers another range of innovative services. These services include *Partners,* an award-winning project to give young mothers encouragement and guidance by linking them with mentoring older women who once were teen parents themselves; *Transitional Learning Center (T.L.C.),* a school set up especially for pregnant teens which meets at the center five days a week, its classes taught by instructors from the local school district; and *Teen Cuisine,* another award-winner, which is an eight-month, five-day-a-week food service training program for single young moms who otherwise have slim prospects for getting off welfare. And the agency staff doesn't just discreetly *offer* the program; they actually track prospective participants down and provide the child care necessary for the parents to be free to attend the classes. "We sought out those we knew weren't doing anything with their lives to provide a last chance to come up with a career," said Delores Holmes, a Family Focus director. "There are always jobs in the food-service area and this was a way to come up with a real job. . . . we let them know they could become a hostess—or even own their own restaurant or start a small catering service" (Family Focus, Inc. 1992, 3; Berkowitz 1987).

Family Focus's services in Evanston include workshops by trained staff on parenting and child development. The strategy is to teach teenagers how to give their very young children the love and acceptance they will need to avoid seeking acceptance through gangs and drug use later. Other offerings include resumé writing, English as a second language, and support groups for new, working, and single parents (Spallone 1992).

In 1990, a Carnegie Foundation survey indicated that more than one-third of children are not ready to learn when they enter school. In all Family Focus centers, emphasis is given to the first years of life, crucial to school readiness. Evanston programs function in co-operation with the local school district. Targeting parents with very young children at risk for school failure, the center offers programs about the importance of early childhood development for school readiness.

Family Focus's Project Early Start—launched in 1991–1992 with Illinois State Board of Education funding and in cooperation with, among others, Evanston Hospital, Infant Welfare Society, Evanston Township High School, and the Evanston Health Department—offers parent training and a free children's program for kids under six including gross-motor activities, stories, and language development. Collaboration with Lekotek (a national resource center for families of children with special needs) provides programs for kids with disabilities. Hard-to-reach families too stressed to seek these services are helped with education and support at home (Family Focus, Inc. 1992, 3–4; Spallone 1992).

The Family Focus center in Chicago's North Lawndale community (home of Yvonne and Charrisse, whose stories appeared earlier) offers a Male Responsibility program which strives to prevent boys from joining gangs.

Their projects increase self-esteem, strengthen academic skills, encourage abstinence, and enhance relationships with parents. In one year alone, activities included school and street clean-ups, car washes, visits to senior citizens, and organizing a community youth conference (Family Focus, Inc. 1994, 3).

Chicago's West Town neighborhood is a largely Spanish-speaking community where in 1989 one in three older teens were neither high-school graduates nor enrolled in school and 42 percent of children aged three to five lived in poverty. There, Family Focus Nuestra Familia works in partnership with the Chicago Board of Education to present an innovative program called *Play 'n' Learn*. Sessions meet for three hours once a week over an eight-week period. After an informational presentation on child development and health and safety issues, the fun begins. Parents and children are videotaped engaging in a planned activity. While the children play separately, a group facilitator helps parents analyze the interaction. Then parents and children together write a story. By the end of the eight weeks, each family has created a storybook to keep and read together (Family Focus, Inc. 1994, 2; 1992, 7).

Community support for youth at risk is particularly strong in Aurora, Illinois, where in 1994 Family Focus collaborated with a number of organizations in a primary prevention program to meet the social, recreational, and educational needs of seventy participants four afternoons a week. Aurora Township, for example, provided weekly transportation to a gym where Township staff joined agency staff in supervising recreational activities. Volunteers from the Urban League tutored youth in reading and math; and representatives from organizations such as the Health Department, the Visiting Nurses Association, and the Juvenile Division of the Aurora Police Department led workshops for teens and their parents (Family Focus, Inc. 1994, 4).

All such community efforts strengthen families at risk and so over time will strengthen our communities. At least that's the vision that inspired Bernice Weissbourd and Irving Harris when they started Family Focus in 1976.

Does it work? The effectiveness of social services is notoriously hard to measure, but because, as *Chicago Tribune* writer Michael Lev points out, a center like Family Focus Lawndale "is always full of parents who say they're being helped, it's probably true. And because local teachers say they noticed an improved attitude from students who went to Family Focus, the program must be working."

NOTES

1. Family Focus is funded by Harris's brainchild, the Ounce of Prevention Fund, a public-private partnership of the Northbrook-based Pittway Corp. Charitable Foundation (Little 1989). Weissbourd, incidentally, was the mentor of Judith S. Musick,

who is vice chairman of the Ounce of Prevention Fund and author of *Young, Poor, and Pregnant: The Psychology of Teenage Motherhood* (1993).

2. Several thousand family resource centers now function in a number of states, including Michigan, Indiana, North Carolina, Connecticut, and Kentucky, which leads with over four hundred centers (Family Focus, Inc. 1994, 5; Lev 1994).

REFERENCES

Berkowitz, Karen. 1987. Teen Cuisine offers job training for teen moms. *Evanston Review,* 14 May.

Claessens, Marilyn. 1993. Working Wonders: Summer day camp helps kids aim high. *Evanston Review,* 15 July.

Family Focus, Inc. 1992. Unpublished Overview.

Family Focus, Inc. 1993–1994 Annual Report. *Children, parents, communities.*

Hoffman, Paul. 1990. No deposit, no return. *Evanston Review,* 19 April.

Lev, Michael A. 1994. Centers of hope for families at risk. *Chicago Tribune,* 24 August.

Little, Anne. 1989. Fund's agencies focus on teenage mothers, children. *Chicago Tribune,* 29 January.

Pesmen, Sandra. 1985. Teen pregnancy foes find friends in business. Crain's *Chicago Business,* 24 June.

Spallone, Jennie. 1992. Neighbors for the '90s. *Chicago Parent,* February.

Weissbourd, Bernice. 1982. Five teen pregnancy myths: Personal view. *Chicago Sun-Times,* 6 December.

————. 1994. Unpublished interview with Louise Carus Mahdi and Nancy Geyer Christopher, editors of *Crossroads.* 13 June.

TEN

LIFE WITHOUT FATHER

Louise Carus Mahdi

*Unless we reverse the decline of marriage, no other achieve-
ments—no tax cut, no new government programs, no new idea—
will be powerful enough to reverse the trend of declining child
well-being.*

—FROM "MARRIAGE IN AMERICA"[1]

The falling apart of families in America is directly linked to the challenge of rites of passage in our times. New values and insights gained from rites-of-passage programs tend to lose their "staying power" in unhealthy home environments, where parents who are not committed to a permanent relationship choose to separate or divorce and no longer live together with their children. Constructive rites of passage are likely to be effective and appropriate for youth where both parents have shared in family life; but unparented youth are not usually ready for such experiences because their more basic need for parenting has not been met. They may search for parent figures and be dependent all their lives, never becoming fully adult.

We must be aware of the special needs of youth without fathers (or mothers). "Dad is destiny" is the opening sentence in a major review[2] of a new book, *Fatherless America: Confronting Our Most Urgent Social Problem* by David Blankenhorn,[3] founder and president of the Institute for American Values, nonpartisan and research-oriented. He is part of a growing movement to train and support mentors as well as to support fathers and reconnect them to their children.

Such efforts are needed, for in 1990, 36 percent of U.S. children did not live with their fathers. This is more than double the rate in 1960. The problem is that "good enough fatherhood" is not possible for most men not living with their children. In the most significant areas, the absent father is not being responsible for his children. He is not recognizable as a father.

Consequently, building healthy marriages will do more to reduce crime, cut violence, and decrease the numbers of adolescent girls having babies than any welfare reform. An indication of this is that without both parents, girls are twice as likely to become teen mothers. Furthermore, only 43 percent of state prisoners grew up with both parents. A missing father is part of the criminal's personal history, more significant than either race or poverty. An absent father is more of a psychological loss than a father who dies. All of these factors lead to negative rites of passage for the children when they come to the major times of transition.

"Divorce is not just an episode in a child's life," we learn from Judith Wallerstein,[4] who has tracked many children over the years. The extended family network helped a lot two generations ago, but now the nuclear family is more typical. The scars of divorce last for decades. Parenting is not like a trade such as plumbing or truck driving. Blankenhorn emphasizes, "It's not a set of techniques. It depends on a human identity." Finding some of one's identity is the goal of rites of passage.

Two generations ago in America there were many more adults available as role models than there are today. Now the neighborhood is often not there to fall back upon. The network of midwives, starting at birth, is also missing. In short, a larger community is not there for many families, and this makes the family more important than ever.

"The good news, largely ignored in today's script, is that married fatherhood is a man's most important pathway to happiness. Being a loving husband and committed father is the best part of being a man. The bad news . . . is that high rates of divorce and out-of-wedlock childbearing, the twin generators of paternity without fatherhood, are incompatible with male happiness and societal success . . . marriage constitutes an irreplaceable life-support system for effective fatherhood. . . . being a real man means being a good father."[5]

The key problem posed by broken homes is that young people often experience destructive and dangerous passages when one of their parents is absent.[6] Rites of passage do not suddenly descend from some other realm at the dawn of adolescence. Many "smaller" passages start before kindergarten in a two-parent family. These small preparatory passages are very difficult to carry out in a one-parent home.

We need to support the two-parent family if we want rites of passage to be effective. We need families, extended families, supportive families. If we want our rites-of-passage efforts to provide lasting initiatory experiences, the need to restore family environments where two parents are present for their children assumes utmost importance. Families can join with other families before their children reach puberty to create an environment and community to support constructive rites of passage for their children.

Blankenhorn believes Fathers' Clubs could invigorate fatherhood through organized father-child activities and through community leadership reaching out to fatherless children. "Security Dads" in Indianapolis go out with their sons to events to make sure "there won't be a lot of trouble." They noticed that being present is what counts. MAD DADS (an acronym for Men Against Destruction-Defending Against Drugs and Social Disorder) has organized other fathers' groups in eight states, starting in Omaha in a Baptist church.

Public housing is surely, next to prisons, the most violent and fatherless place in our country. Perhaps the rules could be changed to give priority to married couples. 1.3 million units are owned by the federal government. Public housing could provide a real test for the "fatherhood idea." This could become a challenge to turn public housing into a more appropriate, less violent environment for children.

Veterans of civil rights and other movements could help us face the challenge of a nonpolitical and deeply human community action.

Interfaith and clergy councils could act on behalf of marriage. New leadership is needed. Communities need to support the fatherhood idea. Athletes need to go out of their way on behalf of the fatherhood idea. Fatherhood is a key factor in the emergence of the human family and of human civilization.

> In the course of evolution, the keystone in the foundation of the human family was the capturing of male energy into the nurturance of the young. . . . The human family is a complex organizational structure for the garnering of energy to be transformed into the production of the next generation, and its most essential feature is the collaboration of the male and female parent in the division of labor.[7]

> Keep the flame burning in the Father's house. . . . And there will always be someone to feel the warmth of the legacy. Keep the flame alive.[8]

NOTES

1. Council on Families in America, "Marriage in America" (New York: Institute for American Values, 1995).

2. Joseph P. Shapiro and Joannie M. Schrof with Mike Tharp and Dorian Friedman, "Honor Thy Children." *U.S. News and World Report,* 27 February 1995.

3. David Blankenhorn, *Fatherless America: Confronting Our Most Urgent Social Problem* (New York: Basic Books, 1995).

4. See Shapiro, Schrof, and Tharp, "Honor Thy Children."

5. David Blankenhorn, *Fatherless America,* p. 223.

6. See Sara McLanahan and Gary Sanderfur, *Growing Up with a Single Parent* (Cambridge, Mass.: Harvard University Press, 1994).

7. Jane B. Lancaster and Chet S. Lancaster, *Parenting across the Life Span* (New York: Aldine de Gruyter, 1987), p. 189. (See also other reports by the Carnegie Foundation and National Commission on Children, as well as Ron Mincy's *Nurturing Young Black Males: Challenges to Agencies, Programs, and Social Policy.* [Lanham, Md.: National Book Network, 1994].)

8. See the essay by Nouk Bassomb, "Baskets at the Crossroads," p. xxvii above.

ELEVEN

THE CODE OF THE STREETS

Elijah Anderson

Elijah Anderson, Charles and William L. Day Professor of the Social Sciences at the University of Pennsylvania, is currently finishing a book on the code of the streets. The culture of "the street" has norms different from those of mainstream society. Respect is believed to be an entity that is hard-won but easily lost. Those invested in the street code become very sensitive to advances and slights. "Being bothered" means being disgraced or "dissed," that is, disrespected. The code of the streets is an adaptation to a profound lack of faith in the police and the judicial system.

An expert on the sociology of Black America, Elijah Anderson is also the author of the widely regarded sociological work, *A Place on the Corner: A Study of Black Street Corner Men* (1978); an award-winning ethnographic study, *Streetwise: Race, Class and Change in an Urban Community* (1990); and numerous articles on the Black experience. Dr. Anderson is associate director of Penn's Center for Urban Ethnography and associate editor of *Qualitative Sociology.*

Interpersonal violence and aggression, such as muggings, burglaries, car jackings, and drug-related shootings, all of which may leave their victims or innocent bystanders dead, are now common enough to concern all Americans. Living in the inner city places young people at risk of falling victim to aggressive behavior. There are two orientations which socially organize an inner-city community: "decent" and "street." Being "decent" means being committed to middle-class values, and being of "the street" means being in a culture whose norms are often opposed to those of mainstream society.

Youngsters whose home lives reflect mainstream values must be able to handle themselves in a street-oriented environment. This is because the street culture has evolved a code of the streets, which amounts to a set of informal rules governing interpersonal public behavior, including violence. The rules have been established and are enforced mainly by the street-oriented, and knowledge of the code is largely defensive; it is necessary for operating in public. Even families with a decency orientation, who are opposed to the values of the code, often encourage their children to become familiar with it to enable them to negotiate the inner-city environment.

At the heart of the code is the issue of respect—loosely defined as being treated "right," or granted the deference one deserves. In the inner city, what one deserves in the way of respect becomes problematic and uncertain. This opens the issue of respect to sometimes intense interpersonal negotiation.

In the street culture, especially among young people, respect is viewed as an entity that is hard-won but easily lost, and so must constantly be guarded. The rules of the code provide a framework for negotiating respect. The person whose appearance deters transgressions feels, and may be considered by others to possess, a measure of respect. With the right amount of respect, a person can avoid "being bothered" in public. Being bothered means being disgraced or "dissed" (disrespected). Those who are invested in the street code become very sensitive to advances and slights which could serve as warnings of imminent physical confrontation.

Many inner-city people, particularly the young, have a profound sense of alienation from mainstream society and its institutions. The code of the streets is actually a cultural adaptation to a profound lack of faith in the police and the judicial system. Lack of police accountability has been incorporated into the status system: the person who is believed capable of "taking care of himself" is accorded a certain deference which translates into a sense of physical and psychological control. Thus the street code emerges where the influence of the police ends and personal responsibility for one's safety is felt to begin. Exacerbated by the proliferation of drugs and easy access to guns, this volatile situation results in the ability of the street-oriented minority to dominate the public spaces.

DECENT AND STREET FAMILIES

The decent and the street family in a real sense represent two poles of value orientation, two contrasting conceptual categories. The labels "decent" and "street" amount to evaluative judgments that confer status on local residents. Labeling is often the result of a social contest among individuals and families of the neighborhood. Although these designations result from so much social jockeying, there do exist concrete features that define each conceptual category.

So-called decent families tend to accept mainstream values more fully and attempt to instill them in their children. They value hard work and self-reliance and are willing to sacrifice for their children. They harbor hopes for a better future for their children, if not for themselves. Decent parents tend to be strict in their child-rearing practices, encouraging children to respect authority and walk a straight moral line. They remind their children to be on the lookout for people and situations that might lead to trouble of any kind.

So-called street parents, in contrast, often show a lack of consideration for other people and have a rather superficial sense of family and community. These families may aggressively socialize their children into the code of the streets in a normative way. They believe in the code and judge themselves and others according to its values.

Children of the street, growing up with little supervision, are said to "come up hard." They often learn to fight at an early age. The children observe anger, verbal disputes, physical aggression, and even mayhem. They learn the lesson that might makes right and learn to hit those who cross them;

the dog-eat-dog mentality prevails. In order to survive, to protect oneself, it is necessary to marshall inner resources and be ready to deal with adversity in a hands-on way. Physical prowess takes on great significance. These children are quick to learn the first lesson of the streets: survival itself, let alone respect, cannot be taken for granted; you have to fight for your place in the world.

CAMPAIGNING FOR RESPECT

These realities of inner-city life are largely absorbed on the streets. Children from generally permissive homes have a great deal of latitude. On the streets they play in groups that often become the source of their primary social bonds. Children from decent homes tend to be more carefully supervised and are thus likely to have curfews and be taught how to stay out of trouble. When decent and street kids come together, a kind of social shuffle occurs in which children have a chance to go either way. The kind of home a child comes from influences, but does not determine, the way he or she will ultimately turn out.

In the street, through their play, children pour their individual life experiences into a common knowledge pool, affirming, confirming, and elaborating on what they have observed in the home and matching their skills against those of others. And they learn to fight, and the child who is toughest prevails. Thus the violent resolution of disputes, the hitting and cursing, gains social reinforcement. The child is initiated into a system that is really a way of campaigning for respect. Experiences reinforce the lessons the children have learned at home: might makes right, and toughness is a virtue while humility is not. Over time the code of the streets becomes refined.

Those street-oriented adults with whom children come in contact—including mothers, fathers, brothers, sisters, boyfriends, cousins, neighbors, and friends—help them along in forming this understanding by verbalizing the messages they are getting through experience: "Watch your back." "Protect yourself." "Don't punk out." "If somebody disses you, you got to straighten them out." Many parents actually impose sanctions if a child is not sufficiently aggressive. For example, if a child loses a fight and comes home upset, the parent might respond, "Don't you come in here crying that somebody beat you up; you better get back out there and whup his ass. I didn't raise no punks! Get back out there and whup his ass. If you don't whup his ass, I'll whup your ass when you come home." Thus the child obtains reinforcement for being tough and showing nerve.

While fighting, some children cry as though they are doing something they are ambivalent about. The fight may be against their wishes, yet they may feel constrained to fight or face the consequences—not just from peers but also from caretakers or parents, who may administer another beating if they back down. Looking capable of taking care of oneself as a form of self-defense is a dominant theme among both street-oriented and decent adults who worry about the safety of their children. There is thus at times a convergence in their child-rearing practices although the rationales behind them may differ.

SELF-IMAGE BASED ON "JUICE"

By the time they are teenagers, most youths have either internalized the code of the streets or at least learned the need to comport themselves in accordance with its rules, which chiefly have to do with interpersonal communication. The code revolves around the presentation of self. Its basic requirement is the display of a certain predisposition to violence. The nature of this communication is largely determined by the demands of the circumstances but can include facial expressions, gait, and verbal expressions—all of which are geared mainly to deterring aggression. Physical appearance also plays an important part in how a person is viewed: to be respected, it is important to have the right look.

Even so, there are no guarantees against challenges, because there are always people around looking for a fight to increase their share of respect—or "juice" as it is sometimes called on the street. In general, a person must "keep himself or herself straight" by managing his or her position of respect among others.

Objects play an important and complicated role in establishing self-image. In acquiring valued things, a person shores up his identity—but since it is an identity based on having things, it is highly precarious.

One way of campaigning for status is by taking the possessions of others. Ordinary objects can become trophies imbued with symbolic value that far exceeds their monetary worth. Possession of the trophy can symbolize the ability to violate somebody—to "get in his face," to take something of value from him, to "dis" him, and thus to enhance one's own worth by stealing someone else's. When a person can take something from another and then flaunt it, he gains a certain regard by being the controller of that thing. But this display of ownership can then provoke other people to challenge him. This game of who controls what is constantly played out on inner-city streets, and the trophy identifies the current winner.

The extent to which one person can raise himself up depends on his ability to put another person down. This underscores the alienation that permeates the inner-city ghetto community. There is a generalized sense that very little respect is to be had, and therefore everyone competes to get what affirmation he can of the little that is available. Among young people, whose sense of self-esteem is particularly vulnerable, there is an especially heightened concern with being disrespected. Many inner-city young men in particular crave respect to such a degree that they will risk their lives to attain and maintain it. The issue of respect is thus closely tied to whether a person has an inclination to be violent even as a victim. Some people may even have the strength of character to flee, without any thought that their self-respect or esteem will be diminished. However, in impoverished inner-city communities, such flight would be extremely difficult for young males and perhaps increasingly females. To run away would likely leave one's self-esteem in tatters. Hence people often feel constrained not only to stand up and at least attempt to resist during an assault but also to "pay back"—to seek revenge after an assault on their person. Their very identity and self-respect, their honor, is often intricately tied up with the way they perform on the streets during and after such encounters. Generally people outside the ghetto have other ways of gaining status and regard, and thus do not feel so dependent on such physical displays.

BY TRIAL OF MANHOOD

Manhood in the inner city means taking the prerogatives of men with respect to strangers, other men, and women—being distinguished as a man. The operating assumption is that a man knows the code of the streets. And if one is not a real man, one is somehow diminished as a person, and there are certain valued things one simply does not deserve. There is thus believed to be a certain justice to the code, since it is considered that everyone has the opportunity to know it. Implicit in this is that everybody is held responsible for being familiar with the code. For those who are invested in the code, the clear object of their demeanor is to discourage strangers from even thinking about testing their manhood.

Central to the issue of manhood is the widespread belief that one of the most effective ways of gaining respect is to manifest "nerve." A display of nerve, shown when one takes another person's possessions, "messes with" someone's woman, throws the first punch, "gets in one's face," or pulls a trigger, can easily provoke a life-threatening response. True nerve exposes a lack of fear of dying. Many feel that it is acceptable to risk dying over the principle of respect. Not to be afraid to die is by implication to have few compunctions about taking another's life. When others believe this is one's position, it gives one a real sense of power on the streets. Such credibility is what many inner-city youths strive to achieve, whether they are decent or street-oriented, both because of its practical defensive value and because of the positive way it makes them feel about themselves. The street-oriented youth, on the other hand, has made the concept of manhood a part of his very identity: he has difficulty manipulating it—it often controls him.

GIRLS AND BOYS

Increasingly, teenage girls are mimicking the boys and trying to have their own version of "manhood." Their goal is the same—to get respect, to be recognized as capable of setting or maintaining a certain standard. Although conflicts over turf and status exist among the girls, the majority of disputes seem rooted in assessments of beauty, competition over boyfriends, and attempts to regulate other people's knowledge of and opinions about a girl's behavior or that of someone close to her, especially her mother. A major cause of conflicts among girls is a form of group gossip in which individuals are negatively assessed and evaluated; the things said can cast aspersions on a person's good name. The accused is required to defend herself against the slander, which can result in arguments and fights, often over little of real substance.

Girls tend to defer to boys in situations of conflict. Increasingly, however, girls are doing their own fighting. One major difference between girls and boys: girls rarely use guns. The ultimate form of respect on the male-dominated inner-city street is thus reserved for men.

"GOING FOR BAD"

Many youths are uncertain how long they are going to live and believe they could die violently at any time. They accept this fate: they live on the edge. Their manner conveys the message that nothing intimidates them: whatever turn the encounter takes, they maintain their attack. A competing view maintains that true nerve consists in backing down, walking away from a fight and going on with one's business. One fights only in self-defense. This view emerges from the decent philosophy that life is precious. It discourages violence as the primary means of resolving disputes. When there is enough support for this orientation, then nonviolence has a chance to prevail. But it prevails at the cost of relinquishing a claim to being bad and tough and sets a young person up as at the very least alienated from street-oriented peers and quite possibly a target of derision or even violence. Many will strive to appear to "go for bad," while hoping they will never be tested. But when they are tested, the outcome of the situation may quickly be out of their hands, as they become wrapped up in the circumstances of the moment.

AN OPPOSITIONAL CULTURE

The attitudes of the wider society are deeply implicated in the code of the streets. Most people in inner-city communities are not totally invested in the code, but the significant minority of hard-core street youths who are have to maintain the code in order to establish reputations. For these young people who are most alienated and lacking in strong and conventional social support, the standards of the street code are the only game in town. The extent to which some children experience, feel, and internalize racist rejections and contempt from mainstream society may strongly encourage them to express contempt for the more conventional society in turn. In dealing with this contempt and rejection, some youngsters will consciously invest themselves and their considerable mental resources in what amounts to an oppositional culture to preserve themselves and their self-respect. Many people in the community slip back and forth between decent and street behavior. A vicious cycle has thus been formed. The hopelessness and alienation many young inner-city men and women feel, largely as a result of endemic joblessness and persistent racism, fuels the violence they engage in. This violence serves to confirm the negative feelings many whites and middle-class blacks harbor toward the ghetto poor, further legitimating the oppositional culture and the code of the streets in the eyes of many poor young blacks. Unless this cycle is broken, attitudes on both sides will become increasingly entrenched, and the violence, which claims victims black and white, poor and affluent, will only escalate.

Elijah Anderson, "The Code of the Streets," from *The Code of the Streets* (forthcoming). Originally in *The Atlantic Monthly* 273, no. 5 (May 1994): 81–94. © 1994 by Elijah Anderson. Reprinted with the permission of W. W. Norton & Company, Inc.

TWELVE

SAVING YOUTH FROM VIOLENCE

Fred M. Hechinger

"Saving Youth from Violence" is from the *Carnegie Quarterly* (Winter 1994) of the Carnegie Corporation of New York. It calls for a new type of commitment from the community, parents, and the schools, in light of sixteen thousand acts of violence each day in our public schools.

Youth violence seems almost a direct response to the missing parents, mentors, elders, and community. The hours after school when parents are not home are especially dangerous.

Fred M. Hechinger is senior advisor to Carnegie Corporation of New York. A former education editor and editorial board member of the *New York Times,* he joined the Corporation's staff in 1991 and has assumed responsibility for writing issues of the *Carnegie Quarterly* on children and youth, among other assignments. He is the author of *Fateful Choices: Healthy Youth for the 21st Century,* published by Hill & Wang in 1992 for the Carnegie Council on Adolescent Development.

"**M**om, can I tell you something? I'm worried. Most of the boys I grew up with are dead. I lie awake at night and think about it. What am I supposed to do?"

The question was from a thirteen-year-old boy in New Orleans. His mother suddenly realized that of a group of six-year-olds who had started school together seven years earlier, only her son was still living. All the others had met violent deaths.

Nearly one million adolescents between the ages of twelve and nineteen are victims of violent crimes each year, and this has been true at least since 1985. The victimization of adolescents, particularly twelve- to fifteen-year-olds, is growing. Teenagers are twice as likely to be assaulted as persons aged twenty and older. The rate and intensity of violence involving children and youths, moreover, has escalated dramatically, and much of it is accounted for by adolescents attacking others in their age group. Adolescent homicide rates have reached the highest levels in history.

In February 1993, seventeen-year-old Michael Ensley was shot to death in the hallway of a Reseda, California, high school, allegedly because he gave his assailant an offending look.

In Houston, two girls, aged fourteen and sixteen, taking a shortcut home from a pool party, were raped and strangled by six teenage gang members, the youngest of them fourteen years old. One seventeen-year-old defendant in the case, when told that he might be charged with murder, allegedly told another boy: "Hey, great! We've hit the big time."

Children are becoming involved in violence at ever-younger ages, according to the Commission on Youth and Violence of the American Psychological Association (APA). In a study of first and second graders in Washington, D.C., the commission reported that 45 percent said they had witnessed muggings, 31 percent had witnessed shootings, and 39 percent had seen dead bodies.

"Clearly," declares Delbert S. Elliott, a leading expert on youth violence, "our children and teenagers are the most frequent victims of violence."

The most dramatic finding from Elliot's research is the sheer magnitude of adolescent involvement in serious offenses.

Marian Wright Edelman, president of the Children's Defense Fund, reports that some African American children are playing a new game called "Funeral"—their own. They discuss caskets, services, and who will attend. Death is a daily occurrence in their lives.

ON BOTH SIDES OF VIOLENCE

An alarming new phenomenon is the rise of violence among girls, often in complicity with violent boys.

Much of the violent activity among teenagers takes place on school grounds. U.S. secretary of education Richard W. Riley has noted that each year about three million thefts and violent crimes occur on or near school campuses. That is about sixteen thousand incidents per school day. Violence at school is becoming almost as much a rural and suburban as an urban problem. A 1993 study by the National School Boards Association found that, of 720 school districts, 82 percent reported an increase in violence in their schools in the past five years. These increases are occurring across all geographic areas.

Violence against girls and young women by males their age is another growing problem. Adolescent girls are particularly vulnerable to date rape and acquaintance rape. Nearly one out of every ten high school students experiences physical violence connected with dating.

THE THREAT OF GUNS

Over all the concerns about adolescent violence hangs the threat of firearms. Guns extort a heavy price from a young person's peace of mind. The psychological harm done to children and adolescents, either by the possession of guns or by fear of those who do possess them, is immense. The vision of guns distorts their behavior and their human relations. The atmosphere around them is charged by the uncertainty of when shots may be fired. They are confined to the safety of the home by their mothers, who caution them to stay away from windows lest they become injured by a stray bullet.

According to the book, *Promoting the Health of Adolescents,* produced under the auspices of the Carnegie Council on Adolescent Development and edited by Susan G. Millstein, Anne C. Petersen, and Elena O. Nightingale, the median age of first-gun ownership in the United States is twelve-and-a-half years of age; often the gun is a gift from a father or other male relative.

"Children can buy handguns on street corners in many communities," says the APA's Commission on Youth and Violence. "In part because of this ready availability of firearms, guns are involved in more than 75 percent of adolescent killings."

In a survey conducted by Louis Harris for Harvard University's School of Public Health, Harris reports that 60 percent of the youths said they could get a handgun; one-fifth claimed they could do so within an hour, and more than a third said they could do so within a day.

Harris points to data indicating that gun violence is not just a problem of inner-city poor children. Just as drugs have come to middle-class youth, so guns have migrated from the city to suburban areas. "It is evident that no part of the country, no area—cities, suburbs, small towns—is immune from the influence of guns among young people today." Yet, he adds, surveys show that a majority of young people, even many who carry guns, would like to see an end to the gun culture.

FAMILY, COMMUNITY, SOCIETY

The Commission on Youth and Violence of the American Psychological Association also stresses that no single factor can be blamed as the cause of violence among children and adolescents: "Youth violence is like heart disease, where many factors build to create the problem," says Alan Kazdin, a psychologist at Yale University who served on the commission. "All the factors matter, but none means that a child will necessarily become violent. Many different paths can lead to trouble."

Among the elements that contribute to children becoming violent, the commission said, were severe frustrations leading to lashing out, doing poorly in school, being stigmatized as "dumb," and lack of social skills that allow youngsters to deal effectively with others, especially their peers.

Growing up in an environment of harsh poverty with a feeling that opportunities for success are closed because of discrimination can lead to hopelessness and rage that find expression in violence.

The American Medical Association reports that about two million children annually experience physical abuse or neglect. One-third of the victims of physical abuse are under one year of age; another third are between the ages of one and six. Estimates of physical abuse of children and youth suggest that as many as 10 percent are assaulted by family members and caregivers each year.

Children who have suffered abuse and neglect while growing up learn to regard it as normal and tend to repeat the behavior toward their own offspring.

Not only are many children themselves abused but at least 3.3 million each year witness parental abuse, ranging from hitting to fatal assaults with knives or guns. As they mature in an atmosphere of violent relationships between men and women—husbands battering wives, women assaulted by boyfriends and other males, mothers maltreated and then abandoned by a succession of men—these children come to adopt the same attitudes and practices in dealing with their peers and eventually their own families as their elders did. At a counseling group session for men who had been arrested for domestic violence, one young man said "he had treated his girlfriend no differently from the way his father had treated his mother."

ROLE OF THE MEDIA

In discussing the cases and causes of youth violence, the role of the entertainment media is a hot and controversial topic. There is an obvious reason for the charges made against the violence-saturated action in movies and on the home screen, and against the often threatening, anti-female sounds of hardcore rap. The expressions of violence are so constantly visible and audible; the gun fire, particularly in movies, so explosive and unrelenting; and the words of hard-core rap ("It ain't nothing you should laugh to/I'll shoot your moms if I have to") so bloody and menacing that the public has begun to object.

One remarkable entry into the arsenal of media violence is "Mortal Kombat," a video game that gives the victor a chance to kill. In its goriest version, the *New York Times* reports, it provides the thrill of ripping out, with bare hands, the loser's still beating heart or tearing off his lifelike head. An eleventh grader from Oyster Bay, Long Island, said his favorite move is pushing an enemy over the ledge and watching him being impaled on a spike. His final triumph comes when he can electrocute his opponent. The game is reported to be number one in popularity at video arcades.

These and other violence-saturated appeals to children and youth in the media seem to justify the American Psychological Association report's warning that "viewing violence increases fear of becoming a victim of violence, with a resultant increase in self-protective behaviors and mistrust of others."

CHARTING NEW PATHS TO SAFETY

There is a growing belief among experts that the trend toward ever more violent behavior in America can be reversed. The report of the American Psychological Association's Commission on Youth and Violence concluded from psychological research that violence is not a random, uncontrollable, or inevitable occurrence: "Many factors, both individual and social, contribute to an individual's propensity to use violence, and many of these factors are within our power to change. . . . There is overwhelming evidence that we can intervene effectively in the lives of young people to reduce or prevent their involvement in violence."

Ronald G. Slaby, a psychologist at Harvard University and a member of the APA commission, concurs: "Violence is learned, and we can teach children alternatives."

Reversal of the trend of violence among the young, Carnegie Corporation's president David A. Hamburg says, calls for the teaching of "prosocial behavior" at home, in child care centers, and preschool programs. "By prosocial behavior, I mean constructive interaction with other human beings—sharing, taking turns, learning to cooperate, helping others. This is very fundamental. It used to be assumed that children got this outside school. This was never a sound assumption, and it is less so now than it ever was. I believe that if you don't get a foundation in the elementary pattern of sharing and cooperation before arriving in school, the odds are very much against you."

At its earliest stage, violence prevention begins with good health care for mother and child and the bonding of the child to a caring adult. It involves stimulating the development of nonconfrontational skills in language and behavior from the start of life.

As they grow up, says David Satcher, director of the Centers for Disease Control and former president of Meharry Medical College in Nashville, "young people must have a reason to believe that they can change the future for themselves and others. Then it is much easier to deal with violence and substance abuse and teenage pregnancy. We've found that those problems were not the problems; they were the symptoms. When young people don't have any hope for the future, they'll do anything."

THE CRITICAL ROLE OF THE SCHOOL

The school remains the institution to which parents look for help in their daily struggle to do the best for their children. It is the place where the campaign against violence needs to be given educational focus and where, in practical terms, children and youth should be able to find protection from the dangerous street culture, not for a few hours but throughout the day.

Under such circumstances, some experts believe schools should expand from the traditional 8:00 A.M. to 3:00 P.M. teaching institution to become all-day community centers concerned with their clients' mental, physical, and emotional needs as well. This is what Joy G. Dryfoos, in her book, *Full-Service Schools: A Revolution in Health and Social Services for Children, Youth, and Families,* written with Corporation support, envisions: schools that link the best reforms with services that children and families need.

Working examples of such community schools already exist. Open from early morning until the evening hours, they take on responsibility for the learning, health, and safety of the children, and they keep their doors open to parents and other members of the community. They are, in Dryfoos's words, "like a big tent into which all other models fit."

More than half a million students, she says, already use school-based health services, often together with their families. Dryfoos estimates that sixteen thousand community schools are needed and that the total cost would be about $1.6 billion to move the concept out of its present demonstration phase into an adequate national effort. But, she adds, a small federal expenditure could embolden states and local communities to speed the movement of full-service community schools.

Turning Points, the report produced by the Corporation and the Council on Adolescent Development (see *Carnegie Quarterly,* spring 1993, "Turning Points Revisited"), recommends the organization of middle schools into small units of approximately 150 youngsters, each taught by a team of teachers who are responsible for the students' academic and personal progress. The result is that every adolescent is known to a teacher and can rely on constant adult advice and support.

Experience with this arrangement shows that it reduces, and often virtually eliminates, violent and other antisocial behavior. By contrast, big schools, where students move about anonymously, give free reign to the kind of adolescent behavior that leads to conflict and violence.

COMMUNITY AND YOUTH ORGANIZATIONS CAN HELP

Focusing on the many hours during which adolescents are not in school and are exposed to the dangers of the streets and the threat of violence, the Carnegie Council on Adolescent Development in 1993 published a report, *A Matter of Time: Risk and Opportunity in the Nonschool Hours.* In the foreword, David Hamburg wrote that youth organizations and programs "can provide young adolescents with social support and guidance, life-skills training, positive and constructive alternatives to hazards such as drug and alcohol use, gang involvement, early sexual activity, and crime, and they can create opportunities for meaningful contributions to the community."

YOUTH CLUBS

Joseph E. Marshall, Jr., a teacher in the San Francisco public schools and head of the Omega Boys Club, believes fervently that people are responsible not only for their own children but for all the children in the community.

"Youth gangs address many of young adolescents' developmental needs, including safety, status, meaningful roles, income, and a sense of competence and belonging," Marshall says. The implied message of the gangs' attraction is that great numbers of adolescents feel cut off from contact with competent and caring adults. Unless they find a voice and a presence that inspires confidence, they are left to drift.

Marshall has established nine conditions for anyone who wants to become an Omega member: no drugs, no alcohol, no guns, no language that could hurt others, respect for women, a caring attitude toward other members, understanding that negative peer pressure often exploits fear and building firm resistance to it, knowledge of the importance of values, and conviction that the family is vital.

A look at Omega's success with hundreds of boys suggests that the club provides the wholesome version of what adolescents look for—the security of companionship and the sense of belonging to something like a family.

MENTORING

For some, the outreach of youth organizations is sufficent; others need more direct contact with a trustworthy adult.

In her annual report essay of 1983, Margaret Mahoney, president of the Commonwealth Fund, urged mainstream adults to devote time to mentoring disadvantaged youth, and particularly young black males from homes without fathers, giving them a sense that "a purposeful life" is possible. She pointed to the needs of children in poverty who "confront too many negative influences, too many bad role models." In that situation, Mahoney observed, one-to-one relationships "can reassure each child of his innate worth, instill values, guide curiosity, and encourage a purposeful life."

In his book, *The Kindness of Strangers: Adult Mentors, Urban Youth, and the New Voluntarism,* Marc Freedman writes that mentors can contribute to the ability of inner-city youth to cope with very difficult circumstances. One of the rich sources of mentoring, Freedman writes, "has been the African American community. Many organizations have initiated projects focused on linking inner-city youth with successful African American men and women—individuals who, in many instances, were themselves raised in inner-city neighborhoods."

For example, the Urban League in Providence, Rhode Island, created the Education Initiative Program that provides about one hundred students with mentors over three years. In Pittsburgh, Milwaukee, and many other cities, local chapters of One Hundred Black Men match their members with youngsters in one-on-one relationships.

Thomas W. Evans, a lawyer and chairman of the board of Teachers College, Columbia University, began his involvement in mentoring in 1983 by pairing five New York law firms with five high schools and taking students to their firms, to court, and to meetings over sandwich lunches. Described in his book, *Mentors: Making a Difference in Our Public Schools,* the program, simply called MENTORS, now operates in over five hundred schools throughout the country, reaching about thirty thousand students.

Because mentoring can have virtually unlimited faces, it enables individuals, as Freedman puts it, "to participate in the essential but unfinished drama of reinventing community, while reaffirming that there is an important role for each of us in it." The beneficiaries of mentoring are less likely to be drawn into the nihilism of violence.

THE LONG VIEW

A review of rapidly emerging developments raises troublesome questions. Are the programs to prevent youth violence beginning to work? How can statistics showing the success of pilot intervention programs be reconciled with equally reliable reports of escalating violence among ever more, and younger, perpetrators and victims?

Part of the answer is that, even as anti-violence actions gain support, violence-creating conditions do not remain static. More guns, the epidemic of crack cocaine, the continuing deterioration of family life, the decline of civic virtue, the spread of poverty and unemployment, the relentless show of violence by the entertainment media—all remain winners in what is still an unequal contest.

President Clinton made this impassioned appeal: "Unless we deal with the ravages of crime and drugs and violence, and unless we recognize that it's due to the breakdown of the family, the community, and the disappearance of jobs, and unless we say some of this cannot be done by government because we have to reach deep inside to the values, the spirit, the soul, and the truth of human nature, none of the other things we seek to do will ever take us where we need to go."

Delbert Elliott puts the matter bluntly: "Once involved in a lifestyle that includes serious forms of violence, theft, and substance use, those from disadvantaged families and neighborhoods find it very difficult to escape this lifestyle. There are fewer opportunities for conventional adult roles, and they are more embedded in and dependent upon the gangs and the illicit economy that flourishes in their neighborhoods."

For the long term, basic answers must be found in broadly conceived education. The crisis calls for the enlistment of schools and communities in offering effective programs of conflict resolution and cooperative learning, providing teenagers with a sense of belonging, giving constructive competition to gangs, creating community schools that operate beyond the normal school day, and fostering responsible family planning, family life education, healthy child development, and the recovery of humane values with a sense of responsibility toward the rights of others. It calls for a personal commitment to mentoring by credible and dedicated adults and peers. It calls for government and business to provide young people with access to community services and to jobs.

In the end, winning against violence will require a public stance that violence is socially unacceptable and that the nation's economic and social policies should reflect a society that despises rather than tolerates and even glorifies violence.

CENTER FOR THE STUDY AND PREVENTION OF VIOLENCE

The center, which Delbert S. Elliott heads at the University of Colorado in Boulder, serves as an information hub, provides technical assistance, and conducts basic research. It has a computerized database for research on all aspects of violence. It also publishes short documents for distribution to practitioners and policymakers that translate its research into policy, treatment, and intervention strategies. Elliott says, "After twenty years of experience of dealing with adolescent violence, we want to see some practical applications of research to really help society deal with this problem."

REFERENCES

Bailey, Anne Lowery. 1993. Group seeks to get Hollywood to change TV and movie portrayals of violence. *The Chronicle of Philanthropy,* 7 September.

Dryfoos, Joy G. 1994. *Full-service schools: A revolution in health and social services for children, youth, and families.* San Francisco: Jossey-Bass Publishers.

Earls, Felton, Robert B. Cairns, and James Mercy. 1993. The control of violence and the promotion of nonviolence in adolescence. In *Promoting the health of adolescents: New directions for the twenty-first century,* ed. Susan G. Millstein, Anne C. Petersen, and Elena O. Nightingale. New York: Oxford University Press.

Evans, Thomas W. 1992. *Mentors: Making a difference in our public schools.* Princeton, N.J.: Peterson's Guides.

The forgotten half: Pathways to success for America's youth and families. 1988. Washington, D.C.: Youth and America's Future: The William T. Grant Commission on Work, Family and Citizenship.

Forum on youth violence in minority communities: Setting the agenda for prevention, summary of the proceedings. 1990. The forum was sponsored by the Centers for Disease Control and the Minority Health Professions Foundation. Atlanta, Ga. 10–12 December.

Freedman, Marc. 1993. *The kindness of strangers: Adult mentors, urban youth, and the new voluntarism.* San Francisco: Jossey-Bass Publishers.

Friedman, Thomas L. 1993. Clinton links gun control to health care savings. *New York Times,* 25 September.

Glassman, Lynn. 1993. *Violence in the schools: How America's school boards are safeguarding our children.* Best Practices Series. Alexandria, Va.: National School Boards Association.

Goleman, Daniel. 1993. Schools try to tame violent pupils, one punch and one taunt at a time. *The New York Times,* 19 August.

Gruson, Lindsey. 1993. It's bloody! It's mortal! It's kombat! *New York Times,* 16 September.

Hamburg, David A. 1992. *Today's children: Creating a future for a generation in crisis.* New York: Times Books.

Hechinger, Fred M. 1992. *Fateful choices: Healthy youth for the 21st century.* New York: Hill and Wang.

Henneberger, Melinda, and Michael Marriott. 1993. For some, rituals of abuse replace youthful courtship. *New York Times,* 11 July.

Kantrowitz, Barbara. 1993. Wild in the streets. *Newsweek,* 2 August.

A matter of time: Risk and opportunity in the nonschool hours. 1992. Report of the Task Force on Youth Development and Community Programs of the Carnegie Council on Adolescent Development. Washington, D.C.: Carnegie Council on Adolescent Development. December.

Northrup, Daphne, and Kim Hamrick. 1990. *Weapons and minority youth violence.* Background paper prepared for the Education Development Center's Forum on Youth Violence in Minority Communities: Setting the Agenda for Prevention. The Center for Disease Control and the Minority Health Professions Foundation with the Morehouse School of Medicine. Atlanta, Ga. December.

Osofsky, Joy D. 1993. *Violence in the lives of young children.* Position paper for the Carnegie Corporation Task Force on Meeting the Needs of Young Children. New York: Carnegie Corporation of New York. June.

Porter, Jessica. 1994. School violence up over past 5 years. *Education Week,* 12 January.

Promoting the health of adolescents: New directions for the twenty-first century. 1993. Ed. Susan G. Millstein, Anne C. Petersen, and Elena O. Nightingale. New York: Oxford University Press.

Prothrow-Stith, Deborah. 1987. *Violence prevention curriculum for adolescents.* Newton, Mass.: Education Development Center.

Sommerfeld, Meg. 1993. About 10% of youths say they have fired a gun or been shot at, new survey finds. *Education Week,* 4 August.

Sullivan, Shawn. 1993. Wife-beating n the hood. *Wall Street Journal,* 6 July.

Thornberry, Terence P. 1993. What's working and what's not working in safeguarding our children and preventing violence. Paper presented at conference, "Safeguarding Our Youth: Violence Prevention for Our Nation's Children." Washington, D.C., 20–21 July.

Turning points revisited: A new deal for adolescents. *Carnegie Quarterly* 38, no. 2 (spring). 1993.

Verhovek, Sam Howe. 1993. Houston knows murder, but this . . . *New York Times,* 9 July.

Violence and youth: Psychology's response. 1993. Volume 1: Summary Report of the American Psychological Association Commission on Violence and Youth. Washington, D.C.: American Psychological Association.

Wilson-Brewer, Renée. 1992. Welcome to your network: A letter from the director. *Connections,* vol. 1, Newsletter of the National Network of Violence Prevention Practitioners. Newton, Mass.: Education Development Center. Fall.

THIRTEEN

PEACE IN THE STREETS

Geoffrey Canada

Geoffrey Canada is president and CEO of Harlem's Rheedlen Center for Children and Families, which serves at-risk inner-city children. Canada is also largely responsible for the Beacon Schools and the Peacemakers program in Harlem and is the East Coast coordinator for the Children's Defense Fund's Black Community Crusade for Children. His recently published book *Fist Stick Knife Gun* (Beacon Press), from which this excerpt is drawn, tells Canada's own story of growing up in a violent South Bronx neighborhood and offers his solutions for turning the tide against gang violence.

It's a Wednesday night in October and I'm early for my martial-arts class in Harlem. I walk into the brightly lit gym and all eyes turn toward me. I'm walking with purpose, quickly and silently. A little boy begins to run over to me and an older student grabs his arm. I see him whispering in the younger boy's ear. I'm sure he's telling him, "You can't talk to him before class." And he's right. I stand in front of my class, looking unhappy and displeased. Everyone wonders who is out of place or not standing up straight. This is part of my act. Finally I begin the class and then I'm lost in the teaching. I'm trying to bring magic into the lives of these kids. To bring a sense of wonder and amazement. I can feel the students losing themselves and focusing on me. They are finally mine. I have them all to myself. I have crowded all the bad things out of their minds: The test they failed, the father who won't come by to see them, the dinner that won't be on the stove when they get home. I've pushed it all away by force of will and magic.

This is my time and I know all the tricks. I yell, I scream, I fly through the air with the greatest of ease. And by the time the class is ending my students' eyes are wide with amazement and respect, and they look at me differently. I line them up and I talk to them. I talk to them about values, violence, and hope. I try to build within each one a reservoir of strength that they can draw from as they face the countless tribulations small and large that poor children face every day. And I try to convince each one that I know their true value, their worth as human beings, their special gift that God gave to them. And I hope they will make it to the next class with something left in that reservoir for me to add to week by week. It is from that reservoir that they will draw the strength to resist the drugs, the guns, the violence.

My two best students usually walk with me after class and stay with me until I catch a cab. I tell them it's not necessary, but they are there to make sure I get home all right. What a world. So dangerous that children feel that a second-degree black belt needs an escort to get home safely.

This community, like many across this country, is not safe for children, and they usually walk home at night filled with fear and apprehension. But when I walk with them after class they are carefree, as children ought to be. They have no fear. They believe that if anything happens they'll be safe because I'm there. I'll fly through the air and with my magic karate I'll dispatch whatever evil threatens them. When these children see me standing on the corner watching them walk into their buildings they believe what children used to believe, that there are adults who can protect them. And I let them believe this even if my older students and I know different. Because in a world that is so cold and so harsh, children need heroes. Heroes give hope, and if these children have no hope they will have no future. And so I play the role of hero for them even if I have to resort to cheap tricks and theatrics.

If I could get the mayors, the governors, and the president to look into the eyes of the five-year-olds of this nation, dressed in old raggedy clothes, whose jacket zippers are broken but whose dreams are still alive, they would know what I know—that children need people to fight for them. To stand with them on the most dangerous streets, in the dirtiest hallways, in their darkest hours. We as a country have been too willing to take from our weakest when times get hard. People who allow this to happen must be educated, must be challenged, must be turned around.

If we are to save our children we must become people they will look up to. We must stand up and be visible heroes. I want people to understand the crisis and I want people to act: Either we address the murder and mayhem in our country or we simply won't be able to continue to have the kind of democratic society that we as Americans cherish. Violence is not just a problem of the inner cities or of the minorities in this country. This is a national crisis and the nation must mobilize differently if we are to solve it.

Part of what we must do is change the way we think about violence. Trying to catch and punish people after they have committed a violent act won't deter violence in the least. In life on the street, it's better to go to jail than be killed, better to act quickly and decisively even if you risk being caught.

There are, however, things that governments could and should do right away to begin to end the violence on our streets. They include the following:

CREATE A PEACE OFFICER CORPS. Peace officers would not be police; they would not carry guns and would not be charged with making arrests. Instead they would be local men and women hired to work with children in their own neighborhoods. They would try to settle "beefs" and mediate disputes. They would not be the eyes and ears of the regular police force. Their job would be to try to get these young people jobs, to get them back into school, and, most importantly, to be at the emergency rooms and funerals where young people come together to grieve and plot revenge, in order to keep them from killing one another.

REDUCE THE DEMAND FOR DRUGS. Any real effort at diverting the next generation of kids from selling drugs *must* include plans to find employment for these children when they become teenagers. While that will require a significant expenditure of public funds, the savings from reduced hospitalization and reduced incarceration will more than offset the costs of employment.

And don't be fooled by those who say that these teenagers will never work for five dollars an hour when they can make thousands of dollars a week. I have found little evidence of this in my years of working with young people. Most of them, given the opportunity to make even the minimum wage, will do so gladly. The problem for many young people has been that they have looked for work year after year without ever finding a job. In some cities more than 40 percent of minority youth who want to work can't find employment.

REDUCE THE PREVALENCE OF DOMESTIC VIOLENCE AND CHILD ABUSE AND NEGLECT. Too many children learn to act violently by experiencing violence in their homes. Our society has turned a blind eye to domestic violence for so long that the smacking, punching, and beating of women has become almost routine. And in many of the same homes where women are being beaten, the children are being beaten also. Our response as a society has been to wait until the violence has gotten so bad that the woman has to go to a battered-women's shelter (often losing the only place she has to live), or we have to take the abused child from the family. In both cases we break up a family, and common sense tells us this ends up costing us more money than it would have if we had intervened early and kept the family together.

The best mode of early intervention for really troubled families is family preservation services—intensive, short-term interventions designed to teach families new coping skills. The family preservation worker spends as much time as needed with a family to ensure that it gets the type of support and skills that it needs to function as a supportive unit rather than a destructive one.

REDUCE THE AMOUNT OF VIOLENCE ON TELEVISION AND IN THE MOVIES. Violence in the media is ever more graphic, and the justification for acting violently is deeply implanted in young people's minds. The movie industry promotes the message that power is determined not merely by carrying a gun, but by carrying a big gun that is an automatic and has a big clip containing many bullets.

What about rap music, and especially "gangsta rap"? It is my opinion that people have concentrated too much attention on this one source of media violence. Many rap songs are positive, and some are neither positive nor negative—just kids telling their stories. But there are some rap singers who have decided that their niche in the music industry will be the most violent and vile. I would love to see the record industry show some restraint in limiting these rappers' access to fame and fortune.

But by singling out one part of the entertainment industry as violent and ignoring others that are equally if not more violent (how many people have been killed in movies starring Arnold Schwarzenegger, Sylvester Stallone, and Clint Eastwood?) we will have no impact on reducing violence in this country. The television, movie, and record industries must all reduce the amount of violence they sell to Americans.

REDUCE AND REGULATE THE POSSESSION OF HANDGUNS. I believe all handgun sales should be banned in this country. Recognizing, however, that other Americans may not be ready to accept a ban on handguns, I believe there are still some things we must do.

Licensing. Every person who wants to buy a handgun should have to pass both a written test and a field test. The cost for these new procedures should be paid by those who make, sell, and buy handguns.

Insurance. Gun manufacturers and dealers should be required to register every handgun they manufacture and sell. This registration would be used to trace guns that wind up being used for crimes, and the manufacturers and dealers should be held liable for damages caused by any gun they manufacture and sell. Individual citizens would be required to carry insurance policies for liability and theft on their handguns, which would increase the pressure on citizens to make sure that their guns were safely locked away.

Ammunition identification. While we are beginning to bring some sane regulations to the handgun industry, we must also begin to make the killing of Americans with handguns less anonymous than it is today. One way to do this is to make all handgun ammunition identifiable. Gun owners should have to sign for specially coded ammunition, the purchase of which would then be logged into a computer. The codes should be etched into the shell casing as well as the bullet itself, and the codes should be designed so that even when a bullet breaks into fragments it can still be identified.

Gun buy-backs. The federal government, which recently passed a $32 billion crime bill, needs to invest billions of dollars over the next ten years buying guns back from citizens. We now have more than 200 million guns in circulation in our country. A properly cared-for gun can last for decades. There is no way we can deal with handgun violence until we reduce the number of guns currently in circulation. We know that young people won't give up their guns readily, but we have to keep in mind that this is a long-term problem. We have to begin to plan now to get the guns currently in the hands of children out of circulation permanently.

The truth of the matter is that reducing the escalating violence will be complicated and costly. If we were fighting an outside enemy that was killing our children at a rate of more than five thousand a year, we would spare no expense. What happens when the enemy is us? What happens when those Americans' children are mostly black and brown? Do we still have the will to invest the time and resources in saving their lives? The answer must be yes, because the impact and fear of violence has overrun the boundaries of our ghettos and has both its hands firmly around the neck of our whole country. And while you may not yet have been visited by the spectre of death and fear of this new national cancer, just give it time. Sooner or later, unless we act, you will. We all will.

FOURTEEN

GANG RITES AND RITUALS OF INITIATION

Dadisi Sanyika

Dadisi Sanyika shows how gang leaders are using traditional steps of rites of passage as they initiate young people into gang membership. The reader is given insight into the power of this process.

"In the different systems of initiation or rites of passage practiced by traditional indigenous people eight fundamental elements are enacted in varying combinations. The basic social strategy was that the elders of the community maintained the cohesion and health of the collective by the systematic transmission of the values and knowledge of the group to the next generation through a system of initiation."

Born and raised in South Central Los Angeles, Dadisi Sanyika was active in the Black Consciousness and Student Liberation Movement of the late 1960s. He then became a student of martial arts as well as Oriental philosophy and healing methods. A founding member of the Mori Nimba West African Dance Company in 1978, Dadisi went on to study the transformational dynamics of traditional African dance through the re-enactment of tribal rituals and ceremony. Currently, Dadisi is Chairman of the Watts Community Policy and Planning Institute, a grassroots think tank in Watts, California focusing on local strategic and sustainable community development. He is artistic director for *Dembrabrah,* West African Drum and Dance Ensemble, dedicated to the study, performance, and preservation of African folklore and culture. He is working on a volume of poetry titled *Rise of the Midnight Son,* to be published this fall. Dadisi is a teacher and facilitator with Mosaic Multicultural Foundation in their work with men and mentoring, and building tolerance and understanding between cultures for healing self and community.

Membership into the Egyptian Mystery System was gained by initiation and a pledge of secrecy. Teaching was graded and delivered orally to the neophyte. The Mysteries regarded the human body as a prison house of the Soul which could be liberated from its bodily impediments through the disciplines of the arts and sciences and advanced from the level of a mortal to that of a God. This was the notion of the SUMMUM BONUM or greatest good, to which all men (people) must aspire and it also became the basis of all ethical concepts.

G. M. JAMES, STOLEN LEGACY

Initiation is a profound spiritual and psychological regeneration as a result of which a new birth, a new beginning, and a new life are entered upon. The word itself, derived from the Latin Initia, also implies the basic or first principle of any science, suggesting that initiates are consciously united with their own first principle, the monad or divine spark from which we all emerged.

BLACK GNOSTIC STUDIES, UNPUBLISHED MANUSCRIPT

Initiation is a body of rites and oral teachings whose purpose is to produce a decisive alteration in the religious and social status of the person to be initiated. In philosophical terms, initiation is equivalent to a basic change in the existential condition. The novice emerges from his/her ordeal endowed with a totally different being from that which was possessed before initiation.

MIRCEA ELIADE

All life-forms, from unicellular organisms to solar systems and galaxies, follow an ordered, cyclic, and dialectical process of birth, growth, maturity, decline, and death. Humans are products of the universal laws of existence. From the dawn of human consciousness in the great-lakes region of Africa at the origins of the Nile, African people developed social systems in conformity with these universal laws. From the earliest sociology of African totemic societies and in all subsequent African communities the puberty rites of passage played an archetypal role in the preparation of the youth for adulthood. Through this initiation process the elders of the community transmitted the accumulated wisdom of the race to the next generation. Initiation is a step-by-step process of re-creation that engages the participant in a new body of knowledge that literally alters one's state of consciousness, producing a transformed state of being. The puberty rites of passage were thus also the process of initiating the youth into the second birth from the profane to the sacred. The rites constituted a path, a road, a sacred journey that all adults of the community had traveled before, stretching back to the beginning of the history of the community.

In allowing the youth to assume their place among the adults of the community, the process of initiation created social cohesion and facilitated collective rejuvenation of the community. Through initiation the ideal was revealed that set the standards for social participation and personal behavior.

Rites of passage were instituted not only to prepare youth for adulthood, however, but also to mark specific phases in the maturation of humans. Initiation is a lifelong process with levels and degrees of complexity. There are rites-of-passage activities at all the major phases of life, in order to mark passage to manhood or womanhood, adulthood, eldership, and death. There are also rites of passage for each specialty group within the social order, that is, men, women, musicians, hunters, artists, healers, blacksmiths, farmers, weavers, fishermen, and warriors. All have special societies with secret rites of initiation. Initiation is the ritualization of the creation process, where a person is changed from one state of consciousness to another. Initiation produces re-created beings.

Later tribal rites and rituals were the prototypes of the Mystery Schools of Antiquity. The ancient clan rites of passage evolved in conjunction with the evolution of human consciousness and civilization. They culminated in the systems of initiation that produced the great sages, hierophants, adepts, and masters of wisdom of the great classical civilizations of Egypt/Kemet, India, China, the Americas, Greece, and Rome. Modern Masonry and the fraternities and sororities are outgrowths of these early rites and rituals.

Whatever the specific type of initiatory system, there are eight phases or elements in the generic initiatory process. These are elders/knowers, separation, sacred place, symbolical death, trials and tribulations or tests, revelation, rebirth, and reincorporation.

EIGHT ELEMENTS OF INITIATION

ELDERS OR KNOWERS

The elders were at the core of African social institutions. They were responsible for the health and development of the family or clan group. The social structure of African people is a direct outgrowth of the family structure, where the parents were the heads of the social group. The elders were the oldest living parents from which the rest of the group came. As the groupings of families multiplied and more complex social institutions developed, the elders from different family clans joined together in secret societies to maintain cohesion and order. These societies of men and women provided the formal infrastructure that permeated the total life of the community. In those indigenous communities that have not been significantly disrupted by Western culture the elders are still central to community cohesion.

In keeping with their cohesive function, the elders also served as guardians of the group's wisdom. This wisdom, gleaned from thousands of seasons of living, resides in the myths, rituals, signs, symbols, and folklore of the people. The elders maintained the knowledge of the sacred history and traditions of the group. They experienced the living truth necessary for the cohesion, survival, and development of the collective.

This knowledge, therefore, enabled the elders to be the teachers, instructors, and guides of the next generation. Thus, the elders were responsible for conducting the initiation ceremony. For a person to be initiated there has to be a body of knowledge and a brotherhood or sisterhood to be initiated into. In turn, initiation was necessary in order for youth to function constructively in the community.

SEPARATION

To be transformed into a new state of being, one must leave the old condition. The separation phase removes the novice from the familiar surroundings that reinforce the old identity. For the youth it is a severance from the protection of the mother and family, indicative of childhood and dependency. In traditional indigenous societies this process is ritualized by having the youth abruptly taken from their homes in the middle of the night, as mother and family symbolically protest. The youth are rounded up together and led from the village to a compound in the bush. In some indigenous villages young girls are isolated in a hut where they are instructed in the ways of womanhood.

THE SACRED PLACE

Traditionally, the sacred place was an isolated circular encampment in the bush. Indigenous rites and rituals of initiation were deadly serious undertakings. In many traditional communities noninitiates were forbidden to enter the sacred place, many times under the penalty of death.

The sacred place is a re-creation of the original space where the gods or original ancestral hero first descended to earth and initiated the history of the family, clan, or particular ethnic group. The sacred place goes beyond the mundane and is a place where the human and the spiritual will commune. It is a return to the ancient days where the ancestral spirits were invoked, a place of dream time. It represents a return to the womb of creation.

The sacred place is where the initiate will reunite with the divine ancestors and relive the original impulse from which the history of the clan was generated. The sacred place comes in many forms. It is the sacred grove deep in the forest forbidden to nonparticipants. It is the cave, the subterranean cavern, the hut, temple, pyramid, bush enclosure, monastery, ashram, dojo, or sacred rug, all of which served as places of initiation, symbolic of the womb out of which a new birth will emerge.

SYMBOLICAL DEATH

A death drama is enacted as the novice enters into the sacred place. This represents entering the world of the dead, death to a profane and mortal existence. Here the neophyte enters the spirit world of the ancestors. In primitive societies this phase was related to being devoured by a great monster or being torn to pieces by a devil or demon.

Death expresses the idea of an end or the completion of a thing. In the case of rites of passage it means the end of a child's life of irresponsibility and the beginning of preparation for adulthood. To be created anew, the old must be annihilated. It is a psychodramatic enactment of chaos and creation, creating the clean slate for the new state of being. This process symbolizes regression to an embryonic condition necessary for a re-creation.

TRIALS AND TRIBULATIONS

The novice is put through a series of ordeals that test his or her character. What is he made of? How does she react under pressure? The ordeals also provide training and conditioning in preparation for the hardships and sacrifices necessary in an adult's journey through life. The novice has to withstand and overcome hunger, thirst, fatigue, pain, fear, isolation, and sleeplessness.

There are periods when the novice cannot speak or is blindfolded and must totally depend on his elder brother or guide. In other situations, the novice cannot use his hands and is fed by his guide. Many of the initial experiences at this stage reenact the helplessness and dependency of infancy. This theme is consistent with the process of birth and is one demonstration of how nature provided our ancestors with the format for social order. At other times the novice is taken to a remote area and expected to make his way back to the camp alone relying only on his own knowledge and ingenuity. In some initiations like that of the Maasai of East Africa, the youth must go out and kill a lion.

The hardships imposed during initiation help to break down the resistance of youth's ego so that they will be receptive to new information and insights. Staying awake for days without sleep, long fasts with repetitive rhythms, chanting, and dance movements also sensitize the novices to altered states of consciousness.

Many of the ordeals are ritualized reenactments of the ordeals the founding ancestor(s) went through in the origins of the clan or tribal group. To relive the original experiences of the heroes and heroines of the group binds the initiates back to the original impulse from which the total community evolved. This reliving of the original exploits of the first organizers of the group reenforces the prime directives or core values of the group. Every adult in the lineage of the clan has gone through the same experiences; this is a powerful technique for the creation of a cohesive and unified group with generational consistency and continuity.

REVELATION

The revealing of the inner meanings of the traditional signs and symbols and explanation of the sacred myths, dances, masks, and ceremonies of the group or community constitute the first phases of a transcendental knowing. Each society has an accumulated body of knowledge, a set of traditions, a sacred history that outlines that particular people's cosmology. This cosmology defines their view of the world and their place and role in this world. This sacred history, this worldview, is revealed in stages as the novice progresses through the various rites and rituals of initiation. The elders explain to the novices that the different spirits that are part of village ceremonies were actually members of the secret societies in masked costumes. They are taught the significance of the elements that constitute the masked figures that are characterizations of spiritual forces.

The revealing of the sacred history and traditions is an ongoing process continuing throughout an adult's life. How deep an initiate can go into the sacred wisdom is in direct proportion to their level of desire, discipline, and dedication to want to know.

During the phase of revelation, the youth also receive training in the ways of adulthood. They are taught their responsibilities as men and women in their age group and to their community. They are provided with knowledge of appropriate behaviors in marriage and in sexual relations. Initiates are shown knowledge of the medicinal properties of plants. They are provided training in the art of warfare and survival skills. They are taught a secret communication system that includes a special language for initiates with signs and symbols, special dances, songs, and rhythms.

In addition, the novices are guided in ceremonies and rituals that induce trance and altered states of consciousness where direct contact is made with the parapsychological/psychic or spiritual dimensions of existence. The new initiates are exposed to magical experiences that provide personal verification of the existence of transcendental realities and existences beyond the normal, everyday world of solid tangible forms.

RESURRECTION AND REBIRTH

The resurrection involves the rites and ceremonies that dramatize that the novice has been re-created. The initiate has been remade into a human, a sacred being that embodies the original knowledge and experience of the ancestors. Resurrection is the other side of the initiatory death, where the novice is torn to pieces or devoured by a monster. In this phase, the novice is reassembled or, in the case of being devoured by a monster, is spit out or escapes back to the world of the living.

The initiate acquires a new title, a new name, a different form of dress, and different ornamentation that differentiates him or her from a child and establishes his or her status as an adult. The initiates demonstrate the sacred initiation dances, songs, and rhythms of their society that are a reenactment of the sacred history of the group. They can now communicate through the secret language and use the signs and symbols with their fellow initiates.

As a part of the adult status they are provided with land to build a home so they can marry and provide for a family. The new initiates will now take their place as adult members of the community, participating in decisions and defending and working for the development of the collective.

REINCORPORATION INTO THE COMMUNITY

There is a coming-out celebration held at the end of the initiation process, where the newly created adults are welcomed back to the community. This community celebration serves to commemorate the completion of the initiation of a new group of youth. The community celebration also serves to bind the total community back to the origins of its beginnings. It is a remembrance for all the adults of the community that have traveled this path before. It is a preview for the children of what lies ahead for them, for one day they will be taken to the secret place to be devoured by spirits in the process of becoming a man or woman. The celebration revitalizes and serves to help to regenerate the total community, by reenforcing the collective ideals, values, and identity of the collective.

SIGNIFICANCE OF THE EIGHT ELEMENTS OF INITIATION

The basic social strategy in traditional, indigenous culture was that the elders of the community maintained the cohesion and health of the collective by the systematic transmission of the values and knowledge of the group to the next generation through a system of initiation. They combined this function of initiation with the need to mark puberty as a period of rebirth. Puberty is the developmental period where young people experience major biochemical, physiological, anatomical, and psychological changes. In the natural wisdom of primal societies this was seen as a period that necessitates a ritualized process that reenacts the sacred process of creation.

The eight elements of the initiatory process are inherent to the process of human transformation. In fact, these elements are expressions of an archetypal pattern of any maturation process. When there is no formal initiation process, an unconscious enactment of a rite of passage will occur. This unconscious initiation will often be antisocial rather than a systematic transmission of values and knowledge. Initiation into urban street gangs is a case in point, where the aspects of initiation appear in a process that does not renew the community or its values.

INITIATION INTO URBAN STREET GANGS

In every major street gang there is a hierarchy of leadership, with the original gangsters or OGs as the honored *elders* of the group. The OGs are the masters of the secrets of the gang and veterans of many missions who have put in much work for their set. They are esteemed in the eyes of young aspirants who seek to emulate their behavior and achieve an equal or greater level of respect in the hood. Their survival has proved that they are *knowers* in the ways of being hard. The OGs or older members of the set are the initiators of the neophytes.

The *separation* takes place when the aspirant starts to identify with the lifestyle of a particular gang and seeks to associate with its members. The aspirant separates himself or herself from the general or civilian population attitudinally and eventually physically.

The *sacred place* in general is the neighborhood or territory of the aspirant's particular set. Within the territory of the set, the gang has specific hangouts that are off limits to nonmembers of the gang. These locations are where the secret activities, including planning missions, teaching new members, sharing information and techniques, debriefing work assignments, disciplining of members, partying, and induction ceremonies, take place.

The *symbolic death* phase is enacted through the act of getting jumped, when the aspirant has to fight a number of gang members at one time. This jumping represents a threshold into the world of the gang. Once jumped you are dead to your old self and enter a new existence. In many instances to exit a gang you must be jumped to cross back through that threshold into nongang life.

The *trials and tribulations* are the various tests the new member is put through to see how much heart he has. These tests can come in various forms, including robbery, jacking (taking someone's car while they are in it), drive-by shootings, beatings, or even an assassination of an enemy. Each gang member is obligated to put in work for the set if he is to be respected.

The phase of *revelation* is the educational process where the new member is indoctrinated into the history, values, standards, and expectations of the gang. Every gang has a history of how the set got started which includes the stories and folktales of the exploits of the heroes or OGs of their hood. The new members are taught how to use firearms, how to burglar-ize, the art of signing, the specific sign and symbols of their set, secret code words, and ways of dress, walking, dancing, and appropriate appear-ance.

Members are schooled on the justice system and expectations when encountering law enforcement. This schooling is both formal, with lecture/presentations and questions and answers, and informal, through observation, conversations, and association with more experienced gang members.

The *resurrection or rebirth* is related to when the new gang member acquires a new gang name, wears the uniform and colors of his set, talks the talk using the keywords of his gang, flashes his signs, walks the walk, and assumes the demeanor and lifestyle of his gang. The new member has been re-created in the image of his set and now has assumed a new identity gov-erned by the lineage and elders of his new family or gang.

The *reincorporation* phase is when the new member publicly acts out his new identity within his community and becomes known as a member of his particular gang. This reincorporation is in one sense a negative factor con-tributing to the further destruction of the greater community. In another sense, the reincorporation of a new gang member back into the greater community is a reminder of the failure of the elders of that community and the greater soci-ety as a whole. The failure is in not providing adequate constructive socializa-tion of the children and youth of the community.

In the final analysis it is the responsibility of the elders of a family, a community, a nation, and the world to initiate the next generation into the wisdom of the group to insure group cohesion and the health of the whole. This responsibility is inherent within the natural order of life. It transcends any materialistic value system that denies each human being's responsibility to all other human beings. In the highest consideration all humans are respon-sible for those life-forms below them or under their dominion, be it due to position, knowledge, capacity, or power. This responsibility follows the eter-nal truth that "*as we sow, so shall we reap.*"

CONCLUSION

The process of initiation is an inherent fact of life, experienced consciously or unconsciously depending on the awareness of the life-form. Our indigenous ancestors ordered their lives in harmony with the natural laws of existence. They recognized the critical role that the youth played in the continuance and continuity of the community. In their natural wisdom they instituted rites and rituals of initiation as the process to ensure the deliberate conditioning of all members of the community.

These rites and rituals of initiation were the formal educational system that transmitted the accumulated knowledge of the group to each successive generation. These rites and rituals provided a clear demarcation at each of the major phases of life. They created a dramatized experience that indelibly imprinted the significance of the event on the psyche of the initiate. The common experiences of initiates bonded them together in a lifelong fellowship consecrated to the service of the collective.

The critical need of today is for rites and rituals of initiation that reunite humans with the truth of their collective humanity. Modern rites of passage must be reinstituted within the context of the present stage of human evolution. They must engage humans in the universal truths and ancient wisdoms that are at the core of harmonious social systems. The sacredness of life and lifeforms must become recognized as the guiding principles for existence.

Those who are "in the know" must recognize that knowledge carries responsibility. We are all interconnected in the grand order of life and are responsible to the whole. The highest level of spiritual work is in rendering service to our fellow humans in helping to create conditions for knowledge, health, prosperity, and peace. Each adult has a sacred responsibility to the collective body of the human race. Each adult carries the legacy of one's ancestors and through one's actions lightens or adds to the karmic load. All people within an age group make up a group with responsibilities to each other, those coming after, and to the whole. If the adult community abandons its responsibility to the youth, it abandons its sacred responsibility to life, and so shall it reap.

The evolution of the human family is an *initiation*. We have been *separated* from our spiritual origins and incarnated in a material world, our *sacred space*. Our psyches have had a *symbolic death* to the unswerving knowledge of our spiritual nature. We have been subjected to eons of *trials and tribulations*. Tests and ordeals of birth, disease, war, famine, disasters, and the rise and fall of civilizations. We have been provided *revelations* by the many teachers, sages, prophets, leaders, parents, and friends from the beginning of consciousness.

It is time for the *knowers* to join together in spiritual fellowship to *resurrect* the ancient wisdom and reinstitute the needed rites and rituals of initiation to reconnect their particular communities to the knowledge of the spiritual origins of all life-forms. It will only be through this knowledge that the fragmented human family will be *reincorporated* into a consciousness of humanity and thus put an end to the willful madness and self-destruction of the industrialized world and all those who follow its ways.

Portions of this essay to appear separately in *Initiation: Levels and Degrees of Transformation,* © Dadisi Sanyika, Golden Thread Productions, 6709 La Tijera Blvd., #454, Los Angeles, California 90045

FIFTEEN

SERVICE AS A RITE OF PASSAGE

Nancy Geyer Christopher

Nancy Christopher, coeditor of *Crossroads*, presents a step-by-step analysis of the dynamics of service as a major rite of passage. Although service projects are important at the end of the teens, a number of high schools are adapting them for earlier high-school years. Those of us who have experienced a major service project know how it has changed and enriched our lives. Here, too, qualified elders are important.

(The biography of Nancy Christopher appears at the beginning of this book.)

The term "rite of passage" has become the cliche of the '90s. If you have any doubt about it, just take a look at its occurrence in print and on the air: A media survey shows one reference in 1976, 107 references in 1990, and 2,624 in 1994. We seem to be fascinated with this term, but why?

At the same time—roughly, since the mid-'70s—we have become more and more uneasy about the fact that our young people seem lost. We know that they are having difficulty growing up, and somehow we are responsible. Is there some connection? Could it be that we're unconsciously trying to find some way to address their crises and so we label activities "rites of passage" as long as they indicate some kind of psychological momentum, any momentum toward adulthood at all?

Think about things like smoking your first cigarette, going to your junior prom, or getting drunk or high for the first time in college. Or hitting the beach during spring break. Or picture what it's like to have your nose pierced, or your navel; or to be initiated into a gang. Or becoming an unwed teenage mother, or going to jail and returning to your neighborhood a "hero." All of these diverse experiences have been labeled a "rite of passage" in the print and broadcast media at some time in the last twenty years. What can they possibly have in common?

These references to "rites of passage" seem also to express the confusion of our teenagers, who seem willing to go to almost any extreme to prove themselves. Most young people seem to realize instinctively that they must earn the *right* of passage into adulthood, as their dramatic attempts do so often show. Surely a society as "advanced" as ours can do better than to leave its young people to struggle on their own through their self-created and often self-destructive attempts at growing up.

To understand all this more fully, we need to remember that rites of passage have a very long and venerable history: For millennia, tribal and religious rites have supported and directed youth on their path to adulthood.[1] Cultures have almost universally held rituals of transformation for their young. Some of these traditional practices—scarification, fasting, headshaving—seem oddly similar to what adolescents do today. Yet these traditional customs endured for centuries as part of a carefully structured and effective transformation into adulthood, enabling initiates to perpetuate their society in a meaningful and orderly way.

The dilemma we face is that our own culture has no concept of what kind of transformation our children should undergo, except possibly to learn the ropes of our "adult" consumer-credit lifestyle.[2] In the absence of community-guided customs, the term "rite of passage" has become like a net we cast out at random: no wonder we fail to catch relevant experiences as often as we succeed. It's as though we're groping for fitting activities to match with a seemingly significant label. At this point in American public awareness, "rite of passage" is a concept in search of a reality.

YOUTH SERVICE AS A RITE OF PASSAGE

Many parents and educators are already discovering that certain socially supported experiences for young people in their late teens or early twenties can be just as transforming as traditional rites of passage were for young initiates in tribal cultures. What they have in mind are *service experiences.* Former Pennsylvania Senator Harris Wofford, who helped set up the Peace Corps in 1961, was present for the founding of AmeriCorps in 1994, and is now CEO of the Corporation for National Service, said he would love to see community or overseas service become "a routine rite of passage" for young people.

One factor that makes this proposal so attractive is that many good service experiences are already available and have proven their worth, so we already have a very good foundation on which to build: volunteer positions are already available through such organizations as the Peace Corps, VISTA, state and county Conservation Corps, urban renewal groups, and volunteer organizations sponsored by religious groups. Very often, participants in such programs have an opportunity to commit themselves to one or two years of service in an area of their choice, such as health, education, ecology, public works, or public safety. A second, very desirable and important feature of service experiences is that just as in traditional societies, these service experiences are, with few exceptions, carefully supervised by experienced and qualified adults.

WHY YOUTH SERVICE WORKS: A COMPARISON OF SERVICE EXPERIENCES WITH TRADITIONAL AND WITH LESS EFFECTIVE CONTEMPORARY RITES OF PASSAGE

Although media allusions to rites of passage are often negative, the experiences they describe often share common grounds with healthier alternatives.

Both positive and negative examples give us evidence about what our young people need during their transition to adulthood.

These needs, it seems, are quite universal, as scholar and writer Joseph Campbell has shown in his studies of myths from around the world.[3] In what follows, I will draw from Joseph Campbell's research. I wish to explore some of the common patterns or elements pertaining to the "psychological momentum" young people seem to feel or to need as they make their journey. I also want to illustrate (by comparisons with age-old, proven rites and contrasts to some less fruitful "rite of passage" activities) the validity of proposing service as a universally expected, culturally accepted rite of passage for American youth.

ONE'S TRANSITION TO ADULTHOOD IS OFTEN SET IN MOTION BY A 'CALL TO ADVENTURE' WHICH INCLUDES CHALLENGE OR RISK.

Tribal rites of passage challenged their youth with tests of courage such as fasting, enduring pain without crying out, or spending long periods of time in training and/or in solitude. On the other hand, teenagers today play "chicken," ride the tops of elevators, or leap in and out of the way of oncoming subway trains in order to prove their courage to their peers. Others do things that land them in prison, seeing prison time as a "rite of passage" and a "badge of courage."[4]

Compare these latter dead-end challenges with the decisions made by youngsters who join City Year (an urban corps started in Boston), for example, or the San Francisco Conservation Corps. These young people daily take on the challenge of working closely, often for the first time, with others from very different racial, ethnic, or religious backgrounds.

RITES OF PASSAGE OFTEN REQUIRE A SEPARATION FROM ONE'S FAMILIAR SURROUNDINGS.

In tribal societies, youth were taken away from their homes to a separate place of transformation—for example, boys were taken to the forest, girls to the menstrual hut. Our ancestors saw that a change in setting is often necessary to bring about the inner changes they were trying to nurture.

Today, young men can join the army or navy as a sure way to find a new, "separate" setting. They can go away to college—or, they can get arrested and go to jail. Even a shopping mall can qualify: "Hangouts [at the mall] have become as much of a rite of passage for teen-agers as braces and Clearasil."[5]

But now, compare *going shopping* with doing conservation work in a distant national park or construction work with an urban corps in the inner city. Or consider: Spending a year in Alaska with the Jesuit Volunteer Corps, or two years in Bangladesh with the Peace Corps must provide enormously challenging but very effective settings for change.

RITES OF PASSAGE REQUIRE THAT ONE ASSUME A NEW ROLE.
Tribal cultures clearly enforced the idea that youth were to begin their rite of
passage as children but would emerge as adults, and their behavior had to
change accordingly.[6] And, during the Age of Chivalry, roles on the path to
knighthood were clearly marked by increasing responsibility: one was first a
page, then a squire, and only then a knight. For teens today, a job at a local
supermarket or department store can help create a new identity beyond that of
son, daughter, or student. Or, initiation into a college fraternity or a gang
would certainly force a youngster to take on a new role, with different attitudes and behavior.

Compared to these, the new roles assumed through youth service seem
to elicit a deeper shift toward maturity. One young woman who joined the
Mennonite Volunteer Corps, for instance, felt a tremendous shift of identity
when she realized that in her work as a job placement officer, clients were
placing their futures in her hands.

**RITES OF PASSAGE EXPERIENCES CREATE NEW
RELATIONSHIPS AND OFTEN A WHOLE NEW CIRCLE OF
PEERS.**
Traditionally, the bonding of age mates was an essential part of youth initiation. Young men and women became part of a closely related group because
of their initiatory status. They were also introduced to a new circle of elders
of the same sex who would become their mentors. In contrast, because bonding with adults other than parents is rare today, peer bonding alone often carries the burden of a youngster's natural need for approval and psychological
support.[7] Peers bond through street gangs, athletic teams, fraternities or sororities, or school cliques. Members often face initiation ordeals and are asked to
prove their loyalty to the group in questionable ways.

The new relationships that form within service corps also create strong
new bonds. One young woman with the Lutheran Volunteer Corps in Washington, D.C. had two non-Lutheran housemates who introduced her for the
first time to very different ways of looking at the world. But their commitment to a simple lifestyle in community, and their common dedication to their
social service work, enabled them to transcend their differences.[8]

**RITES OF PASSAGE EXPERIENCES FORCE US TO ACCEPT NEW
RESPONSIBILITIES OR OBLIGATIONS.**
In tribal cultures, the rite of passage into adulthood is irrevocable; the new
adults know their new responsibilities will be permanently expected of them,
and that they can't excuse themselves from them simply because they "don't
feel like it today." Or, in the Jewish tradition, growing maturity means accepting more complex laws, stricter dietary prescriptions, and a more demanding
spiritual discipline.

Most religious groups offer fine opportunities for young people to accept new obligations, but all too often, youngsters today impose a host of new responsibilities upon themselves by becoming parents. Given their perceived lack of other options, parenthood is often the only way to adulthood they believe open to them.[9]

Parenthood seems such a premature choice when compared with the direction taken by youth service volunteers. Their new responsibilities include replanting forests, evacuating victims of floods or hurricanes, and even working as Peace Corps representatives of the United States in distant countries such as Togo, West Africa.[10]

SUCH EXPERIENCES LEAD TO AN EXPANDED SENSE OF POWER AND AUTONOMY.

Native Americans of the plains and other hunting tribes traditionally empowered their young people through the Vision Quest. They make their quest in solitude and by fasting, often going to "the breaking point of physical suffering in the hope of entering into communication with the sacred world."[11] Today, our youth express their autonomy by owning a car, having a baby, or with alarmingly growing frequency, acquiring a gun.

In contrast, a program in East Harlem has been working for over two decades to train youth in leadership. This effort makes it evident that young people will be authentically empowered only when they share legitimate decision-making roles with adult leaders.[12] Inspired by the East Harlem program, youth corps leaders around the country are building empowerment into the corps experience.[13]

OFTEN, RITES OF PASSAGE ACTIVITIES ALLOW ACCESS TO PRIVILEGED KNOWLEDGE OR TEACH NEW SKILLS RESERVED FOR ADULTS ONLY.

Tribal rites often focus on wilderness survival techniques. The hunt is an important criterion for manhood, for instance. Knowledge of tribal myths and secrets is essential to the initiate's coming of age. Today, the driver's license represents an adult form of privilege as well as driving skills that *ought to* reflect a level of self-discipline and emotional maturity sufficient to the responsibilities of safe motoring. Street gangs teach new members the rules of their turf that will increase their chances of survival.

On a more meaningful level, youth service volunteers develop skills and knowledge applicable *beyond* their home turf. And while many of the youth corps work in teams, their focus reaches beyond the team. For instance, the team members of City Year in Boston, and now in Chicago, develop skills in ecology and social service, in math and English for GED completion where needed, and in negotiation and conflict resolution. Above all, through their work projects, they are developing a wisdom about how a society works or doesn't work.

RITES OF PASSAGE EXPERIENCES INVOLVE RECOGNITION BY OTHERS OF ONE'S NEW STATUS.

In tribal cultures the newly emerged young man now accompanies his elders on the hunt and into the battlefield. The young woman has now been accepted by the community as eligible for marriage and motherhood. This is the stage of the journey that Joseph Campbell calls "the return." The young person has been transformed forever and now has a new status and a new self-perception. This new status is recognized and validated by the community. Today, high-school and college graduation ceremonies, debutante balls, getting a driver's license, or registering to vote offer varying levels of community recognition.

Completion of a term of service also creates a new status for American youth. Most programs have a ceremony or celebration of closure to express public recognition of their accomplishments. This is especially true of Peace Corps members, who are often regarded as experts in the culture of their service. Many are asked to give talks on their experience. Many service programs function as a bridge to further educational or vocational training. One young woman who worked on a literacy program in VISTA decided to become a reading specialist following her term.

SUCH EXPERIENCES BRING ABOUT A NEW PERCEPTION OF THE SELF.

The youth's world has moved beyond the home and into a wider arena. The tribal youth undergoes a permanent change in his or her self-perception that is often symbolized by a new name, a new hairdo, or a tattoo. Sol Yurick mentions oaths of allegiance, secret insider slang, certain styles of clothes, and gold ornaments as "symbols of [the street gang's] rite of passage into manhood."[14]

In youth service experiences a deeper transformation—one not so reliant on external symbols—often takes place. Work with a conservation corps is almost sure to generate a change in a young person's self-perception. Or, one young man who entered a parole service program saw himself much differently when he realized he could make a great impact on the success or failure of the mentally challenged youngster he was helping to train for the Special Olympics.[15]

Isn't it *just possible* that youth service can be the reality we've been seeking to give concrete meaning to the concept of a rite of passage for coming-of-age in America? If service programs were to become universally accepted as an expected phase of adolescent development, youth would not be the only ones to benefit: by tapping the rich supply of creative talents and energies of our youth, whole communities could discover valuable new ways to meet their needs for constructive social and economic change. And (as I hope the above comparisons have shown), youth service programs honor the traditional wisdom of past ages although they are fully contemporary—offering to today's communities something of value while helping to empower our young people's heroic journeys to adulthood.

NOTES

1. See Arnold van Gennep, *Rites of Passage* (Chicago: University of Chicago Press, 1961). van Gennep introduced the term "rite of passage" in his 1908 book, *Les rites de passage,* and, in his analysis, identified three stages: separation, transition, incorporation.

2. See Ray Raphael, *The Men from the Boys: Rites of Passage in Male America* (Lincoln and London: University of Nebraska Press, 1988) for a discussion of the impact of consumerism on the development of youth.

3. Joseph Campbell, *The Hero with A Thousand Faces* (Princeton, N.J.: Princeton University Press, 1968 [1949]).

4. *Washington Post,* 24 June 1990.

5. *Los Angeles Times,* 6 January 1991.

6. See David D. Gilmore, *Manhood in the Making: Cultural Concepts of Masculinity* (New Haven: Yale University Press, 1990).

7. See Mihaly Csikszentmihalyi and Reed Larson, *Being Adolescent: Conflict and Growth in the Teenage Years* (New York: Basic Books, Inc., 1984), p. 62.

8. Urie Bronfenbrenner emphasizes that mere interaction, as pleasant as it may be, will not reduce hostility between alien groups; what will is working together on what he calls a "superordinate goal," an important task that pulls the participants out of their personal boundaries toward a cooperative relationship. (*The Ecology of Human Development: Experiments by Nature and Design* [Cambridge: Harvard University Press, 1979], p. 100.)

It should also be noted that peer relationships, important as they are, are not sufficient as a substitute for good adult mentoring and guidance. For example, one young woman participated in the American Friends Service Committee in post–World War II Berlin. She was to help with a building project, but once there, she found absolutely no adult mentoring nor guidance. Her memory of this experience is still painful.

9. *Washington Post,* 22 January 1991. See also Leon Dash, *When Children Want Children: An Inside Look at the Crisis of Teenage Parenthood* (New York: Penguin Books, 1989).

10. See Amitai Etzioni, *The Spirit of Community: Rights, Responsibilities, and the Communitarian Agenda* (New York: Crown Publishers, Inc., 1993). See chapter 3 for a discussion of national service.

11. Louise J. Kaplan, *Adolescence: The Farewell to Childhood* (New York: Simon and Schuster, 1984), p. 240. (See the chapter in this book by Kohl.)

12. Dorothy Stoneman with John Bell, *Leadership Development: A Handbook from the Youth Action Program of the East Harlem Block Schools* (New York: Youth Action Program, 1988).

13. Another group, the National Youth Leadership Council in St. Paul, Minnesota, is dedicated to developing service-oriented youth leaders.

14. *Newsday,* 9 October 1990.

15. Alec and Mora Dickson, *Volunteers* (London: The Furnival Press, 1983). Alec Dickson founded the Overseas Volunteer Service, the British predecessor of the Peace Corps and its domestic counterpart, the Community Service Volunteers. A remarkable aspect of the latter program is young offenders helping physically and mentally challenged youngsters. The impact on the helpers is extraordinary, leading the Dicksons to ask, "Who helps whom?"

A similar program was started in 1988 in Los Angeles County, matching delinquent students with disabled, mostly younger students. They work together for two hours, five days a week, for about six months. The delinquent youngsters have an option whether to participate in this program or to attend one of the more traditional community day centers. A six-month follow-up of the student participants indicated twice the success in staying out of trouble as nonparticipants.

Adapted from *Right of Passage: Heroic Journey to Adulthood* (Washington, D.C.: Cornell Press, 1996). © 1996 by Nancy Christopher

SIXTEEN

WHY APPRENTICESHIP MATTERS

John R. McKernan Jr.

John R. McKernan Jr., governor of Maine, has investigated apprenticeship as successfully practiced in several European countries. This chapter presents some of his findings in Maine and elsewhere in the United States. This selection is from Governor McKernan's book, *Making the Grade: How a New Youth Apprenticeship System Can Change Our Schools and Save American Jobs.*

McKernan's focus is on the rapidly growing number of high-school graduates who are unprepared for the demands of today's global skilled labor market. Drawing on Maine's new youth-apprenticeship program, McKernan offers a step-by-step plan for reforming educational and vocational training.

McKernan is chairman of Jobs for America's Graduates, Inc. and former chairman of both the Education Commission of the States and the National Education Goals Panel.

People often ask me why all this matters—whether a youth apprenticeship program is really necessary to meet our nation's needs. "Our schools weren't so different when I was a kid," someone will say. "Why change something that worked so well for me?"

The answer, of course, is that the times are different, very different. The fact is that our country is changing—and not always changing for the better.

The wage gap between the educated and the uneducated is growing—to a point that makes society as we know it unsustainable.

Rather than just accepting change as something we can do nothing about (except putting more police on the streets and building more prisons), we must examine the root causes of the changes we are seeing.

I believe that the cause can be found, generally, in the lack of jobs that pay a decent, living wage. And why is that?

The reason, to me, is clear. We cannot hope to compete successfully in the global marketplace without sophisticated technology that enhances productivity. To operate that technology, however, requires workers with the most developed skills. But too few of our workers or graduating high-school students have those skills. The Commission on the Skills of the American Workplace gave its report the apt title "High Skills or Low Wages." I believe that those are indeed our stark options as we approach the twenty-first century; we face a choice between jobs that demand high skills for high salaries or low-skill jobs whose pay falls far below the standards to which Americans have grown accustomed.

Those who care about the future of our country ask how and where we are going to find a remedy. I am convinced that we need to reform both the U.S. school and workplace.

During the Industrial Revolution, productivity grew by a factor of about one hundred from 1850 to 1950. Since the microprocessor revolution took off in the early 1970s, productivity in some areas has increased by a factor of more than one million.

Many of our larger businesses have already begun the painful process of catching up with this latest revolution. They have invested billions of dollars in new technology and in intensive training of their employees. These improvements caused their productivity to increase, and today U.S. business leads the world. Our improvements have far outpaced gains in Japan or Germany.

There are warning signs that we should watch. In recent years, the annual growth in productivity has been cut in half. From the end of World War II up to the 1970s, the annual growth rate ran about 2.5 percent. Since then—throughout the 1980s until the early 1990s—growth shrank to 1 percent or less each year. At the same time, the gap in productivity between this country and its competitors also diminished; it is now less than 10 percent higher than Canada, Norway, and Sweden; less than 20 percent higher than Japan, Germany, or France.

The good news, however, is that productivity trends in America have improved.

U.S. business has learned over the past few years that to improve productivity, it must readjust three fundamental business structures: the production process (making it possible for workers to produce more per hour), investment in technology (the production of better products in the same amount of time), and the education and retraining of workers—which alone can account for about a quarter of all growth in productivity in a given year.

Although businesses know where to target their investments, most of them have not resulted in new jobs. Instead, our new surge in productivity has resulted in *fewer* new jobs, accompanied by a greater demand for higher skills, both in the new jobs available and in existing jobs.

This reality creates the great paradox of the productivity gains made in America over the last few years—these gains have not been accompanied by a corresponding increase in our standard of living. This phenomenon is caused by the inadequate skill level of American workers, who are often rendered obsolete by technology. Once workers are laid off, they begin looking for new work. The good jobs, however, require the very skills which they do not have.

In order for our standard of living to increase it is necessary that we address in the short term the need for increased skills among our unemployed. For the long term, we have to ensure that students coming out of our schools have a strong work foundation upon which they can build. A youth apprenticeship system begins to take them down that road.

There is no doubt now that U.S. business is staying competitive—but at the expense of the unskilled American worker. A survey of middle-sized businesses conducted by Grant Thornton in 1990 found that more than two thirds of the companies interviewed felt that they had a problem with productivity. Yet more than half of these companies looked upon the problem as a minor one, probably because they believed they could solve it simply by replacing their workers with new machinery.

Today, much more than a basic skill like reading is needed. There are few jobs for those who do not know algebra, and fewer jobs still for those who lack basic problem-solving and teamwork skills. No, the days of the unskilled worker in a high-wage job are finished.

Yet despite these harsh realities, our schools have frequently dragged their feet about change. Though our schools do recognize that the best students need a better education, they still overlook the "forgotten half" of the student body, those children who don't plan to continue their education toward a four-year college degree. Yet it is just these children who need our schools to teach them more and better skills if they are to be equipped for today's job market. Left to fend for themselves, as they so often are today, they constitute the greatest threat to our future standard of living. Youth apprenticeship can change all that.

We can only be successful, however, if we also address the equally urgent necessity to change the way U.S. businesses operate—especially the kind of small and midsized companies that are predominant in my state. They must adjust to modern technology and to the demand for a highly competitive workforce.

Not surprisingly, there have been myriad reports and studies that have examined our changing times and the implications they bring in their wake. From the news media to individual corporations, from state governments to the federal government, all eyes have been focused on ways to improve the modern workplace.

One such study, "The Secretary's Commission on Achieving Necessary Skills," was ordered by the U.S. Department of Labor. The final report, issued in 1992, found five "essential" requirements for good job performance today:

1. **RESOURCES:** A student must be able to identify, organize, plan, and allocate resources, such as time, money, material, facilities, and human resources.

2. **INTERPERSONAL:** A potential employee works well with others; understands the demands of teamwork, teaching, customer service, leadership, and negotiation; and knows how to handle change and diversity.

3. **INFORMATION:** A student must be able to use computers to process information and to evaluate, organize, interpret, and communicate the information he or she has acquired.

4. **SYSTEMS:** The student must understand, monitor, and know how to improve or design systems.

5. **TECHNOLOGY:** A student must be able to select and apply appropriate technology, and maintain and troubleshoot equipment.

A *Fortune* magazine survey, published in June 1993, identified trends affecting businesses, especially those that are becoming more productive by downsizing. According to *Fortune:* The average company will become smaller and employ fewer people; traditional hierarchical organizations will give way to a variety of organizational forms, especially networks of specialists; technicians—from computer repairers to radiation therapists—will replace the manufacturing workforce; horizontal divisions of labor will replace vertical divisions; the pattern of doing business will shift from making a product to providing a service; and last, work itself will be redefined to encourage and even require constant learning. The old nine-to-five mentality will be replaced by a higher order of thinking.

There will be, ultimately, a shift in the approach of business to better and better quality in its products. Continual improvements and customer satisfaction will be valued more highly than mass production by rote. During 1991 and 1992, I served on Secretary of Labor Lynn Martin's National Advisory Commission on Work-Based Learning. The commission came to these same conclusions about business trends and our economic future.

During my tenure on the commission, I realized that many of our larger companies were already modernizing their work sites and their workforces. The pace of that modernization has only increased since then. Other businesses, however, are taking what I believe is a shortsighted step. To lower their costs, they are simply moving operations to third world countries. I am convinced that this action is ultimately self-destructive. If enough companies follow suit, we will gravely undermine the United States' standard of living. Instead of enjoying the fruits of a productive, technological revolution—as we once enjoyed the fruits of the Industrial Revolution—we could instead experience ever-increasing crime and an ever-widening disparity of income, leading to civil disobedience and social unrest. We cannot allow this to be America's future. We must, rather, adopt policies that allow businesses to be competitive and hire American workers. This will not be easy.

It is achievable, though. One of the leading advocates of apprenticeship programs around the world is the president and CEO, managing board, of Siemens AG in Germany, Dr. Heinrich von Pierer. The ability of American workers to respond to the apprenticeship concept is obvious from Dr. von Pierer's words:

Siemens does not believe in apprenticeship merely for its educational value. We believe in it because it makes a bottom-line difference. We have practiced apprenticeship for over 100 years, and, in our collective judgment, it gives our company a worldwide competitive edge. Today we have apprenticeship programs in sixteen countries. Among those are three different models established in the United States for testing.

Some have suggested that American workers do not meet the standards of workers elsewhere in the world. This is not so. In fact, the first-year apprentices at our test site at Lake Mary had collectively the highest test scores after the first year of any of our apprentices anywhere in the world!

The American workforce will clearly benefit from a major investment in apprenticeship. The "raw material" in America has proved second to none when properly trained and prepared. This is why we are aggressive investors in America and in the American workforce.

For small businesses, meeting the challenge of modernization is a daunting prospect. They lack the facilities, expertise, and resources to upgrade their workforce. Therefore, if the system does not change, they too will contribute to our worsening economic climate.

The work-based learning commission found out, very quickly, that the key to achieving first-rate skills and good wages does not lie with worker training and education as separate pursuits. Rather, learning should be based on the integration of school and workplace, so that future workers can use their knowledge and training to solve problems and also be stimulated to continue the learning process. It is a revealing statistic that, over the past fifty years, fully 60 percent of the growth in workplace productivity can be traced to work-based learning.

Japan and Germany are two countries, among others, that have invested heavily in work-based education. We must do the same if we are to compete in world markets. To build a well-trained labor force, we, too, must invest in education, both in schools and at U.S. work sites.

Throughout the pages of this book, I have tried to build a case for the importance of forging a new dynamic relationship between school and business. Without it, youth apprenticeship programs cannot hope to succeed.

During my lifetime, schools have remained isolated from business. Historically, teachers have done their job to educate students; business has then taken the graduates and taught them what they needed to know to do their jobs. As a result, a school staff member still does not truly understand the needs of business, nor does the business community truly know how youngsters are taught in our schools.

Youth apprenticeship creates a direct connection between workplace and education. I am convinced that this is an important first step toward building a link between one community and the other and developing a new U.S. system for improving the skills of our labor force.

A dynamic relationship between business and schools will ensure that one can learn from the other. U.S. business can establish standards for the skills they need to be competitive, and schools will be able to upgrade their capacity to meet these high standards. Educators will be able to develop appropriate curricula while business can keep them informed on its changing needs.

As educators and the business community continue to work together, the standards demanded of students will become clearer and clearer. With such standards, it will ultimately become possible—sometimes as early as the tenth grade—to certify students according to their mastery of their studies. Then, when a student graduates, his or her diploma will truly mean something, spelling out the range of skills possessed by the student.

A youth apprenticeship system will also influence and improve the in-house training of existing workers. As meisters teach apprentices, coworkers will recognize the importance of improving their own skills. That, in turn, will easily lead to a dialogue between schools and businesses on the best ways to meet the training needs of existing workers.

The result of the dialogue will be a realization that the structure established to support a youth apprenticeship system can easily be modified to establish a work-based learning program for existing employees. And that will set in motion a series of new partnerships designed to integrate training of future workers while upgrading the skills of those already in the workforce.

I do not believe that this country is prepared to spend the billions of dollars necessary to create a completely new—and expensive—infrastructure to train employees now working in small and middle-sized companies. But a youth apprenticeship system can put in place the necessary facilities, expertise, and resources that businesses need to design a process of lifelong learning and skills enhancement for all of their employees.

Students in a youth apprenticeship system spend about half their time at a work site; during that time, schools are left with a partially unused physical plant that could be used for classes to upgrade the capabilities of existing employees. And when youth apprentices return to the classroom, those employees can return to their jobs with new skills. Such a venture between businesses and schools can produce a synergy that supports youth apprenticeships and also meets the needs of businesses to improve the current workforce.

Maine's youth apprenticeship program has already shown how this process can work. Jurgen Kok of Nichols/Portland is the chairperson of Maine's Skills Standards Board. He told me that his company's participation in the program has inspired some of his workers to develop their skills further.

"Our employees have always seen overtime as the only way to make more money. I have always told them that if they were to spend the same amount of time enhancing their skills—and we pay tuition up front—then their paychecks would *always* be bigger." Since his company began its participation in youth apprenticeship, more and more workers have chosen additional training. "Because of its focus on education and training, we believe this program will promote lifelong training for our current workers as well as for our apprentices," Kok said.

As this reciprocal system develops, and our schools and businesses integrate complementary programs, we will build a true, lifelong learning system. Schools will work in concert with employers, and the worlds of practical work and education will be linked, giving our children, as well as our current workforce, a training that is both academic and work-based.

That accomplished, I believe we will credit a new youth apprenticeship system with having helped America turn the corner, bringing with it increased productivity, reinvigorated schools, and, especially, renewed prosperity.

SEVENTEEN

EDUCATION AND THE WORLD OF WORK

William Raspberry

William Raspberry, a Washington-based urban- and minority-affairs columnist, writes a warmly personal twice-weekly column which has appeared in *The Washington Post* since 1966.

Time magazine has written: "Raspberry has emerged as the most respected black voice on any white U.S. newspaper. He considers the merits rather than the ideology of any issue. Not surprisingly, his judgments regularly nettle the Pollyannas and militants."

Raspberry's newspaper career began with a summer job at the *Indianapolis Recorder* in 1956. His duties there as a reporter, photographer, and editor inspired him to join *The Washington Post* after serving two years in the Army.

His coverage of the 1965 Watts riot earned him the "Capital Press Club's Journalist of the Year" award, and in 1967 he received a Citation of Merit in Journalism from Lincoln University in Jefferson, Missouri, for distinction in improving human relations. In 1994, William Raspberry was awarded the Pulitzer Prize for Distinguished Commentary.

Georgetown University, in honoring him with a doctoral degree in 1984, said that William Raspberry "has shown us what we are, but has also shown us what we might be."

Raspberry and his wife, Sondra, live with their three children in Washington, D.C.

Berlin—Young Germans, aside from the university-bound minority, leave high school ready for work. Their American counterparts graduate from high school ready for college—or nothing.

The difference, I am convinced after a few days' looking at German schools, could shed more useful light on what has gone wrong in American schools—and American society—than all our frenzied attention to school reform, reorganization, and deteriorating academic standards.

Americans, though troubled as never before about the quality of our schooling, remain ambivalent as to its purpose. We fret that our schools routinely fail to produce workers of the competence our industry requires in order to remain competitive in the international market, but it strikes us as somehow wrong to gear our schools to industry's requirements. Education, we tell ourselves, should be its own reward.

The Germans suffer no such ambivalence. For them, work is what responsible citizens do, for themselves and for the state, and education is the means by which they learn to do it more efficiently.

One result of that assumption is that they do a much better job than we do of preparing their young people for the school-to-work transition. German youngsters are at once more serious about work and better at it than their American counterparts.

Are there lessons for America in the German approach?

The premise of this trip is that there are. I am traveling with a group of Indianans who hope to adapt elements of the German system to the needs of their state. The group, which includes educators, legislators, union officials, and employers is looking both to improve the quality of Indiana's work force and to enhance the work skills and attitudes of its young people, particularly its disadvantaged youth.

Their focus is Germany's "dual system" of combining academics and apprenticeships, particularly for the 75 percent of German youngsters who will not pursue university education, for real jobs in the German economy.

Young Germans typically spend the first 10 years of their schooling on academics (though even at this stage there is heavy emphasis on the world of work) and the last two years pursuing on-the-job apprenticeships for three or four days a week with a day or two of formal instruction in public school classrooms.

Perhaps most intriguing to an American visitor is the loose tie between the apprenticing employer and the apprentice. In general, the youngster himself will find a sponsoring employer, who then may train him for as long as three years. At the end of this costly training, for which the employer pays, the apprentice is free to seek full-time employment wherever he chooses.

The training, in some 380 apprenticable skills, is standardized across Germany, so the skills are fully transferable from one company to another. Employers consider the training outlays an unremarkable investment in the competency of Germany's work force and, therefore, an investment in their own long-term survival.

German supervisors are themselves master craftsmen, unlike in America, where first-line managers are likely to be recent college graduates with little on-the-line experience. The result is an unusually competent work force, which is proud of its technical skills.

While the government closely regulates the quality and content of the apprenticeships, there is no legal requirement that employers maintain apprenticeship programs at all. Most do, however, including small companies of which Germany has an unusually large number. It is rare to find a large company—even with parent companies based outside of Germany—without an excellent apprenticeship program that routinely trains far more workers than it intends to hire.

The dozen Hoosiers are the second group to make this tour under the sponsorship of the New York-based CDS International and the German Marshall Fund. The first group, largely top-level policymakers, decided that any successful effort at implementing any part of the German approach would require the enthusiastic endorsement of workers, employers, legislators, and educators. Thus, this second tour, which so far has included Cologne, Bonn, and Berlin, and which will end in Copenhagen.

The Indiana visitors are uniformly impressed by the work-seriousness of German high schoolers, the quality of their academic instruction, and the dignity accorded non-college trades. Nor, given the unquestioned quality of German products, do they doubt that America would do well to emulate major aspects of the system.

Their question—and mine—is whether a system that grows out of the medieval craft tradition can be transplanted in substantial part to America, with its vastly different traditions and assumptions.

PART THREE CONTEMPORARY RITES OF PASSAGE: GROUP EXPERIENCES

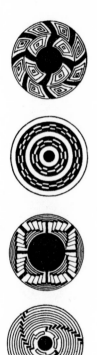

EIGHTEEN

THE JOURNEY: AN EXPERIENTIAL RITE OF PASSAGE FOR MODERN ADOLESCENTS

David Oldfield

David Oldfield describes "The Journey," a program he developed for adolescents of many different backgrounds and circumstances including hospitals and mental institutions. His approach involves young people in a symbolic adventure as they confront the "necessary crises" of adolescence. He presents several case histories in depth and gives some examples of practical techniques he uses.

David Oldfield is Director of The Center for Creative Imagination at The Foundation for Contemporary Mental Health in Washington, D.C. He holds a master's degree in religion from Yale Divinity School, and a master's degree in special education from Southern Connecticut State University. He is the author of several books: *The Journey: A Creative Approach to the Necessary Crises of Adolescence; The Legacy; Bridging the Gap: A Life Transition Program for Teenagers and Their Parents; Private Paths, Common Ground: An Adult Rite of Passage* (a multimedia tool to mark and honor the significant passages of the middle and later years); and *Seven Islands of Experience* (a multimedia program of renewal for education, mental health, community planning, and the world of work). His workplace series, *The New Basics,* has been used by government agencies, financial institutions, corporations, and nonprofit organizations, as a means for breaking old paradigms and developing more efficient and meaningful strategies for meeting the challenges of the future. Mr. Oldfield has designed specialized programs for schools, business and industry, mental health institutions, government, and service and religious organizations across the country. Under his guidance since its founding in 1980, The Center for Creative Imagination has become internationally recognized for its contribution to our understanding and use of imagination, myth and ritual, and creativity in our personal, professional, and organizational lives.

I've been a "closet" rites-of-passage advocate ever since I began work in the field of mental health. The programs I use are, in fact and in spirit, rites-of-passage programs, although some mental health professionals might disagree. Perhaps I can best describe myself as a professional "story-listener," because I listen to the inner stories of adolescents—particularly adolescents in crisis who are struggling deeply with the issues of growing up.

I have found that working with adolescents requires much ingenuity. What works for one youngster or group may fail miserably with another; so I have learned much and borrowed shamelessly from many disciplines, and I appropriate the right to do this not only for myself but for all of us who work with adolescents in crisis. Any means or methods are "fair game" because the challenges we face in this work are so great. I have tried to design "The

Journey" as a modern rite of passage accessible to modern youngsters of all
backgrounds.

THE SCIENTIFIC VIEW IS NOT ALWAYS BEST

Over the last fifteen years I have listened to the stories of youngsters who
want to describe their deepest inner feelings. They seem to have a natural talent for creating their own rites, and they often seem to heal themselves in
spite of our current mental health system which sometimes actually prevents
them from doing this work for themselves.

In our world today, society has come to view practically all problems or
issues of human life from a scientific point of view. I have seen this attitude
wherever I have worked: in psychiatric hospitals, residential treatment centers, and in a variety of state agencies that deal with the mental health of adolescents. Unfortunately, this scientific approach to adolescent crises (with its
demands for quantifiable results, statistical verifications, and concrete, replic-
able experiments) often reduces the adolescent soul to a mere biochemical
machine. Although young people going through this troublesome period
deserve to be treated with respect and dignity, the scientific view with its
emphasis on rationality seems unable to accept the fact that adolescence is a
turbulent, "messy" time very ill-suited to neat categories or descriptions. As a
result, it often demeans adolescents by seeing them as wayward kids who
need help while we adults and professionals are *experts* who provide it. The
usual procedure is to diagnose the youngster as having this or that technically
labeled problem, and then to prescribe "cures" or "treatments," all in purely
quantitative, scientific terms.

I can understand to some extent why many highly trained professionals
would feel most comfortable when they can use scientific language and back
up their views with quantitative, statistical studies. But when we try to measure the ways and means of the adolescent spirit, I'm not convinced that the
prevailing diagnostic categories are appropriate nor that this way of talking
lends much dignity to the deep anguish our youngsters often experience. We
live in a society that seems to believe that all knowledge is based on "head
learning," but it is not.

Our ancestral elders have shown us that the value of rites of passage for
adolescents in crisis cannot be measured scientifically, as though we can
quantify "how much better" a person becomes for having undergone them.
They teach us that rites of passage impart a form of self-understanding that is
felt in the heart rather than learned in the head.

In ancient cultures, people understood that the wisdom of the heart is
accessed by the imagination; that imagination is the thought of the heart. Our
imaginations show us what our hearts know about life, and we can express
this knowledge in terms of image, symbol, and metaphor. I think we're at a

point in history where more than ever, we need to learn what is in our hearts. More than ever, we need to work with our creative imaginations.[1]

RITES OF PASSAGE ARE ART FORMS

Rites of passage are much more like an art form than a science. And like many art forms, they have two basic functions. One function of art is *curatorial:* it preserves the ancient traditions of the past. And as many writers on this subject have shown, traditional rites of passage did contain very special, powerful, and effective traditions well worth preserving and rediscovering.

But like art, rites of passage are not solely curatorial. We make a grave mistake if we focus only on what once made sense in other cultures. Art and rites of passage both have a second main function, a *creative* function. They must be recreated constantly to fit the needs of the present time.

At some point we need to gather up all our data about the rich traditions from the past and ask ourselves how we can "reinvigorate" them for use in our own, modern American rites of passage. In urban and suburban and rural life, in a world that has shrunk incredibly in the last decade, in a world that has grown increasingly complex socially, economically, and technologically, how can we address the issues of the 1990s in terms of rites used centuries ago? I believe what we need to do is focus on the *spirit* of these traditional practices, and strive to carry that spirit forward and make it once again a vital part of our lives. We must strive for a balance between the curatorial and the creative— between what we can learn from the past and what we must create or invent for ourselves. It is this balance that keeps a rite vibrant and filled with power.

CONTEMPORARY AMERICAN RITES OF PASSAGE

It is certainly not easy to design rites of passage appropriate for Americans in the 1990s. For instance, we must try to avoid cultural, subcultural, and ethnic biases. We must also stay aware of the great diversity of ethnic contexts America embraces: What works for adolescents in the Pacific Northwest doesn't necessarily have meaning for those in Orlando, Florida, or for youngsters living in Hawaii. If we set out to develop a program to be used nationwide, we must try to make sure it will work in a very wide range of situations and settings. The best way to do this is, I think, to work with elements and concepts that are universally meaningful, that we all can share in common.

I have found much inspiration in the work of Margaret Mead's *Coming of Age in Samoa,* a great classic that helped introduce the idea of rites of passage in our times.[2] In the last chapter of that book, she reflects on how rites of passage for Americans would differ from those practiced in Samoa. She observes that in a nontechnological, stable society like Samoa, the object of a rite of passage is to educate youth into the reality of the adult world. The elders would teach them what is real, what it means to be a man, what it means to be a woman, who God is and what the proper relationship to that Godhead is—all within the context of the living myth of that society.

But America is a pluralistic society and each ethnic group within America prizes its uniqueness. Our great battle cry is freedom. So we really cannot justify dogmatically imposing our own values on the younger generation, telling them what they must value and what they must believe in. Margaret Mead realized that such an attitude will not work in modern American society; she proposed that instead of imposing answers on our youngsters, we pose questions that will help them discover their own values. Instead of telling them, for instance, "This is what it means to be a man (or woman)," we should ask, "What does it mean to you to be a man (woman)? What do you see as the main differences between being a boy (girl) and a man (woman)?" We cannot dictate answers to such questions; we can only share our own experiences and feelings about these things. If we patiently work to create an atmosphere of openness and mutual respect, we can create a "circle of wisdom" where people can instruct each other and no one has the right to dogmatically impose his or her own views on all the others.

THE LANGUAGE OF THE HEART

Years ago, I became frustrated with the pervasive scientific approach taken by mental health agencies in this country. I'm not a scientist, and I have difficulty understanding the scientific language so often used by psychiatric researchers and practicing psychiatrists. Many of the patients who received treatment in mental-health institutions seemed as alienated as I was.

When I first started working at a residential treatment center in Connecticut with emotionally disturbed boys, I was fresh out of Divinity School, and very, very naive. After my very first class I was excited and relieved that I'd made it through the hour without too much difficulty. But when I began to assign homework, a thirteen-year-old boy in the front row raised his hand and said, "You're new here, aren't you. Don't you know, you can't give me homework! Didn't my doctor tell you that I *perseverate* under stress?"

Now, in Divinity School we never even heard of "perseverating"; the word just wasn't in our language. This student had learned just enough quasi-scientific, psychological terminology to excuse himself from any responsibilities he found distasteful. But in a way, I think he was actually catching us at our own game: his doctors focused only on their diagnostic labels, so he merely played this "diagnosis game" back at us. Clearly, this method of treatment was unable to engage the creative spirit and energies of this young man to heal himself.

The adolescent rite of passage is, in my opinion, about power: marshalling one's own personal power and finding its limitations, discovering how it fits in relation to other powers in the universe and within the community, and in times of trouble, using one's personal power to heal one-self and others. Every adolescent needs to discover his or her personal power and how to use it wisely. But many standard, "mainstream" psychiatric prac-tices actually tend to take power away from our youngsters. We use a lan-guage and therapies that they cannot begin to understand.

That is why one of my first goals in developing a rite-of-passage experi-ence for adolescents was to find a *common* language. I also began to focus more on experiential learning, because I found this is one of the most natural kinds of learning for teenagers. Teenagers are usually not "verbal" people. For many, adolescence is not a time for analyzing and talking about one's feelings. Although adolescents use more sophisticated language than young children, they have not yet mastered many of the highly abstract or complex concepts that deal with the inner life of the emotions. For example, when an adult asks his or her adolescent son or daughter, "How do you feel?" the youngster might not know how to respond other than to say, "I feel like shit." We tend to feel surprised and disappointed by such "uncommunicative" responses, failing to realize that at that age, a youngster simply might not have other, more appropriate words in his or her vocabulary to express his or her feelings more adequately.

So the crux of the matter, as I saw it, was to first find a language that would put adolescents and adults on an equal footing so that neither would be more fluent or linguistically advantaged than the other. In time I found that the language of the imagination is just such a language: imagery is a natural language to all of us, but we don't become more fluent in it merely by grow-ing older. We all have internal images swirling around in us, but they are all equal in value—no one person's imagery is any "better" or any "worse" than anyone else's.

It is precisely in the change of self-image and the changing of one's image of the world and how one thinks one should relate to the world that a rite of passage takes place. What changes whenever we make an important transition in our lives, is our inner image of self and of our relationship with the world around us. Therefore, not only is the language of the imagination useful for egalitarian reasons; it is also the language best suited to express what we experience in times of transition.

MYTHS AND HEROES

In my research about how other cultures in other times helped adolescents in crisis, not only did I find that they used rites of passage; I also found a pro-found and consistent use of *stories*. Stories were told to the young to help them reframe their experience. One listens differently to a story than to a lec-ture or to matter-of-fact conversation. Stories frame experience. Archetypal psychologist James Hillman observed that patients who have a sense of their lives as an unfolding story usually have a much better prognosis than patients who have lost touch with the sense of story in their lives.

The stories we find most appropriate—and which hold the most fascination for us—tend to change as we grow older. The richest form of the language of imagination is mythology. In myths we find the greatest sense of awe and we ask the biggest questions about life, and in myth we give shape to our most essential understanding of how we fit in the grand scheme of things. So, in many cultures, mythology is a most powerful teaching tool for adolescents. Historically, the myths told most frequently to adolescents were hero myths.

Every society on earth has its own hero myths. These myths have two major functions: first, they provide role models. They show what it means to be a good woman or a good man or a good human being. We look at what happens to the hero and see how he or she handles his or her life's problems, and in this way we learn what is expected of us. We learn how to take responsibility for resolving problems that arise in our own lives.

The second and more important function of hero myths is that they tell us what to expect out of life. We need to be honest with our children and admit that sometimes life hurts and that part of being alive is learning to face life's sorrows as well as to embrace its joys. Joseph Campbell, in his book *The Hero with a Thousand Faces,*[3] describes how he spent the better part of the Great Depression reading myths from around the world. He discovered that fundamentally, all hero myths are instances of the same story: all heroes go through the same basic phases in order to complete their heroic tasks.

Now, if you compare the stages of a hero's journey with the stages of a rite of passage, and then compare these with a psychological understanding of the developmental tasks of adolescence, you find that *they're remarkably all the same!* For example, the first stage in a hero's experience is a *call to adventure,* leaving the known world for the unknown, where the great adventure awaits. The first adolescent crisis is also one of separation, and the first stage in an effective rite of passage is often a literal, physical separating of the initiate from his or her normal surroundings or routine.

Now this was very interesting to me, especially when I began to notice that most of the troubled youths I was working with suffered from what our professionals call *separation anxiety.* I gradually came to see this as their "call to adventure," similar to what happens to a hero. As to the value of this approach, just ask yourself this: Would you rather suffer from "separation anxiety" or would you prefer to be "called to adventure"? I don't mean this facetiously; I truly believe we have done a terrible disservice to the innate workings of the human psyche by framing them in the cold, sterile, "psychobabble" type of language so often used in the mental health profession. This language often alienates youngsters so much that they don't even feel as though they are participating in their own symptoms. In contrast, when we use the language of myth and describe their experiences in terms of a heroic rite of passage, they begin to take a more active, interested, and effective role in their own course of development. They begin to discover their personal power to heal and find new directions for their lives.

THE JOURNEY

Over the years I developed a program for adolescents which uses these ideas, called "The Journey." As will be described, there are five stages to this process, each one taking a name from the corresponding stage of heroic myth, and each dealing with one of the major aspects of rites of passage as well as the developmental challenges of adolescence. I believe part of the reason this program seems to work is because when one sees the particulars of one's life in the context of universal mythic themes, something electrifying happens; one becomes empowered to move forward.

Naturally, working in the context of myth means working with one's imagination. But the more thoroughly one explores one's imagination, the more time it takes to fully understand the meaning of specific images that arise. Often a youngster's experiences contain too much imagery to process at once. That is why "The Journey" has a workbook to document their experiences; one needs a document to come back to over and over again to help the learning sink in.

In The Journey, we rely heavily on guided imagery: Through guided imagery, youngsters can often access that deep realm of imagination that is so transformative. The human mind may well be better suited to using the language of images than more "logical," discursive language. Robert J. Lifton, a Yale psychiatrist, speaks of the "mytho-poetic zone of the psyche"—that deep, deep zone where we find meaning for ourselves. I believe one way to gain access to that realm is by using guided imagery.

In The Journey, we also use the activity of mask-making as a therapeutic tool. We make masks of plaster and surgical gauze. These are "life masks"; they represent the person, but they are not exact. They are like a crude approximation of the person behind the mask. We found mask-making helpful for a number of reasons.

First, the whole process of coming into adulthood is a matter of deepening one's self-awareness. Now, in adult therapeutic circles, self-awareness is usually a familiar concept and readily understood. Adults can access self-awareness through introspective reflection. But introspection is a very abstract and difficult task for many teenagers. If we ask them to reflect upon themselves by posing direct questions ("Who are you, anyway?"), they are at a loss to begin. Plaster face masks are very concrete representations of who they are, and as such, provide a clear and tangible starting point on an inner journey of self-discovery.[4]

Since the masks clearly define features indicating family resemblances, they provide a prime opportunity to initiate discussions about family ties, traditions, and tribulations. The enduring paradox facing all adolescents is the balancing act of discovering one's uniqueness while renegotiating one's connections in the world. The family unit lies in the middle of this paradox: most adolescents feel the need to become "other" than their parents, but must also become aware of the "baggage" (genetic, emotional) they have inherited. One's familial inheritance often appears quite unmistakably in these masks: one sees one's mother and father in such a mask as well as oneself.

Young children often approach life as though they are the center of the whole universe. But by the time a child reaches adolescence, he or she must move to a more mature understanding of life, move beyond the childlike egocentric perspective. One of the most concrete and effective ways to help teenagers come to realize that they are not the center of the universe is to have them exchange and wear one another's masks. In some instances this can be tantamount to putting a youngster "into someone else's *skin.*" It is especially interesting to watch what happens when males and females exchange masks. It is often enlightening to temporarily change one's gender identity; we can learn very much about human nature this way. It is good to try to feel what life is like from perspectives other than one's own.

THE ROLE OF PARENTS

We also have a book for parents. They have to be part of the process, particularly in this day and age, because no matter how much a youngster might grow and change while in our care, if we then return him or her to a dysfunctional family, all of that learning and changing will be lost because the family will not be able to support it. So we need to get parents actively involved in their children's transitions.

We give the parents a book called "The Legacy." It's basically a blank book with some interesting questions on the top of each page. (It's designed really beautifully so that a parent wouldn't dare throw it out!) Most of these questions ask them to reflect on their own adolescence. We take the parents through the five stages of The Journey but unlike their children, the parents undertake their journey by remembering how they handled their own adolescent crises. They write their stories as a legacy to their children.

The final phase of The Journey is a ceremony of passage that the youngsters themselves create. Parents are invited. Usually the parents bring their Legacy books to present to their youngsters after reading aloud a few of the stories they have written about their growing up. These books lend a sense of continuity between the two generations: Youngsters see that they aren't alone, that their parents went through difficult times too.

Some of the questions in The Legacy are easy; for example, "What are some of your nicest childhood memories? What were some of the fads and fashions of your day, especially those your parents disliked?" But some of the questions are very difficult, questions like, "What is the biggest mistake you made in your teenage years?" Sometimes a parent will call me on the phone and say, "Could I write about the *third* biggest mistake I've made—I can't possibly tell her about the first two!"

Parents, too, often feel threatened by their inability to deal with life's difficulties. But teenagers don't necessarily want to see their parents as wonderful, perfect role models. They want to see them as authentic people who have made mistakes just like themselves. Actually, it is better in the long run for a parent to acknowledge his or her failures because in this way the child is then able to say, "My mom (dad) screwed up just like I screwed up, but she (he) made it. Maybe there's hope for me, too."

THE FIVE STAGES OF THE JOURNEY

STAGE ONE: THE CALL TO ADVENTURE

As I mentioned earlier, there are five phases to The Journey which correspond to five phases in hero myth, rites of passage, and the developmental stages of adolescents. The first stage of The Journey is what we call the "Call to Adventure." All heroes begin a quest by leaving the known world to enter the "Great Unknown." You don't need to be a Greek scholar to observe this. If you have seen *Star Wars* or other movies that portray modern heroic myths, you see how they all begin: Something happens that makes it impossible for the hero to stay where he or she is and so he or she has to go forth into a much larger world on a quest of some kind.

Ninety percent of all heroic myths begin with a call to adventure that is negative; very few heroes go forth simply because they want to find the Golden Fleece, for instance. More often, they are called away because something has fallen apart. For example, in the myth of the Holy Grail, the king has a wound in his side that won't stop bleeding. As long as his wound bleeds, the land is fallow and nothing will grow. So someone has to go forth to find the secret that will stop the king's wound from bleeding.

The first crisis of adolescence is a crisis of separation, *which is precisely the same task.* The adolescent has to let go of the safe, familiar world of childhood and enter into the as yet unknown world of adulthood, not merely a passage through time, but in quest of a whole new way of *being.* In traditional rites of adolescent passage there is a very concrete separation: often it is not only quick and efficient, but it can be rather brutal. For instance, the initiate might be kidnapped—forcibly removed from the mother's hut and led into the wilderness, there to spend several days alone. An event like this shows the youngster in no uncertain terms that from now on, life is going to be different. The youth can no longer expect adults to care for him or her as a child. "Caring" no longer means being protected from harm. As a young person moves through adolescence, the great irony is that adults may now express their "care" by leading the young person *directly towards* what terrifies most. In this way he or she is forced to become more independent and responsible.

Kids today are wrestling with the very same kinds of issues in their own lives. But how can they accomplish this separation and move out into their own world? What calls the youth of today to the adventure of their lives? Sometimes it is a first boyfriend or girlfriend, or a first transgression of a curfew rule, or an after-school club—or much more dangerously, drugs or alcohol, that nudge a youngster away from hearth and home. But inevitably, *something* will provide the final push that leads a young boy or girl away from mother and father, to venture forth into the wide world.

As an example, I remember a boy who came to the hospital because he was severely depressed and "school phobic." He stopped going to school in the middle of his senior year. We didn't know at first but found out later that he quit school because in his family, when one graduated from high school, one was expected to move out. He was utterly terrified of moving out and becoming independent, so with typical adolescent logic, he reasoned that if he were never to graduate, he could stay at home for the rest of his life.

We asked him to imagine himself as a hero being called to go forth on a great adventure. He was about to begin the first leg of this journey. We asked him to frame his own images: What did his call to adventure look like?—He saw himself in his home, a safe and comfortable place, which is where all heroes' journeys begin. We then asked what happened that called him out into the larger world. He told us that as he sat in his home, his "safe place," he heard a knock at the door. A man's voice boomed out his name. At first the young man cowered inside and answered that he was not at home, but the man outside didn't believe him. Magically the stranger opened the door, and the young man, room and all, was sucked out into outer space.

With the help of these images the youngster came to realize that his home was no longer a "safe place." All had been suddenly uprooted and flung out into space, there to float, spinning, as he said, like Dorothy's house in *The Wizard of Oz*.

And this is just like what happens in reality: if you don't receive the call to adventure and move forward on your own, then life will make you get moving in its own way, which will usually be much less agreeable. We have many traditional motifs in heroic myths where the hero refuses his or her call to adventure—and the consequences are never very pleasant. In the Judeo-Christian tradition, the story of Jonah captures the essence of what one can expect if one chooses to refuse the call to adventure. These motifs show us that we *must* go forth when we are called.

Parents can make the separation easier or more difficult for their youngsters. The greater the unconditional love and acceptance the parent has for his or her child, the more confidence the youngster will have to face his or her transition. Conversely, if the parents themselves are emotionally immature and dependent on the love of their child *as a child*, it will be much more difficult for the child to separate. It is interesting that many societies incorporate rites of passage that parents must undergo in order to prepare them for the jolt of their child's coming of age. I think such practices are very valuable, because the parents' lives must also be totally reorganized as their children reach adulthood. They must restructure their previous self-images at the same time that they restructure their relationship with their sons or daughters. Indirectly, this changes their relationship to their spouses as well, and offers a unique opportunity to reinvigorate old interests, values, and attitudes that they had to "put on hold" during their primary parenting years.

In parts of Melanesia, there is a very powerful ritual for mothers of girls coming of age, called "Letting Your Breast Hang." Prior to the daughter's rite of passage into womanhood, the mother ceremonially releases her upper garment and no longer covers her breast, so that it is exposed. This signifies her change in status to that of "old woman." It signifies that she is passing her active sexuality on to her daughter. This is a graphic example of an internal truth: the future of the tribe depends on the passage of fertility from mother to daughter, from father to son. We adults are not always emotionally ready for such passages; that's why rituals exist. Many mothers today, because of their own unfulfilled needs, feel great pain in letting go of their adolescent children, and could well benefit from a sanctioned, formal occasion to help them transform this relationship.

For example, I remember a boy who was admitted to a psychiatric hospital where I was working, who had just slit his wrists—a very serious suicide attempt. When I asked him to represent his feelings pictorially at that time, he drew a figure that was split in two. Half of him wanted to become independent and go his own way. But he also drew his mother, a single parent, standing naked on his left, beckoning him to stay with her. In reality, every time this boy would move toward independence (for example, make plans to get his driver's license), his mother would go into an emotional tailspin: she would go to bed and make her son stay home and take care of her.

The son became extremely depressed and attempted suicide, which led to his being admitted to the hospital. But as soon as he came to the hospital, his mother spontaneously became "well" and began to behave like the perfect parent. As long as he was sick and dependent upon her, she was fine. But if he started to move toward independence, she would again fall apart.

Although this is an extreme example, the theme itself is very common: When youngsters and their parents begin to separate, parents sometimes sabotage their children's progress unless they are given an opportunity to ritualize the letting go. That is why parental rites of passage are needed just as much as rites of passage for their children!

PHASE TWO: FINDING ONE'S PATH

The second phase of The Journey is called "Finding Your Path." It focuses on the second crisis of adolescence, the crisis of independence. This phase of The Journey correlates with ancient adolescent rites of passage in which youngsters were sent into the forest to spend time in solitude, as they sought their personal vision. More and more people are becoming aware that at adolescence especially, we need to search for and to discover our unique vision of life.

After a youngster begins to separate from his or her parents and previous attitudes, the next question is, "Now what?" Typically, the teenager asserts him or herself by choosing new friends, for example, or rebelling against a previously set curfew. They need to find their own set of values independently. Often they will express this transition by transferring previous dependence on their parents to dependence on their peers. For example, although they may not be concerned about what their parents think of their appearance, they become *very* concerned about dressing acceptably in the eyes of their peers. They talk the talk, they walk the walk of their peers. At this stage, no real revolution of independence has taken place: the youngster has merely transferred his or her dependency from one group to another.

As we know, adolescent peer pressure can often deter a youth from discovering his or her individuality and creative abilities. So at some point we must try to refocus the youth's attention back to him or herself and ask, "What is it like when you come face to face with your self? What is *your* value system, what are *your* goals, regardless of what your parents *or your peers* want you to be?" These are very, very difficult questions. How does one find one's own path? How does one become an explorer of one's own life?

We approach this stage of The Journey in a number of different ways. One way is to ask the youngster to look at his or her life as though it could be depicted on a map. We ask the youth to describe the path he or she has followed so far: What has he or she seen in life, what has life already shown, and what still lies ahead?

Now, some youngsters will take these questions quite literally and talk, for instance, about "when I lived in Cleveland and we moved to upstate New York . . ." and so on. But more often they use metaphors to describe their lives. I recall one such map, for example, made by a youth who drew a maze, a labyrinth. The boy called this stage of his life "The Garden Maze of Confusion" and he associated it with his experiences in middle school. He said that in middle school, all the students seemed to move around a lot but no one really got anywhere; everyone was lost. (". . . We all got stuck in there.") Above this labyrinth he drew a cliff, which he called the "Ledge of Insecurity." He explained that he needed to climb this ledge. He went on to talk about how insecure he felt, a topic which is usually embarrassing for kids. But because he used a metaphor that many of us can naturally relate to, it opened up a group discussion where we talked about the "ledges of insecurity" in our own lives. Such metaphors universalize these youngsters' experiences and show them that they are not alone.

I believe the single biggest problem with growing up in America today is that there are so few opportunities for youngsters to go on a quest for their own uniqueness. Time and again they have complained that "People don't want to be bothered with me; nobody is interested in helping me discover what is uniquely me. All they want is that I get good SAT scores or get into the right school or fit into this group or that group and behave as they want me to. But no one really wants to hear from me, to find out what is deep inside me."

In The Journey, we play improvisational games to help youngsters find their uniqueness. Improvisational games require spontaneity: you don't have time to reason at length how you ought to move next, but somehow you engage your inner talents to help you through each situation.

In early adolescence, the development of identity is easily confused with the creation of a persona, or social mask one can use as a front to the world. We need to get behind the masks, the personas of youngsters who feel they must always act "cool" or "tough." Improvisational games help with this, too. For example, we do some exercises where we move our facial muscles in some very silly-looking ways. When one has one's face screwed up into a ridiculous arrangement, it is just impossible to remain "cool"! Doing things like this makes it easier to take further risks: if you've already lost your persona, you may as well keep going along your path of self discovery.

We also have a mirror game: One girl or boy looks into the "mirror." The other girl or boy *is* the mirror. The job of the girl or boy who is the mirror is to "flush his or her own personality out of his or her feet" so that he or she is nothing more than a reflection of the person who is looking at him or her. The job of the person who is looking into the mirror is to move in such a way that the "mirror" can stay with him or her at all times. This game inevitably leads to much eye contact and it helps to establish the basis for interpersonal trust.

Some of the improvisational games are quite powerful. For example, we play a game called "How Angry Can You Get?" I think this is a very, very important exercise for adolescents especially, because anger is still a taboo emotion in our society. So we don't deal with it a lot, and we don't teach young people how to cope with it.

The game "How Angry Can You Get?" allows a person to modulate the intensity of anger that he or she expresses to another person. This is a "reversal" game, a typical improvisational strategy of exaggerating what we have been taught to suppress in order to break through the taboo and see it more clearly. Most of us spend little time "playing" with something as volatile as anger, but only by doing so can we begin to master this impulse. We find it instructive to videotape these episodes so the youngsters can review how they behave at different levels of anger with each other. Other youngsters observe the process, paying special attention to body language, tone of voice, and the different strategies kids use in order to win an argument. This can be a very powerful game and useful in many different settings.

PHASE THREE: IN THE HEART OF THE LABYRINTH

Phase three of The Journey is called "Entering the Labyrinth." This is traditionally the time of *ordeals* in ancient rites of passage. At a certain point in any rite of passage the initiate must endure certain ordeals to prove to him or herself and the community that he or she is worthy of moving on. One of the differences between growing up in modern America and cultures where rites of passage were or are practiced is that in the latter societies, adulthood is something you earn. It is never bestowed automatically—not because one turns twenty-one, or starts menstruating. One must earn adulthood because it signifies an important change in status, in identity and responsibility: when you attain adult status, you are no longer the same person. The ordeals prove you are worthy of the new status. You must face very difficult tasks and find your own way through them.

We don't give our youngsters enough opportunities to prove themselves—so they create their own rites of passage by pushing themselves in their own ways. Sexuality, drugs, alcohol consumption, and interpersonal violence have become all-too-frequently used arenas for the playing out of the need for ordeal. For instance, a drinking "game" now popular involves "beer bongs," where one shoves surgical tubing down one's throat, holds a funnel to one's mouth, and gulps down six to eight beers in a half hour. I'm convinced that this is a perversion of a rite of passage: These adolescents are trying to show they can now handle more life than they could in the past.

In ancient cultures it was necessary for youngsters to go out and prove they could hunt and track and snare animals and build their own shelters because doing these things showed they were self-sufficient. Self-sufficiency was needed for adulthood.

But that type of self-sufficiency is not often an issue for adults today: We do not necessarily need to show that we can kill and capture the animal in order to survive. Instead, many threats to our self-sufficiency today are internal. For instance, some youngsters become suicidal out of a fear of failure, or because they feel so insignificant as to be totally invisible to those around them.

In The Journey, when we ask youngsters what issues they need to face in their lives and how they propose to deal with them, we suggest that they begin finding their answers by exploring images that arise for them naturally.

One boy traveled on his Journey as a cat. He was what one might call "sneaky"—very feline—in reality as well. Although he had a very high IQ, he never made his own decisions; instead, he always tried to please other people.

Eventually he became involved in a Neo-Nazi organization where his "please others" attitude became dangerous.

This boy depicted his life situation at the time as a transitional place where he came up against several closed doors. His ordeal was to select the right door to pass through: Only he could make this choice, and he had to make it on the basis of his own reasons.

Hanging on the walls surrounding these doors were the pelts of many animals. He explained that these were animals who came to this transitional place but were unable to choose their own paths. His picture showed how important the boy considered this turning point in his life.

Another image adolescents often use to represent their entry into the adult world is downward movement. One must go "down and in" before one can come "up and out again" as a transformed human being. Parents often worry when their sons or daughters, who may have been vivacious and outgoing as children, suddenly become quiet and withdrawn. Such children often cloister themselves in their room immediately after school, not to emerge until supper time. Parents hastily conclude that the child is suffering a deep depression. Maybe the child *is* depressed—but on the other hand he or she may simply be "going down and in" in a quest to find new sources of energy or creativity.

One teenage girl drew a picture of herself as "Niambi the Exotic." In reality she was very much the opposite, an extremely quiet and introverted girl, not prone to conversation, who seemed to have little energy or enthusiasm for life. But her picture showed that she felt there was an exotic part deep inside her, her "Niambi" personality. She drew Niambi trapped inside a bottle; the problem was therefore to think of some way to get Niambi out of this bottle.

Metaphorical language like this is often useful in opening up group discussions, so we brought these images to the group in which the girl participated and asked for help in freeing Niambi from her bottled-up state. One young man in the group remembered how an audiotape company once made commercials in which a singer would hit a very high note and shatter a glass. He said, "Niambi, maybe you need to find your voice; maybe you need to sing your song in order to shatter the glass from the inside."

His remark made a strong impression on the girl, who said she would work at finding her voice. As the weeks went by we noticed that she was not as quiet as she had been.

One Friday she announced to the group, "I think you'll be surprised when I come back Monday morning," as the session ended. And indeed we were surprised: This quiet, shy little girl showed up on Monday with bright green, spiked hair and wearing the wildest clothes one could imagine. This was her way of telling us "I'm out!" (Incidentally, not too much later both of her parents showed up demanding, "We'd like to see David Oldfield!")

This example shows that growing up is not always a smooth process; youngsters rarely grow up gracefully. Yet we must give them the freedom to explore and experiment, and not hold them accountable for everything they do while they are in the process of smoothing out some of their ragged edges.

Wounding is often a part of traditional rites of passage. Today, youngsters often feel an *inner wounding*, typified in terms of imagery as, for instance, a bird whose wing has been broken or some other wounded animal. Adolescents often feel like wounded animals, and like them, are often dangerous to be around because they are scared. They act as if to say, "Don't come near me in this wounded state—I might lash out at you."

One of my favorite adolescent drawings takes a popular teenage phrase quite literally: youngsters often say that they "feel like shit," and their major task in life is to somehow discover how to stop feeling this way. In the picture in question, the boy's father is on his right. He has bug-eyes and is vomiting as he looks at a big pile of shit in the center and says, "That's not mine!" The mother is there too, and on the left are his peers in the form of big yellow noses. They are spitting on him. This picture clearly expresses the youngster's feelings of absolute and utter worthlessness.

When we work with a person's deep-seated images, we would be very much mistaken if we tried to make him or her change them. For example, it would be wrong to say to this boy, "You're not *really* a piece of shit, are you?"—and then suggest that he change to some other way of looking at himself. We have no right to do this because these images accurately express how the youngster feels at that moment, and we need to work with those feelings exactly as they are.

The particular young man who drew the picture mentioned above continued to work with his original images. As his story progressed, a forest fire wiped out his house and all the land surrounding it—a very good metaphor for the devastation that had taken place in his family life. And then something incredible happened: He was the only organic matter to survive the fire in the whole area, so he spread himself over the ground and became fertilizer! In his final drawing, new shoots of grass were growing up through him. Eventually with the guidance of his (very insightful) social worker, he was able to help his whole family grow into a new way of felating to one another.

We also deal with death in The Journey. In fact, the idea of death is central in my work. Death holds a central place in most rites of passage. It is still a fairly taboo subject in America and it is entirely neglected in our educational system. This is a very serious omission, especially since children today are so overexposed to unrealistic images of death in the media. In most movies and television programs, death is cast in very bizarre, fantastic terms. But our children are given no opportunities to learn about death as a meaningful part of real life. As a result, our children are at once terrified of death yet naively unmindful of the value of human life.

This phase of The Journey culminates in a symbolic experience of death. In ages past, nearly every rite of passage for adolescents included a similar symbolic experience. I don't think the elders subjected their children to these ordeals just to be morbid or to frighten them, but rather because they knew that their adolescent sons and daughters were undergoing a spiritual and an emotional death at this time. In order to give these experiences outward expression and to acknowledge just how momentous these changes were, therefore, they allowed their children to experience a ritual death and a subsequent rebirth to mark their passage into a wholly new and different stage of their lives. The symbolic experience of death made it clear to the adolescent that one phase of life was over, and another, radically different phase, filled with new demands and new understandings, was about to begin.

PHASE FOUR: THE WOOD BETWEEN THE WORLDS
In this part of The Journey, we focus on balancing the intensity of the inner experiences of the first three phases with an outward journey toward actively caring for and sharing in the world outside oneself. In this phase, we ask the youngsters to focus on the discoveries they made on their inner journeys that can now be translated into actions and contributions to the world. What they have learned on their inner journey must give meaning to the practical concerns of living, or all of their inner travels will have been in vain.

The wisdom of balancing inner experience with outward expression comes to us, once again, via ancient rites of passage. After dealing with the ordeals of passage into adulthood, the youth of ancient times would then distill from these experiences a "new vision" of life. This new vision was understood to be the way the deity or the universe revealed itself to each person individually—no two visions were alike. The youth was then charged to find the "natural expression" of this vision, the best way the vision could be made understandable to the community. Telling a story, writing a song, painting the vision on a shield, dancing the vision—these were the common ways to share the uniqueness of one's vision with others. Now the challenge is to bring this into life. A vision is a beginning.

PHASE FIVE: THE CEREMONY OF PASSAGE
In the final phase of The Journey we invite adolescents to shape a ceremony or celebration that honors the knowledge and insight they have acquired along the way.

Ceremonies are celebrations that stand outside of time's normal flow. They are occasions for stepping out of our routines and preoccupations so we may touch something essential in life. We seek ceremony when we feel that something powerful and profound is happening.

The "passage points" in life require something more from us than our normal ways of being offer. And so we dress differently, perhaps, or speak special words, in a voice different from that which we normally use. We change the atmosphere: the lighting, the sounds, the adornments—to create "a space apart." And we do things in ceremony that are consciously symbolic: tell symbolic stories, enact symbolic dramas, eat symbolic foods. Symbolism allows the depth of what we feel to shine through. Ceremony is a visible means for honoring that unseen world that we feel within.

But ceremony is never imposed from external sources. The structure and content of the ceremony should grow out of the shared experience of those who gather. A ceremony that does not arise from and speak to the experience of the adolescents who have made this journey is a dead ceremony, and a dead ceremony is far worse than no ceremony at all.

One of our groups gathered with their parents and guardians in a final ceremony of passage that included a unique "gift-exchange." Gathering all the participants into a circle, the youngsters explained that they had placed an invisible box in the center. One at a time, the teens approached the box and picked an imaginary gift from it. One of the girls, for example, reached into the box and pulled out a brick and a hammer, describing them in mime. She carried the brick to her parents and placed it at their feet. Then she whacked the brick with her hammer. It crumbled into sand, which she tossed over her shoulder, brushing her hands clean of the "brick wall" she had come up against—in her case, drugs—for good.

I have no doubt that as we learn more and more through our experiences with youngsters in the future, they will help us to develop The Journey and other programs like it into better, more useful, and more effective tools for coping with transitions at adolescence.

Traditionally, rites of passage initiated the young into the sacred heritage of their community, village, tribe, or clan. But just what is our modern community?—If anything, it is humankind, the all-encompassing global village *into which few of us have been initiated as yet!* In creating or helping to create truly modern rites of passage for our children, we thus have a marvelous, unparalleled opportunity to open up an ongoing dialogue among all our planet's ethnic and cultural voices.

It is probably impossible to describe the true spirit of a rite of passage in literal terms, but one Hawaiian boy expressed the matter very eloquently after sharing the symbolism of his mask with one of our recent groups: "This has been a journey deep within me, to a place where I am fully Hawaiian, and deeper still, to a place where I am a human being."

NOTES

1. Another great value we can learn from ancient rites of passage that focused on adolescence is the sense of *mutuality* that arises when one understands that the whole community is renewed when its young pass into adulthood. What I like most about borrowing from ancient rites of passage is that they usually invite participation by all of us—not just the immediate family, not just teachers or youth ministers, but the whole community—in helping our young people find themselves.

2. Margaret Mead, *Coming of Age in Samoa* (New York: William Morrow and Co., 1961).

3. Joseph Campbell, *The Hero with a Thousand Faces* (New York: Bollingen, 1949).

4. Each person's mask is made by a partner who works with the surgical gauze and plaster to completely cover the person's face. This is an incredibly intimate process, because the person making the mask has to work, for example, around the subject's nostrils and other facial features not normally touched by another except perhaps in sexual encounters. But the mask-making process is nonsexual. It is, in fact, a wonderful way to learn to touch another person without sexual innuendo.

NINETEEN

AFRICAN AMERICAN RITES OF PASSAGE TODAY

Artemus Taylor and Ronnie Wooten
Introduction by Nancy Geyer Christopher

INTRODUCTION

Contemporary rites of passage programs, over the last decade or so, are changing the way young people are moving into and through adolescence. Nowhere is this more true than in the African American community. During the 1980s and early 1990s, there has been a veritable explosion of programs based on Afrocentric culture, mythology, and ritual to link black youth to their African heritage and provide them with a sense of their own inestimable worth.

While not the cause of this movement, certainly a call to action took place at the 1982 annual meeting of the National Urban League. At this meeting, sociologist Bruce Hare released his youth development discussion paper entitled, *The Rites of Passage: A Black Perspective.* Dr. Hare drew national attention to the fact that public policy must increase life chances "by providing both rites and rights of passage." He reemphasized to the African American community the crisis of a generation of young black men. Dr. Hare, now with the Department of African American Studies at Syracuse University, posed this question: How can young people move into adulthood when the very definition of adulthood—the ability to care for oneself and for one's own, which is accomplished through employment—is denied them?[1]

When inadequate education impedes mental readiness for high-skill jobs, and when appropriate employment for uneducated workers has disappeared, a society is in trouble. Furthermore, when the traditional male roles of protector and provider are denied to large numbers of young men, we should not be surprised that self-destructive behavior takes over. Every healthy culture should provide its young people with adequate training for employment and opportunities to contribute to the community as they move into adult roles. U.S. society has denied both to a large segment of its youth and then wonders why we have a crisis.

The unemployment situation, quite obviously, cannot be solved without changes in the educational system. Education will not improve until serious racist conditions are healed. These problems, according to Hare, must be dealt with by the society at large and the African American community in particular.

In response to this and to other such calls, the African American community, during the 1980s and early 1990s, has been taking responsibility for the education of its own youth: by mobilizing its resources and setting up mentoring programs, by instituting Afrocentric education in both public and private schools, and by developing rites of passage projects. Churches around the country are incorporating rites of passage rituals as part of coming-of-age celebrations. For instance, the Union Temple Baptist Church in Washington, D.C. celebrates its culmination of manhood and womanhood training at the age of eighteen through *Orita,* which in Swahili means "crossroads" (*The Washington Post,* 17 February 1986).

"Building Black Men," a community program begun in 1981 at Trinity United Church of Christ in Chicago, stresses history, group activities, decision-making skills, and community service (*New York Times,* 4 May 1989).

The Hawk Federation, which stands for "High Achievement, Wisdom, and Knowledge," founded in 1986 in Sacramento by the Institute for the Advanced Study of Black Family and Culture, is an in-school program for ninth graders. Through the study of African culture and participation in enrichment activities, the program instills confidence, competence, and black consciousness (*New York Times,* 4 May 1989).

The Simba program in Oakland, California, founded in 1988, is an unusual blend of Afrocentric and New Age approaches. Intensely dedicated mentors who have completed sixty-six hours of training make a commitment to interact with their ten- and eleven-year-olds until they are eighteen. The boys—and since 1993, girls—and their mentors meet weekly at local community centers to work on nonviolent survival skills, self-discipline, and responsibility. What makes Simba in Oakland distinctive is the conviction that the solution is internal: changing the way people think about themselves. According to founder Roland Gilbert, when adult men and women take responsibility for the way they think, feel, and act towards themselves they will then be ready to mentor boys and girls and lead them toward maturity. Hence the critical importance placed on mentor training.[2]

A year-long rites-of-passage program is open to all the boys and girls of Simba. It usually takes place at the age of twelve. The process unfolds through twelve levels during which the youngster achieves a higher sense of self. He or she engages in external activities such as researching African and African American topics, attending religious services regularly, and doing community service. But the major emphasis is on internal activities—a self-analysis—by learning centering exercises and keeping a journal.

Even public school administrators, especially in the inner city, are realizing that something is needed to turn around the cycle of education failure and early, high drop-out rates among minority students. A hopeful trend is gaining momentum: bringing rites-of-passage programs to preadolescent youngsters in their public-school classrooms.

Two examples of such rites-of-passage projects in the public schools follow, one in Chicago and one in Washington, D.C.[3] They share many similarities: an emphasis on parent involvement, a recognition of the need for healing as well as for educating, a use of the symbolic power of African names, and initiating training before adolescence. But there are also some significant differences: While the Chicago program started with boys only, it has moved to a coed format, team-taught by men and women. The D.C. program has chosen to remain gender-specific: the girls are taught by women, the boys by men. While both share a concern with psychological healing, the Chicago program is culture based, the D.C. program explicitly therapeutic. The Chicago program uses voluntary enrollment; the interested students must meet certain criteria. The D.C. program works with the whole class. The Chicago program puts emphasis on learning African languages, the D.C. program on learning African principles. The Chicago program brings personal tasks into the classroom, such as instructions on hygiene and practical matters like folding underwear. The D.C. program takes the students into the community to open their eyes to neighborhood challenges and what they could do to help. Each program has its rationale for its approach. Both are finding better ways to lead our children through the passage to maturity.

RITES OF PASSAGE IN SOME CHICAGO PUBLIC SCHOOLS

Artemus Taylor has worked with youth for almost twenty-seven years. An active member of the Urban League for many years, he started a male-responsibility group in the Chicago Urban League. He conducts workshops and conferences for African Americans and legal groups as well as for the Illinois Department of Children and Family Services and the Centers for Disease Control. He is an experienced lecturer, trainer, program designer, and counselor and works with colleges, hospitals, churches, and other civic agencies. Some of his workshop, lecture, and conference topics include the following: The Media as Monarch: How the Media Shape Our Opinions of Blacks; To Be Popular *or* Smart: Black Peer Pressure; The Forgotten Half: Teen Fathers; Urban Turf: Gang Codes and Colors; Manhood Training; and Rites of Passage.

In the following adaptation of an informal interview conducted by Louise Mahdi and Nancy Christopher for this book, Mr. Taylor describes his work as director of A-MEN, the African Male Educational Network, which he founded in 1988.

The mission of A-MEN (a nonprofit organization) is to promote, encourage, and assist in the improvement of the social and economic conditions of African American men and women. To achieve this goal, A-MEN has become an advocate for the rights of young, minority men and women and has developed a culture-based curriculum. In addition, A-MEN is working to heighten public awareness of the obstacles to success facing young African Americans. A-MEN seeks to empower groups of individuals, community organizations, schools, churches, and hospitals to work for change. The group receives no federal or state funding.

To contact Mr. Taylor's organization, write to A-MEN, 9824 S. Western Avenue, Suite 175, Evergreen Park, IL 60643, or call (708)-720-0235.

SANKOFA: SYMBOL OF THE WISDOM IN LEARNING FROM THE PAST IN BUILDING FOR THE FUTURE

Proverb: It is not taboo to go back and retrieve if you forget.

GOOD INFORMATION!

There was a twelve-year-old boy in one of our programs who seemed to tyrannize the other students. We could see that somehow he was exerting a certain power within the group: For instance, whenever we would line up at the end of a session to go back to class, the others would save a space up front for him, and he would walk through the whole line to that privileged first place. He was obviously a leader.

One day, he sat at his desk and diagrammed accurately the whole social structure of our class. Once, when we were writing information on the blackboard, we turned around to find that everyone was already taking notes without being told. Naturally I wondered what they were all doing, so when I asked them, this same boy yelled, "We are taking notes, Brother Taylor. This is some good information!"

We thought it was interesting that the information we were sharing stimulated these young brothers to go to the library on their own and do research. We had tapped into something certain of these young men were already doing on their own: finding ways to gain information about their own heritage.

That incident made me realize that I had to go back and do some more studying myself, just to match this powerful energy of these kids. After we started the A-MEN program in the elementary schools in the Chicago area, we very soon discovered that we had to do a lot of studying and research just to become as knowledgeable about African history, for instance, as some of the leaders of the local gangs. Many of them actually knew more about African culture, African American history, politics, and economics, than the average college professor!

I am by no means glorifying gangs, but I don't think many people are aware of the fact that gang leaders are very intelligent. On their own, they get information from books, bibliographies, the media, and many other sources. And as you rise in status in a gang, you are expected to know more and more. You cannot be a dummy. I am not praising what they do but only stating the fact of the matter: We must acknowledge what is called their "sankofa," their "twin image." The twin image of bad is good. If they appear to be living out the bad side, "sankofa" means there is another side that contains something good. Sankofa is the symbol of the wisdom which is unafraid to go back and learn from the "good side," to build for the future.

A-MEN'S MISSION

"Deeds not words" is the A-MEN motto. Our mission is to help our young brothers—or as we call them, our Simbas (young lions)—get in touch with their sankofa.

The A-MEN program is offered primarily in the elementary schools in the Chicago area. As far as I know, A-MEN was the first organization to use rites of passage for boys and girls in the Chicago public schools. We think of rites of passage as processes that promote successful entry into a new life situation; rites of passage help youth grow into a new position or status, or grow out of an undesirable way of life or a disturbing life crisis.

Rites of passage programs are spreading. We have a group of eight men teaching in Milwaukee. They are creating programs similar to ours. We also have a group in Atlanta and in Biscoe, my hometown in North Carolina. But since we aren't able to be there often enough or long enough to work closely with them, they have developed much of their program by themselves.

Usually, schools contact us to begin a program for them, rather than vice-versa. Since we are certified by the Chicago Board of Education, most school principals are willing to give us the opportunity to work with their students. For example, a school might be having serious problems with their boys—and since we focus on working mainly with males, our program is attractive to these administrators. Every school has its own personality, so when we are invited to a school, we meet with the principal to discuss the details of our program and how we will design it to meet that particular school's specific needs.

Next, we usually meet with the teachers who will participate, as well as with the local school council. We like to begin early in the school term (early fall) so we can be with the children for the whole school year. We try to work with each group of students continuously, twice a week for at least four years. We find it necessary to use this longer time frame in order to see some actual changes in the children. It also allows us to evaluate our own progress, establish good working relationships with the teachers, and, most important, get to know the parents.

It is impossible to overstate the importance of parent participation! We urge parents to attend at least four workshops if they enroll their children in our rites-of-passage programs. We want all parents to be fully aware of what we are doing, because for both children and parents this will be something new, something different. Our parents know they can come any time to see exactly what we do in our work with their children.

While we have focused mainly on boys, we have begun to work with girls in the last two years. We now have an excellent group of well-qualified women on our staff. Most of our programs take place in a coed setting, girls and boys together in the same room. In the real world, girls and boys will not be by themselves, so we separate them only when it is time to discuss certain topics where the boys need to be alone with the men, and the girls need to talk with the women.

Another way we integrate the girls with the boys is through team teaching. In many schools, we will assign a man and woman teacher as partners working together. One advantage of this is that the students can then see healthy male-female relationships firsthand. And yet at the same time there is an adult man for the boys (Simbas) to emulate, while the young girls (Angels, we call them) can turn to the female teacher for specifically female questions and issues.

Our facilitators have all been trained in *Ntu* rites-of-passage work. *Ntu* is an African principle and philosophy that refers to the whole person and promotes a holistic view of life. (*Ntu* is also the name of our Chicago rites-of-passage group.)[1]

STRUCTURE OF THE PROGRAM

During the first years, beginning in the fourth grade, we meet for only twelve weeks with the children and schedule home visits with their parents, but we increase the time we spend with them as the program continues, so that by the eighth grade we work with them very intensely—two or three times a week in sessions that last two hours. It takes time to build their self-worth, which has not always been nurtured in traditional Eurocentric schools. Since we meet with the students during their regular school day, attendance is not only expected but required, once they sign up.

From beginning to end, we do all we can to ensure that each student will be an active participant. To give everyone ample opportunity to participate, we sit in a circle. This is the African way, the Circle of Life. In the circle no one feels left out; all are seen as equals. If a child refuses to participate on his own, we find ways to involve him.

An important logistical question we had to address is whether we wanted to offer our programs to all students, or to accept only those who met certain qualifications and were interested in participating. Although some schools ask us to work with the entire class of eighth-graders, for example, we find that such groups are usually too large. Also, when we work only with children who enroll on a voluntary basis, the whole group seems to interact much better. We eventually realized that whenever we included all students in a certain grade without exception, those who did not want to enter the program tended to cause a great deal of conflict.

THE SELECTION PROCESS

As we discovered our own limitations and developed more realistic expectations, we began to suggest limiting our enrollment. We asked the teachers, parents, and school councils to help in the selection process. Now we ask them to give us referrals so that we work only with kids who really want to be in our program and who therefore have a greater chance to benefit from it.

I should add that limiting enrollment in this way has certain beneficial side effects that seem to pay off in the long term. For instance, because the students who enroll are already motivated, their group will become more and more enthusiastic about what they are doing as they continue in our classes. They feel as though they have come into a new, special status. Word gets around quickly, and before you know it, more and more kids actually want to join us. So we get free advertising, in a sense, and in the long run we are able to reach more youngsters than if we had tried to require attendance. Our rites-of-passage groups acquire a certain reputation around the school, and the participants seem to stand head and shoulders above the rest. Both the program and the participants come to be seen as having a unique importance. Often this leads to a point where our main issue becomes not, "What right do you have taking me away from my regular classes in school?" but rather, "Why can't I be in your program too?"

This is why, as time went on, we found we had to develop some restrictions, standards, admission requirements, so to speak, just to keep the groups small enough for our staff to handle them effectively. For instance, if you are a young boy or girl who wants to enter our program, besides convincing your teachers and the group to write you recommendations, you must also make a commitment to meet certain challenges: You must turn in your homework consistently. You must strive for at least a C average, and you must meet it if your grade level has been below a C. You must refuse to be involved with gangs. You must also refuse to be involved with drugs. You must make a commitment to follow the instructions of the elders, willingly and without causing conflict in the group.

Naturally, for one reason or another, not all those who want to enroll are able to meet these requirements. And not all who enroll are able to maintain our scholastic standards. We try to enforce them as a general rule, but sometimes it does not seem reasonable to do so. For example, if a youngster has a D average but shows that he or she is putting forth a sincere effort, we acknowledge that they still have the potential. We keep them in the program and try to give the extra help they need.

In any particular school, by the time we do initiation ceremonies in the eighth grade, we've been at the school so long that everyone already knows about our requirements. They already know who has been in the program: who made it through and whose behavior was so impossibly disruptive that they were dismissed. The group makes the decision to dismiss a student if it becomes evident that he or she refuses to accept some of our fundamental moral or ethical principles. One of our most basic principles is that we will accept one another and learn to appreciate what each person brings to the group: "I am my brother's keeper."

We want to create strong, healthy relationships that build a sense of community, belonging, and trust. So when a student demonstrates that he or she is not willing to join us in this way, that he or she will only weaken the group, the group makes the decision to let that student go.

GENERAL PRINCIPLES

We base the structure of our program on some general principles about human development. For example, we like to begin when the children are in the fourth grade or earlier.

At the fourth grade or pubescent stage, the main questions these kids need to work out revolve around their sense of self. In the fifth grade, they start to work on history: both African and African-American history.

BONDING

One of the benefits of our program is that it seems to generate strong bonds among the students. Those who participate break down the tyranny of gang turf. We set up a "brother/sister system" and give life to the spirit of "I am my brother's keeper."

For instance, we pair everyone up with a "brother/sister." We have them exchange phone numbers and learn about one another. It's remarkable that so often people can live in the same community for years, and yet not know a thing about their neighbors. So when we pair up the boys—our young Simbas—we give them get-acquainted assignments. They learn about each others' families, how many brothers and sisters each one has, what their favorite colors are, and other personal details that make another person interesting.

Another aspect of this brother/sister system is that we strongly encourage students to help each other in whatever appropriate ways they can. For instance, studying together—not copying homework assignments, of course—but peer-tutoring. In turn, the teachers make sure each child can demonstrate in class what he or she has learned.

TEACHERS AS FACILITATORS

We are not "traditional" educators; rather, we think of ourselves as "facilitators." We make sure there is never a situation where a student who needs help with something is passed over with no one to help him or her. We also make sure that they have the right information; for instance, we teach them how to take and keep notes. For those who have trouble taking accurate notes in class, we write the most important information on the board so everyone can be confident that they have accurate information.

Through the years we have also discovered that African American children learn more by seeing and touching and listening. This is why we use music in our teaching. For instance, we listen to taped music—rap as well as other kinds—and learn to evaluate its message. We've discovered that nonverbal methods often prove more effective than traditional classroom formats.

SIXTY SIMBAS

In spite of our efforts to use caution in selecting participants, we have encountered our share of disruptive challenges! For instance, a certain school invited us to come in and work with sixty of their most recalcitrant students—behavior-problem students, you might say. But to our surprise, we managed to gain their attention and eventually they became captivated by what they were learning. When we began to talk about African culture or about African American history, for example, you could just feel a hush descend over the classroom. I think one of the reasons we were able to get through to these youngsters is because the issues we deal with are of real, immediate concern to them, to their own identity.

They changed some of their habits outside of school as well. We taught them simple things at the beginning, for example, about cleaning up their room at home; or we would have them bring their underwear to class and learn to fold it, along with their socks and T-shirts. We taught personal hygiene at a very basic level. And they went home and they emulated what they did in the classroom.

Our experience with these sixty boys helped us to transform and improve our own program in many ways. But at the same time, we were able to assist in their personal transformation as well. There were some who had behavior problems, and some had learning disabilities, but our staff at A-MEN helped turn their behavior around. In those days we did not have the "evaluation tools" nor the "controlled environment" that many professionals might think necessary.[2]

But we did find that most of these students wanted to do the right thing. In fact, ten of them consistently made the honor roll, and of these, four received special scholarships to a very fine private high school in the city. And one of these four was chosen Freshman of the Year at that high school—a youngster who had been labeled as having a behavior problem and who, in the sixth grade, had been in and out of the principal's office regularly for misbehaving.

Another young Simba in that group won first place at the science fair for the district, and the fair was scheduled for the same day as our own initiation ceremony. He had been in our program with the same group of students for three years, and he refused to miss the ceremony. His parents asked me if I had persuaded him to come to our ceremony at the expense of missing the science fair. Actually, I had advised this young Simba to go to the fair, but he felt the ceremony was more important, and his parents agreed.

This was one of our first ceremonies together, a special moment not only for our organization and staff but also for the school, the kids, the parents, and the community. From that time on, we never had to worry about attracting the kids. Quite the reverse, we had so many who wanted to participate that we couldn't accept them all.

GANGS

You are probably aware that most of the communities we serve have serious problems with gangs. As we continued to learn and refine our programs and our methods, we came to a rather profound realization: The gangs were already doing many of the things we found most effective in our own work! The gangs were talking about African history. The gangs were communicating through symbols. By the way, the first written language the world knew was symbols. So we decided to utilize many of the same concepts that made gang membership attractive: concepts like family unity and nationalism, discipline, order, and responsibility. But, of course, we applied them in positive ways.

Did you know that the gangs do a lot of recruiting from fourth and fifth grade? From the perspective of these youngsters, everything—the whole world—revolves around the self. The energy of Self makes them feel they can conquer the world. For example, my own son is ten years old. When I come home after a day's work, he always wants to tell me how strong he is: "Daddy, see how strong I'm becoming." So my "home program" for him as his father is to help him to deal with self, to deal with his body, to help him put all that energy he has into perspective. So far, his mother and I have been able to bring a healthy balance to his understanding of himself.

We always discuss the pros and cons of gangs in our rites-of-passage program. Unfortunately, the gangs often are the only male figures in our children's lives.

THE ELDERS

In our work we emphasize the importance of parents and "the village" and "the elders." Very young children need bonding with both a female/mother and a male/father, and at a very young age they must learn respect for the elders. Too many of our families have no adult men, with the mother as the only parent; so the young boys automatically turn to other older males for their definition of manhood. For instance, the gang leaders impose discipline and order, essential in all young boys' lives.

That does not mean that a single mother cannot raise or educate her son. But a single mother should never have to do this alone: Whether she can get help from her father, uncle, brother, or cousin, we need some positive men in our boys' lives. If a mother does not choose a man to guide her son and to be a role model for him, he will choose one himself. Often the only place they can find men in the neighborhood is on the street, in the gangs. In those cases, the gangs give them their definition of manhood.

How can a boy become a man if he has never seen a man? How can a teenager be a good father if he has no one to relate to as his own father? Boys make babies, but men take care of them.

We try to supply an alternative for the Simbas in our village, to establish a balance between the masculine and feminine influences in their lives. To compensate as much as possible for the lack of fathers at home, our program gives the kids a chance to be with responsible, "tribal" fathers on a regular basis.

AFROCENTRISM AS A RESPONSE TO RACISM
We utilize the African *Fante* principle and philosophy of life.[3] I would like to clarify how our program came to have an Afrocentric focus.

As you know, contemporary American society is Eurocentric. Because of this, our black youth feel they do not fit into American culture in many ways. As their mentors and teachers, we try, therefore, to accentuate the African values that will strengthen our Simbas'/Angels' self-identity to help them survive in contemporary America.

Seven or eight years ago the school programs brought into the community were mainly Eurocentric. These programs were successful in communities whose people were of European descent, but in our communities they never worked because our sojourn in America was different. Eventually we began introducing Afrocentric elements, inspired by Dr. Anthony Mensah's work at the University of Wisconsin (Milwaukee),[4] and the Simbas took interest immediately. We had youngsters coming out of the woodwork to enroll in our rites-of-passage programs. From that time on, we have developed this Afrocentric focus.

We try to deal with problems of racism throughout the program. As we see it, racism is the biggest hindrance to the healthy development of our children and the greatest form of violence in this country. We define racism as any instance where people of one ethnic group deliberately and systematically treat another ethnic group as inferior. Racists in this country foster the idea that blacks are child-like, dependent, and incapable of doing things for themselves, as though they always needed the guidance of white people. This racist attitude led to such widespread oppression of African American people that they had to develop self-help strategies for sheer survival and development.

We try to instill confidence in our young Simbas and Angels—confidence in knowing that they come into the world with certain qualities that make them unique, and that can tie in with the African experience. Some of the traditional Ghanian ways of expressing character through one's name give us an interesting way to convey this sense of uniqueness or individuality. For instance, if you are born on a Sunday, you are talented and creative. If you are born on a Saturday, you are a preserver of the past.

Another ancient Ghanian value that goes back thousands of years is the idea that everyone is "birthed into the world with a purpose." For example, my name is Kweku. That means that I am a messenger. I think of myself as being born into this world for that particular reason. In our activities with the children, we try to reinforce ancient African cultural values such as these. For instance, *sankofa,* or "twin image," which I mentioned earlier. Another meaning of *sankofa* is "don't be afraid to go back and fetch what has been lost."

As our programs at A-MEN continue to evolve, and as we continue to learn what works best, we have begun to hope—with some degree of confidence based on our results—that A-MEN offers a process that can truly qualify as a constructive rite of passage for our fine young Simbas and Angels.

RITES OF PASSAGE IN SOME WASHINGTON, D.C. SCHOOLS

Ronnie Wooten has worked with young people for over three decades but, for the past six years, through the Progressive Life Center in Baltimore and Washington, D.C. Progressive Life is an agency which takes a holistic approach to mental health by working with the whole family, dealing with the full life cycle, and encompassing all ages. Established in 1983, the Progressive Life Center is a private nonprofit human-services firm that provides therapeutic services as well as staff-development training. Using humanistic and Afrocentric models of intervention, the Center draws on principles of balance, harmony, and interconnectedness to help develop satisfying and healthy human relationships, particularly within a family context.

The Center is staffed by clinical social workers, family therapists, licensed psychologists, and medical consultants. Therapeutic retreats play an important role in programs for groups and families, and in the Rites of Passage programs for adolescents. An equally important program is focused on preadolescents in Washington, D.C. classrooms. In the following article, based on an interview with Nancy Geyer Christopher, Ronnie Wooten describes the various Rites of Passage programs run by the Progressive Life Center.

To contact the Progressive Life Center, call or write 1123 11th St., NW, Washington, DC 20001, (202) 842-4570, or 100 E. 23rd St., Baltimore, MD 21218, (410) 235-2800, and ask for the *Rites of Passage Manual.*

HESHEMA: THE PRINCIPLE OF RESPECT

How did I get into working with rites of passage? I read Kwanza Jawanza Kunjufu's books. That's probably what enlightened me. It's not a new concept. I think people are trying to find out what's going to work for their kids. The way things are going now in society—the way we rear our children—it's different from the way it was traditionally for us. I think people are realizing now that grandma's ways are better than those of the people on Oprah. I think that people are waking up . . . it's like a reawakening . . . it's happening all over the country. Rites of passage is not a new concept. All cultures had their own rites of passage.

I think of the case of the Indians where the boys were sent off to an island [each alone for a year] as a punishment for their crime. [The Seattle case in 1993 involved two Native American adolescents who mugged a pizza-delivery man.] You see, that's part of their tradition. They know what works for their people. I have always appreciated things that work for people as a group.

The Progressive Life Center leases the space from the AME Church (Washington, D.C.), but we are a totally separate entity. Progressive Life is a mental health agency. All of our work has to do with healing. Our Rites of Passage programs are therapeutic—which is different from a lot of other pro-grams—because this is a mental health agency, a healing program.

The Rites of Passage programs deal with various ages: with latency-age youth in the D.C. public school system—that's usually fifth and sixth graders, ten to twelve years old. We go into one particular school, Smothers Elemen-tary School, over in Northeast, which has been very receptive. This is our fourth year there. At the time we started working with Smothers that wasn't part of my assignment, but my understanding was that the administration was open to the idea of a Rites of Passage program. I now coordinate the effort for the fifth grade. The sixth grade is a continuation of the fifth-grade program. The sixth grade—the same group that was with us as fifth graders—gets the Afrocentric education (African history, arts, and culture) along with the drug-prevention unit.

In the Smothers program the administration controls the selection of stu-dents. They give us a fifth-grade class and everybody in the class is part of the program. Our Rites program is set up for one day a week right after school for ninety minutes to two hours. We may have a cultural outing during the week—so some weeks it may be two meetings a week.

All of the programs, fifth grade through adolescence, have cultural out-ings. We may go to the Blacks in Wax Museum, the Frederick Douglass House, and other museums, but socialization is also a part of our emphasis. We go out to eat, especially to ethnic restaurants. In addition, we go skating, swimming, horseback riding, on nature walks, anything where our kids inter-act with other young people.

We also have a middle-school project at Turning Points at Douglas Junior High School. Turning Points is the name of Sharon Pratt Kelly's [for-mer D.C. mayor, 1990–1994] program at Douglas. [The program was cut along with the D.C. budget.]

Our middle-school project is under a CSAP grant—Committee on Sub-stance Abuse Program. I'm coordinator of the Rites of Passage program under that grant. Our substance abuse program is based on Afrocentric educa-tion and the African values system. We go into the classroom at 11:00 during the day. Even though the drug program is separate from Rites of Passage, we manage to combine the two so they complement each other.

Everybody in our Rites of Passage programs gets the values system; all of our groups have basically the same theme. We try to instill a new value system by using the seven African principles—[Umoja = unity, Kujichagulia = self-determination, Ujima = collective work & responsibility, Ujamaa = cooperative economics, Nia = purpose, Kuumba = creativity, Imani = faith]— but we've added an eighth principle, Heshema, the principle of respect.[1] We put together a whole curriculum to teach the principles. Using modules for each session, we teach the youngsters how to use the principles in everyday life.

But the junior-high level is more intense than that for the younger people. Seventh and eighth graders are mature enough to be able to handle more. We meet with them the same amount of time: ninety minutes a week. They may have more outings. They may have more community-based pieces as part of their requirements for their graduation. We do a community-awareness piece where we take them out into the community and they are quizzed: What do you see? What's happening? What needs to be changed about what's happening? Where do you fit in? What do you need to change?

We also deal with another age group—of fourteen- to eighteen-year-olds—in our adolescent Rites of Passage. This program is court-based not school-based. We work with different projects throughout D.C., Baltimore, and Prince George's County [D.C. suburban area]. These youngsters are court adjudicated. They come in through some kind of program where they're deemed out of control. They come to us from the courts because they need therapy. The nature of our package is holistic: we deal with the family, community, and child. Every aspect of their lives should be covered. We deal with ten to fifteen youth at a time in a group.

The high-school kids are not the ones who have been in the elementary- and junior-high programs. Hopefully, we've done a good enough job at the elementary level that they won't become court adjudicated. I haven't yet seen one of our kids from the lower level come back to us through the court. That's a good sign. We get referrals from the court. These programs are done here. We have a Substance Abuse program. We have a Foster Care program. We have a Gateway Group Home program.

All programs are designed to fit the needs of the young participants. The curriculum is similar, but there are modifications to fit the specific issues related to the life circumstances, for instance, foster care or group housing. The Foster Care program runs a Rites program here at the Progressive Life Center. We use the basement facility here. But we've used churches all over D.C. and other recreational centers. We do not run the group home but rather we run the clinical piece, including the Rites of Passage. We have a contract with the Gateway Group Home for service.

So they all have their own separate Rites package. The adolescents are screened by us. We need to know who's group-ready. Who's going to be able to handle the material? How should we cluster them? But everybody's eligible that's referred by the court.

We have a parenting program aimed at the parents of all the youth in Rites of Passage which is part of our complete package. I think all families in America could use a little help, some families, a lot of help. But as part of the Rites program itself, parents are asked to be participants on certain levels. At the present time teenage parenting is not a formal part of the program although we do deal with it as needed. But I would like to see it expanded.

We have an orientation for the parents, and presentations in the schools, and I'm always available for questions and answers. We find we have more success with oral presentations than with letters or even handouts. When people are allowed to ask questions and respond to ideas, they seem to take a better piece of it home with them. We let them know what we do firsthand; we do rituals with them. During the course of a program we meet with them maybe half-a-dozen times.

THE RITUALS

Our program begins with what we call *Rites of Separation.* The parents bring their young people to us and hand them over to us for our care—much like in the tribal culture where the elders are entrusted with the care of the growing children. All parents are encouraged to participate in that.

Rites of Separation takes place with a ceremony at the school. The parents present their children to the leaders of the program. All of the community who are present witness the event and give their affirmation. The parents are then seated and we [the leaders] are left with the young people. The youngsters are then taken to another room and receive the instructions of the leaders. There is a lot of symbolism. Then we all come back together and celebrate. Other programs we do, we've used churches, rec centers, police-sponsored boys' and girls' clubs for various ceremonies, because it gives us a chance to give to the community, to let them see, to let them experience part of this. We find that an important part of this is to connect the community and the family with the young person.

Next comes a *Naming Ceremony.* We ask for input in the naming. The parents identify positive traits in their children or qualities they would like to see their young people move toward. We formally hook it up with an African name. Each individual knows and has the feeling that he has been individually named and not just given a name from a hat. It's a name that has individual meaning. Everything we do we try to connect to everything else. In the beginning we were using only Swahili names from East Africa. But that had to change because if we had two or three with the same traits, we didn't want to give them all the same name in the group. So I explored different naming books. I talked to a couple of priests who do naming to check whether or not that was okay to do. They said it was fine, that whatever African names we wanted to use that would be fine.

The *Naming Ceremony* occurs during the first half of the year, depending on how the program is set up. We do that so the kids can familiarize themselves with the name by using it. The second half of the year, they'll be using that name as opposed to their birth name. Many people, both young and older, are not familiar with the sound of African names and the meaning. Sometimes kids will laugh at them. But once they get used to it, it becomes a matter of pride. In fact we had a *Naming Ceremony* for the adolescents last night. We celebrated at a Senegalese restaurant with parents and guests. There was drumming. It was fantastic.

At the end of the year we have a *Transformation Ceremony*. The idea we emphasize is moving to another level of life—not completing something, as is implied in graduation. Graduation usually means the end. We want to take you on. We have you for the fifth grade; we want to take you to the sixth. The *Transformation Ceremony* happens at the end of each year. It's very elaborate and ceremonious. There's a big feast at the end. Everybody's invited, from parents to friends, anybody in the community that wants to come or is involved in the young person's life. The door is open to everybody. We as an agency provide the main course and ask people to participate on the level that they can, as far as desserts or things like that. We find that that makes them feel a part. Ceremonies like this have been done at churches or boys' and girls' clubs. We're fortunate that when we do a Rites program here [AME Church, Washington, D.C.] that we can use the facilities here.

All during the program itself we have different intervals where we have family projects, such as a dinner. We also have an elderly unit where we adopt an elder in the community and go over and possibly paint his house—anything he or she cannot do for themselves. This kind of experience makes our young people think about their own existence in the community. It also gives them hope that some things can be changed. Things can be done. We all have to be a part of the process.

All of the young people are required to keep a journal in the Rites of Passage program. We use handouts during our sessions to help them reflect on their personal feelings about their experiences. I review all the journals, but the kids keep their journals.

For all age levels, we have both male and female groups. All groups are gender specific. We have women leaders working with the girls and male leaders with the boys. That's also related to the tribal traditions.

We do in-house training. Since I'm the coordinator, I'm responsible for preparing the facilitators, assessing their level of knowledge, and selecting appropriate material. I monitor and set up all material used in the program.

We have ongoing training: two hours every morning. In addition, we have clinical training every Thursday. Certification is required, but everything else is ongoing. We are adamant about our staff being well trained. Not only are they trained in Rites, but they must take the introduction to psychotherapy. It's a must for anybody who works here.

All of our Rites programs are therapeutic, even those in the schools. We find it works better because you've got to meet these young people where they are. If you don't do that then you don't capture them. Most young people today . . . there's some sort of dysfunction in their lives, if not in their homes, then in their communities. You have to correct the problems and still give them the cultural base for their self-esteem building. But we must always move forward.

Most of the national programs aren't therapeutic programs. They're culture based, which is fine. I'm in alliance with the national program of the Rites of Passage. I attend their conferences and have presented at different times. Although we are not a part of it, we are in complete support of it.

We're in the process of setting up some kind of evaluation system. In the past we've had a lot of our material duplicated before it was completed and tested, so we're real careful about that now. When people try to run away with things before they have the complete information, it takes away from the credibility of the whole thing. If it's done improperly, then people say, "Well, that doesn't work."

I have just completed a *Rites of Passage Manual* that should be out very soon. It's in the final editing stages now. That will provide our framework for all our Rites groups across the board, but the curriculum in the manual is geared specifically for adolescents. I'm a person who believes that all that's done in Rites should be shared with communities and other Rites groups.

NOTES TO INTRODUCTION

1. Bruce Hare's original monograph was updated and published as "Black Youth at Risk" in *The State of Black America 1988* (New York: National Urban League, Inc., 1988), pp. 81–93.

2. "Training Mentors for African-American Teens," *Crossroads,* A National Weekly Radio Newsmagazine, National Public Radio, 22 April 1994. See also Roland Gilbert and Cheo Tyehimba-Taylor, *The Ghetto Solution* (Waco, Texas: WRS Publishing, 1994), the story of the founding and philosophy of Simba by Gilbert, who conceived the idea.

3. The D.C. program was cut in 1995, several months after the interview, because of the financial crisis faced by the district.

NOTES TO "SANKOFA"

1. *Ntu* is the cosmic universal force that never occurs apart from its manifestations. It was picked by a group of forty-seven social workers and police officers at Chicago Police Precinct no. 15 who went through the rites, to identify it and distinguish that process from all other types of rites or initiation processes going on in the continental USA. With the help of Wright College, one of the city colleges of Chicago, they went through the course, which was taught by Dr. Anthony Mensah, a Ghanian, with the assistance of Mr. Reuben Harpole, the Senior Outreach specialist from the University of Wisconsin, Milwaukee. As a result, several who participated in this course became full-time rites-of-passage facilitators.

2. We conducted our own survey with the parents and also the teachers. Before the program started, we asked parents, teacher, and child to write down what behaviors they thought should change, or wanted to change, in the child. After the first year, we asked about this behavior and found that all of the kids' behavior changed—not only in the classroom but also at home. The parents would begin to notice, and then they would call the school, asking what this program was, and who the people were who were presenting this program at the school.

3. This principle deals with the African philosophy of existence and includes these beliefs: we are all one people; to be human is to belong to the community; we are all children of God; we are one with nature; all the people are born to succeed; no one is born to be left behind. More information about the principles we promote and the philosophy we use in our training can be found in our manual, *Rites of Passage and Initiation Processes with Akan Culture,* compiled by Dr. Anthony Mensah. For further details, please contact A-MEN.

4. I wish to acknowledge Dr. Anthony Mensah as the tribal elder who introduced Rites of Passage to us and as the man who is guiding me on the spiritual path to becoming the man that I am yet to be. Dr. Mensah is a professor in the departments of Africology and of Education Policy and Community Studies at the University of Wisconsin, Milwaukee.

NOTES TO "HESHEMA"

1. Roland Gilbert discusses in *The Ghetto Solution* (Waco, Texas: WRS Publishing, 1994), p. 100, the "Seven principles of Blackness," or *Nguzo Saba,* developed by Dr. Maulana Karenga.

TWENTY

THE "SENIOR PASSAGE" COURSE

Shelley Kessler

Called by Daniel Goleman in the *New York Times* a "leader in a
new movement for emotional literacy," Shelley Kessler currently
directs the Institute for Social and Emotional Learning. She provides workshops for educators and consults to schools around the
country to develop curricula for strengthening emotional and
social capacities, as well as rites-of-passage programs. As first
chair of the Department of Human Development at Crossroads
School in Santa Monica, California, Kessler led a team in pioneering one of the first curricula to integrate emotional, social, and
spiritual capacities with academic learning. Author/editor of *The
Mysteries Sourcebook* and producer of *Honoring Young Voices*,
Kessler is an active member of CASEL—the Collaborative for the
Advancement of Social and Emotional Learning, based at the Yale
Child Study Center.

Kessler also leads workshops with her husband, Mark Ger-
zon, on gender issues and on initiation into the midlife quest. They
are writing a book on the stages of long-term intimacy—*Man,
Woman, Earth: Reclaiming Spirit and Wildness in Intimate Relationship* (San Francisco: Harper.)

What am I going to do with my life?
Why do I let people step over me?
Who am I?
Will I get AIDS?
Will I marry?
Will I live long?
Will I be successful in life?
Why do I hate people so easily?
Why do I get so angry?
What do others think of me?
Why do my parents fight so much?
Why do I use drugs?
Am I as destructive as they say I am?
Will a bullet come in my window and kill me?
Will I ever find someone to love?
Do I believe in anything?
What is my purpose in life?
Am I "normal"?
Why do I worry?
Am I really the future?
Why are some people so mean?

Why do people hate others?
Will blacks and whites make peace?
Why do people suspect our generation?
Why do people hurt those who love them so much?
Why are people so friendly when you are doing well, and forget you in the
bad moments?
Why is it so hard for people to forgive?
Is racism ever going to end?
Is the killing going to stop?
When will kids stop shooting kids?
When will kids stop having babies?
Where did life really start?
What is God? Man or Woman?
Is being dead better than living?
Is the government responsible for AIDS?
Will they find a cure before my aunt dies?
What is there after death?
Is there a God?
Will there ever be peace?

These are some of the questions written by a group of high-school seniors at
University Heights High School in the Bronx in the fall of 1994 when they
were asked to write anonymously their personal "mysteries" about themselves. Capturing their wonder, worry, curiosity, fear, and excitement at this
moment in their lives, these questions are central to the curriculum of the
Senior Passage Course, which I first brought to this school in 1992.

Plagued by the usual, nationwide problem of "senioritis," this alternative
public high school was also struggling with another problem. Students at
University Heights knew they had found a sanctuary and they didn't want to
leave. Nurtured by a community of dedicated teachers committed to progressive education, students felt cared for and safe—sometimes for the first time.
At precisely the time they were being encouraged to take flight, some would
sabotage their own success. Attendance would fall dramatically, quality of
work would falter, and completion would become impossible for many students.

I learned of this problem from two faculty members who attended an
introductory "Mysteries"[1] workshop I had facilitated with my colleague
Zackery Terry for thirty teachers and administrators from the New York City
system of public alternative high schools. I was impressed with the remarkable opennessnes of these two teachers—Marion Fuller and Judy Wechsler;
they exemplified everything I had heard about University Heights. Viewed as
a model of alternative education by fellow educators in both the local New
York system of public alternative high schools and the national Coalition of

Essential Schools, this urban high school is known for the adventuresome spirit of a faculty committed to making whatever changes are necessary to serve the needs of their students.

These two teachers were immediately enthusiastic when I told them about "the Senior Passage Course"—a curriculum designed to guide students through this vulnerable transition so they could discover the inner strength and peer support that would make it possible to step courageously into the adult world. In the 1980s and early 1990s, I had been part of a team of educators at the Crossroads School in Santa Monica, California who developed the core curriculum for this course designed to be a "rite of passage" from adolescence to adulthood. Over the previous decade, a thousand students had completed this course. Seniors and parents loved it immediately. Based on this response, administrators decided to implement an entire human development curriculum for grades seven through twelve based on a model of the senior course. Faculty were skeptical at first but soon gained respect for the program as they witnessed the new quality of leadership and personal character that the seniors brought into the school.

In 1991, I left my position at Crossroads determined to make the tools and philosophy of this unique program available to a broader audience of American students and educators. The retreat in New York was one of my first opportunities to share this approach with educators in the public schools. After Marion attended the training and heard about the Senior Passage Course, she invited us to a meeting of the decision-making body of the school. Coming from a private school in California with a program explicitly naming its spiritual dimension, Zackery and I were filled with trepidation as we approached University Heights. After all, Marion and Judy trusted our work from the weekend retreat. But these other educators—what would they think of our offer to partner with them in piloting a senior passage course? We were startled when they said they wanted the course and they wanted it immediately. And they would not consider piloting it with a small group of seniors—after hearing about the curriculum, this faculty wanted training and curriculum assistance as soon as possible so that all of their seniors could have this opportunity.

But would this course work for teachers and students in the inner city? Could the curriculum and methodology be adapted to meet the needs of a public school? Unlike the primarily affluent student body of Crossroads, the seniors at this Bronx high school are, according to the magazine of the Coalition of Essential Schools, "near-dropouts, chronic truants, and classic underachievers who did poorly at other high schools, both public and private. . . . On their way to University Heights, by train and bus and on foot, they pass nodding addicts and spaced-out crackheads. Each day they run a gauntlet of their less-motivated peers, who lounge on street corners and call to them to skip school, hang out, and have some fun."[2]

By the spring of 1995, as the third year of Senior Passage drew to a close, founding principal Nancy Mohr and team leaders throughout the school looked at their seniors with such satisfaction and pride that they decided to implement "Passages" courses throughout the school. "They were such a team," says Risa Marlen, M.S.W., of the seniors. (Marlen now coordinates the Passages Program that is being extended to meet the needs of students in grades seven through twelve.) "Our seniors had never had such a spirit of mutual support and empowerment. And the self-sabotaging had stopped. We just weren't seeing it anymore. Having a place and a formal way to work through the emotional challenges they were all facing allowed them to focus on their work. They were determined to graduate and they had the confidence and concentration to do so."

Already in the second year, teachers were seeing results. "They want to work for us in a way I've never seen before," said English teacher Marion Fuller, who team-taught her senior passage section with Francisco Garcia-Quesada and Michelle Disilvo. "They believe us now when we say the academic work is for their own good. We've listened to what is in their hearts. They have felt our compassion for the larger issues in their lives. So they know that when we are doing academics together, we can also be trusted as guides."

For Francisco, the methodology of this course was so compelling that he decided immediately to adapt the course for a church youth group he led in his own Hispanic community in a small town outside the city. "The spiritual quality of the exercises makes this curriculum so natural for my community," Francisco says, still amazed at his discovery. Before he took over a hundred students on a retreat designed to be a rite of passage, he insisted that parents agree to come to a ceremony honoring the students upon return. "The church had never been so full as we were that day. There were people sitting in the aisles, leaning against the walls. And the students were so proud."

To understand why high-school seniors so urgently need this kind of support and why the Senior Passage Course is effective, I will describe the needs this class addresses and some of the most important dimensions of this curriculum.

THE NEED

Throughout this volume, authors have called us to recognize the importance of "rites of passage" for the health, wholeness, and safety of our youth and our communities. In working with teenagers over the last twenty years, I have seen that in this culture, teenagers experience not one but several "passages":

1) the major transformation at puberty when they are awakened from childhood into adolescence,

2) a challenging transition as they enter high school, and

3) the "senior passage"—when students step over the threshold into adulthood.

Without appropriate support, this last stage can be one of the most fragile moments in the life cycle. Guided and validated by caring and creative adults through this passageway from adolescence to adulthood, young people blossom with character, compassion, and the capacity to make decisions that serve their own growth and the health of the community.

The senior year of high school is a time of enormous transition—not only for the student, but also for family and faculty. As students prepare to move into college or the world at large, they must cope with the pressure of crucial decisions at a time when their identity is just beginning to form. For students who have felt cared for, they are anticipating the emotional shock of leaving behind nurturing relationships at every level—parents, siblings, teachers, or friends. For those who have missed this sense of connection and support during their childhood, there is an urgent need to establish some real experience of belonging before they will be willing to let go of their childhood. On the threshold of the unknown, seniors must say good-bye not only to relationships with others; they are challenged with letting go of a childhood self and an adolescent identity that will no longer serve them in the adult life that awaits them.

Anxiety is normal for the high-school senior. Mood swings are common among both the student and parents who are also feeling the shock of letting go. Family relationships may become volatile at this time—familiar patterns between parent and child often change and even reverse, bringing much confusion in their wake. Even the most disciplined students may lose their capacity for focus at this time—there is no faculty unfamiliar with the hazards of "senioritis" to both the quality of learning and the once harmonious climate between student and teacher.

While seniors are facing these losses, there is also an exciting awakening occurring at this stage of development. Students begin to glimpse the possibility of larger purpose and deeper meaning in their lives and in life itself. They begin to ask, and have insight about, the larger questions of existence and human relations. They begin to have the acuity of mind of the adult while still bubbling with the vitality, playfulness, and humor of the child. Given the opportunity to explore these depths with adult guidance and peer wisdom, high school seniors gain access to strengths of character that help them meet with grace the challenges described above.

The Senior Passage Course is designed to guide students through the turbulent waters of this major transition. The class provides a structure in which to address their deepest yearning and concerns that arise at this time, allowing students to see the commonality and normality of these issues. The curriculum guides them to recognize and honor the change that is taking place.

Students prepare consciously for the impending losses and learn some tools for healing the grief from previous losses that are often activated by this letting-go stage in their development. They learn skills for coping with stress and for making decisions that can minimize the stress in their lives. The social and emotional skills that can be gained through this class provide a foundation for creating satisfying relationships in the new environments they will enter upon graduation.

OVERALL STRUCTURE OF THE SENIOR PASSAGE COURSE[3]

The course is designed to meet once a week for a two-hour session. It lasts one semester in its original setting at Crossroads; I have continued that tradition in the after-school program I have been facilitating with my colleague, Jeffrey Duvall, for seniors in Boulder, Colorado. At University Heights, it has been extended to a full-year program, adding writing projects and other activities focused on practical preparation for college and the job market.

Each class follows a similar structure and rhythm: For the first fifteen minutes or half hour, there are warm-up activities which help each individual to become fully present and which bring the group together. Then the group sits in a circle for an hour or more, sharing stories or reflections on a theme set by the guide. After each student and teacher has had one turn to speak, about twenty minutes are taken for responses—to an individual or to the experience of witnessing or being witnessed in this way. The class ends with five or ten minutes of a closing exercise, designed to help students make the transition out of what has by now become a very intimate and vulnerable way of being together so they feel ready for whatever will greet them outside our door.

GETTING STARTED

Play is an important element at the opening of each session. Many warm-ups are games, borrowed and adapted from either theater or adventure-based learning. We carefully select games designed to foster alertness, focus, cooperation, and laughter. We talk with the students about "presence," about how unless we are fully present, we are not able to learn, to listen, to love, or to receive love. (Workshops for teachers pay particular attention to developing what I have called "The Teaching Presence"—the capacity to come to students with an open heart, with a willingness to protect them through discipline, and with a capacity for clearing away whatever keeps us as adults from being fully present and open to the moment. The games help us all become present so we can be ready for something new to happen.

A playful game may then be followed by an art activity, such as drawing, sculpting, or movement, which encourages students to express themselves through metaphor and symbol. Students might be given pastels and paper and asked to draw a symbol of their past week, or a lump of clay to sculpt a symbol of how they're feeling right now. Later in the course, they might be asked to sculpt a symbol of what "intimacy" or "letting go" means to them. The homework assignment for the second class is to bring an object which symbolizes something that is important to them in their life right now. Concealed in a paper bag, these objects are then placed in the center of the circle of students. One by one we go around the circle, with each person choosing an object that interests them, telling the group why they were drawn to that particular object and then asking the owner to reveal its story. In a recent group, these objects included a chocolate mousse cupcake, an engraved gold ring, an oil painting of a landscape, a new tattoo, and an Eagle Scout medal. The stories brought laughter, sighs, and tears. When one girl told the story of the ring she bought and engraved with her brother's name, date of birth, and date of death last spring, the bonds of compassion began to weave from one tearful eye to the next around the circle. In this exercise, the symbol "game" shifts from being a warm-up to becoming a storytelling ritual at the heart of the class.

Symbolic expression is central to the Senior Passage course, because it naturally and quickly takes students to the deeper levels of communication with self and others that meet the budding adult's yearning for authenticity, meaning, and connection. Moving to symbols early in the session when we are still playing helps facilitate a richer, more meaningful level of sharing when we shift into the storytelling circle.

Other tools which help the seniors move easily to this deeper level of communication are relaxation and visualization exercises. In the early weeks, students are introduced to relaxation as a way to deal with the high levels of stress that are common in the senior year and as another way to become present. Students experience a marked shift in their energy and focus after a few minutes spent in deep breathing or muscle relaxation activities. Later, after an introductory sensory awakening exercise begins to stimulate the long neglected imaging part of the mind, we use visualizations that relate to a particular theme we are addressing in the circle. Visualization helps students develop capacities for activating their imagination and creativity—strengthening these facets of intelligence helps not only in academics and the arts, but also with the significant life decisions to be made at this time. And these same tools can be used for exploring the natural "highs" that can substitute for the more self-destructive "highs" that students seek through substance abuse and courting other dangers.

SACRED CIRCLES

Each session includes an hour or more of sitting in a circle, speaking and listening from the heart. In the early weeks, this circle is introduced very simply as a time to listen and let people speak without interruption or immediate reactions. We take each group through an "agreements for safety" process:

what do they need to be able to speak authentically here about things that matter deeply to them? Then we are ready to speak in the circle.

Themes for the first five weeks are set by the guides with a focus on looking back to childhood, to origins and ancestors. We evoke early positive memories and encourage interviews with parents so students can fully celebrate and honor their childhoods before beginning the journey of letting go.

Around the fifth week, we do "the Mysteries Questions," a crucial turning point in the course. These questions, like the ones you read at the beginning of this chapter, are elicited anonymously from students in a reflective process in which they are asked to write their "personal mysteries" about themselves, about others, and about life or the universe. "What are you worried about, curious about, afraid of, excited by? What do you wonder about when you cannot sleep or find yourself walking alone, lost in thought?" The guides collect all these questions, type them up verbatim by category, and then read them back the following week to the group in a ceremonial tone. The reading of the Mysteries Questions is always a powerful moment for the group—they feel honored to hear their own words read aloud, amazed at the wisdom and depth in the questions of their peers, surprised at the repetition of certain themes, and profoundly connected as they realize that they are not alone in their deepest yearnings and concerns.

At this time, we introduce Council*—shifting the quality of the circle from the secular to the sacred. Council. Council is adapted from indigenous peoples throughout the world who created forms for building community through speaking from the heart, sitting in circles close to the earth. In Africa, in Hawaii, among the Native Americans, and in ancient Greece, people passed a sacred object to empower the speaker to speak without interruption. We begin our Council by asking a student to light a candle at the center with words of dedication for our council. Then a theme is introduced linked to the questions posed by the students in their Mysteries Questions. In this way, the curriculum becomes "student-centered," created and re-created by each new group of students to meet their particular needs. Of course, certain themes persist for virtually every group: preparing for loss and learning about grief; learning to live with regrets and disappointments; fear, excitement, and decision making about this next crucial step in their lives; exploring kinship and differences between men and women; and forgiveness, intimacy, stress, success, meaning, and purpose.

Around the tenth week, we begin to prepare for the retreat. We give students a brief conceptual framework about rites of passage, and through exercises and themes in class and between classes, we begin the journey.

THE RETREAT

Embedded in this course is a journey into the wilderness designed to be a "rite of passage" from adolescence to adulthood. As others in this volume have explained, the absence of such adult-guided and sanctioned experiences in our present culture has led many students to seek their own badges of adulthood which are often quite destructive. For many girls, losing virginity or actually bearing a child has become a self-determined rite of passage; for boys, going to the furthest edge with alcohol or the speed of a car, or even a first murder, have become emblems of their passage. Young people need at this time to face challenges that stretch them to their larger capacities—the courage, stamina, and responsibility that defines genuinely adult character— and then to be honored and welcomed into the adult community.

In the original course in California, this retreat is a five-day journey cosponsored with the Ojai Foundation. In our Boulder program, where we do not have school sponsorship, we limit this retreat to three days. In the Bronx, a one-day retreat has best served the students and faculty. Students there have been extremely apprehensive about spending an overnight in nature, so faculty have decided it is best to build slowly towards a longer journey. Students and faculty alike have been astounded at the impact of just one day in a beautiful landscape with a ceremonial design.

Each of these journeys use periods of solitude and reflection as well as group activities that build to a pitch of intensity in releasing childhood. The California and Colorado journeys have also used an adaptation of a Native American sweat lodge as part of the passage experience. The retreat and the weeks of follow-up with students, parents, and faculty provide a ceremonial experience of the transit that the course itself nourishes over a longer period.

CLOSING MOMENTS

We have found it essential to end each session with five or ten minutes of an activity which brings a sense of closure and which helps us all make the transition from this very open, connected place to a more self-contained way of being in the world. Early on, this is done with great simplicity. Students may be asked to reflect silently on what they have heard and felt during this session, on where we have just been, and where they are going now. Or we may all rise, stand shoulder to shoulder, and call out one word that describes how we each feel right now. As time goes on, we are more likely to close by holding hands and looking into each other's faces for a moment of sweet silence. Or we ask the group what they feel they need for closure. The last few sessions focus the entire class on the task of learning to say good-bye in ways that foster completion and wholeness. These not only serve to help the group complete their relationships with each other but also become a model of how to approach good-byes in other spheres of their lives.

WHAT THE STUDENTS SAY

Only recently, in my hometown, did I begin to systematically gather from seniors their written reactions to their senior passage experience. Some preferred to remain anonymous. Others, the voices that follow, were delighted to tell the world how they felt.

From Maya: *It is difficult for me to express the depth and meaning of this group in a way that does it justice. As I look back, I am amazed at how much I have grown as an individual. I am so thankful for the friendships I have developed as well as an understanding of other people.*

I feel that I am now a much stronger person and the group has contributed to that. It has taught me that I have the power to control my destiny, but also let it guide me when necessary. I have learned to see the beauty in myself, others, the world—everything, to recognize it and be thankful for it. Along with this I have become more accepting of my weaknesses. The group has created an environment for all of us to see and learn things that have always been present, just not recognized. Once this knowledge has been seen, it continues to be a major part in our lives.

From Esak: *The Senior Rites of Passage has provided me with an environment that allows me to clear my head, slow down, and make healthy choices for me. A Senior Rites of Passage meeting is a place where people listen to me and where I am taught to listen to others. It makes me realize just how unique each individual's experience is, and the importance of listening. I get so much respect for what it is that I say that I never feel wrong. Even when I do not think I have eloquently, or adequately, expressed myself, I know that I have been heard. Whether I feel good or bad, loving or hating, energetic or tired—I am not wrong. And when I cannot be wrong, I can analyze situations as they relate to my life, and I realize what is important to me.*

A senior in high school must make colossal decisions whether he or she is ready or not. It is now that we decide where it is that we will make our place in society and how we will get there. The more people who can be honest about and aware of their own needs when making these decisions, the healthier the decisions will be.

From Alex: *I think the group has allowed me to see myself for who I am. I have learned to respect myself and accept who I am. I have also seen ways in which I would like to change—ways I'd like to be more like others in our group. The changes I have made in the past few months have been possible because of the support of the group. Thank you all.*

Sharing in council is the most important skill I have learned from this group. It seems simple at first: listen when the other person speaks. But it's harder to fully listen to someone than I ever thought. I am finally learning to really listen with my heart and know how it is the only way to benefit from someone else's experience. Through council, I have also learned how to listen to myself speak what is inside without censor.

And from Ari: *What has been such a pleasant surprise about this class is that I have learned that each person has special qualities and gifts to give when you see who they are behind the surface. One important thing I have learned this year is the enormous value and healing power true listening can have—understanding, showing compassion, and truly getting into another person's shoes and leaving your own for a while. Sadly, in our society, the only time we really get into another person's shoes is when we are abso* *in some television show whose characters are both superficial and unrealis-* *tic.*

Senior Passage meetings give me a feeling of being at peace, being a part of a community (a family of brothers and sisters), and having a great respect and love for life. The bonding and unity within Senior Passage not only cheers me up after a hard day but also restores my faith in humankind and in each person's potential for goodness.

WHAT I HAVE LEARNED

At this point in my life, having worked with every age group in the life cycle, no teaching has felt so satisfying as the senior-passage work. I have taught preschool children, junior high pre-teens, teenagers, and women as they become mothers. In partnership with my husband, I have helped to guide young men and women in search of the deep masculine and feminine, women and men in mid-life, and even elders as they explore the spiritual quest in the second half of life. Each has stretched me and stirred me. But none has inspired me, moved me, enriched my heart and soul the way these young seniors have—fresh from the terrain of childhood and perched on the brink of adulthood. Whether they were students I had known for years at Crossroads, witnessing their entire passage through adolescence, or seniors I met with once for a demonstration council in the Bronx, or students I met only as seniors and then worked with for five months in Boulder, young people who are given a safe space for authenticity at this particular moment in the life cycle bring a vulnerability, passion, playfulness, and intensity of aliveness that makes this work deeply nourishing to my soul.

And over the years, they have taught me two of the most important teachings of my life. They have taught me the meaning of spirit. And they have altered my understanding of the process of change and the possibilities for the future by demonstrating the "evolution of consciousness."

When I began this work, my lifelong avoidance of organized religions as well as spiritual books and teachers had left me with a great sense of wonder and mystery about the meaning of spirit and the question of whether it was possible to nourish the spirit of young people in secular settings. It was the seniors, through their stories, who taught me that spirit may be nourished and developed in many ways. They taught me that connection—deep connec- tion—was the most pervasive longing of the human spirit. Deep connection to the self, to another, to a group, to nature, or to a higher power were each described by one senior or another when asked to tell a story about a time when their "spirit" was nourished. I also saw in them a longing for solitude and silence, despite the initial resistance that would rise in many of them after living in a culture which suppressed both so thoroughly. And their Mysteries Questions showed a great need to explore or at least name the search for meaning and purpose, the mystery of origins and endings in life. Finally, I learned that the human spirit yearns for nonordinary experience, for states of mind that are radically different from everyday waking consciousness. If we guides and mentors will not speak of such territory and give them healthy, integrated ways to reach these lands, I learned that our young people will go there any way they can and mostly in vehicles that may produce lasting damage to the body and the spirit as well.

The second lesson I learned astonished me at first and has come to give me great faith in the future. Sitting in circles with young people of seventeen or eighteen, I have been privileged to hear wisdom I did not dream possible in the young. And I have heard wisdom, insight, and compassion that I rarely or never heard from my own generation. Sometimes a seventeen-year-old would express an awareness that came to me only in my forties. Sometimes my colleagues and I would struggle and struggle with a problem in the group until we let go and discovered that some students knew exactly how to handle the situation with grace and compassion beyond our ability to imagine. I also saw an integration of the masculine and feminine within both young women and men that my generation has struggled for years to hold together.

I realized that I was seeing before me the "evolution of consciousness"—a term that was once meaningless to me. I saw that teaching young people how to create a container that is safe enough for authenticity allows an outpouring of truth that might otherwise be long hidden or doubted. And as each student is witnessed and honored in his or her wisdom, that wisdom grows in them and calls forth the wisdom from others. The confidence and empowerment of students that emerges from this process is deeply satisfying and inspiring to any guide that engages in this work. Over and over, I have watched new teachers and apprentices have their first stunning encounter with this wisdom, and be forever moved.

A generation of young people is yearning for adults and elders who are willing to give as much importance and care to their hearts and souls as their academic success and athletic prowess. While it is not always easy to incorporate such courses into schools, it is deeply rewarding to do so. And when schools are unwilling to take this on, after-school programs can be created. I believe that the health of future generations, as well as the health of our democracy, depends on a new commitment to our young as they strive to join us as adults—a commitment to listen, to learn, and to teach what we have learned about the journey to personal wholeness and caring community.

NOTES

1. A senior "Mysteries" course in 1984 was introduced by Jack Zimmerman, President of the Ojai Foundation, with the help of Ruthann Saphier and Maureen Murdock. The following year, under the visionary leadership of Paul Cummins, Cross-

roads created a Department of Human Development to coordinate existing prog in Ethics and Community Service and to develop a Mysteries Program to serve dents in grades seven through twelve. I was hired to chair that department and teach Mysteries at all grade levels. Working as a team with Zimmerman, Saphier, Murdock, Peggy O'Brien, and Tom Nolan, we refined and expanded the Senior course over the seven years of my tenure as chair. The rich curriculum of the "Senior Passage" course reflects the unique gifts and creativity from each of these educators as well as new contributions from the Boulder faculty and the University Heights faculty adapting it for their inner-city population.

2. Anne Diffily, "The Electric Company," *Brown Alumni Monthly* (March 1991).

3. For those who are interested in exploring this course in further detail, see *The Mysteries Sourcebook*, a three-hundred-page guide for teachers which provides curricula, sample lesson plans, and a wide range of articles on methods used in the Mysteries Program—the birthplace of the Senior Passage Course. The Sourcebook can be purchased by contacting the catalogue Great Ideas in Education at 1-800-639-4122. Resource Center, P.O. Box 298, Brandon, VT 05733-0298. This catalogue also carries the video *Honoring Young Voices* which I produced to illustrate the principles of Mysteries and the responses of students, faculty, administrators, and parents to this program at Crossroads and at an inner-city school in Washington, D.C.

---

*For a thorough introduction to council, see "Council," a booklet by Jack Zimmerman and Virginia Coyle, published by the Ojai Foundation, Box 1620, Ojai, CA 93023. Intensive workshops in leading the council process are also provided by the Ojai Foundation.

TWENTY ONE

VISIONQUEST

Bob Burton and Steve Rogers

Through rites of passage specially designed to meet their needs, youth who enter VisionQuest embark on a meaningful journey. They are given a wide variety of opportunities to accept responsibilities and complete them—and through repeated experiences of success they learn they can make positive choices in their lives.

VisionQuest is a private corporation that contracts with public agencies to provide programs for troubled teenagers. Youngsters are referred to VisionQuest primarily through juvenile courts, probation departments, and social-service agencies. Under the careful supervision of VisionQuest staff, young people are given opportunities to discover their own self-worth through participation in team quests ranging from cross-country mule-driven wagon trains, to sailing in tall ships where they learn the strict discipline of teamwork, to productive community service in needy neighborhoods or for victims of natural disasters.

In one of the VisionQuest programs, the Buffalo Soldiers, young people travel throughout the United States to steer school-children away from the drug abuse, crime, and violence that had often characterized their own lives. A special report about the Buffalo Soldiers is included in the chapter presented here.

The old blue and white bus rumbled through the Pennsylvania countryside . . . Near the front of the bus sat Ron Roberts, oldest of the group at nineteen, an ex-gang member from Philly who had committed more felonies than he cared to remember. Becoming a Buffalo Soldier, he said, changed his life. In school he had learned about the Rev. Martin Luther King Jr., but nothing about black soldiers. Never before had he encountered men who cared about him or been around horses and other animals. "This is my family now," he said.

Behind Roberts was eighteen-year-old Dormen Lisby, tall, sensitive, and bespectacled, a high-school graduate serving time in VisionQuest for vehicular manslaughter. Being a Buffalo Soldier meant so much to Lisby that when his sentence expired a week earlier he asked the judge for permission to stay another six months. Lisby, a talented artist, said the judge thought he was crazy, but granted his request. "Being a Buffalo Soldier gives me a pride I can't really explain," he said. "When the Gents [Buffalo Soldier staff leaders] talk to us about what the old guys did and what we can do to stop drugs and violence, it brings tears to my eyes. It's great to be a Buffalo Soldier. I love my race. It means a lot to me, finding out about my people and my ancestors. This should be for everyone, not just those of us who get in trouble. It changed me."

From his thirteenth birthday to the time a few months ago when he arrived at VisionQuest, Dominick, whose parents had been killed in separate violent incidents, spent most of his nights out on the town looking to beat up people and fight with cops. He said he had more anger than he could release. When he appeared before little kids and told them to say no to drugs and violence, he said, it sent chills up his spine with contradictory sensations: a sense of pride at being a positive role model and a sense of concern that he was really talking to himself.

The peer leader of the group, eighteen-year-old Sgt. Maj. Steve Bryant, had been scheduled to leave the program a day earlier, but like Dormen Lisby, he had gone to court and asked to stay. Most of the drills these guys had learned, he had taught them. Bryant was incorrigible, it seemed, when he arrived in the program two years ago. Now he was a leader, determined to stay off the streets and attend Temple University.

At 12:30 P.M. they marched out to the bus, with Sgt. Maj. Bryant barking out the orders: "Heeeere we go again! Buffalo Soldiers back again!" When they arrived at the Rayburn Building for the Congressional Black Caucus ceremonies honoring black veterans, the boys still had a few hours to kill. So they performed outside on Independence Avenue. The professionals of Capitol Hill eyed them with puzzlement. Who are these kids? How do they fit in?

Soon they were inside, standing proud as honor guards as [ex-Commander-in-Chief of U.S. Armed Forces Colin] Powell spoke to the caucus and the black veterans. When he mentioned the Buffalo Soldiers in his speech, Dormen Lisby felt an overwhelming sense of pride. When the address ended, the Buffalo Soldiers marched down to the foyer, where Sgt. Maj. Bryant introduced them to Powell and said they wanted to be soldiers of peace. Then Bryant lined up his troops and got rolling, twenty minutes of step-dance drills.

They were dazzling, moving in flawless unison from one step to another. Bob Burton, the VisionQuest founder, stood to the side and smiled. "And the psychologists say they can't do this," he said softly. As the late afternoon shadows darkened the foyer, the Buffalo Soldiers performed an encore step. They finished frozen in place, heads down, fists triumphant in the air.*

PERSONAL BEGINNINGS

I want to give you a little background to explain how VisionQuest began. In a way, our whole organization was born out of human failure, and the particular human failure I'm referring to is—myself!

---

*Excerpt from David Maraniss, "Buffalo Soldiers: Forgotten Black Heroes of the Old West: Due Recognition and Reward," *The Washington Post Magazine,* 20 January 1991.

As a child, I had a very difficult time in school and was labeled a "special ed" student. Because of my dyslexia, I could not read or perform the kinds of mental tasks in school that our American educational system prizes so highly. But I learned how to play football and, with the help of some wonderful, caring people I was given a football scholarship for college. I didn't realize at the time that my worst failures and my biggest crises were yet to come.

I managed all right until my senior year. In that one year, I lost eligibility for the scholarship (which meant I had to quit college), and I also lost the election for captain of the football team (a failure which to me was more important than graduating or having a future career in football). At that time I returned to my parents' home, despairing and devastated.

It was then that my father helped me turn my life around. He was a union leader, very much respected by his fellow workers and well suited to his work as a machinist. He said, "You've got to deal with your failures by facing them head on. You have got to confront them and turn them into advantages; you cannot give up on yourself just because you don't feel you are a perfect success." Then he explained to me how he, too, had to face many failures as a child. His stepfather put him in a reform school at the age of twelve and abandoned him there, where none of his family visited him. Although my father's grandfather later rescued him from that place, he never fully overcame his sense of rejection. The haunting dishonor of that time remained with him all his life, but the strength he took from moving beyond his pain eventually enabled him to become a wonderful, supportive father.

MY FATHER CHANGED MY LIFE

This conversation with my father really changed my life; I became interested in finding out more about how our correctional institutions affect the lives of the young people who are sent to them. I decided to enter VISTA (Volunteers In Service To America) and work with troubled, delinquent Native American kids. Later on, I became a caseworker in a boys' reform school, then a probation officer of the juvenile court, and then program director of a juvenile-detention center.

In all of these institutions I felt as if I could understand the pain these young people felt and I saw how they were treated, in so many ways, with disrespect and dishonor. But I really didn't have any answers. I really didn't have a clue how anyone, let alone a rather less-than-brilliant individual such as myself, could remedy any of the countless inadequacies of "The System."

In searching for alternatives I was reminded of what I had learned while I was working with VISTA on the Crow Reservation in Montana. The Crow Indians had ceremonies and traditions such as the "vision quest," a traditional rite of passage, to guide their children to adulthood. It became clear that our elders today have no *honorable* ways or means to help kids become adults. I began thinking that these ancient ceremonies and structures could offer a new direction to take with kids.

Steve Rogers and I had been working together in a "locked" juvenile-detention center. We found that we shared many of the same frustrations in trying to make a difference with kids. We started our work in VisionQuest in 1973 in an effort to change the system by building on Native American ideas about how children become adults. With this rite-of-passage approach, and with the help of a juvenile-court judge in Tucson, Arizona, we signed a contract to take six local youths from a state reform school on a wilderness quest. Over the next twenty years, we grew into an organization with eight hundred staff members, and we've worked with over eight thousand youngsters. Currently, close to eleven hundred youth are enrolled in VisionQuest programs across the United States I am still amazed whenever I think about how we have grown. We have a high rate of successful participants who do not fall back into old behavior patterns when they return home.

VISIONQUEST'S PHILOSOPHY AND METHODS

Although the details of our philosophy and methods have evolved through the years, our original basic concepts remain the same. We take young people out of their familiar neighborhoods and bring them to nature. Kids can't manipulate the weather, or a mule or a horse, so they have to learn to deal with these realities cooperatively. At the same time members of our staff help them focus on the underlying issues causing their "acting out" behavior.

Troubled youngsters need to succeed at something positive in their lives. That is why our programs help ensure success. Our goal has been to counteract the dishonor of their past and to provide them with a sense of personal dignity. We focus on a sense of family, a positive connection with one's heritage, a sense of self-worth, and a respect for nature and for values beyond one's self.

As VisionQuest has evolved, so have some of the concepts and methods we use in training staff. Because the young people who enter VisionQuest programs come from so many social, cultural, and ethnic backgrounds, it helps when the counselors and program leaders who work with them reflect a similar diversity in background. For example, at any one time there might be three or four different Wagon Trains on the road. Of these three or four, one "Wagon Master" might be Hispanic, one African-American, one or two of European descent. Some quests might be led by Native Americans, others by Americans with Jewish or other backgrounds.

Part of VisionQuest's philosophy includes the belief that we learn most when we participate actively in our own training process. Training of Vision-

Quest staff begins with an orientation period and continues throughout their work in the organization.[1] We meet with staff regularly for "talking circles" in which we discuss selected training issues. Although these discussions are guided by senior or more experienced staff, all are encouraged to participate, sharing what they can about the topic from their own previous training or from any relevant personal experience. In this way the older staff members are able to "keep current" regarding new ways of accomplishing treatment goals, while younger staff members receive the guidance of those with decades of firsthand experience.

We stress that *all tribes are necessary to make the world complete.* Everyone has something unique to bring to life. VisionQuest programming has always stressed race and heritage esteem as a way to better know oneself and interact with others—who may or may not be particularly tolerant or who may be prejudiced or racist in attitude. VisionQuest participants are treated with respect and dignity, something they are not offered in many traditional locked facilities. Any employee who displays prejudice—toward other staff or toward a program participant—is terminated on the spot. Likewise, in the kind of environment VisionQuest leaders strive to provide, there is an implicit but unmistakable understanding among the program participants that all expressions of racial or ethnic intolerance will be strongly censured.

GUIDED CENTERING

Central to our method is a process that helps youngsters face and find their way through their own dilemmas. We call it "Guided Centering." We help youngsters to identify their issues and release the pain they cause, in a secure emotional and physical place where they can meet their darkest fears head on. Often, they come to understand the "why" of their issues and learn how to stop the incorrect thinking that causes them to repeat the past. We also focus on re-education and learning how to make positive choices for the future. We try to show them a way to "find their personal center" by first going out and facing the storms of nature in the real world outside, so that they can then face the storms of reality in their own lives. Many of the concepts we use in Guided Centering are based on the Native American Medicine Wheel.[2]

FOUR MAIN ISSUES FOR ADOLESCENTS

The issues these teenagers have to work through usually fall within four main categories: abandonment, boundaries, abuse, and esteem.

ABANDONMENT

The death or departure of a parent, for example, or the parents' divorce early in a child's life, often leads to anxiety and depression. The abandoned child continues to feel somehow responsible or guilty. Children who feel abandoned tend to fall into drug or alcohol addiction.

BOUNDARY ISSUES

Boundary issues often originate from a failure to respect externally imposed limits. Equally damaging can be limits that are too rigid. Often children without strong parents, or with only one parent, have few limits to help them control their behavior. They've had little guidance to help them make decisions for the long run. They have had little chance to incorporate a set of values internally from their parents. Children with boundary issues act on impulse; they feel an impulse and instantly act with no buffer, no thought. They can be very manipulative, and they always want attention.

ABUSE

Many teens in trouble have suffered from some form of abuse—either at the hands of others or self-imposed through addictions to drugs or other unhealthy habits. Abused youngsters often feel shame as well as a loss of self-worth and personal power. Some children begin to feel they deserve the abuse because they are repeatedly told how bad or wrong they are. Abused children lack healthy egos. They do not trust, they repress feelings, and they refuse to talk about their issues; denial is critical to maintain an outward face of normalcy.

SELF-ESTEEM

Almost all troubled youth have low or no self-esteem. They set themselves up for abandonment or abuse and then feel they deserve what happens to them because they have a negative idea of who they are. We strive to encourage a healthy esteem for self and others. We teach these kids to be proud of who they are and where they came from. We use appropriate practices of the Native Americans, for example, sweat lodges and smudging, to help convey this sense of pride and respect for their ancestors.

A SYSTEM BUILT ON HONOR

One of the main points I want to make is that these youngsters have rarely disappointed us once they have made a commitment to finding out who they are. Our philosophy is based on honor. And I guarantee, these kids return honor for honor. When they go on a wilderness quest, they find out very quickly that they cannot compete with nature; they learn that they must harmonize with it. And the wilderness, the woods—the long roads or trails through storms and all types of weather—have a way of softening the pains they have experienced because of fragmentation in their families or confusion in their communities.

Our present juvenile-justice system leaves so much to be desired! If a youngster in America breaks the law a number of times, chances are that sooner or later he or she will be confined in a locked institution. And chances are that the "treatment" offered there will be inappropriate for rehabilitation and clearly incapable of meeting that young person's real needs. And so he or she will go on to a life of further crimes and further punishments.

I believe this is a very serious mistake and a tragic waste of human potential. We must stop incarcerating our children behind bars. We cannot expect them to act honorably while we continue to treat them as hard-core criminals.

VISIONQUEST'S CHALLENGE

VisionQuest offers a variety of opportunities to learn self-discipline, independence, and respect for others in an atmosphere without cells, barred windows, or controlling drugs. These include impact camps, wagon trains, specialized quests, sailing programs, group homes, and in-home supervision and education. All are designed to break the old patterns of failure and institutionalization. VisionQuest replaces the negative influences of the streets—drug usage, gang behavior, police involvement—with positive recognition for individual accomplishment and cooperative effort.

A PERSONAL COMMITMENT IS REQUIRED

Our first contact with a youngster often occurs when a member of our staff comes to interview him or her in jail. During this early interview we present a challenge, an opportunity to experience a modern-day quest designed for such young people. Before we will accept a youngster into VisionQuest, we require that he or she make a commitment to remain with us for at least one year, to complete at least three of our high-impact programs, and to abstain from sex, drugs, alcohol, and tobacco. This is usually very difficult for them, but it teaches them that they have an inner power; they are able to abide by restrictions they impose upon themselves. We encourage them to be willing to face—rather than to run away from—the issues raised in family and Vision-Quest life.

We also seek the parents' involvement and support from the beginning. We encourage them to face family conflicts honestly and discuss problems.

Our main goal is to build the youngsters' self-esteem by providing a series of experiences where they can succeed. These successes gradually build to a point where the young person can recognize his or her accomplishments and take credit for them. Eventually, they are able to develop a new, positive self-image.

IMPACT CAMPS

Typically, a youth begins in an *Impact Camp* and remains there for three to five months. During this time, participants enter into a structured routine, physical training classes, and group and individual counseling, with the overlying goal of preparing for a quest experience that will last several weeks. Organized as tipi villages, these camps provide a fresh, unspoiled environment in which each youngster can achieve physical fitness while learning to deal with issues and problems away from the pressures of his or her former surroundings. They introduce youngsters to some of the philosophies and methods they will use to sort out personal problems. Impact Camps provide many youngsters with one of their first opportunities to build positive relationships with peers and adults.

QUESTS

Quests provide specific challenges and opportunities to discover the satisfaction of success as one learns to develop self-control and trust. Quest experiences are intense. They challenge participants physically, mentally, emotionally, and spiritually. Each quest centers around a primary activity such as hiking, marathon running, bicycling, riding horses or camels, or rock climbing. Differing in theme, scope, and duration, a Quest may be a three-week guided trek through national-forest land with time for solitude and introspection, a cross-country horseback or bicycle expedition, or the extended Buffalo Soldier program which fosters pride and community involvement.

WAGON TRAIN

Our modern *Wagon Train* program offers a sense of community and sharing in a common goal. Youngsters travel across the country in ten to twelve mule-drawn wagons, setting up camps along the way every night. Wagon trains blend pioneer adventure with disciplined educational and counseling programs.

Many of our youngsters come to us with anger, aggression, emotional pain, and a poor sense of self-worth. Youngsters who come from the city must learn new ways to cope with weather, animals, time, and distance. For instance, those who have become adept at conning everyone and everything around them discover that their manipulative skills won't work with a mule! Each day that mule determines whether or not they will move down the road smoothly to camp, so they must consider their animal's needs before their own. Often they form a special bond with these mules; for some, it is the first "friendship" they have ever had.

Interdependence, cooperation, and a strong work ethic are the core of life on the trail. Each youngster's job on the Wagon Train requires cooperation with staff, other youngsters, and the animals. Additionally, each youth attends four hours of school daily.

THE BUFFALO SOLDIERS

Pride in one's ethnic and racial heritage is a major focus for the *Buffalo Soldiers.* These precision-drill units honor the historic all-Black Ninth and Tenth

Cavalry Buffalo Soldier troops, the first African Americans allowed to be soldiers in the U.S. Army. In the late 1800s, they had to overcome racial prejudice, defective weapons, and inadequate supplies, but these adversities did not deter the Buffalo Soldiers from establishing a tradition of excellence and service. Eventually, they won twenty-six Congressional Medals of Honor. Because of their great pride in who they were, they had the lowest desertion rate as well as the lowest rate of alcoholism in the army.

VisionQuest's Buffalo Soldiers carry on that tradition. Our troops embark on a schedule of several public appearances a day where they encourage other youngsters to say no to drugs, stop violence, and stay out of trouble. They perform at elementary schools, high schools, colleges, neighborhood centers, state legislatures, and in parades. The violence they refer to is the domestic or often gang-related street violence found not only in the inner city but in just about every corner of this country. During their training, our Buffalo Soldiers learn that their former ways of responding to situations with unfocused anger and aggression are self-defeating and counterproductive. They develop responsibility, tenacity, self-discipline, and a solid work ethic. These modern-day Buffalo Soldiers are a new kind of warrior: they are Soldiers of Peace.

OCEANQUEST

The basic tenets of sailing—the development of a sense of responsibility, teamwork, rigorous self-discipline, and respect for authority—form the foundation for *OceanQuest*. Under the direction of a licensed captain and crew, youngsters learn to direct and navigate tall ships, maintain them in top condition, deal with emergencies, and cope with demanding circumstances such as weather. They begin to function effectively as a team in stressful situations, handling issues that arise from living in the close quarters on the ships that serve as their home at sea. OceanQuest sails in the Chesapeake Bay, up and down the Atlantic coast, and in the Gulf of Mexico.

Youngsters who complete the OceanQuest program develop a self-confidence and assurance characteristic of those who have successfully met the challenge of the sea. They acquire important skills that will help them direct and navigate their own lives.

Before going on a tall ship, youngsters must complete a dockside training course which includes instruction in water safety, basic rescue techniques, survival swimming, and shipboard safety procedures. They also participate in "day sails" where they practice safety procedures and develop confidence as sailors. New participants are paired with more experienced youngsters during day sails. When everyone has gained the necessary experience, the tall ships put to sea.

At sea, sailing training is ongoing. The young people continue to acquire new skills while improving and refining old ones. Daily programs reinforce the experiential learning and training aboard ship.[3]

HOMEQUEST

The process of reintegration with family and community is the final step. Following accomplishments in high-impact programs, some youths move to group homes where they begin the transition back to their homes and to more successful family and community relationships. They are supervised by live-in staff while they attend school or go to work. All cooperate in chores around the house as well as community service. In a nurturing, family-like setting they learn skills to prepare them for more independent living when they return home.

HomeQuest is an intensive program designed to support young people whose primary residence is in the family home. Participants may enter the program directly or after completing other VisionQuest programs. Home-Quest aids the process of reintegration by helping them transfer values and ethics they have learned to practical applications in the home and community. The young people attend public school or, when appropriate, a VisionQuest school. Their school and work progress is closely monitored, as are their home and neighborhood relationships. In the evening, they gather at a Vision-Quest facility for counseling and recreation. There are weekly parents' group discussions, family conferences, and individual counseling.

EDUCATION AT VISIONQUEST

Each VisionQuest program has an on-grounds school that operates according to the applicable regulatory authority. Classes are generally small, involving up to fifteen students. There is a core academic curriculum including English, math, science, history, electives, and physical education. VisionQuest also has an approved GED curriculum; some youths graduate from high school while attending a VisionQuest school. Each school also offers special education services for students who need them.

COMMUNITY SERVICE

Both youth and staff participate in community-service projects wherever their specific VisionQuest programs are located. These volunteer projects range from recycling programs and building trails in state and national parks to visiting senior citizens' homes and helping physically challenged children to ride horses. We have also taken part in work with the Habitat for Humanity, an organization which coordinates the building of small houses for people who need them. Some of us helped with the clean-up effort in the aftermath of Hurricane Hugo: VisionQuest youth spent several weeks on St. Croix, U.S.

Virgin Islands, helping poor residents rebuild their homes. They also helped the school district clean and rebuild a high school as well as several elementary schools. All participants volunteered for this duty.

Through hard work, VisionQuest youngsters develop a sense of pride in work well done and a sense of security in a predictable and disciplined environment. As they experience new ways to express themselves through their work with us, they begin to turn negative energies in positive directions: They begin to envision more productive goals for their personal lives. They develop more mature and responsible habits, and they learn to focus on values that foster physical, psychological, and spiritual growth rather than self-destruction.

Participating in VisionQuest is a challenging adventure for staff as well as students. We are constantly learning new ways to strengthen our programs and discovering ways to revise or supplement the services we offer. Our hope is that troubled youth everywhere might some day have an opportunity to benefit from "rites of passage" like those we strive to provide.

A NOTE ON VISION QUEST CEREMONIES

Native Americans had a traditional rite of passage which marked a youngster's transition from childhood to responsible and self-respecting adulthood. "Vision quest" is now the accepted term in English, although various tribes had different terms for this journey of self-discovery and self-realization. Parents, uncles, aunts, tribal elders, grandparents, and other mentors taught and guided the young person along the way. Upon returning from the ritual experience, the youth shared thoughts, dreams, and visions with tribal elders. These experiences were often healing and creative. It was then up to the youngster to progress through a cycle of further challenges. The entire process was designed so the youngsters would succeed, with guidance, in their own unique ways.[4]

VisionQuest takes its name and many of its key concepts from the vision quest. We also use several traditional symbols and ceremonies which, because they are so unfamiliar to our young people, make a startling but effective impact. These ceremonies can clarify and heal as they have for centuries. They involve all the senses; they invest the intellectual changes these young people go through with a physical reality as well as a meaningful metaphor.

THE MEDICINE WHEEL

The Native American symbols and ceremonies we borrow for our program supply a new frame of reference for our participants. One of our most frequently used symbols is the circle; specifically, the Native American *Medicine Wheel.*

For the Native American, the Medicine Wheel symbolized a way of life representing the order, harmony, and philosophy of the universe. A Medicine Wheel was usually laid out with stones on the ground. Like the Earth, the Medicine Wheel had the four cardinal directions: north, east, south, and west. Each direction had subpoints using both color and animal symbols. These varied from tribe to tribe.

The center of the Medicine Wheel represented all living things, people included. The spokes of the wheel connected the outer circle, representing the universe, to its center. There was also "Father" Sky above and "Mother" Earth below.

At VisionQuest, the Medicine Wheel provides a frame of reference and symbolic representations of contemporary values. It provides a structure that enables our youngsters to describe their issues, fears, plans, and confusions in a meaningful way.

THE SWEAT LODGE

Another Native American concept we have incorporated into our program is the *Sweat Lodge* ceremony. The Sweat Lodge is an ancient cleansing ceremony, a purification of body, mind, and spirit. It also fosters closer relationships between youth and staff, a significant bonding. VisionQuest has obtained permission to perform this ceremony from Crow Medicine Elders who have guided us.

A Sweat Lodge is a small structure built with willow branches and covered by canvas tarps. It provides a closeness in spirit to all that is within the lodge and within the person. In the Sweat Lodge, people are more open or willing to listen. The Sweat Lodge helps to improve communication by creating an opportunity to begin a deeper dialogue concerning sensitive issues.

In the center is a fire pit in which hot rocks are brought from a fire outside the Sweat Lodge. Water is poured over heated rocks to produce steam. The person who pours the water is known as the sweat leader or the one with "the right to pour." The "fire-man" builds and tends the fire that heats the rocks. To the Crow people, the rocks are the "ancient ones," the ancestors. The fire puts the heat of the sun into the rocks to purify those who take part.

At VisionQuest, we use the Sweat Lodge ceremony to develop closer relationships between youth and staff. Inside the Lodge, one begins to sense a safety and intimacy that enables us to address issues which may be too personal or painful in ordinary conversation. We also use Sweat Lodge time to discuss goals and to connect the various aspects of the VisionQuest experience. We use its symbolism to help our youngsters leave behind their previous habits of aggression, manipulation, and self-destruction, and to build their self-confidence and optimism toward the future.

NOTES

1. We recruit men and women with varied college and experiential backgrounds to work directly with program participants—for the most part college graduates and persons holding advanced or specialized degrees in social service professions. But we also encourage people with other skills and backgrounds to join our staff, since we also need business managers, accountants, truck drivers, technical and maintenance workers, skilled craftspersons, food service specialists, and creative groundskeepers.

2. See section on the Medicine Wheel near the end of this chapter.

3. See the chapter by Edward Carus on a special Coast Guard sailing program.

4. See the book by Frank Linderman, *Plenty Coups: Chief of the Crow* (Lincoln: University of Nebraska Press, 1962), for a carefully recorded description of an authentic American Indian vision quest.

TWENTY TWO

OLD MEN, MUSKRATS, AND ADOLESCENT DREAMS

David Knudsen

David Knudsen has been working with adolescents since 1970, first as a high-school teacher in Media, Pennsylvania and now full time in a camp in Temagami, Ontario. He is director of the leadership school "Temagami Experience" and works with North Carolina Outward Bound in leadership training. He trained with Native American Medicine Men, particularly in the use of the Sioux Sweat Lodge.

David Knudsen tells about his own personal experiences as a sixteen-year-old sailor on a Scandinavian freighter as a rite of passage. In the early 1970s he began developing a program for adolescents using canoe trips and camping in the wilderness of Ontario and Quebec. He now offers the counselors and others in his camp special training in leadership so that the camp experience builds on events each day that lead into a meaningful rite of passage for the participants as well as for the staff.

Each year, Northwaters on Lake Temagami, Ontario provides the opportunity for hundreds of adolescents to come to terms with themselves in a canoe-camp setting. There are also week-long programs for adults. For more information, Mr. Knudsen can be contacted at P.O. Box 477, St. Peters Village, PA 19470, or by phone at (610) 469-4662.

I was up and out of bed early that morning in late December. The clock read 3:50 A.M. so I canceled the alarm for 4:00 and quickly got dressed.

After putting on my coat, heavy mittens, wool hat, and hip boots, I threw my pack basket, loaded with an assortment of traps, stakes, and lures, over my shoulder and began the long walk to the river around dawn. This was my favorite time of day. It was so still and filled with mystery. Somehow I felt freer at that time of day than at any other. School seemed so confining and had many rules that seemed unimportant. As a nine-year-old boy, I would walk about ten miles that day, checking and rebaiting forty traps or more, stopping only to eat a lunch of sardines, bread, and cheese, with maybe a thermos of lukewarm tea and an apple which would double for muskrat bait.

Every day in the fall and winter started this way except that I traveled shorter distances on weekdays because of school. At the end of the season I might have seven muskrats, a few opossums, a skunk or two, and a raccoon. Each would be skinned and stretched, and then my parents would drive me to a distant farmers' market where a man would buy my furs.

I would always stand back for a moment hoping a small crowd would gaher. Then I would proudly walk up to the table with all the dried furs hanging over my back on a string, heave them onto the table, and wait for the buyer to perform his ritual. He would look at the pelts, blow on the fur, separate them into piles, and examine them again. The longer it took, the prouder I felt. Finally, he would say something like, "Nice pelts. Did you notice the fur market is down a little this year?" It didn't matter because I just heard "Nice pelts." Opening a tin box, he'd begin to count out $82.00 mostly in ones. Then he'd look me in the eye and say, "Deal." I'd agree, "Deal," and we would shake hands firmly. It was even more special if there were a few old men around when all this happened and especially if they said things like, "Nice job, kid," or "Where did you get 'em?"

Perhaps my early career as a fur trapper developed because of another talent I had, that of "striking out" at the plate. I was the exception growing up in a small blue-collar community in southeastern Pennsylvania where everyone played and talked baseball. One Saturday morning in late spring, when a group of friends and I met at the school to try out for the local Little League team, a very large man with a cigar in his mouth looked at me and said, "Sorry, son, but we can't use you." At that age, maybe seven, I wasn't very conscious about things like competition, failure, or loss of membership in a group. I just know I felt left out.

Probably out of feeling sorry for myself, I started spending time in the woodlot near our house. That was an important time in my life—a time of solitude, a time to sift through the ashes by myself. As time went on, I became totally fascinated with the forest. It was very nurturing, somehow like being connected to a "Source," and it became most important in my early development.

When I was about eight, I met an old man whose wife had died some years back, who lived across the valley from our house. Born in Yugoslavia, he now lived in a shack right in the middle of suburbia. Words could not describe just how out of place this man was in terms of his neighbors. He had no running water, no electricity, and no indoor plumbing. He had a bird dog, the first I had ever seen. Everyone else had poodles and cocker spaniels, but he had a real bird dog that he kept chained up to a wooden barrel.

Whenever I could, I would spend time with the old man. He would teach me how to catch eels on nights when there was no moonlight, how to trap and skin muskrats, how to identify animal tracks, and how to move quietly through the forest. We would play five-card stud together every Saturday morning. I would work at odd jobs to save pennies for the "big game," and each week, I would watch my hard-earned money pass hands. He taught me patience and respect for elders, how to do without, and how to stand my ground; he also taught me how to drink black coffee.

I never understood why my parents would allow me to spend so much of my time with this man. My mother told me later that the other mothers were horrified. (It is a wise mother who can let her son go to be with a mentor.)

Perhaps on an intuitive level she knew she had to let me go so I could develop more independence.

My father must have known this too, because when I turned sixteen, he got me a job on a Danish freighter bound for Argentina. I don't think he was ever able to verbalize anything about rites of passage, but somehow he understood this concept instinctively. My father gave the carpenter on the ship twenty dollars and told him to watch out for me. No one spoke English and for the first three weeks out to sea, I went from being homesick to being seasick, never deciding which one was worse. I learned so much about life and about myself during the next six months, saw such poverty while in South America, and was astounded by the joy in peoples' eyes, joy I had never seen on the faces of the adults in my neighborhood. It was as if they spoke from their hearts rather than their heads. When I came back, my parents had a special dinner for me and we had champagne. We *never* had champagne, but we had champagne that night. Some of my father's friends came—men whom he had sailed with during the war. They listened to my stories and I realized that something in me had changed. I had somehow grown up. Men were listening to me in a different way, men I respected.

By the time I reached eighteen I was working for a company making helicopters. It didn't take long for me to realize that working indoors was never going to be fulfilling, so I ignored the advice of others, packed up my old car, and drove to Colorado. I decided that I wanted to be a cowboy—if there were still such a thing. A man who owned a ranch in the Four Corners area offered me a job: sixteen hours a day, seven days a week, at a dollar a day. I jumped at the offer and bought a new hat and boots. In retrospect, I must have looked ridiculous. But one round-up, two cattle drives, and endless months in the saddle finally began to make a difference in how I viewed life. I learned about hard work, perseverance, and being comfortable in silence.

Because I worked hard for this man each day, I looked for some kind of indication of how I was doing, but at the end all I received was a handshake and a thank-you. About two months later my father received a letter from him complimenting my work. That felt good, but the message I got from his restrained compliment was that "real men" don't show emotion or give compliments directly.

WORKING WITH RITES OF PASSAGE IN THE WILDERNESS: THE BEGINNING YEARS

My work with rites of passage began in 1971 when I was working as a teacher and decided to take a group of young men on a canoe trip into Canada. While there I heard about an old man selling an island that was used as a small canoeing camp. When I landed on the dock I knew that somehow this island would have a lot to do with my life's work. I walked up the hill from the dock to meet this old gentleman. We talked about our hopes and respect for the land and finally we shook hands to close the deal.

I started a camp program for young men ages ten through nineteen. The first canoe trips were very difficult, but it was my philosophy to experience hardship without complaint, exactly as I had been taught. Being tough was what mattered. In those early years, my small staff and I put in some very long days with the boys. We pushed the trips so hard that there was never a moment to slow down and look at the country or take the time to talk with one another. Silent endurance is still a characteristic that I value, but it was so out of balance in those days. No doubt many young men learned some important lessons from this approach, but we turned an equal number away from ever learning to be with the wilderness. We maintained our approach with a degree of stubbornness for a number of years. It was, at the time, more important to be right than to be honest, so we surrounded ourselves with those who either agreed or were too afraid to challenge our system.

After seven or eight years of being involved in the business, I felt stuck—of course, because I *was* personally stuck. (Someone once told me that there is no such thing as a "grown-up": There are only those who are growing up or those who are stuck.) About that time I met a woman who talked to me about being "conscious." Native American philosophy, ritual, rites of passage. I didn't have a clue as to what she was talking about. Our intuition, however, told us that we should team up and work together.

In 1979, a year later, I was in North Carolina with a friend who had asked me to attend a spiritual-healing conference. I had never heard of such a thing. After attending and listening to a number of speeches about spiritual approaches that I did not understand, I decided to leave. Just before leaving, however, a Lakota spiritual leader by the name of Wallace Black Elk spoke. What he said made a lot of sense to me. He talked of Nature as I had experienced it during those earlier years in the forest. I wanted to go to him after the lecture and somehow make a connection, but so many others rushed up to meet him that I held back.

Late that same night, after trying to sleep in a bunkhouse with about forty snoring men, I decided to go for a walk. I ran into Wallace Black Elk and he told me then about a dream he'd had that I would be there, and a vision: he wanted to send his adopted son to our island to share some ideas. He told me that a long time ago the young men of his people would go on a vision quest when they were only twelve or thirteen, seeking a vision for their lives. From this time on they would know why they were here and what their lives would be about. He also told me that it was time for his people to begin to share their beliefs so that my people could find their way back to their own path of spirituality. I didn't understand much of what he was talking about then, but I was certainly excited about the possibilities. Perhaps I could finally find more balance and bring it into my work.

From that point on things began to change dramatically in my life and also in the life of the camp. A shift in consciousness can make such a difference! Everything had been there, yet for years we had struggled. Suddenly it all began to change. What began with eight young men and a few canoes and buildings suddenly began to grow. Last summer we worked with 450 people including people from eleven foreign countries. We have expanded to two island base camps now offering a variety of programs.

WHAT WE HAVE LEARNED ABOUT WORKING WITH RITES OF PASSAGE IN THE WILDERNESS

Each summer since 1971, we have operated wilderness camp programs in which boys struggle with the issues of becoming men. We have learned that the wilderness represents a place of balance, and that using a wilderness experience as a metaphor for one's life can be extremely valuable. For one thing, it helps people get over thinking they are victims. As we tell our participants, "When you're canoeing and it's raining, you can make the next hour miserable, or you can make it wonderful. It really doesn't have much to do with the weather. The solution is in the conversation that you have with yourself." The experience can also teach the art of living life in the present. How many of us spend our lives looking forward to the next event that we risk missing out on the moment. Think of the expressions: "I can't wait until . . .", or "Thank God it's Friday," or "I can't wait to finish this so I can . . ."

When we experience our lives as victims we often use blame as a means to survive. For ten years I ran Alternative Programs for two public school systems and worked with young people who blamed parents, teachers, the society. It's a way of not being responsible for creating one's own reality. I found that time spent in an outdoor setting, with a leader capable of diagnosing where the group is and who could design appropriate interventions to help the group or individual to the next level, greatly speeds up the process of personal growth. We need to process and develop questions regarding the event that maximize learning and application back home. If time is not taken to sit together and discuss the meaning of this experience for everyday living, then much will be lost. It will just be a trip to the woods, not much more.

Our team began to study rites of passage. There was still much we didn't understand, but we did know that the old model of strong charismatic dominating leaders who made most of the decisions and who had participants follow them through the wilderness, was definitely not working. As change began to occur in our organization (a balance of power between leader and participant), there was resistance from leaders who had worked hard within the system to finally reach the top. Training staff to a new way of thinking and behaving became crucial. How many creative approaches to education have failed because no one thought to work with the staff first! Unless people are invested in the change, they will usually resist or undermine—not consciously, but nevertheless, with disastrous results.

Training of staff became the primary objective for the next four years. During this time, we also became coeducational. First we taught our leaders how to create a safe container for participants and how to honor the individual by giving each person the time to share their thoughts and the opportunity to tell their story. In everything we do, we try to build a feeling of accomplishment and success. We began to offer an environment that was less authoritative and more nurturing. Communication and compassion led to trust and sharing, which led to cooperation and a willingness to risk not only physically, but also emotionally.

Many times, each summer, I watch groups of ten-, eleven-, and twelve-year-olds sitting in a circle sharing their learning while a group of seventeen- and eighteen-year-olds, who have just completed a six-hundred-mile trip to the Hudson Bay, surround them and listen and applaud their stories and learning.

I have come to understand that rites of passage seem to take place when we return from an adventure, when the experience is embodied in a ritual, and when there are older mentors there to hear the story and honor it. The sequence of these ingredients is important.

The significance of meaningful ritual cannot be emphasized enough because ritual affects the unconscious part of the individual: growth and change take place when this area of our psyche is thus affected. After a very meaningful ritual (a sweat lodge), a sixteen-year-old girl came to me the following morning to share a dream. For many years she had had a recurring dream of a small bird with little lights all over its body that was trapped behind a wall of glass. In her new dream, she told me, the bird came through the glass and took off.

HOW WE WORK WITH RITES OF PASSAGE TODAY

At camp, we begin working with boys when they are about ten or eleven. This is a good age to begin the transition away from their mothers. A strong sense of independence is difficult to achieve in our young men if they are too much mothered and not enough fathered. I applaud the mothers who understand this and are willing to allow their eleven-year-old sons to attend a wilderness experience. We watch over them carefully, and around the evening fires we fill their heads with appropriate myths and stories. By the time our participants are fourteen we begin to push a little on the trips. Going beyond one's own limitations builds self-esteem. We work with fears that block us from reaching our dreams, or that part in all of us which sometimes wants to quit or give up, the part that just wants to crawl back under the covers some mornings and not face the world. We work on setting goals and avoiding the excuses, justifications, explanations, and opinions that keep us from ever reaching them.

Later, at about sixteen to eighteen, we provide an experience which has to do with becoming an adult. After a long and difficult expedition to Hudson Bay and hundreds of miles of canoeing white water, we take the group into a sweat lodge ritual. Soon after this experience, each talks about the kind of person he or she is. The idea is not to think about what you are going to say, but rather to allow the words to come from deep within. Often these young people will talk about a dream or vision. They talk of compassion, sensitivity, balance, and responsibility. Hearing them speak from their hearts is always one of the most moving things we experience each summer.

Finally, we stress service to others and the environment. It seems that when we receive an important understanding we can only hold on to it by being willing to give it away. A group from last summer cut and split a few cords of wood for an older native person too ill to gather what she needed for the winter. This way of service continues throughout one's life.

The last day of each summer for the past twenty-five years I have stood alone on the cliff side of our island base camp. Just at dusk I watch a formation of canoes coming down the lake. Our oldest section of voyagers is returning from a month-long trip to the Hudson Bay. Birch bark torches light the way and each canoe is adorned with moose and caribou antlers. The canoes cut fast through the water and I can feel pride within each of the paddlers. Waiting patiently on the dock, the younger ones watch with respect, knowing that someday they too will have such an opportunity. Upon arrival, hugs and greetings are exchanged and later each section of voyagers is honored.

Finally, I remember a young boy age sixteen, who came to talk to me the morning after a rite-of-passage ritual. He shared a recurring dream in which he entered a burning building on Thanksgiving night looking for a small boy trapped in the fire. He would search and search but never had any success; then he would be driven out by the heat and flames. He said that in his latest dream after his rite-of-passage experience he came out from the fire and there was the young boy standing outside with a smile on his face, safe and sound.

TWENTY THREE

UP WITH PEOPLE

Paul Colwell

 Although "Up With People" is for participants in their late teens and early twenties, similar projects on a smaller scale would be possible for younger people. All who have worked with youth creating a performance production know what it does for strengthening the self-esteem, skills, and self-confidence of everyone involved. The people participating in the "Up With People" program are in many ways self-selected. Those who know and work with them can see how their skills, practical know-how, and maturity develop during their year with this organization, guided by adults like Paul Colwell, songwriter and cofounder of Up With People.

Up With People's World Headquarters are located at 1 International Court, Broomfield, Colorado 80021 (phone [303] 460-7100).

Up With People entered the world scene in the mid-1960s and became established as an international, nonprofit educational organization in 1968. It began as a musical show with the intent of expressing some of the hopes, aspirations, and concerns of a young generation and grew into an innovative experiential learning program in which more than seventeen thousand young people from seventy countries have participated. Over the past three decades millions of people around the world have seen the Up With People productions live and on television, from the Great Wall of China to the plains of Kenya, and from the Royal Albert Hall in London to four Super Bowl halftime spectaculars.

The purpose of Up With People is to build understanding and cooperation among people around the world, to break down racial and cultural barriers, and to develop in young men and women the skills necessary for leadership and service in a world that is increasingly becoming an interdependent global community. Each year approximately seven hundred college-age youth representing twenty-five to thirty nationalities and diverse backgrounds travel in five casts to different countries and continents. They live in homes with host families everywhere they go, providing them with a unique opportunity to learn about the people and places they visit.

This experience is exciting and personally challenging. It combines musical performance, community service, educational activities, career exploration, and direct involvement in the technical, logistical, and promotional aspects of the day-to-day operation. A typical day for one cast might include performing at a high school, a visit to a drug rehabilitation facility and a senior citizens' home, and taking down the stage equipment late into the night following their full-length two-hour show.

The participants are able to take advantage of the educational opportunities each community offers. In Brussels, Belgium, they are frequently briefed by officials of the European Community. In Belfast, Northern Ireland, they have met with members of the city council. In New Mexico and Arizona they are often guests of tribal leaders on the Indian reservations.

As part of its ongoing expansion and outreach, Up With People recently launched an urban schools project, first in the elementary and junior high schools of Los Angeles, and then in other cities, including Denver, Tucson, and San Antonio. It features interaction with the students through a musical presentation and in classroom workshops that focus on respect for others, self-esteem, conflict resolution, and introducing the students to the cultures of the world. The Up With People cast members also benefit from this face-to-face activity with their students; and whether from other countries or the United States they come away with a better understanding of the rich diversity of the American culture.

One could describe the unique Up With People experience as a rite of passage to adulthood, with all its responsibilities. In this respect, Up With People's alumni have put their leadership skills to work in their communities. For example, one alumnus founded an orphanage for street children in Mexico City. Another established a grassroots self-help organization to revitalize his economically depressed town. Yet another has created a highly regarded curriculum for at-risk teens. As elected officials, lawyers, teachers, physicians, social workers, journalists, entertainers, businesspeople, and community volunteers, alumni all over the world are proving daily that their spirit of idealism, tenacity, and leadership continues to burn brightly long after their year with Up With People ends.

TWENTY FOUR

WALKABOUT IN HIGH SCHOOL

Maurice Gibbons

This chapter is taken from Dr. Maurice Gibbons' book, *The Walk-about Papers: Challenging Students to Challenge Themselves* (Vancouver, British Columbia: EduServ, 1990). Creator of the highly acclaimed "Walkabout" model of teaching and learning, Dr. Gibbons focuses on creating more meaningful and effective learning environments in our schools by nurturing students' natural curiosities, talents, and interests.

This article is of great current interest since Walkabout schools and programs founded in the seventies are still operating and more are appearing every year in high schools throughout the United States and Canada.

As Dr. Gibbons recently wrote, "Today adolescents have a hard time finding a rich and transforming means of initiation to adulthood. Because they must make that passage, they do find their ways, with mixed success and disaster. The renewal of our society begins with a vision of the culture we want and ceremonies by which we can convey that vision to our citizens in the making. Perhaps we can see a hint of the transitions of the future in the struggles of our young to save the earth and its people, often with their lives or futures on the line. In the process we may learn a new definition of adulthood ourselves. . . . Initiating our youth successfully may be the essential ingredient of education designed for the 21st century."

Maurice Gibbons is an independent educator, consultant, writer, and sculptor who was until recently a professor of education at Simon Fraser University, Burnaby, British Columbia. After twelve years teaching elementary school and high-school English and drama, he began teaching curriculum development and instruction at the university level. Gibbons holds a doctorate from Harvard, where he was a Harvard fellow and served on the editorial board of the *Harvard Educational Review.* A specialist in the creation of innovative approaches to instruction, he is best known for his work in the theory and practice of new program development emphasizing self-direction, challenge, and excellence. The first Walkabout article is still the most requested reprint in *Phi Delta Kappan*'s history.

His books most often referred to are *The New Secondary Education* and *Toward a Universal Curriculum for a Global Generation.* He is presently a member of the Institute on Learning How to Learn sponsored by Northern Illinois University. *Slashing a Pathway to the Year 2000* appeared in August 1991. His *Self-Directed Learning Sourcebook* was published in 1995.

Recently, he has developed programs in Challenge Education, Becoming an Expert, and The Working Journal. He is codirector and cofounder of World Citizens for a Universal Curriculum, a nonprofit society devoted to empowering students with the processes they need to address global issues and take action on them. He and colleagues are currently developing "Skool-Aid" to supply basic learning materials to less developed countries. Gibbons is currently a writer, an exhibiting wood sculptor, and a consultant, often to international sites where his programs are being used.

As a consultant, speaker, and workshop leader, his main educational theme is equipping students for the pursuit of competence and excellence now and in the future. His video, "Walkabout: Challenging Students to Challenge Themselves," was released by The Open Learning Agency, fall 1995.

WALKABOUT: SEARCHING FOR THE RIGHT PASSAGE FROM CHILDHOOD AND SCHOOL

Recently, I saw an Australian film called *Walkabout* which was so provocative—and evocative—I am still rerunning scenes from it in my mind. In the movie, two children escape into the desert-like wilderness of the outback when their father, driven mad by failure in business, attempts to kill them. Within hours they are exhausted, lost, and helpless. Inappropriately dressed in private school uniforms, unable to find food or protection from the blazing heat, and with no hope of finding their way back, they seem certain to die.

At the last moment they are found and cared for by a young aborigine, a Native Australian boy on his Walkabout, a six-months-long endurance test during which he must survive alone in the wilderness and return to his tribe an adult, or die in the attempt. In contrast to the city children, he moves through the forbidding wilderness as if it were part of his village. He survives not only with skill but with grace and pride as well, whether stalking kangaroo in a beautiful but deadly ballet, seeking out subtle signs of direction, or merely standing watch. He not only endures, he merges with the land, and he enjoys. When they arrive at the edge of civilization, the aborigine offers—in a ritual dance—to share his life with the white girl and boy he has befriended, but they finally leave him and the outback to return home. The closing scenes show them immersed again in the conventions of suburban life, but dreaming of their adventure, their fragment of a walkabout.

The movie is a haunting work of art. It is also a haunting comment on education. What I find most provocative is the stark contrast between the aborigine's Walkabout experience and the test of an adolescent's readiness for adulthood in our own society.

The young Native faces a severe but extremely appropriate trial, one in which he must demonstrate the knowledge and skills necessary to make him a contributor to the tribe rather than a drain on its meager resources. By contrast, the young North American boy or girl is faced with written examinations that test skills very far removed from the actual experience he or she will have in real life. He or she writes; he or she does not act. He or she solves familiar theoretical problems; does not apply what he or she knows in strange but real situations. He or she is under direction in a protected environment to the end; does not go out into the world to demonstrate that he or she is prepared to survive in, and contribute to, our society.

The isolation involved in the Walkabout is also in sharp contrast to experience in our school system. In an extended period of solitude at a crucial stage of his development, the aborigine is confronted with a challenge not only to his competence, but also to his inner or spiritual resources. For his Western counterpart, however, school is always a crowd experience. Seldom separated from his or her class, friends, or family, he or she has little opportunity to confront anxieties, explore inner resources, and come to terms with the world and his or her future in it. Certainly, he or she receives little or no training in how to deal with such issues. There are other contrasts, too, at least between the Australian boy and the urban children in the movie: his heightened sensory perception, instinct, and intuition—senses which seem numbed in the children; his genuine, open, and empathic response toward them in saving their lives, and their inability finally to overcome their suspicious and defensive self-interest to save his. And above all there are his love and respect for the land even as he takes from it what he needs; and the willful destruction of animals and landscape which he observes in disbelief during his brushes with civilization.

Imagine for a moment two children, a young Native looking ahead to his Walkabout and a young North American boy looking ahead to Grade 12 as the culminating experiences of all their basic preparation for adult life. The young Native can clearly see that his life will depend on the skills he is learning, and that after the walkabout, his survival and his place in the community will depend upon them, too. What meaning and relevance such a goal must give to learning!

The Native's Western counterpart looks forward to such abstractions as subjects and tests sucked dry of the richness of experience, in the end having little to do directly with anything critical or even significant that he anticipates being involved in as an adult—except the pursuit of more formal education. And yet, is it his test-writing ability, or even what he knows about, that is important—or is it what he feels, what he stands for, what he can do and will do, and what he is becoming as a person? And if the clear performative goal of the Walkabout makes learning more significant, think of the effect it must have on the attitude and performance of the young person's parents and instructors, knowing that their skill and devotion will also be put to the ultimate test when the boy goes out on his own. What an effect such accountability could have on our concept of schooling and on parents' involvement in it!

For another moment, imagine these same two children reaching the ceremonies which culminate their basic preparation and celebrate their successful passage from childhood to adulthood, from school student to work and responsible community membership. When the aborigine returns, his readiness and worth have been clearly demonstrated to him and to his tribe. They need him. He is their hope for the future. It is a moment worth celebrating.

The Walkabout could be a very useful model to guide us in redesigning our own rites of passage. It provides a powerful focus during training, a challenging demonstration of necessary competence, a profound maturing experience, and an enrichment of community life. I am not concluding that our students should be sent into the desert, the wilderness, or the Arctic for six months—even though military service, Outward Bound, and such organizations as the Boy Scouts do feature wilderness living and survival training. What is appropriate for a primitive subsistence society is not likely appropriate for one as complex and technically sophisticated as ours. But the Walkabout is a useful analogy, a way of making the familiar strange so we can examine our practices with fresh eyes. And it raises the question I find fascinating: *What would an appropriate and challenging Walkabout for students in our society be like?*

Let me restate the problem more specifically. What sensibilities, knowledge, attitudes, and competencies are necessary for a full and productive adult life? What kinds of experience will have the power to focus our children's energy on achieving these goals? And what kind of performance will demonstrate to the student, the school, and the community that the goals have been achieved?

The Walkabout model suggests that our solution to this problem must measure up to a number of criteria. First of all, it should be experiential and the experience should be real rather than simulated; not knowledge about aerodynamics and aircraft, not passing the link-trainer test, but the experience of solo flight in which the mastery of relevant abstract knowledge and skills is manifest in the performance.

Second, it should be a challenge which extends the capacities of the student as fully as possible, urging him to consider every limitation he perceives in himself as a barrier to be broken through; not a goal which is easily accessible, such as playing an instrument he already plays competently, but a risky goal which calls for a major extension of his talent, such as earning a chair in the junior symphony or a gig at a reputable discotheque.

Third, it should be a challenge the student chooses for himself. As Margaret Mead has often pointed out—in *Coming of Age in Samoa*, for instance—the major challenge for young people in our society is making decisions. In primitive societies there are few choices; in technological societies like ours, there is a bewildering array of alternatives in lifestyle, work, politics, possessions, recreation, dress, relationships, environment, and so on. Success in our lives depends on the ability to make appropriate choices. Yet, in most schools, students make few decisions of any importance and receive no training in decision-making or in the implementation and reassessment cycle which constitutes the basic pattern of thoughtful growth. Too often, graduation cuts them loose to muddle through for themselves. In this Walkabout model, teachers and parents may help, but in the Rogerian style—by facilitating the student's decision-making, not by making the decisions for him. The test of the Walkabout, and of life, is not what he can do under a teacher's direction, but what the teacher has enabled him to decide and to do on his own.

Fourth, the trial should be an important learning experience in itself. It should involve not only the demonstration of the student's knowledge, skill, and achievement, but also a significant confrontation with himself: his awareness, his adaptability to situations, his competence, and his nature as a person. Finally, the trial and ceremony should be appropriate—appropriate not as a test of the schooling which has gone before, but as a transition from school learning to the life which will follow afterwards. And the completion of the Walkabout should bring together parents, teachers, friends, and others to share the moment with him, to confirm his achievement, and to consolidate the spirit of community in which he is a member.

POSTSCRIPT ON CHALLENGES, STRATEGIES, AND PROGRAM STRUCTURES

In the years that followed the publication of the Walkabout article, many programs were launched, and each added some new dimension to the concept. The following is a brief catalogue of some useful practices that emerged:

THE WALKABOUT COURSE: The many delivery systems developed to offer the program include complete Walkabout senior-high-school programs in which all courses are also conducted as individual challenges; a Walkabout theme pursued for one day a week throughout the year; a Walkabout Time of one or two weeks broken out of the school schedule on one, two, or three occasions; and a Walkabout course with a regular place in the school schedule. The course includes training in such self-directional skills as decision-making, goal-setting, planning, problem-solving, and self-evaluation. Students are organized into small support groups for the planning and execution of their challenges. When they are prepared, students negotiate time out of school to do their fieldwork.

ADDITIONAL CHALLENGES: In addition to adventure, logical inquiry, practical application, creative expression, and community service, several additional challenges are also considered appropriate. They include the following:

1. **Academic Concentration:** Students choose an academic field in which to become particularly knowledgeable and proficient, such as: trigonometry, electronics, the novel, Russian history, the

Impressionists, existential philosophy, or the remote exploration of space. Topics may be very narrow and detailed, or broader and more focused on a structural overview of a field. Students determine how they will study the topic and how they will demonstrate that they have become specialists in it.

2. **Self-Knowledge:** Students learn about themselves through reflection, discussion, and action. They address the basic personal questions: Who am I? What do I stand for? Where am I going in my life? How should I relate to others? How can I determine quality or excellence? What is reality and what is the meaning of life? What do I believe? This challenge includes keeping a journal, regular experiences of solitude, a search for role models, and a solo experience— 24, 48, or 72 hours alone, without distraction, preferably in a natural setting. The focus is on "the person I am, and the person I want to be." Since work on all of the challenges is relevant to this topic, it becomes also a summary of "what I have learned about who I am from what I have done." Reflection, with inner dialogue, is a vital part of the Walkabout process.

3. **Life-Planning:** Young people often leave school unaware of what they intend to do in their lives and what preparation is required for what they choose. In this challenge they explore their own abilities and passions, and they explore the options available for applying and expressing them. They consider work, recreation, lifestyles, travel, and relationships; they find out what is required to pursue the choices that they find compelling; and they make tentative plans for the future they seek.

4. **Networking:** The focus for this challenge is relationships. It includes friendships, partnerships, teamwork, sharing information and interests, service to others, and relationships with the planet and its peoples. Students may work with a small group on one or more of the other challenges, or they may develop a group challenge of their own, using their shared power to reach beyond easier and more familiar tasks. The challenge is both to become socially competent and to use that competence toward a worthy end.

THE NEGOTIATED CONTRACT AND THE WORKING JOURNAL: Students need help in the demanding task of designing, managing, and enacting their own learning activities. The contract outlines the steps in the process of pursuing a self-directed challenge activity. The journal is a companion-book to the contract, and acts as a record and guide for the thinking, decision-making, planning, action, and reflection involved in becoming an aware, productive person. The contract can begin simply with only a goal and a plan, and may develop into an extensive document with many steps and considerable detail.

The journal is the student's workbook outlining his or her thinking, planning, and action, and what he or she is learning from the process. The challenges, contract, journal, support group, mentors, and training in each new skill that students must apply, all help them to create their own structure when the structure provided by regular courses is taken away.

BASELINE EVALUATION AND THE PROOF PORTFOLIO: With every student potentially pursuing a different learning program, a different approach to the evaluation of accomplishment must be taken. One practical and appropriate method is to establish a baseline measure of students' level of performance at the beginning of the activity, and to negotiate with them what measure will constitute a satisfactory and an excellent improvement beyond that baseline. Since most activities will lead to some form of product, accomplishment, or specific performance, another useful instrument of evaluation is the personal portfolio, in which some acceptable form of proof of each of those achievements is kept. This may include such things as testimonial letters, certificates, photographs, newspaper clippings, and official reports. Building an impressive portfolio both for course evaluation and for later use in applying for jobs and college entrance, contributes to evaluation, to motivation, to learning, and to the students' future success.

Reprinted with permission from the educational journal, the *Phi Delta Kappan,* May 1974.

Walkabout Papers, the Walkabout video, and other books on self-directed learning are available from Personal Power Press Inc. at Bow V-49, Bowen Island, B.C., Canada, VON 1GO.

TWENTY FIVE COMING OF AGE AT SEA

Edward H. Carus Jr.

 Many features of military experience are recognized as providing effective rites of passage and initiation—whether in the army, the navy, or the air force. Edward Carus describes his personal rite of passage in sailing and working on the U.S. Coast Guard cutter *Eagle* as part of his training at the U.S. Coast Guard Academy in New London, Connecticut. The men and women in training sailed across the Atlantic four times, that is, two trips to Europe and two trips back to Connecticut. This is just one example of "creative anachronism" and its effective use in our times.

Edward Carus' training aboard the square-rigged U.S. Coast Guard Cutter *Eagle* has continued to serve in his professional life. He has organized and led several research voyages in the Pacific aboard the sailing vessel *Aeolus,* and then produced documentary television programs based on those expeditions. Mr. Carus has also published articles about those research voyages as well as produced a number of films relating to the cultural and natural history of the Pacific Basin.

During the summers when I was a Coast Guard cadet (1951–1955), I made one short trip and two long cruises to Europe aboard the United States Coast Guard Cutter *Eagle.* At least once a week in the wintertime, along with several hundred other cadets, I did manual labor aboard the ship. The 296-foot sailing vessel has three tall masts, two of which are fitted with ten large square sails and seven jib-like fore-and-aft sails; the third and aft mast is fitted with a total of five fore-and-aft sails. The bark *Eagle* is rigged similarly to those famous sailing vessels of the nineteenth century when "Iron men and wooden ships" plied the oceans.

Why would a modern service academy with high academic standards use an old-fashioned square-rigged ship to train future officers of the U.S. Coast Guard? There are several excellent reasons for this. First, maintaining and sailing aboard the *Eagle* is a relatively inexpensive way to keep several hundred cadets productively occupied while they learn about the mysteries of the sea and gain practical work experience; secondly, manning a complicated sailing vessel with a total of twenty-two sails requires skilled leadership and extensive teamwork; thirdly, visiting foreign ports of call broadens the young cadets' knowledge of the world; finally and possibly the most important reason, completing a two-month cruise on the high seas *develops a very high level of self-confidence and a strong sense of one's identity.*

I want to concentrate on the last, maybe unrecognized, but possibly most important, reason why the bark *Eagle* is an excellent training environment for gaining self-confidence and respect for oneself as well as one's colleagues.

For hundreds of years, going to sea has been an excellent training ground for individuals to grow up and develop their own identity. There are many examples of this in literature. Who can forget the vivid descriptions in Richard Henry Dana's autobiography *Two Years Before The Mast*, the complex drama in Herman Melville's *Moby Dick*, or the pathos in Joseph Conrad's novel *Lord Jim?* All three of these authors acquired their life's philosophy while on the high seas. The same sort of thing happens to the hundreds of cadets who sail across the wide ocean on the USCGC *Eagle*.

Being at the mercy of the weather and the elements over which you have no control is both a powerful and a humbling experience. Surviving a wild storm with waves crashing over the bow of a large sailing vessel, heeling over at a thirty-degree angle and feeling the wind blow in your face at fifty miles an hour, makes you feel insignificant and God fearing. At the same time, you come through these tough experiences: you climb to the top of the 100-foot mast and help reef the royal sail while hanging on to the yardarm for dear life, or take the steering wheel with one of your classmates and hold a steady course despite the difficulties, or get up in the middle of sound sleep and go out on deck because a sail has to be changed, or stand watch on a beautiful clear night and talk quietly with one of your friends. These adventures are not easily forgotten. Experiencing the joy of beautiful weather, the difficulty of trimming a sail in a gale, the delight of watching the sun set and the moon rise, the exhaustion of standing the midwatch from midnight to 4:00 A.M. and still getting your homework and chores done, the comfort of getting back into your bed while others get up and do the work for a while, the challenge of organizing and managing a work party to carry out an important assignment, the excitement of entering an exotic new port of call after several weeks at sea—all of these experiences in a period of two months transform most boys into men.

Over the centuries, seeing the world by crewing aboard a sailing ship provided an effective means through which young people developed into mature young men and women with a solid sense of identity. Today, it is difficult for our youth to experience a similar adventure. Training aboard the USCGC *Eagle* is an excellent example of a creative anachronism which promotes the coming of age so badly needed in a culture of very advanced technology. In this case, going back to sailing takes us forward in terms of helping adolescents become adults.

PART FOUR RITES OF PASSAGE: RESOURCES

WHAT A WOMAN IS

Erica Helm Meade

As a child Erica Helm Meade learned the healing power of story and has worked with healing tales in her personal and professional life for over twenty-five years. She is the author of *Tell It By Heart: Women and the Healing Power of Story* (Chicago: Open Court Publishing Co., 1995), from which this chapter is adapted. Erica gives presentations and workshops on creativity, initiation, and healing in the United States, Canada, and the United Kingdom. Her use of story incorporates rhythm, ritual, psychology, and art. She has developed and led therapeutic story groups for children and adolescents in numerous residential and outpatient treatment settings.

Erica Meade selects just the right story for Nita, a 17-year-old African American girl, as she inches toward maturity, recognizing and coming to terms with those qualities which create her own uniqueness. What blossoms is her love of her own feminine nature. The story told within the case story is told in many versions in Africa. (See "An African Tale" in *Betwixt and Between*.)

HORMONES

I walked through the door of the teen residence center to lead Tuesday night story group. The familiar smell of fried chops wafted from the kitchen, but a strange quiet filled the hall where raucous teenage voices usually echoed. Silence in the house made me uneasy. It followed calamity, concealed smoldering conflicts, and preceded uproars. I hoped for a smooth evening, but knew better than to expect it. If emotions didn't erupt during dinner; they'd likely explode in group.

The girls lived at the residence center because their home lives had gone awry. What was best in them was badly wounded and scabbed over with ugly defenses. If they didn't get serious help now, they'd become troubled young women, dangerous to themselves, and maybe to others.

The staff hoped to help them outgrow stormy childhoods and root themselves solidly in adult life. This was no easy task. In her first few months, a girl would typically act out family traumas, trying to pull the staff into hurtful battles and stubborn stalemates. But after a year or two, most of the girls let go of destructive routines to find more creative ways to cope. At that stage, a girl became a role model for new residents, demonstrating that their stay there had a purpose: to strengthen and cultivate what was best in them. That winter we were grateful to have one such role model in the house, a seventeen-year-old African American named Nita.

Nita had come to us wearing a studied "tough-girl" guise, and understandably so: Since she was ten, her father had been in prison for violent crimes, and her mother had several younger children by men who tended to treat her roughly, and then drop out of the picture. By age eleven, Nita stood taller than her petite mother. With Dad gone, it seemed only right to try and fill his shoes as the family protector. This wasn't easy in a neighborhood ruled by gangs. For Nita, shielding Mama and the babies meant imitating Dad—staring people down, sticking out her jaw, tossing back her head, and puffing up the broad shoulders and imposing chest she'd inherited from his side of the family. She set out to earn a "rep" on the block by "talking mean," making threats, and occasionally proving she meant business by roughing up kids who messed with her siblings.

But the fact was, she had no real heart for bullying. After a few months at the center she'd happily stopped shoving and hitting altogether. The more we got to know her, the more she stood out as exemplary, making the best of school, her job, and life at the center. Unlike most of the girls' parents, Nita's worked with us and not against us. They'd each begun their own soul-work and they viewed her stay at the center as a chance for Nita to heal. Mom's visits and Dad's letters encouraged just that.

At the dinner table that evening, Nita's seat was empty. It seemed odd, for she never missed a meal, especially chops and gravy.

I sat across from Kate, my story group assistant. She was a full-time staffer with her finger on the pulse of the house. It amazed me how much sense Kate could make of the girls' testy moods, unruly conduct, and strained silences. We always met before group so she could fill me in on house news. Then we'd plan group according to the predominant theme among the girls that week. Whether it was rape, rivalry, or self-esteem, my job was to come up with a story that opened doors for exploration and learning. Neither I nor the staff had ever before seen anything quite like our ritual evolve. Though it was unusual, the administration stood behind it one hundred per cent, because it was the only therapy group run by an "outsider" that had withstood the test of time. It was less threatening to the girls than traditional group therapies. Their fascination with stories expanded their tolerance for talking about painful themes.

We'd tried different formats over the years and finally settled into a routine that worked. It started with dinner. On Tuesdays, the girls set a place for me and I joined them as a way for us to "hang out" together. This enabled them to warm up to me a little before we stepped into story work. It also gave me a chance to acclimate myself to the unpredictable emotional weather, whiff the general mood, and note any oddities before starting group. That night as always, we made chit-chat as we passed steaming platters family style.

"Where's Nita?" I asked Kate.

"She's late getting back from the doctor," Kate said, offering no more. That was my cue that it was confidential, not a cold or flu. Suddenly the chop on my plate didn't look so great. In the past year we'd dealt with pregnancies, AIDS, overdoses, and attempted suicides. I hoped this particular silence wasn't pregnant with tragedy. Kate read my mind and said, "Not to worry. It isn't life threatening."

Shelly, the girl on my left, looked at Kate, and then at me, her eyes growing wide enough to pop. She couldn't hold her tongue long enough to swallow. "It's hormones!" she blurted, ripping the strained silence wide open. Out of her mouth flew half-chewed chunks of food.

Jessica, to my right, snorted in kind. Milk shot out her nose and mouth, "It's *hormones!* Get it? *Whore moans! Like, 'ahhh, ahhh, oohhh . . . Harder, Baby, harder,'*" she howled, throwing her head back, clutching her ribs. The gut force of her laughter spewed a mouthful across the table, splattering Suzanne's angora sweater. Their grotesque display started a chain reaction. Rene's bulimic gag reflex kicked in and she rushed out of the room to barf. Suzanne, covered in milk and little dabs of green—probably half-chewed peas—demanded Jessica pay her on the spot for dry cleaning. Waves of nausea, indignation, rage, and hysteria rolled in both directions down the table. All five staff members had to pull a tight rein to get the girls settled down for the rest of dinner. I can't tell you how relieved I was to leave the table. I envied the cook, alone in the kitchen, peacefully gnawing her chop.

Kate and I met in the remodeled closet we called a consultation room. "Which chair do you want, the wobbly one or the broken one?" I asked. (We shared a long-standing perturbation at the underfunding of youth agencies.) "And remind me next time to lay off the inquiries at dinnertime, will you?"

"I should have forewarned you," she said. "You walked in on a bomb waiting to go off. We've never dealt with a hormone problem before, not since I've been here anyway. We don't know if it's strictly medical, or psychological, and as you saw, the girls come unglued about it. It's dead silence, or total eruption with no middle ground. So we haven't figured out how we're going to discuss it."

That made perfect sense to me. There probably wasn't one of us under that roof—staff, girls, storyteller, or cook—who wouldn't, at some point in life, get anxious about hormones.

"Nita's periods have been sporadic since she started at age eleven," Kate said. "She gets cramps and spotting, but no real flow. She's had tests and x-rays, but they've never found any actual cause for it. This week it's all come up again. That's what the commotion was about. We found out she's got quite a bit of facial hair, and she's mortified about everyone knowing."

"Now how in the world did she keep that hidden around here? I mean, with privacy practically nonexistent, and razors prudently rationed, and all."

"The secrecy is what's sad," Kate said. "Before dawn every morning, Nita's been creeping into the bathroom with razors, tweezers, and a flashlight. That's where all her spending money goes! She saves up, and when she goes

on pass, she buys razors, batteries, and special creams. She's got a whole suit-
case full of hair removal stuff."

"Good God! Imagine her getting up at that hour every day. Put that
together with how hard she works at Dairy Queen to earn a few bucks, and
the picture breaks your heart. It also explains why she's always broke when
we take the girls shopping."

"Exactly," Kate said. "It explains a lot of little things, and it's been going
on the whole time she's been here. Jessica got up early Monday morning and
stumbled in on her. They scared each other half to death. Nita broke down
crying. She was so mortified I took her aside and we had a long talk about it.
She poured her heart out. She feels badly about the facial hair and the fact
that she has no real menstrual flow. She thinks it means she's not a real
woman. Nancy took her to see Dr. Matock. They ran more tests and still
found no organic cause. The doc says it's possible her flow got blocked up at
the onset of menses due to emotional instability or trauma, and she had plenty
of both at the time. That's when Dad went to prison and Mom was hospital-
ized for another miscarriage."

"Yeah, and when she first came here, remember how often she said boys
were lucky because they didn't have periods?"

"She also said she was never going to get pregnant, because it led to
nothing but trouble and pain."

"So if we entertain Doc's theory, we might take it a step further and say,
basically, it wasn't safe to be female. With Dad gone, Nita had to be macho to
take his place."

"Right. She had to have balls to protect the family and had to put her
ovaries on hold, because functional ovaries might lead her into the same trap
Mom was in—pregnant, broke, beat-up, and alone with six kids. So anyway,
Doc talked about trying a minute dose of hormones to see if it boosts her
cycle. He sent her to a specialist today, to get a second opinion. Nita was real
hopeful about it."

"This all makes a lot of sense. Nita's at a crossroad. She's reevaluating
femininity. Before it seemed deplorable, so she rejected her budding womanhood; but now it's looking better, so she wants help bringing it forth. Her attitude shift makes total sense. Her mom's getting stronger and building a better
life. And here at the center, Nita's got a broad spectrum of female role models. Look at us. We're a multi-ethnic staff of intelligent, beautiful, skilled,
professional women." I winked at Kate who was always ready for comic
relief, "We probably make femaleness look like a veritable piece of cake,
don't you think?"

Kate nodded, "Right on! Hysteria, corns, Midol, hair spray, varicose
veins, low end of the pay scale . . . and talk about broad spectrum, I'm broad-
ing all the time," she said patting her hips. We both felt beat from a full day's
work, but a little sarcasm perked us up no end. In truth, we loved hashing
over whatever happened to be stewing among the girls. Story group themes

came together like specialty soups, based on the available stock, staples, and seasonings of the day. On this particular night we had a lot to work with: fresh turmoil, Nita's desire for change, Doc Matock's down-home insight, Kate's meaty observations, and my storytelling. It was my job to act as a wise grandmother would—to come up with a fitting story—one that would nourish Nita, and provide a context for healing. But as often is the case, the story hadn't yet come to me. Kate and I were close to the wire. I closed my eyes and pictured Nita, hoping the right tale would bubble to the surface.

In a recent story group, the others had fallen silent as Nita spoke in a near whisper. "I hadda walk Mama to the store cause she was scared to go alone at night, and I was too young to buy her wine. It was kinda dark at the bus stop and a old lady says to me, 'Excuse me sir, do you know the time?' I kep' walkin' and Mama says, 'Nita, help the lady. You gotta watch on.' Nobody around but me and Mama. I felt bad cause the old lady thought I was a man. After that I asked Mama, 'Do I look like a man?' Mamma said, 'No, baby, you just a big girl, besides, it's dark and that old lady can't see.'

"I feel bad at school too, cause girls in gym class say I'm like a guy. I wanna be more ladylike cause I wanna ask this one boy Gerry to the Sadie Hawkins dance, but I don't want him and his friends to say I'm like a guy. I don't wanna be no Miss Priss, like that frat girl Whitley on TV. I wanna be still sorta outrageous like Tina Turner. Or ladylike, but strong, like Jackie Joyner."

Clearly, it was my job to tell a story which would give Nita permission to be both "ladylike" and strong, like her favorite singer and athlete. The tale should affirm her African roots, as well as her female essence. It should welcome her into the society of womanhood. A popular African tale came to mind. Sobonfu Somé, a West African teacher and a dear friend of mine, had explained the subtle meanings of the tale's myriad variations. Now I prayed my tired memory could recollect one for Nita's sake.

Through the narrow window of our closet, Kate and I had a view of the parking lot. We saw van headlights pierce the fog outside. It was Nancy, bringing Nita back from the doctor. When they passed under the floodlight on the way to the door, we could see crumpled Dairy Queen bags in hand. That meant Nita was fed and ready for group. It also meant she hadn't been too upset to stop by her workplace for food.

Kate yawned ferociously, telegraphing her exhaustion from a long day. "Tell me you're not brain-dead," she pleaded.

"Okay," I nodded, "remember that wonderful African tale we worked with a couple of years ago, about a girl who's both strong and beautiful? That story's pertinent to Nita, because the heroine is also a protector, and the story's about her courage through the difficult passage into womanhood."

With that said, there was no need for further discussion. Kate and I had been doing group together for years. Planning group meant identifying the theme of the day and selecting a fitting story. The rest had become an ingrained ritual that varied little. Kate rang the bell and rounded up the girls while I arranged the group room. I moved the sofa, fluffed pillows, and softened the lights, as if readying my living room for guests. The fact was, I was the visitor. The center was their home. But it's important to arrange a room for stories: dimming harsh lights to a softer glow, drawing seats in toward the hearth, clearing away distractions.

Evoking the mythic requires subtle attention to the surroundings. Our ancestral storytellers knew better than to compete with noise, food, or bright lights. The African story would evoke mythic presences: the virtuous heroine, the river hag, and the river monster. These beings are disinclined toward fluorescent lights and plastic chairs. They're much more likely to join us in the half-light where candles flicker and shadows dance. Stories require their mystique, and it's the teller's duty to guard it. Nighttime, gathering together time, fireside or hearthside: These are the times and places for story, and the settings most conducive to the mythic imagination.

Adolescence also has a mystique of its own, and the girls made it their business to guard it. They didn't just enter the room. They tried new walks, overstated gestures, emitted sighs, exuded auras, brooded silences, unleashed moods. They strutted, trudged, stomped, and crept into the room. One posture begged, "Notice me!" while another said, "Look at me and you die!"

Rounding them up took Kate a good five minutes. The first arrivals were antsy, impatient, eager to start. Several asked to *brag* first. *Bragging* was our opening ritual, each girl's opportunity to announce prideful accomplishments, small pleasures, and the week's good fortune. Brags helped start group on a positive note, which wasn't easy with girls who saw life as hell, families as torture, and themselves as the cause of other people's pain. Gathering around the hearth, talking about their talents and blessings didn't come naturally, but over time, most of them came to relish the chance to display their gems for admiration.

But there were always those who couldn't pull it off. That night, Shannon was stuck in an old round of self-hate. She tried to make it a team sport. "You all hate me!" she screamed. "None of you care about me! I don't have any fucking brags! How could I, stuck in this jail? . . . Erica can go ahead and tell the dumb story, but I'm not listening!" Sometimes when a girl couldn't brag for herself, others in the group could. At such times, they bragged for her, and she basked in their praise. But Shannon was so steeped in self-loathing, that praise hurt. It brought forth too many hunger pangs for what had always been missing. She was like a starving child who'd have to sip weak broth before she'd be strong enough to digest real food. Listening on the sly while pretending not to need us was about all she could take.

As latecomers filed in, and the brags wound down, the girls prodded, "What's the story?" "What's it about?" "What kind of story is it?" "What nationality?" These questions were also part of our ritual. The cataloging gave them a gratifying foothold in the story. Nita came through the door just in the nick of time. I held off answering until I knew she could hear.

"I'm hoping to tell an African story," I said with deliberate emphasis on *African*. Nothing awakened their souls like the mention of ancestral roots. They were forever begging me to tell tales from their particular ethnicity. Since they saw family heritage as a disaster, the notion of coming from a larger family moved them deeply. It was my job to unearth the tales their grandmothers would tell if lost traditions had remained intact. Celebrating ancestry through lore became a matter of esteem—affirming their origins—making each girl a heroine for a night.

The three African American girls beamed. It was their night. Nicki smiled and said, "My ancestors were African."

Nita plunked down beside her and piped up, "Of course they were! Did you think they were Swedish?" She seemed full of moxie for a girl whose best-kept secret was out on the table.

Nicki snapped back to prove she was heritage-wise and nobody's fool, "Coulda been from Brazil or Haiti."

But Nita got the last word, "They all from Africa, girl! Haiti, Brazil, Cuba, Jamaica, Costa Rica: They all from Africa." It was settled.

"Sorry I was late," Nita went on, "but, can I tell my brag before the story?" Kate gave her the go-ahead. She spoke softly, almost whispering, "Dr. Matock sent me to a special lady's doctor, I guess you call her. And I'm real happy cause she's real nice and she's helping me with a problem I have." Nita spoke without raising her eyes. Kate shot me a subtle glance, sharing my surprise that Nita addressed her theme head on. "She explained something to me. Lotta girls have facial hair." Again I felt Kate's surprise, but we avoided checking each other's eyes. "And it's a girl's prerogative if she wants to let it show, or get rid of it, or whatever she wants. So, I'm happy, cause if I don't want to shave, I can have hormone pills or 'lectrolysis that won't chafe my face." Nita smiled like it was Christmas. There wasn't a distraction in the room. The other girls kept their eyes averted, and tried to look casual, but their ears hadn't missed a word. A mixture of fear, awe, sympathy, and respect filled the silence. It'd be a long time before *hormones* were the butt of in-house jokes.

"Tell the story," somebody said.

Nita was off the hook for the moment, and I was on. I hadn't told the chosen tale for over two years. How could I be sure it would surface on call? Like everyone else, the storyteller lives in a state of constant amnesia. Just because you knew a tale at one time, there's no guarantee it will always come back to you. I knew dozens of tales by heart and if pressed, could have roughly summarized several more. But knowledge once held at the fingertips, can easily fall out of reach like a lost book. I needed a moment to focus on retrieving the tale from the dusty shelves of my memory. Luckily Kate had a few announcements to make. While she talked, I closed my eyes and tuned inward.

Our ancestral storytellers saw memory as a sacred function. They believed memory endured like a mountain, yet flowed ever onward like a great river. The memory goddess was said to imprint the soul by placing her indelible mark on the storyteller's heart and senses. This explained memory's link to odors, textures, images, sounds, rhythms, and strong emotions. Numbers can be learned by rote, but stories must be learned by heart. To awaken her memory of a tale, the teller must picture the first scene, smell its landscape, and hear the first word. This is how we prime the well of memory, coaxing the first scene out of the rock. First it trickles, then begins to flow down the mountainside forming a stream, gradually gathering the momentum of a river. But I was tired and the riverbed was still dry.

Kate wrapped up the announcements. The girls adjusted their pillows and nestled into their seats. They nagged me, just the way I like them to. That too, was part of our ritual. They listened better when they had to work to get a story. "C'mon! Are we having a story tonight or what?"

I still didn't have a solid enough footing in the story to tell it with confidence. "I hope we're having a story," I said, "but I forgot how to get hold of it. What are the instructions from Sobonfu?" Sobonfu had coached me on the ways of storytelling in her village, and had encouraged me to share them with the girls. They'd never met her face to face, but they loved her nonetheless because her methods held great delight. Nicki said, "Take your basket to the land of the ancestors and see if they'll lend us a story." I often teased that if we didn't ask politely, the ancestors would put a recipe in the basket instead of a story, and we'd have to spend the evening making crocodile stew. I looked around the room at the girls and settled my eye on Nita. "Nita," I said, "would you like to do the asking?"

"Okay," she said grinning. "Please, Honorable Ancestors, put a good one in Erica's basket so we won't get bored and fall asleep or have to cook stew."

RETRIEVAL: PLUNGING DEEPLY

I closed my eyes and pictured Sobonfu's radiant face. Then I saw her grandmother, a consummate elder storyteller. I held my basket and prayed for a story for Nita. Luckily, when I peered inside, the first scene was there. I saw African women standing at the river's edge. I heard flies buzz, felt gritty wet sand on my feet and velvety brown water at my ankles. I smelled the yeasty sweet river. I now felt confident the story wanted to be told. Word-pictures began to surface, trickling up from memory, falling forth from my lips.

There was once a village alongside a great river in Africa. The water rolled along the sand each day as it had the day before, the year before, the century before, and all the time before that which

no one even bothered to count. And all that time, people lived in the village. And all that time, when girls reached a certain age—the age when nature began to work changes in their bodies—their elders gave them a gift. The gift stood for female beauty, and with it came certain powers, status, and responsibilities. The gift was a belt, with beautiful stones and shells, and each girl wore hers to protect the generative powers within her body. No girl received hers until womanhood came upon her from the inside out.

One girl's elders gave her a fine belt with golden amber, red bloodstone, and hundreds of coral beads sewn together in a swirl, like river water 'round a rock. It comforted the girl to feel it 'round her waist in the morning when she filled her urn at the river's edge. She wore her belt so proudly, and it looked so beautiful encircling her hips, that all the people who saw her turned their heads to take a second look. Looking at her made them notice all the beauty around them: the trees, the river, the sky, and the distant mountains.

This story had endless variations depending on the time and purpose of the telling. Sobonfu said, "You don't wear the same dress each day, well, the story doesn't either." That day the point was to enhance Nita's wardrobe, and the belt was no mere accessory. It carried the power of the mountains and the never-ending flow of the river. It protected Jackie Joyner's power-source as she leapt hurdles. It was the outrageous fringe shimmying at Tina Turner's hips as she sang.

Other village girls were jealous of her belt. When the girl walked by, one whispered, "She thinks she's better than us." The jealous girls decided to trick her. The next morning they gathered in the center of the village. A clever one called out, "Oh, did you hear the wise woman's prediction? I'm so frightened!"

"No," said the girl with the belt, "I didn't hear. What did the wise woman predict?"

"She said the river god is angry and the river will flood its banks! All of us will be washed away and drowned, unless we girls throw our belts to the river god as gifts. That alone will save the village."

"Is it true?" asked the girl.

The others nodded, "Yes, it's true!"

"Then we must go at once!" said the girl with the belt. She ran to the river. The other girls ran too. She unhooked her belt. The other girls unhooked theirs. The girl hurled her fine belt far out into the middle of the river. Then the other girls laughed. They had only pretended to hurl their belts. Now they put them back on and walked back to the village.

Being fooled like that made her eyes sting with tears. She wanted to get her belt back. She took a deep breath and dove into the river, swimming further and further into the dark water until she came to the deepest spot.

Our heroine was willing to sacrifice her belt when she believed it would protect the village. Nita, too, was a courageous protector, willingly sacrificing aspects of femaleness when she believed it would help protect the family. Now came the time for both heroines to retrieve what was lost. Nita, too had leapt into the river—going to doctors, learning about hormones, talking about it in group. She'd plunge again and again before the issue was resolved.

THE RIVER HAG

There at the depths of the river, the girl saw the river hag with green slimy hair undulating all around her. The river hag was covered with sores. The sores oozed slime, and in the slime small snails crawled, and worms burrowed.

"Greetings, Grandmother," the girl said respectfully. "Have you seen my belt?"

"Belt?" asked the river hag in a loud, raspy voice. "Did you say belt?"

"Yes," said the girl and she told the whole story of how she'd been tricked.

"I can help you," said the river hag, "but first, you help me. Lick clean my sores."

The girl was wise enough to know she was speaking to a river spirit in hag form, so she took the hag's hand, and licked the slime from the sore on her wrist. Then she licked clean all the sores on the hag's arms. Then her back, and so on until all the sores were clean, and the river hag was happy.

The point of the river hag was not to force the girls to revel in morbidity, but to tell them in no uncertain terms, that old wounds must be tended before the radiant belt can be restored. Now that her secret was out, Nita had begun to lick clean the sores of her bruised female identity. In doing so, she was bound to taste her mother's uncleansed wound, and perhaps her grand-mother's, for there was no telling how long the female branch of the family had been ailing.

Like our heroine, Nita would have to overcome squeamishness. She'd have to accept certain physical realities if her menses started flowing as she hoped. In sex ed class she learned that nutrient-rich menstrual blood had the power to give life, but she also noted that discarded menstrual pads smelled like "something dead dragged outta the river." Her nose read the paradoxical news of the natural world. Fertility's next of kin is a black sheep called decay.

Hidden in the river hag scene is the knowledge that the passage toward womanhood links us not only to beauty and generativity, but also to the mysterious depths, the very source where the river of life is inextricably linked to decay and death. Our ancestors understood this, so much so, that whether Aztec or Persian, they worshipped the cycle of life, death, and rebirth, all in one goddess, the Great Mother. Her fruitful womb was also the tomb where the dead were digested and regenerated to continue the cycle.

The river hag is a vestige of the revered African river goddess. She teaches what schooling does not: that the passage to womanhood is a powerful step from which we must not shrink, but it also takes us one step nearer to old age, decline, and death. Sobonfu says this teaches a young woman to respect elders because in them she sees her future self. The ancestors felt it imperative to impart this knowledge to young women. That's why their stories convey the full spectrum of what it means to be a woman.

The girl heard a loud slurping sound coming from upstream. She felt the river floor shuddering beneath her feet. Slithering toward them was the river monster . . .

The river hag said, "Hide beneath my hair." The girl did just that. The river monster slithered up to the hag and said, "I smell a human being! I want to eat it for my breakfast!" The river hag pointed downstream and said, "She went that way." Luckily the river monster moved on in search of lunch. After he was gone, the hag gave the girl a belt more beautiful and more laden with powerful gems than the one she'd had before. She thanked the hag, put the new belt 'round her waist, and swam back to shore. She dried herself in the sun and then went back to the village to complete her daily chores.

When the jealous girls saw her new belt they asked, "Where did you get that belt?" She told them about the hag at the bottom of the river.

All the jealous girls ran to the river and hurled their belts far out to the middle. Then they dove in and swam deeper and deeper until they met the slimy hag. "Give me a belt!" they cried. The hag told them they must help her first. But when she told them to lick clean her sores, they said, "FORGET IT!"

Just then the river monster came back upstream. He smelled lots of human flesh and was by now very hungry. The river hag warned the girls. They swam as fast as they could to get away but were never heard from again. As for the girl with the special belt, she never again fetched water from the river without thanking the

river spirit in all her forms. She lived to a ripe old age and became a medicine woman. People came from far and wide to seek her advice. When the time came, she taught her granddaughters that the strength and beauty of womanhood grow from the inside out. And that is the end of the tale. Thank you Ancestors for lending it to us. Now we give it back.

JEALOUS GIRLS

"Thank you, Ancestors!" the girls said clapping their hands, as was our custom. I scanned their faces in order to read Nita's without singling her out. She wore a knowing smile as if the tale had brought her a personal message.

"Round-robin?" Suzanne asked.

"Yes," I answered, "round-robin." This meant everyone would have a chance to make a personal comment.

Suzanne wanted to start. "Lots of girls at school are jealous of me," she whined petulantly, "because they'll never have my hairstyle and clothes. I'm really used to people being jealous. And I don't care if they hate me because I know why. They just wish they had my looks, that's all." There were myriad reasons for Suzanne's superficial self-image, but that's not where we were headed that night. I glanced Nita's way to see if she was ready to speak yet, but she avoided my eyes.

Kim wanted to go next. She launched into a hateful diatribe against her mother and sisters. They were bitches who hated her because she was beautiful and got more attention. Kim's tone was crass, and it echoed Suzanne's focus on surface appearance. The story spoke of inner beauty, and yet there we were, right back in the covergirl/pin-up mentality, where beauty equals slim young blondes, waif-like poses, and pouty lips. Kim and Suzanne set a stiff cosmetic code in the house, which many of the younger girls tried to emulate. For all of them, but especially for Nita, we needed an expanded standard of beauty.

"What kind of beauty are you talking about Kim?" I asked, "an outside shell, or something that shines from the inside out?"

"Well the story is about the inside kind," Kim said with a shrug as if we were out of her league. She looked around to see if anyone was going to help her. Luckily, Nita's hand popped up. She said, "I'll speak about that 'cause that's my problem." Kim looked relieved to be off the hook.

"I won't name names," Nita said, "but I get jealous of some of them girls at school who wear short skirts and flirt with guys. I'm not talkin' about none of you girls, here. You're all mostly good friends of mine. But I get mad when guys pay attention to girls like that—girls who just hang around the mall and buy stuff with money from their folks. They don't respect no elders, and yet they got tons of belts to wear, know what I'm sayin'? I usta intimidate some of them girls. But I'm trying to make a change. I wanna get over my old 'intimidation tactics' like the school counselor calls it. But when I get jealous like that, I just get mean, like I don't know no other way."

"Is it fair to say, Nita, that there are two parts at work?" I asked, "One as courageous and kind as the belt girl, and one that can be mean like the jealous girls?"

"Yep, that about says it," Nita grinned.

"In the story, the meanness washes down the river. Who knows what happened to the jealous girls? It's the belt girl who goes back to the village and puts down roots. Which is taking root in your life?"

"You mean like, the kind part or the mean part? The kind part, for sure. It's going that way more and more. That's the way it's gotta keep on, too, if I wanna make my sports goals and go to the dance and all.

"See, I guess everyone knows I'm sprung on this guy, Gerry. I feel all soft when he's around, and I don't wanna hide my inside beauty any more. I wanna have my inside beauty show like the belt girl."

"Nita, I think it's working. Right now, for instance," I looked around at the others and added, "I'm probably not the only one to notice."

Several voices piped up. "Yeah, it shows." "Heck, yeah, all the time."

"That's what I really want," she said smiling. "I don't want to go all sissy and quit track or nothin', but I wanna be more ladylike 'cause I don't wanna be all dressed up at the dance and have Gerry's friends say I look outa place."

TESTING THE WATER

The hormone thing would be worked out later, and so would her worry over the facial hair, but at this moment, among her peers, Nita bared her soul to reveal her most immediate fear: that of a possible wisecrack at a fragile moment. She was testing the water, but she wasn't going to plunge into serious dance plans until she felt some assurance of safety. She'd outgrown the old intimidation tactics, but what new shield would take their place? I didn't know the answer, but I knew how to respect the question. I knew how to wade along the edge of it, watching the water for clues. From previous talks I'd learned Gerry was an excellent candidate for Nita's first date. There was no reason to suspect treacherous waters there. His good intentions didn't form a complete shield, but they strengthened the potential safety of the first date.

"You don't want to be embarrassed," I said, just to let Nita know I was still wading beside her. "As I see it, Nita, you have two things in your favor." That statement drew all the girls' attention like fish to a fly. Nita wasn't the only one worrying about the dance.

"First off, you know Gerry respects you. No doubt he sees your inner beauty." Her eyes grew wide, she held her breath and nodded stiffly. "His respect, that's one big thing in your favor. And he's no dummy, either. Is he the type to respect someone who doesn't deserve it?"

She looked to the group. "No!" "No way, not Gerry," chimed those who knew him. Nita took that in and smiled.

"What's the other thing?" she asked, her eyes pinned to mine.

"The other thing you already named yourself. You have friends here, people who love and respect you. Perhaps their love is like an invisible belt, one that gives you strength and self-respect." I waded out a little deeper, and hoped there were no jagged rocks. "Some of your friends will be at the dance. I don't know for sure, but it seems to me they might be the types who'd stick up for you if anyone said anything rude." Again, the girls nailed the bait. They found calls to loyalty irresistible.

Kim made a fist and said, "Yeah, if that pig Dwayne says anything, I'll kill him, Nita. You have my word."

Shannon hollered, "We'll torch their lockers!"

"I'll put hot sauce in their jockstraps!" Jessica yelled.

We teetered on the old familiar verge of chaos. Kate gave me one of her *How-you-gonna-get-out-of-this-one?* looks. She had no intention of rescuing me. I had to think fast. "Quiet!" I yelled. "Quiet!" The girls weren't used to me yelling and they hushed more out of surprise than obedience. "The loyalty is excellent," I said, "but you have to express that appropriately."

"Bla, bla, bla," said Christine. "You're just like staff."

"Hey!" I said. "We're talking here about supporting Nita. She wants to let her inner beauty show at the dance. She wants to feel ladylike and she's trying to get away from intimidation tactics!" I turned to Nita to get the focus back to her. "Is that right, Nita? Is that what you mean by ladylike?" Some of my feminist friends might balk at my repetition of Nita's phrase, "ladylike," but she used it in a positive sense, and echoing it was more respectful than substituting a word of my choice in its place.

"I don't want to pour hot sauce on no jocks, if that's what you mean," she said grinning.

"Okay then, peanut butter, get it, *penis* butter?!" Jessica whooped, whirling hysterically away from the point once again.

That was it. Kate had had enough. "Jessica, one more outburst like that and you're out of group for the rest of the night."

"They did it, too," Jessica pouted, settling back into her seat. "Okay, I'll shut up, but I don't think it's fair. Kim called Dwayne a pig."

"Look," I said, "the loyalty and enthusiasm are great. But this point about being ladylike is important too. Aren't there any ladylike ways to stick up for a friend?"

"See, that's what *I* want to know," Nita said. We had six minutes before group ended, and in that time I wanted to respond to her question, or at least try. To drop the tough-girl guise, and embrace the softer side of womanhood,

Nita would have to feel safe. To release her hold on the protector role, she'd have to feel protected. Staff helped her feel safe at the center, but they couldn't follow her to the dance. I was wary about putting the other girls in the protector role, but if they couldn't stick up for her, who could? Nita needed to learn that no woman is an island, sufficient unto herself. She needed to learn the type of strength one gains from relying on trusted others. Among the girls, as in families, individual healing requires group support.

I took a breath and plunged headfirst into deeper waters. "What we're talking about here, is how to stick up for a friend without attacking like a gang of vandals." I looked each of the girls in the eye. None of them had the level of sophistication I was talking about, not even Nita. They'd had assertiveness training, and could distinguish assertiveness from hostile aggression, but when the heat was on, the timid ones hid, and the fighters lashed out. I knew the role model in this instance would have to be Kate.

"Kate," I said, "say you had a friend like Nita, and you overheard mean remarks about her. What would you do?"

"Hmmm," Kate said. "Well, I guess I'd say something to stick up for my friend. Like I might say, 'Hey! You don't really know Nita but I do, and I can tell you straight up, she's a fine person. That's all there is to it.'"

"I like that," I said. "It's strong, without getting overly hostile." I turned to Nita. "How would you feel with a friend sticking up for you like that?"

"I'd feel good," Nita nodded approvingly.

"Do you think that's ladylike enough for a dance?"

"Yep. See, that's what I'm talking about, but that's hard for me 'cause I'm used to intimidation tactics."

"What about your friends here? How would you feel if one of them stood up for you that way?"

"I would feel very happy as long as they didn't embarrass me with no hot sauce," Nita grinned.

Jessica piped up, "Kate, can I please say something now? It's not about hot sauce. It's totally appropriate." Kate nodded. Jessica said, "I'm not going to the dance, but if I was, I'd say something appropriate to stick up for Nita."

Kate encouraged, "Well, okay, Jessica, what would you say?"

"Like, say Dwayne said something really gross like . . ." Kate raised a finger in warning. Jessica caught herself, "Well, just say somebody made a comment that wasn't appropriate. Then I'd say, 'Hey, Nita's my friend and she looks good in a dress. What's a matter—are you jealous?'" She checked Kate to see if she'd won any approval and Kate nodded. Nita nodded too.

"Some of your friends will be there, won't they, Nita?" I asked. She nodded again, "Yeah. Nicki, Charmaine, and Shelly."

"I wonder if they might support you at the dance," I urged, looking their way. Charmaine spoke up, "I wouldn't let some creep get away with raggin' on Nita." Nicki and Shelly felt the same way. They agreed to meet with Kate before bedtime, to start planning how they might support Nita at the dance, appropriately, of course.

"It's nearly time to go," I said. "Thanks for a good group. Nita, you're brave to face things head on. I'd say you're as courageous as the belt girl, plunging right into the river. Going to a dance is one of many plunges you're taking this year. There's no guarantee you won't meet the river monster, but with support from others, you have every reason to believe in yourself and follow your hopes, just like the belt girl." Nita beamed and looked around to make sure everyone heard.

"Okay, group's over," I announced. "You ladies can go." Sometimes group ended with a rush of sweatshirts and hairstyles racing out the door. That night, the girls just sat. They asked for another story. They asked why I had to leave—why we couldn't have a slumber party. Kate and I had to peel them out of their chairs in order to get back to our closet to debrief.

Weeks later Nita did go to the dance with Gerry. They looked big, sweet, and shy in the photos she showed at brag time. It was the first of a few outings with him, none of which ended in humiliation.

In the months to come Nita's hormone supplements needed a bit of adjusting. But her menses finally flowed to her satisfaction and for the facial hair she chose electrolysis. After a year Doc Matock stopped the hormone supplement altogether. He'd been right. A little boost did the trick. After that Nita's blood flowed with the moon, of its own accord.

She continued to bring a gentle openness to group and set a supportive tone for others trying to make changes. She channeled her fierceness into athletics, gaining the admiration of her team. She won several track awards and her coach helped her seek college scholarships. I went to her last high school track meet and saw her scathing glare unnerve the competition. It delighted me no end to see her intimidation tactics put to good use. She shook her well-formed limbs, looking as confident as Tina Turner and as focused as Jackie Joyner. Nita had found her own way to weave *sweet* together with *tough*. She gave the word *ladylike* new meaning, and taught us all something about what a woman is.

TWENTY SEVEN | GUIDELINES FOR CREATING EFFECTIVE RITES OF PASSAGE

Robert P. Eckert

Bob Eckert is founder and director of the Learning Institute for Functional Education (the LIFE Institute), located in the northern Adirondacks in New York. He is a holistic therapist specializing in addictions, delinquency, and wellness. Besides having worked as a family therapist, he has been a consultant to health care and educational institutions, business organizations, and individuals.

Training programs offered at the LIFE Institute include Stress Management in the Workplace, Drug Proofing Children: A Parents' Guide, Healthy Alternatives to Addictive Lifestyles, Preventing Drug Abuse and Delinquency, and many other special request topics such as adolescent depression and suicide and creative problem solving. A special course on rites of passage draws on anthropology, archetypal theory, and experiential education techniques to develop criteria for effective contemporary rites-of-passage programs.

In the paper presented here, Mr. Eckert presents a model for constructing modern rites of passage based on the idea that rites of passage should promote not only physical, but psychological, social, and spiritual health as well. His suggestions apply not only to adolescents but to all major stages of life.

Although we have had rites of passage within our culture for quite some time, we have not been as focused on rites of passage as we need to be. Specifically, we have not yet decided exactly what we want to occur as the result of such rituals. Consequently, often there is no power in them; or worse, they orient the initiate in directions which are less than healthy. As a West African proverb says, "It takes the whole village to raise a child." The elders of the village must come together to discuss how they will raise their children into young adults and initiate them in a healthy direction.

Another problem is that many of our current rites of passage seem unrelated to our contemporary culture. They are not performed in the context of a value system which informs a mature, responsible movement through developmental cycles. Likewise, too little of the currently available literature on rites of passage focuses on how to introduce them into American culture.

Responding to these issues, I wish to discuss how we might implement constructive rites of passage within our contemporary society, utilizing systems and supports already available. I will also suggest a generic template which we can use to judge the efficacy of any rite of passage we might wish to design or examine.

Implementing rites of passage is wonderful, yet somewhat frightening work. My concern is that we might teach people the techniques and power of

rites of passage *outside of* an appropriate ethical standard. There are many
people in the world today who use the power of ritual and group process in a
negative way. We need to be careful that we don't do the same thing. If properly applied, the template which I will present will prevent our doing so and
will facilitate successful life-enhancing experiences for those whom we guide
and the community to which they belong.

ELEMENTS OF EFFECTIVE RITES OF PASSAGE

If a rite of passage is to be successful it must be strong. When you look at any
passage ritual, irrespective of the culture which facilitates it, you will find
many "power generators."

What makes an effective rite of passage? First, there must be very
strong standards for the movement of an initiate from the preinitiated state
to the new status he or she achieves by undergoing the ritual. There must
be absolutely firm standards about what qualifies the initiate to move to a
higher level of functioning, responsibility, or privilege within the society.
Often in the United States, Canada, and most of Western society, in our need
to move young adults to higher levels of responsibility uniformly and collectively, we initiate people who are not yet ready. We settle upon a specific age,
rather than more appropriate criteria such as demonstrated emotional maturity, problem-solving skills, and ethical behavior as determinants of an initiate's readiness. We must take a more individualized approach if we are to
empower the rite of passage. No one should be initiated until he or she is
ready. No one is ready until he or she has met the standards that the culture or
group has laid down for the initiation—and the standards must never be
weakened.

The second characteristic of effective rites of passage is that of *congruence:* congruence between the adult and the youth, the initiator and the initiate. We adults must embody the lifestyle, the standards, and the ethics we recommend for our young people. There can be no hypocrisy. In the United
States, for example, we are trying to initiate our young people to a drug-free
lifestyle in all of our drug-prevention programs, but the adult community
itself is not drug free. American adults use legal drugs, for instance, which we
know are killing as many or more people than all of the illegal drugs combined. There is no congruence between our injunction to younger people to
"Just Say No" and our actual behavior. Adolescents are skilled at finding
adult hypocrisy and throwing it in our faces. We call that rebellion. In this
way adolescents are our teachers and what they have been teaching us by
their difficulties with drug abuse and sexuality is that we are hypocrites, for
what we are asking them to do is incongruent with what *we* do. In this double
standard, we see a portion of the genesis of youth drug problems. Unless we
adults exemplify the value system we hope to instill in our young people,

there is very little likelihood that we will see long-term positive effects through any form of ritualized initiation.

Next, when we look at the more effective rites of passage, we notice that very frequently the power of the ritual itself creates a *nonordinary state of consciousness* which acts as a unique marker, indicating that a change has occurred. Many of us have experienced these nonordinary states, this altered form of consciousness precipitated by various rituals: A well-run funeral process which places us in deep connection with our grief; the tingles that run up and down our bodies when we hear/sing the national anthem at sporting events; the feelings conjured at the movies when we see people doing things to care for others in distress; the intense emotion in parents at the birth and during milestones of growth/accomplishment of their children. Somehow there is some *connection to that which is greater than I.* Whether we want to call that thing God, the Holy Spirit, the collective unconscious, kundalini, love energy, or team spirit, these feelings clearly evoke some deep sense of connection to that which we experience as being external to self. Rites of passage, when utilized appropriately, evoke just this sort of feeling. And insofar as they do, they increase in power and effectiveness.

The power of the ritual is not the ritual itself. The power is in the nonordinary state induced in the direct participants, and in us as we watch.

Recently, I experienced a fire walk. Although it is sad that such a powerful ritual is used outside of appropriate cultural contexts (and because of flexible standards and poor preparation a number of people got second- and third-degree burns), it serves nonetheless as an example of the anchoring of change with a nonordinary state. The powerful preparation, using techniques as diverse as neurolinguistic programming and karate, placed us in the nonordinary state necessary to walk eight feet across flaming and glowing coals without being burned. Those who were *ready* and able to sustain the nonordinary state suffered no consequences. Those who were not ready were burned. The power of the ritual lies in learning to reach the nonordinary state. The fire walk is just a test to see if you've achieved that state.

There seems to be an innate drive to experience nonordinary or altered states of consciousness, this sense of connection to that which is greater than self. However, when people attempt to achieve it through the use of alcohol and other drugs, the ability to experience connection is decreased if not lost entirely. Effective rites of passage allow the initiate to experience these nonordinary states of connection, and thus the *initiation becomes a strong emotional marker of change.* We have not done a very good job in our culture of teaching our young people how to have such experiences in a drug-free way, and consequently we see many adolescents self-initiate with various experiences in unguided, immature ways.

As we look at the history of rites of passage and at initiations in other cultures, we notice the fourth element which seems to invest them with power and increase their effectiveness. This element is typically a *symbolic death/rebirth experience*. As the initiate moves from one state of being to another within the community or family or self, there should be a death of that which was, prior to the birth of that which will be. This death/rebirth cycle can be symbolized in ritual, it can be experienced through the imagery of a nonordinary state, and it can be facilitated through periods of withdrawal followed by a welcoming into the new level of social integration. Initiations of adolescents into adulthood, for instance, frequently include a statement made symbolically or directly to parents in the presence of their child, to the effect that they will never see that child alive again. In fact they will, but they will never see their son or daughter *as* a child again, because upon completion of the particular rite of passage which is about to begin, they will accept the child as an adult. Recently I helped initiate a young man into the mature masculine. I symbolized this shift by asking him to burn a picture of himself as a young boy which his mother had given him after it had been hanging on the living room wall for many years. When she gave us the picture, I said to her as she looked at it that she would never see her boy alive again. Although she was prepared for this statement, it nonetheless caused her to cry. As her son saw the tears, his confidence in his safety with me was shaken. This created a fear which marked the event emotionally, and emptied him of the self-assured "hero"; this prepared him to integrate a more mature form of this ego structure (the warrior) during the ordeal phase of his rite of passage. We took a new picture on a mountaintop, after he had survived the ordeal of climbing. This new picture was then placed in the old frame and rehung.

A fifth quality is the *health of the initiator* or initiators. A healthy rite of passage requires a guide who has internalized the concept that at no time in our development are we complete. At no time are we all grown up. At no time are we anything more than a human being. This attitude implies that the rite of passage, too, is only a marker in overall development, and that development must continue afterwards. Too frequently today the initiate, upon completion of his or her particular task, assumes and is supported in assuming that he or she is now a complete, elite human being. Such pretentiousness can be dangerous to the initiate and to others, emotionally and, in some cases, physically.

Healthy initiators create humility in the initiate. As elders we need to be careful not to perpetrate the myth that once one passes through this initiation one's life will be easy. It will not. It will be different. The initiate will gain a level of respect and responsibility that he or she did not have before, but he or she will continue to encounter challenges. I think often we lose the power of our initiations because the adult initiators attempt to put themselves across as "having it all together." This is exactly what happens in cults. A charismatic individual cons people into believing that they have at last found someone who has it all together, when in fact they have not. Any of us who do rites-of-passage work need to be fully aware of who we are. We are not perfect, so we need to do this work with an attitude of humility. We must be willing to explore our personal shadows.

The sixth condition which makes rites of passage effective is a *sincere desire* of the uninitiated to attain the rights and privileges associated with having successfully negotiated that particular rite of passage. Initiation has to be something people want. In America today, for instance, there is a very strong and almost universal desire among middle adolescents to have a driver's license and to own an automobile. Their desire itself affords an excellent opportunity to require that they demonstrate readiness through the successful completion of a healthy rite of passage into adulthood. If a rite of passage is to be challenging, there must be motivation to go through it. The family, subculture, or society must extend some privilege to the initiates or they will not do the work required to move to a higher status. This work is always difficult, always challenging, and willingness to do it must be proportionately compensated.

The seventh component is a *period of preparation*. Rites of passage do not occur outside a context of growth. There must be some form of learning and development involved. The initiate must prepare to meet the criterion for recognition at the new level of being. Medical school is an excellent example of this. Often, then, there is a preliminary period of isolation, or an ordeal or a trial to overcome, such as the residency period for young doctors.

Finally, there is often an outer symbol, some form of *outward ornamentation* which indicates to others that the individual has completed a particular rite of passage. For physicians, the right to place the honorific "Dr." before their name, and wear the white garments of their craft. In American culture, the wedding band for married couples.

A VISION FOR GROWTH

Earlier, I mentioned my fear that rites of passage techniques can be used inappropriately. Now I would like to present a model of ethics by which we can examine any rite of passage to test whether it assists the initiate to move in a healthy direction.

We remember that in the Old Testament story of Moses, after he spent time on the mountain he came back carrying the tablets, the standard by which he was told to live. Any rite of passage must be informed by some strong ethical standard. When we go to the mountain we must return with something we can live by. There are many useful, positive, healthy, ethical systems. What is needed is a template by which they can be judged, one specific enough to provide guidance, yet general enough to preclude offending the various orthodoxies.

The work involved in preparing for a rite of passage is very much like the ordeal of climbing a mountain. Climbing brings us to a place to view and understand that which is not always easy to see. But we have to come back down. There is every indication that well-designed rites of passage assist the initiate in living a life based on the memory of what was seen on/from the mountaintop.

That is the essence of what a rite of passage will do, but to do so it must effectively supply a focal point at which the initiate can aim.

The question is, does this rite of passage that I am leading move the participants to a higher state of health? To answer that question, I propose that we use a model based on the concept of health in all of its aspects.

HEALTH

A good rite of passage will lead to a healthier state. But health is not a destination—it is a process. It is not a place you get to, it is an ongoing activity.

BIOLOGICAL ASPECTS

First, we need biological, i.e., physical health. For example, a person becomes more biologically healthy as his or her immune system responds more appropriately to insults from the environment. One might ask, "What's this got to do with making a person more valuable and functional in a culture?" As the immune system improves, the person is more capable of being fully who he or she is. Think of the times you are sick: are you as functional as you would like to be? Are you as good a husband or wife, lover, parent, or worker as you could be? Are you at your greatest potential? No. So we need to focus on the health of the immune system.

We also need to take a look at our cardiovascular and musculoskeletal health; not primarily so that we might run faster or lift more weight, but rather because regular exercise will increase our awareness of our body, our kinesthetic awareness. This is valuable for it enables us to tune in to our body's responses to our thoughts about the environment around us. Effective rites of passage help us develop such body awareness.

Another constituent of biological health is the ability of the organs to work in complex harmony as an integrated organ system. Other than our genetic endowment, our organ systems' health is influenced primarily by what we eat. So we need to think about food and what that has to do with becoming a better, healthier person.

In short, in the biological arena we want to remove physical limitations and maximize the initiate's potential by making him or her more physically healthy. If your preparation and rituals require this, whatever your particular technique, you are moving in the right direction.

PSYCHOLOGICAL ASPECTS OF HEALTH

Second, we must focus also on psychological health. Again we should remember that this is a process, not a destination. I would like to emphasize three psychological goals.

The first is to increase our ability to learn. As we become more psychologically healthy, our learning skills increase. Anything which increases this ability moves us in a healthy direction. We need to train initiates to extract the maximum amount of wisdom from every experience they have. We need rites of passage which focus on increasing a person's ability to learn.

A second psychological goal is to increase inner awareness. As we look cross-culturally at various rites of passage we notice that most include some process designed specifically to do just this. Ritual, movement, breath, narrowly controlled use of drugs, meditation, journal writing, and prayer are all designed to help us access inner awareness. Effective, healthy rites of passage are characterized by an increase in self-awareness for the initiate. Whenever we help people to be more aware of their subconscious process, we improve their likelihood of moving in a healthy direction. I would suggest that the preparation phase help the initiate develop life-long skills in this regard.

A third psychological goal is to increase our ability to experience a full range of affect or emotion. American society today does little to help its young people experience emotions in appropriate and healthy ways. My idea of a healthy rite of passage is one which allows a person to access deep feeling and express it. We would learn to feel angry, sad, glad, and afraid completely, so that we might move through the feeling and not be restricted by not fully experiencing it or remaining stuck in it. How many people today, for instance, are raging internally, holding it in as long as they possibly can, then becoming violent? How many people in our culture do not allow themselves to fully experience sorrow and to do the work of grief? How often have we set up and facilitated rites of passage for families to grieve a lost loved one and then excused an adolescent from going through that process? It is abominable that we would do such a thing! We don't want our child to go to the funeral because *it will make him feel sad.* Exactly! A well-designed funeral should assist us in accessing our sadness; it should help us to cry. If it doesn't, the mourning process has not fulfilled its healing function. When my younger brother died in 1992, I felt that my surviving brother, my father, and I needed to do something that would assist us in mourning. I created the opportunity for us to dig his grave together so that we could honor him and push our grief to the surface. It worked. It strengthened the rite of passage for the loss of a loved one.

Children must be given the opportunity to grieve. So often when I am doing deep intuitive or creative work with young people, I find unresolved grief that they have to work back through because they didn't have a chance to deal with it the first time. Or, think of how much joy we could bring to our lives if we were fully able to experience the feeling of gladness, to access our inner playful child, to "let our hair down" and have fun. Think of the lives we could save if we were to help "workaholics" access their fear and tension, examine its roots, and thereby discard that fear and tension, moving beyond it.

Healthy rites of passage should facilitate growth in all three of these areas of psychological health. They should help us be better learners, more fully aware, and more able to fully embrace our emotional and feeling selves.

SOCIAL ASPECTS OF HEALTH

Rites of passage also ought to increase social health. There are many ways to define social health, but for our purposes I will define it as mutually constructive interaction within a life-enhancing ethical standard.

In order to be initiated to the rank of Eagle in Boy Scouts, a powerful rite of passage for many young boys, one of the requirements is community service. By requiring service of these young men and the consequent joy of giving we increase the likelihood that they will continue to do as the Scout motto says: "A good turn daily." Typically such experiences increase the sense of connection to that which is perceived as external to self. Because of that, what I do to that which is external to self, I experience as doing to myself. When I care for that around me, I am also caring for myself. When I harm that around me, I am harming myself.

Some rites of passage unfortunately do not focus effectively on social health. Some use the selection and subjugation of a scapegoat to mark the rite of passage for a particular individual or group. When a gang says "Because you now belong to our gang you are better than others," it allows the member to attack nonmembers, thereby condoning socially unhealthy behavior. When a religion describes its members as "the Chosen," it sees others as "not chosen" and thus indirectly condones bigotry and potentially, violence. It is important that our rites of passage are inclusive rather than exclusive; that they affirm the sense of connection with and love for others rather than engender feelings of superiority.

SPIRITUAL ASPECTS OF HEALTH

The fourth and perhaps most important aspect of the health model is spiritual health. In our culture we might call this the "S" word: you are not supposed to say it in a secular arena. How can we identify the spiritual? Is it religion, God, church? "Mine's the best" is the way we tend to think: "Mine's the best!"

I will not attempt to define the spiritual or spirituality. Rather, we can talk about what spiritual health might look like and we can judge our rites of passage on the basis of whether or not they facilitate development of spiritual health. Again, this is a process, not a destination. Perhaps it is the quintessential process.

We become more spiritually healthy as we become more comfortable with the fact that life is difficult. Our various orthodoxies are designed to help us deal with life's difficulties. The ultimate question, "Why was I born to live, suffer, and die?" is one of the main questions of religion. This problem of our mortality, common to us all, is made easier in many cases by our faith and religion.

The serenity prayer, often used in twelve-step support groups, is an example of an answer to difficulties as they arise. In it we ask God for the ability to "accept the things I cannot change, the courage to change the things I can, and the wisdom to know the difference." The first part of the prayer, in which we ask for the ability to accept the things we cannot change, the serenity to live with difficulty, points us in the direction of greater spiritual health. A good self-test for spiritual health is to ask what happens to you when you are standing in a grocery store express lane and the person in front of you has twenty five items and is writing a check which he did not get preapproved. Some of us might say, "Huff, huff, well I don't believe this" and turn to the next person and say, "Count those items!" and we count out loud so everyone can hear. A more spiritually healthy person thinks, "There is nothing I can do about this" and lets it go. We need to work with young people and help them connect to that serenity, help them realize that the person in front of them in the aisle did not do that to attack them, so there is no need to attack them back.

Another way to look at spiritual health is to look at its antithesis. As an example, we have what I call "The Myth of the Grown-up." There is no such thing as a grown-up, there are only growing-ups and stuck people. To the degree that we are constantly examining and attempting to improve ourselves, we are demonstrating spiritual health. To the degree that we think we have it all together and there is no need for self-examination and we are right and that is it, we are exhibiting spiritual malaise. It's a sad truth that our culture tells its young people that at some time in their life they will be grown up and they will have no more difficulty. The media and our pervasive commercialism perpetrate this myth: If we just buy the right things, look the right way, and use the right telephone company our lives will be easy. If we are to create healthy individuals and a healthy society, we must help promote inner serenity in our youth and their spiritual health in general.

Finally, the experience of *connection* is symptomatic of spiritual health; connection to self, others, the natural world; connection to that which is greater than self. We are very unlikely to harm that to which we are experiencing connection. Suicide, murder, war, and environmentally damaging behaviors can only occur where there is disconnection. When rites of passage increase connection, they are helping the initiate move in a useful ethical direction.

I propose that this health model should inform any rite of passage. I believe it can help us design systems for improving our selves and those in our charge so that we can create healthier individuals, families, communities, and nations. If the rites of passage we implement conform to this model, I believe they will greatly enhance the lives of the people they touch.

FIVE HEALTHY HABITS

I wish to describe a program that we do at the LIFE Institute which incorporates rites-of-passage technology and is guided by the health model I have just outlined. Our program makes use of five key strategies by which individuals can facilitate healthy development. These five strategies were developed from research on high achievement and resiliency, in answer to the question, "What do people who seem to succeed in life do specifically to maintain healthy growth, development, empowerment, and altruism?" These strategies clearly are not exhaustive in helping us create effective initiatory programs for our young people; they constitute only one approach among many. Yet we have found that they are very helpful.

RISK

First, let us consider the habit of risk taking. People who continually improve and excel seem to be innately comfortable with taking risks as a process of development. There are two types of risk taking, physical and emotional.

After observing many people who seem to excel, I have come to believe that the benefit of taking physical risks lies largely in making one aware of one's mortality. If I place myself in physically risky situations, I become aware that this experience may be my last. I believe this awareness is initially subconscious, but with frequent, consistent risk taking it gradually moves into consciousness.

This concept was clearly delineated in the movie *Casualties of War*. In one scene, two of the main characters had been "in-country" in Vietnam for quite some time and had become hardened emotionally due to their direct involvement in combat. As they walked along a road during a troop movement and civilian evacuation, they were approached by an awkward young man who had recently come to Vietnam and had been separated from his unit. He interrupted their conversation to ask them for guidance in finding his unit, but they had little patience with him and basically told him to "get lost." He continued up the column looking for his squad.

Moments later, as the two continued talking, there was an explosion. Everyone hit the dirt and the word was passed back that it had been caused by a land mine. Having been "in-country" for quite some time they knew that if a land mine had been stepped on or tripped, it had been off the road and they could continue along. About a hundred yards up they came across the same young man who now lay dead on the side of the road. One of the companions now turned to the other and said, *"We have been living as if because we could die at any minute, nothing mattered. Perhaps, because we could die at any minute, we need to live as if everything mattered."*

This is the essence of the wisdom that seems to come from physical risk taking. What is interesting is that the *actual* risk need not be very great; it is the *perceived* risk which is important. Programs like Project Adventure,

Outward Bound, and various rock-climbing experiences which are perceived to be extremely dangerous (when in fact quite safe) create the experience of intimacy with our mortality. They make us begin to question, "Why are we here and what should we be doing?" They precipitate existential crisis and move us to a greater self-awareness.

The second type of risk taking is emotional. Very frequently as adults age and become more aware of their bodily vulnerabilities, they seem to take more emotional risks but fewer physical risks. Rapid developers often seem to reach a point when physical risk decreases while emotional risk increases proportionately. When we take an emotional risk, we place our ego in a vulnerable position. We risk "death to the ego." When the ego momentarily dies, and we emerge as a somewhat wiser survivor, we learn that risking ego death is not the real risk we thought it was. Our growth rate begins an exponential curve of improvement. We expose our frailties with the goal of receiving feedback in order to improve.

The habit of "being proactive" which Steven Covey speaks to in his bestseller, *The Seven Habits of Highly Effective People* (New York: Fireside, Simon, and Schuster, 1990), is one of taking the risk of responsibility. When we have an interaction with others which is uncomfortable, the high performer takes personal responsibility for improving that interaction rather than reaching for the emotional safety that blaming the other (proacting) provides. If it's someone else's problem, I don't need to change, I need try nothing new, I need not risk.

In our developmental work with young people at the LIFE Institute we create opportunities for perceived physical risk taking and actual emotional risk taking. Under the guidance of an elder there are opportunities to increase self-awareness, feelings of connection to others, and a sense of our own mortality. Rather than wait for some day in the future when we will finally begin to do our work, we must realize that that day is now, and risk taking helps us remember.

INSIGHT DEVELOPMENT

Rapid developers and altruistic contributors to our society seem also to be "insight motivated." They place themselves regularly in situations which will provide opportunities to increase their intellectual understanding of self, others, and the natural world.

This attempt to develop insight into the connection between one concept and another, one animal and another, one ecosystem and another, typically fosters a sense of connection to some system greater than the self. As long as there is a sense of something greater than self, one has a sense of direction which leads to development and a continued focus on that development.

We need to create opportunities for young people to experience the excitement of insight to the point of motivating them to continue to crave that excitement. In our rites-of-passage work with young people, we constantly challenge their thinking. As they begin to construct a worldview, we challenge their ideas so that they are constantly expanding in new directions. We must continue this perpetually, not only for our students but also for ourselves as elders.

DIET

Many of us grew up during the refined, convenient, fast-food movement of the last few decades. But now we have access to research that shows the amazing impact diet has on physical, emotional, and cognitive performance. If we look at the lifestyles of the truly powerful altruists we can get a sense of the power of diet. We are what we eat. If our organ systems are to function at their highest capacity we must be aware, insightful, and concerned about what chemicals, food, or nutrients we put into our bodies.

An awareness of diet has two primary payoffs. First, appropriate nutrients increase cognitive function and overall biological health, thereby decreasing disease and uncomfortableness within our body. The first benefit, then, is that we think more clearly, our brain works better, our organ systems work better, and we are more capable of moving toward our potentials.

The second major benefit of a healthy diet is that it can help us to better understand our emotions. Emotions are windows to our subconscious, but if my emotion is caused by eating too much fatty food, too much sugar, not enough complex carbohydrates, too much protein, too much of a particular nutrient and not enough of another, it is very difficult for me to know whether my emotion stems from a subconscious process or from a physiological/metabolic process. As we control our diet, we can begin to trust our emotions as guides into the subconscious.

So diet relates to personal insight and development in two ways. First, with a healthy diet, the brain works better and we have greater access to its memory. For example, we sometimes find ourselves in a situation where we know something and it is "on the tip of our tongue," but we cannot quite access that information. We can almost feel the presence of that information but we are unable to make it conscious. The primary controllable factor in such situations is the neurochemical balance we create in our central nervous system based upon the nutrients we have taken in. Second, with a healthy diet we can attain greater personal insight because our emotions will stem from our subconscious rather than from mere indigestion.

I predict that over the next decade, parents of school-aged children will be focused far less on forcing them to "cram" for exams and far more on helping them modify their diet to optimize cognitive performance. Our programs with both young and older people intentionally modify diet to include more complex carbohydrates and less fat. In only three to five days, they begin to experience the beneficial changes which can be precipitated by this simple modification.

EXERCISE

High-level achievers often adopt a regular, habitual body awareness or exercise program which will have the benefit of increasing kinesthetic or somatic awareness, an attunement to the sensations of the body because of regular frequent focus. Exercise such as yoga or Tai Chi can be as effective as running, weight lifting, rowing, walking, or aerobics. I recommend that people do not attempt to distract themselves from the sensations of their body by using music when exercising. Rather, if we are to increase kinesthetic awareness, we must focus intensely on the subtle sensations of the body.

The benefit of this kinesthetic awareness is to enable us to consciously control physical tension by monitoring the thoughts that give rise to it. Stress is not what happens to us, it is what we think about what happens to us. We find that high-level achievers and altruists generally do not experience much stress because they make conscious choices about the thoughts they allow themselves to have about the impact the external environment is having on them.

In our programs, we attempt to present our students with opportunities to increase their kinesthetic awareness through a variety of methodologies, hoping that at least one will be attractive enough to motivate them to continue on their own. Cardiovascular and musculoskeletal fitness and increased joy in the capacities of the body often accompany, but are not prerequisites for, a more effective kinesthetic awareness.

SPIRITUALITY

People who excel in life frequently use regular, habitual rituals to help still their minds and focus in a conscious, concentrated manner. They might use prayer, meditation, a body-awareness technique such as Tai Chi or yoga, reading Scripture, or some form of creative imagination. This stilling of the mind increases awareness of self and one's connection to others and that which is greater than self. I like the motto of Teen Peacemakers, a group originating in central New York: "Peacemaking with self, peacemaking with others, and peacemaking with the natural world." We can create peace by monitoring our thoughts in a quiet state and moving them toward more peaceful patterns. We might even say a person is well-developed spiritually only insofar as he or she is able to be at peace with self, others, and the natural world. In fact, that is one of the primary goals we see in the perennial philosophy which underpins our major religions.

At the LIFE Institute, our programs use culturally specific technologies to still the mind and to experience connectedness to others, self, and that which is greater than self. We have found that many stress reduction techniques such as progressive relaxation, creative imagination, and guided imagery are also useful.

RIDES

These five areas of focus—Risk, Insight, Diet, Exercise, and Spirituality (RIDES)—provide a template for daily personal development which moves one in the direction of biological, psychological, social, and spiritual health. At the LIFE Teen Institute, a week-long peer leadership and drug-abuse prevention program, we use this model in group work with young people around the country, and it has worked very well for us. Under the guidance of wise elders, young people graduate from this program with a more mature sense of who they are and what is expected of them as adults. The program's high standards, the congruent behavior of the adults, the powerful experience of the opening of the unconscious mind, the growing sense of connection to self, others, and the natural world, the rituals of community formation and separation, and a desire for the respect of the adult community—all allow the participants to wear their graduation T-shirts with pride and knowing—the essence of healthy initiation.

What we are about is helping people to learn, to move beyond the limitations of ego to a higher state of knowledge and awareness. We need to keep in mind and believe in our ability to do so. Let's utilize healthy rites of passage, appropriate methodologies, and the guidance of mature elders to help us all find out how much better we can be. A young woman who graduated from an Outward Bound program said it this way: "We are better than we know. If we can be made to see this, perhaps for the rest of our lives we will be unwilling to settle for less."

TWENTY EIGHT

WHAT YOUR DREAMS CAN TELL

Robert Moss

Robert Moss spent his early childhood in Australia, where he survived a series of near-death experiences and first learned about the
practices of a *dreaming* people through contact with Aboriginal
friends. He has been a war correspondent in Vietnam, a college
professor of history, an actor, but above all has been interested in
dream work and healing.

Dreams are very helpful at times of transition and during
rites of passage around the world. Dreams are referred to in Australian "Dreamtime." They are used in African healing (see the
chapter by Vera Bührmann in *Betwixt and Between*). In Colombia,
South America, dreams were believed to have caused the very creation of culture. Native Americans have long been aware of the
significance of dreams for people of all ages, particularly at times
of transition such as puberty and later (see the chapter by Steven
Foster in *Betwixt and Between*). Native American elders have an
inspiring understanding of people's dreams at transitions. In the
words of Dr. Ernst Rossi, dreaming is "an endogenous process of
psychological growth, change, and transformation" that is "a lab-
oratory* for experimenting with changes in our psychic life."

We all dream. On average, we dream for about two hours every night. We
dream in cycles. On a typical night, we'll experience between four and
seven dream sequences, whether or not we remember them. These data are
derived from the study of Rapid Eye Movement (REM) sleep, pioneered by
Eugene Aserinsky and Dr. Nathaniel Kleitman at the University of Chicago
forty years ago. The REM phase, in which the eyeballs may be moving as if
we're watching a tennis game, is associated with strongly visual dream images.

Given the amount of time we all spend dreaming, dreams may be our
most underutilized resource. In modern Western society, we've tended to dis-
parage dreams as a possible source of insight and information.

Yet, in most cultures, dreams are honored as a source of more important
knowledge than is available to the ordinary waking mind. The authors of the
Upanishads—the Hindu scriptures compiled from 1000 B.C. to 600 B.C.—
maintained that dreaming is a higher state of consciousness than waking.

Among American Indians and other indigenous peoples, the first business of the day is often to share dreams within the family circle. Individuals
are encouraged to seek their purpose in life, and specific guidance in life's
passages, through dreams.

Maybe the hunger for meaning and the sense of emptiness that afflict so
many people in our society are related to the fact that we are out of touch
with our interior lives because we don't make room for our dreams.

Reprinted with permission from *Parade*, © 1994.
*E. L. Rossi, *Dreams and the Growth of Personality* (New York: Pergamon, 1972), p.

I've worked with an active dream circle for years, and I've learned that to start harnessing the power of your dreams, you need only two things: the ability to recall and the willingness to be open-minded about what your dreams are telling you.

The kind of dream dictionaries found in drugstores won't tell what your dream symbols mean to you. Theories often get in your way, especially when they reduce dreams—which are multilayered—to only one level of significance.

I like what Carl Jung, the founder of analytic psychology, said about that: "I have no theory about dreams. I do not know how dreams arise. On the other hand, I know that if we meditate on a dream sufficiently long and thoroughly—if we take it about with us and turn it over and over—something almost always comes of it."

You are the ultimate authority on your own dreams. Your gut feeling about what your dream means is your first and best guide.

There are "big" dreams and "little" dreams. It can be a bit like watching TV: You get a news report in between a soap and a game show, interrupted by commercials. But I've observed that nearly all dreams—including the scary ones—come to help us, and they tell us more than we already know.

Once you've begun catching your dreams, what can you hope to find? Here are a few possibilities:

1) *Dreams can be a road to our creative source.*

Dreams, as Freud remarked, are "the royal road to the unconscious," from which creativity springs. People in all fields of endeavor have found that creative breakthroughs come through dreams. This is as striking in the sciences as the arts.

HOW TO CATCH YOUR DREAMS

Before we can use our dreams, we have to catch them. Here are a few tips on improving dream recall:

- Tell yourself, before sleeping, that you are going to remember a dream.
- Be ready to record your dream with a pen and notebook—or a tape recorder —close at hand.
- Arrange your life, if possible, so you'll wake spontaneously. If you must use an alarm, use a buzzer instead of the radio.
- Dreams fade fast. You need to catch them within ten minutes of waking, or you'll probably find they're gone.
- Record your dream right away. Start with any names or phrases in the dream; they can be especially revealing.
- Transcribe your notes later into a dream journal, adding your feelings and associations. Date each dream and give it a title.
- Share your dreams with a partner or circle of friends.

Elias Howe credited his invention of the modern sewing machine to a nightmare. On accepting his Nobel Prize, Niels Bohr declared that his dreams had shown him the structure of the atom. Another scientist, Friedrich Kekule, realized the molecular structure of benzene was a closed carbon ring when he dreamed of a serpent swallowing its tail.

Our dreams sometimes alert us to purposes and possibilities beyond the ego's waking agenda. I had an experience of this kind when I was working on an idea for a thriller with a Russian theme that would follow the formula of a previous best-seller I'd written. I thought the book would be a commercial success, but I felt the urge to work on more original—and therefore riskier— projects.

In my dream, I walked into a banquet hall where the tables were laid for a huge gathering. But there was trouble in the kitchen. The master chef had gone on strike because he refused to work with my menu. His message for me was, "I don't feel like cooking stroganoff." If I insisted on this dish, I could only count on mediocre cooks. I got the message and dropped that book idea!

2) *Dreams can put us in touch with our larger selves.*

Dreams can help to move us beyond the limits we impose on ourselves or which are imposed on us by others. They can put us in touch with aspects of ourselves we may have repressed or denied. "We are a battlefield of many selves," says the Jungian analyst Robert Bosnak. We cease to be a battlefield when, through dreams, we recognize the parts of ourselves we have been denying and make peace with them.

3) *Dreams can be early warning systems.*

Many of us recall dreams in which we seem to glimpse events, both trivial and momentous, before they take place.

Two weeks before his death in 1865, Abraham Lincoln dreamed that he entered the East Room of the White House and found a body laid out in state. A guard told him that the President had been assassinated.

Rita Dwyer, former president of the Association for the Study of Dreams, credits the fact that she was saved from being burned to death in a chemical fire to a friend's prophetic dream.

I dreamed recently that a toddler in a friend's house in England was in danger because an unscreened window that came down almost to the floor was often left open. I checked and found there was a similar window in my friend's new house, which I had never visited.

Such dreams provide early warnings. But we don't need to regard them as cases of ESP. Lincoln obviously knew he was an assassination target. In some part of my memory, I "knew" about the design of a certain type of

London house, having lived in that city for several years. My dreaming mind, like a hyperefficient secretary, simply brought a possible problem to my attention.

4) *Dreams can be rehearsals for future challenges.*

Research suggests that pregnant women who frequently dream of child-birth spend less time in labor—presumably because they've been rehearsing overtime!

Jack Nicklaus, practicing his swing in his sleep, dreamed a new golf grip that made a winning difference in his game. Dr. Stephen LaBerge, a leading dream researcher at Stanford University, reports the case of a surgeon who rehearses difficult operations in his sleep and says he performs them in less time than normally would be required.

5) *Dreams can be tools for healing.*

Most physicians agree that the mind has a powerful influence over the body. Healing dreams may point out problems or suggest treatments and may come before the symptoms of a disorder have appeared. Kathleen O'Connell, a psychologist, calls these "intervention dreams." "These are our danger signals, warning of a coming crisis," O'Connell says. "They'll get more threatening until the dreamer wakes up to the danger."

6) *Dreams can be magic carpets.*

Dreams are adventures and creative experiences in their own right.

Susan Novotny, a successful but overworked businesswoman in Albany, New York, had been planning for years to take a Caribbean vacation in mid-winter but never managed to find the time or money. "Then," she told me, "I discovered that dreams can be magic carpets. One winter night, I flew off to St. John's. I lazed in the sun for seven days. Everything was vividly real. The softness of the air, the lapping of the water. When I woke up, I was completely refreshed. I thought, 'I couldn't have had such a fabulous vacation if I'd spent $2000.' And I didn't have to wait for my bags at the airport!"

7) *Dreams can be a gateway to the soul.*

Dreams can be an immense source of inner strength and spiritual guidance. Since the dawn of consciousness, humankind has sought clues to the purpose and destination of the soul through dreaming. In the dream yoga of Tibetan Buddhism, conscious dreaming is taught as a preparation for the soul's journey after death and as an education in the nature of reality and illusion.

8) *Dreams can remind us that we are all related.*

Sharing dreams in groups can build a sense of community and shared humanity. The Ullman Method, developed by Dr. Montague Ullman, invites each member of a group to explore a shared dream as if it were his or hers. I've found in my own workshops that this approach builds a sense of connectedness on a vital, human level.

TWENTY NINE

PERSONAL SHIELDS

Kaye Passmore

Traditional shields have been a way of shielding the bearer in many warrior cultures, but can also be used as a symbol of identity. One's main symbols may change at different stages of life. Drawing or painting our symbols, in shield form or otherwise, can greatly strengthen and nourish our inner life, and also improve our dreams. (See the chapter on the wolf by Herb Martin.) The arts, in general, are important in helping us find our identity, one of the main tasks of adolescence.

Kaye Passmore, Ed.D., teaches art at Notre Dame Academy in Worcester, Massachusetts and has worked with colleagues in music, theater, and dance to build an integrated arts program there. She has also published an article describing this integrated arts program in *School Arts* (December 1993), and one about combining Native American art, writing, and symbolism (*School Arts* [April 1995]). She is a consultant with Davis Publications, who specialize in books for art education. Ms. Passmore is also an artist in her own right, and regularly exhibits her oils and acrylics.

Our school is making a push to encourage all students to write more in every course. An introductory project relating Native American art and symbolism with writing helped my students to improve their writing skills while stimulating their art historical imaginations.

We began our project by looking at prehistoric art and Native American art, and discussing the origins of art forms all over the world. We discussed symbolism and how every culture has symbols, many of which are universal. We also considered the decorative symbols on personal objects, such as pots, utensils, blankets, and shields. Symmetry and asymmetry in design were attended to before the students undertook the task of designing personal shields that symbolized themselves.

DESCRIBING THE DESIGN

Either below the shield or on the back of the shield, they wrote a description of their design, explaining the meaning of their symbols. They rendered their shields on 15-by-20-inch (38-by-51-cm) illustration board in watercolors, acrylic paints, markers, inks, or colored pencils.

Before the students started to design their shields, I showed them the charms on my old charm bracelet and told them what each represented. There was a palm tree from a trip to Miami Beach, an eagle from a visit to the Air Force Academy, a palette for my painting, and my high school graduation ring. Some of the students were wearing charms on necklaces, and they

Senior Miranda Holmes elected to use black ink for her shield.
"The drop of water is for that in which I swim.
The note is for music which turns my life to
    bright from dim.
The heart is for friends whom I hold so dear.
The moon is for love of the night as it nears.
The 'M' is for Miranda, my name.
This is my identity."

Senior Adria Polletta wrote, "The triangles represent the structure of my life. However, they are facing inward pointing to my insides which are out of control and full of emotion."

shared their significance. We talked about what symbols they could use to represent their interests, hobbies, and sports.

SYMBOLIC USES OF COLOR

We discussed the symbolic uses of color like we find in flags, such as red for courage and blue for loyalty. We reviewed some of the symbols we had seen during the past week, particularly the Kiowa shields in George Keahbone's *The Mud Bath Ceremonial.* I pointed out the shields in the *Bayeux Tapestry* and the Ravenna mosaic, *Emperor Justinian and Attendants.* I also told them the story about Leonardo da Vinci painting a monster on a shield when he was a young boy. Supposedly, the monster was so real it terrified his father, but his father was so impressed with it that he sold it to a Florence merchant.

SUGGESTED MEDIA

The students began their shields by listing the symbols they would use. Then, they traced around a hubcap to get a round shape. They drew their designs in pencil on tracing paper and transferred them to illustration board. They added color to their projects with markers, watercolors, acrylic paints, or colored pencils. Some of the students combined media. This wide choice of materials helped to accommodate the wide range of art expertise in the class.

For some of the students, the written descriptions became part of the art. One senior wrote a poem describing the symbols of her life and mounted it neatly under her design. Others wrote the description on the back, and a few scribbled it on the front.

Then, the students wrote evaluations of their completed projects. For myself and the majority, it was an enjoyable success. I learned about the students' interests and hobbies from the symbols. (French fries are very important to teenagers—one girl incorporated McDonald's fries into her design. That's what she likes to eat on her free periods.) Their designs were creative, showing a great deal of thought.

First published in *School Arts* 94, no. 8 (April 1995).

George Keahbone's *The Mud Bath Ceremonial,* part of the *Bayeux Tapestry,* and the Ravenna mosaic, *Emperor Justinian and Attendants,* are illustrations in Gerald Brommer's *Discovering Art History* (Worcester, Mass.: Davis Publications, Inc., 1988).

THIRTY

REENACTMENT OF TRADITIONAL RITES OF PASSAGE

Edith Turner

Edith Turner tells of her experiences with groups enacting different rituals of passage from different cultures, with meaning on
several levels. She discusses the surprising empowerment of ritual.
As a musical score needs to be played, so ritual needs enactment.
   A lecturer in anthropology at the University of Virginia,
Edith Turner has had extensive field experience both as companion and colleague of her late husband, Victor Turner, as well as in
her own right as an anthropologist studying rites of passage in
indigenous societies around the world. She has done fieldwork
among the Ndembu of Zambia, the Iñupiat Eskimos of Northern
Alaska, and in Mexico and Ireland, observing and participating in
many rites of passage. She has lectured widely on aspects of her
fieldwork and on the general principles derived from it. One of her
specialties has been the organization of the actual performance of
a variety of traditional rituals from the world's cultures (Africa,
Bangla Desh, Korea, Israel, Morocco, Brazil, Haiti, Papua New
Guinea, Nepal, Bali; also, in the United States, rituals of the North
West Coast Indians, East Coast root doctors, and mainstream
whites)—an experiment which has proved extraordinarily effective for the participants.
   Particularly fascinating is her sense of the mysterious way
performed ritual takes on a life of its own, larger than our intention and not altogether subject to our control—having to do with
"entities out there"—so that it is essential to proceed with respect
and care. Her accounts of reenacting girls' puberty rites with university students (contrasting those of the African Ndembu and
Bemba tribes to American sorority rush and pledge rites) lead us
to understand how ritual can bring about the joy of release, create
a reverential sense of *communitas,* and produce "what is finally a
sacred human being— as all humans can be."
   Some of Edith Turner's publications include *Image and Pilgrimage in Christian Culture: Anthropological Perspectives*
(1978); "Performing Ethnography" (1982); "Religious Celebrations" (1983); "The Milk Tree" (1985) and "Zambia's Kangkanga
Dances: The Changing Life of Ritual" (1987), both on girls' initiation among the Ndembu; "Rites of Passage" (encyclopedia article,
1987); "The Carnivalization of Initiation in Zambia" (1987, on
boys' and girls' initiation); *The Spirit and the Drum* (1987); "Poet-
ics and Performance as a Dialogue between Enactors, Spectators,
and Analysts" (1989); "Comparative Symbology, Interreligious
Tolerance, and Education" (1989); "Childhood among the
Ndembu: Liminal Play and the Magic of the Adult World" (1991);
Experiencing Ritual (1992); and *The Hands Feel It: Healing and
Spirit Presence among a Northern Alaskan People* (1996). She is
editor of the journal *Anthropology and Humanism.*

If, lacking our own rites of passage, we are to benefit from those of another culture, we must actually reenact its rituals. Questions arise concerning ethics and logistics. First, would not performing a true ritual as a kind of experiment or therapy belittle serious religion? Also, would it not be a mere simulation—and if so, with what value? Moreover, would reenacting a traditional ritual merely repeat some outworn form which we might more usefully ransack for a new invented ritual or good bits of theater? Worst of all, would not such performance reduce rituals into mere objects of inspection—museum pieces—given that we don't live in the mythic ambience of the culture of an enacted ritual ourselves?

In considering these questions, it is important to understand that, when performed, ritual takes control in surprising ways. In the first place, we could not possibly belittle the powerful force of religion as living ritual expresses it—if anything, it makes *us* feel small, regardless of our attempts to control it as an experiment or therapy. Secondly, as anyone with experience knows, the written description of a ritual is rather like a musical score—neither has life until performed. In reenactment, ritual ceases to be mere simulation and develops a reality that quickly takes over. Anthropologists without this experience miss a wide area of living human culture. To understand a culture, we must lend ourselves to it and participate as much as possible from the inside—and this we can do through the high play of performing ritual. Thirdly, ritual is not just a matter of outworn forms; rather, the structure of its three-stage pattern—separation, transition or "liminal" period, and reassimilation—creates a large, dynamic whole continually renewed in reenactment and concerned with "entities out there." This internal organization is complex, unique, and sensitive to ill-intentions and misuse: witness the destructive use of its power in Nazi Germany, the Soviet Union, and Yugoslavia. In performance, events transpire the way the ritual wants—not necessarily the way we want—and do not always turn out the same. This phenomenon we must experience to fully understand. And fourth, given how performance revives ritual, it can't possibly reduce it to being a mere object of inspection. To the contrary, the performed ritual leaps out of its museum case—or library book covers—rather like a stolen and recovered Mexican image parading anew through the streets, its efficacy come alive once again.

Ritual has to do with behavior based on beliefs in mystical beings or powers. From the religiously subjective point of view it is more: it is actually plugging into those powers. Once we understand this difference, the reason for performing ritual seriously today—whether as true initiation or true therapy—becomes clear. As ritual is enacted, it renews life for the participants who, in handling materials existentially powerful, begin to sense that power at their own fingertips. This phenomenon has occurred during a number of ritual reenactments for educational purposes led by the anthropologist Victor Turner and myself at the University of Chicago, New York University, and the

University of Virginia, and by myself alone since Turner's death in 1983. For instance, here is the experience of Linda Camino, a student who during a class reenactment of a puberty rite took the role of the girl initiate ("guinea fowl") among the Ndembu of Zambia:

> Around and around they danced, again and again with punctuated cries and claps. Beneath the blanket I lay still and quiet, firm and "cool," patiently awaiting the next stage, which I knew would be to escort me to my seclusion hut. Then a strange thing happened. Time lengthened, expanded, and my wait seemed interminable, for as the singing and cries of the women grew lustier, as the pulsation of their feet and hands quickened to the driving beat of the insistent drums, I began to fear that they had quite forgotten all about me, guinea fowl. They were having fun; I was not. The drums beckoned me. Their wrenching beats filled my muscles with tension, demanding a response, a response I could not give as guinea fowl. The women's enthusiasm and boisterous cheers challenged me to spring out from the blanket to join them. At this point, a desire to be like those other women, a desire to move my body freely to the sounds of drums overwhelmed me. I longed to be a woman—alive, vital, responding, moving; not a dull guinea fowl, still before a tree, unseen, stationary, alone. (Turner and Turner, 1982:46–47)

In another example, a couple "married" in a simulated American wedding went around together in real life for some weeks after the "ceremony"— such is the power of the ritual form.

For we were not dealing with performance as a simulation only, but with techniques which effect transformation in the individual—techniques developed through long eras of time, weathered now, flexible with age, closely adapted to the human condition. These performances are at one and the same time experiments and efforts at actual initiation, divination, or healing. In breaking outworn taboos against taking religion seriously, they also can be the long-desired invocation of deity, the actual sacralization of people and things.

I had a major bout with ritual at the department of performance studies at New York University in 1985. When invited to organize a two-week workshop there to perform women's rituals, I accepted with enthusiasm because ritual performance was my specialty; I wanted to further explore matters to which my ear had been keyed from previous occasions. At the same time I saw that it would be a grueling task. The group would not consist of anthropology students; they came from dance, theater, folklore, earth science, and photography, and differed from each other about the nature of ritual. We would all have to work hard, because the opportunity to focus on women's rituals was a rare one to be used fully. I could help them with the African Ndembu girl's initiation, the American wedding, Korean shamanism, sorority rushing and pledging, and the American birthday party—all with which I had had prior experience—but I wanted to pioneer another that had never been performed outside its own culture before—the Bemba girl's initiation, called

Chisungu. A further ritual fell into place of itself—the challah rites of the Jewish sabbath, and there were even more, including the Bangla Desh wedding—too many to mention. All demonstrated characteristics of rites of passage, including a threshold phase or, as it is now called, "liminality," with its touch of the sacred; *communitas* (human fellowship); polarized symbols— that is, symbols that have emotional and bodily power on the one side and carry moral teaching on the other; and jokes of reversal recombining elements in a humorous way, the value being to change the initiate's perspective in order to make her receptive to teaching and transformation. A common example in our own culture are the fantastic masks and costumes worn at Mardi Gras.

I wondered if our performances might highlight new principles. For instance, would we find out through our subjectivity—for this would clearly be involved—what would work for us and what would not, and why? Through the hurly-burly of the busy course I tried to catch answers to these questions, and so did the students as soon as they understood. As women we were proud that *we* might break the ritual barrier. Women, I believe, are the more flexible sex, less structured, and take to religion more easily. A considerable body of knowledge has already grown up among women about sisterhood and the value of their bodies, without which such a study of ritual would be useless. So we were preadapted for the task.

After a brief prestudy, we plunged right into the girl's initiation among the Ndembu, a ritual traditionally taking three months, but which we replicated in three hours. Most of the participants were used to rehearsal, but we had none. The Ndembu themselves learned the ritual by participating in real ones. Like them, I felt that rehearsing the ritual was unthinkable, just as rehearsing the giving of Christmas presents would be unthinkable. When we got started there was a kind of impetus which could not be stopped. Some students were bewildered and tried to resist being carried away. They wanted to slow down and savor each symbolic act, a temptation because the sequence of rites was so rich. Others gave themselves up to the process and let it take them where it would. Those who had no prior expectations had a better time.

The ritual consists of laying the girl initiate under a milk tree in the woods, a tree that represents the matrilineage of the tribe. For a whole day, the village women dance around her as she lies covered with a blanket. At evening she is picked up by her "midwife" instructress (for she is like a baby about to be born) and carried pick-a-back with a dancing step, amid a bunched crowd of women, around the village plaza, and into her seclusion hut. After three months of training in dance and sexual proficiency, she makes her debut as a grown woman—even as a being greater than that, for she is decorated with many beads and an earthen crown, feasted, and led like a spirit into the crowd from an unexpected direction. Her dance before them all is the great moment of her life.

Appropriately, the day we performed this African ritual was Martin Luther King's Day. When the students in the role of mother, midwife, and girl "wandered in the bush in search of a milk tree" in the basement of Tisch Hall on Broadway, they were seeking for the roots not only of Black culture but of human meaning itself. They reported that in the wandering dance itself they found meaning—and poetry. Once established around the tree, with the girl under the blanket, they would have liked the dance to go on forever and ever—achieving the true ritualist's long attention span, if not to say trance, transcending time.

When in the final stage the group of women converged on the newly trained girl to dress her and load her with beads from the whole community, the sense of reality about the ritual was strong: "It was efficacious," said Jane Kelton who took the role. "My face was altered. I felt that distinct sense of *communitas.*" A passive beautiful creature was becoming the creation of all of us women; as we tended her, the realization of our kinetic acts grew. From the time she disappeared from our midst to when she reappeared from an unexpected direction to enter the circle of drummers and singers, her spirituality had grown vastly. The impression of this shimmering outreaching form, reddened with "earth," stayed in the mind and combined with our consciousness of her new sexuality to become somehow a metaphor for climax itself, the moment of orgasm.

The next ritual was the rushing and pledging rites of an American college sorority. This ritual is in its deepest essence secret. How were we to perform it in a group which could not claim sorority membership? And why would we choose this kind of thing, from white middle-class American culture—a well-nigh taboo class for the members of my workshop, themselves pioneers of performance who had nothing in common with the mores of the middle class? But we tried it. The difficulty of secrecy was overcome by inventing a new sorority, called "Pi Sigma Kappa," and this sorority was different, because its open motto was "Nothing human is alien to me"—which rather dished the critics. The task of invention and directing was undertaken by an anthropology graduate student at the University of Virginia, Mary Gelber, as an experiment in subjectivity. Because it had new, hitherto unused, secret elements, no secrets of an existing sorority would be given away. It was constituted like other Greek letter societies; it opened with the usual rush party, and pledging time involved the rites of ordeal, the oath, and pin presentation. But it was shifted just enough to be unique. We were thus able to look into and experience for ourselves what goes on in the heart of such a secret society. The comments went like this. Jane Kelton found her persona was slipping in and out of role. Her notes ran, "I momentarily regained my slightly sneering persona during the readings. I asked my neighbor, 'Do you understand any of this?'" (The readings were from the great masters of anthropology, corresponding to Mary Gelber's highest loyalty.) Kaite Ringer felt that the sorority emphasis was all on the group, that group power ran away with individuality. Everyone, on the other hand, appreciated receiving at the outset a letter personally written to each, inviting her to pledge (Mary Gelber had labored over the letters all morning). Ann Allbright, commenting on the pledge ceremony, said that it was like a wedding. There was a white tablecloth, candles, flowers, an altar (on which a woman as homemaker was "sacrificed"), and then the binding words. Mary Gelber likened rush to courtship, thus pledge might be like marriage. Others saw how a sorority seeks total friendship, and it was agreed that such friendship might be possible. Women in a closed group could make it happen—more so, the members felt, than in any ordinary life situation, even real marriage. Here was the creation of a "circle of trust," the concretizing of *communitas*—a paradigm for most ritual.

The rushing and pledging constituted a tough exercise in empathy. There were many occasions of great solemnity, even an episode of swearing on respected books (not, this time, the Bible). The dramaturge Mary Gelber revealed an unexpected side to her personality—a fierce and unquenchable dignity and seriousness, very like a religious gift. What were theater people to make of these religious touches? Was it impossible for them to take them seriously? For most of them it was. On the other hand it was important for them to experience the elitism of the Greek-letter society, to feel the fear that one might not be selected, to experience the disgruntlement of the disappointed ones, to know in one's fiber what American college students undergo. To my surprise I found myself not the only person with a "don't-shut-me-out" complex activated by the situation.

Again the question arises: "But aren't we all pretending, as actors do—using the 'as if' of Stanislavski, the method of putting oneself in the place, in these instances, of ethnic persons or persons of a particular class?" In practice the performance of ritual was different: we often let ourselves through the frame, like Alice through the looking glass, and took a walk there in the looking-glass world. The rim of the frame, the threshold of the door, as it were, was none other than the limen of the rite of passage. Jane Kelton was the youngest of our group, so in our acting out of the girl's ritual of the Ndembu, it was fitting that *she* be the one initiated. In this performance, we weren't pretending. We really *wanted* to initiate her, to prepare her for adulthood. The seeking after the milk tree in the basement of Tisch Hall was a true preparation for the liminal phase. The dancing in the liminal phase was too short for the participants; they were experiencing the joy of liminality and wanted to savor it. As for the sorority ritual, for some it worked, and there remained the feeling of actually belonging—in this case to an anthropologically generated society of love, with founders chosen from the beloved old masters of the science, who may not be named, though anyone could guess them.

These experiences made it clear that we seriously needed the rite-of-passage pattern. We needed to enact carefully the preliminal entry in the sacred sphere, so as to truly arrive in it, and to achieve *communitas* for the return to the world at the end, so as to come out safely. Both theater and ritual give release. The theater, almost totally free of taboos, releases the imagination; it plays, it is never deadly serious. Ritual can literally release the soul, but it needs theater—our enactments, for instance—to break down our modern skepticism. Theater can be very near to seriousness, as is the Bread and Puppet Theater,* for instance, but it is always like a butterfly ready to fly off. Ritual needs this unencumbered sense of freedom to become more flexible and dare to revert to what it really is—a deep, uninhibited, often sexual or scatological hot-blooded affair. Interestingly, the one who began the performance of ritual as an educational experience was Vic Turner, the son of an actress. In Chicago around 1970, when his student David Blanchard and the seminar performed the Iroquois False Face Midwinter Ritual using actual "False Face" masks—lo and behold the wearers experienced the "dreaming" as they danced. These experiences of enlivened ritual benefit the anthropologists themselves and so in a sense are a payoff for all the difficulties undergone in the field. And where do ritual and theater meet? Vic Turner had the answer. He knew that a society with its regular structures can use living performance as a major means of becoming conscious of itself. Performance here includes ritual, theater, and the well-known list—dance, poetry, oral sacred history, carnival, sport, and so on. In this era we are able to explore a variety of rituals in a sympathetic spirit, understanding that they have a special power. We are no longer afraid of them. We urgently need personal experience of the rituals of other societies, for the relationship between the religions may freeze or become dangerous without that necessary sympathy.

My next subject highlights a principle which is not often recognized today; that is, the power of sacred objects. This principle revealed itself in the course of the performance of a largely obsolete girl's initiation ritual, *Chisungu,* performed by the Bemba tribe of Zambia at least until 1934. Audrey Richards' book *Chisungu* (1982 [1956]) is a painstakingly honest and well-reported account of the initiation and won the admiration of anthropologists everywhere. The style is dry and academic and exegesis is thin in many places, but the events—and they are complicated—are written down clearly, and there is plenty of background material. Greatly daring, I included Chisungu in my list of rituals to perform and was very glad I did so.

It is a ritual of ordeal. The overconfident green and callow girl is taken over by the women, shrouded with a blanket, teased, tested, praised briefly, teased again dreadfully—in many cycles of testing, praising, and teasing—until she is finally presented with an array of sacred pottery emblems and becomes a woman. How should I arrange this so that the group could perform it? There was no problem. The participants, who had been given the text to read, immediately seized on the salient issue, the making of the emblems—carefully described and illustrated by Audrey Richards. One of the group brought in a large mass of flour-and-water dough, our "clay." Whilst we sat on the floor discussing and familiarizing ourselves with the rites that we were to perform, we pulled the illustrations close and made the emblems. I looked at the clay being formed. "That's the crocodile, the chiefly clan totem," I said, surprised. Ann Allbright was making a squirming croc and was painting it in black and red. The book was coming true. "It means the chieftainship," I told them. "Audrey Richards says that the chieftainship—in fact the entire country's unity—depends on Chisungu being performed." I was reminded of the Apache, whose girl's puberty ritual was identified by Claire Farrer as "the crucial factor in their ethnicity and success in coping with the rigors of survival as a people" (1987, 240–41); and there were more examples of the same kind of vital link.

Object after object took form under the women's hands. The peculiarity of the emblems, all knobs, penises, pregnant protrusions, simple round humps, bird forms, tortoise forms, reptile forms, began to work on us. What were we at? It was like the day of creation. "Among the Agni of West Africa, God is a female, and a potter," I told them. They seemed to know it already.

After we were finished we took the girl, shrouded her with her blanket, and brought her into her "initiation hut"—again in the basement of Tisch Hall. How sorry she felt to be secluded and left out of our activities! We could see her hunched back, animal-like under the blanket. The Bemba girl experiences rejection for a time and then is received into the community of adult women, now sane and whole. She will not be left out forever, unlike those not chosen for sorority pledging. The American who does not get invited has to resolve her sense of isolation without the aid of a well-defined group.

Next, the "mistress of the pots" (that is, mistress of ceremonies) carried a bowl of seeds with her mouth from woman to woman, presenting, honoring, sacralizing—as Audrey Richards explains—both the seeds and the one to whom they are offered. Why the mouth? In another context Richards tells us that the mouth stands for the vagina. But it is unspoken in this rite. Neither do we speak of it, but are aware of it as we struggle to pass the bowl from one mouth to another without spilling the seeds. The girl stays on one side; she only enters the women's rites to be tested, praised, and teased. After the seed rite we scold her, pummel her, and drive her out to the "gardens" in order to make her leap over a heap of brushwood. She can't do it. We urge her again and again, the voices threaten and cajole. "C'mon!" When she succeeds the praise is inordinate, she's taken up and carried home like a chief—it's just that she has shown willingness, she wants to belong, she'll strive to win our love. This inevitably reminds one of brainwashing techniques, which I brought up in discussion. You make the subject suffer, then discontinue the cruelty, apparently showing great kindness. The subject in spite of herself begins to feel grateful and gradually goes the way the masters intend. Did the Bemba women in some sinister way plot to hold their young girls to their way of life in case they should escape? (It should be added that this was a society based on chiefdom and status was highly emphasized.) Let us look at the initiation as a whole. The series of ordeals is intended to raise her as if by a series of canal locks (to use a Western metaphor) high into another level of life, adult womanhood. As she is raised to one level, she is still low by comparison with the next stage. She must be punched down like dough (to use another Western metaphor) so that she will rise up all the better (this humbling before status elevation is discussed in Victor Turner, 1969; 157–60). Such acts, long drawn out and lasting for a whole month, work the effect of increasing her desire and culminate in her sacralization as she is presented with the sacred emblems, made sacred by the very act of their reverent presentation. Rather than brainwashing it appears to be a beautiful and subtle way of producing what is finally a sacred human being—as all humans can be.

The actual performing of the Bemba girl's initiation brought to life one rite which was obscure to Audrey Richards herself, the making of the large clay emblems on the floor of the initiation hut, particularly the Snake. For years after reading *Chisungu* the image of that Snake haunted me, as did the mystery of the pottery emblems. The Snake is enormous, obsessively decorated all over with ordered rows of pumpkin seeds and corn grains. It is only shown once to the girl initiate, and two hours after its making it is destroyed. The episode disturbs one in a curious way, the pottery emblems too, with their knobs and excrescences—you could say they were phallic symbols. Of course they were, and the Snake was too, according to the Bemba. Why not mold a phallus, then, and have done with it? Let us follow the rites.

In an interval between the girl's ordeals we gathered for the task—the first time to my knowledge that this rite had been performed outside Bembaland. It was certainly the only occasion when the making of the Snake was the focus of a group of academics. Would the dry words of the now-deceased Audrey Richards be sufficient to teach us anything if we carried out the instructions? The women were forming a slender snake. "It should be wider, fatter," I exclaim and point to the picture. "It's huge." They lay on all the clay they have, the Snake writhes, powerful. We bend down to decorate it. It seems to be creating itself. My eyes water. What is this we're seeing? In the midst of the women a brilliant object is revealed, triumphal, central, absolutely riveting. Everyone is excited. The pumpkin seeds are all erect, with no skimping and no gaps; the maize dots adorn the body as it writhes. It is royalty and glory. The Snake. How could we tell from the book that that was going to happen?

We brought the girl up to have her look at it, and shortly afterwards I said, "We must destroy it." We took out the seeds, sadly at first, then savagely; then, joyous by this time, pressed together the beautiful body into a dull mass again. Everyone felt exhilaration in this deed, the same joy of sacrifice I experienced among the Ndembu at the "killing" of the effigy of the thunder god, or at the Samaritans' Paschal sacrifice of lambs at Shechem in 1983, or at the symbolic killing of the Yaqui deer dancer in Tucson in 1981. The Hopi also destroy their carefully created sand paintings as soon as the rites are over.

Isa Kopelman asked, "Why is it made and destroyed so soon?" We began to talk about ephemerality, process itself, the ambience of time. To us women the image of menstruation seemed appropriate to connect with this Snake which was so superb and then was destroyed. We discussed how the periodicity of our bodies enables us to be released at certain times, so that we could reach realms of feeling and poetry not available at other times. The building up and the release of breaking down, breaking down the tautness which structure induces—in this we women can reach levels of trance where there is no resistance to the coming of the gods, a time of real connection. The menstrual cycle itself is only another image of the release of tension. The Snake, an image of both flexibility and high art, says more than menstruation, more than verbal poetry can, or any use of words.

It should be noted that the above experience happened in 1985, fifty-four years after Audrey Richards's observations of Chisungu. We were not Bemba tribeswomen, and it is very possible that we placed certain of our emphases incorrectly. However, it is my opinion that *"anamnesis"* (not forgetting) is involved here. The old experiences in fact were not forgotten; they were written down by Richards and, as we found, could be revived. But it was only by means of performance that we could plumb the levels reached in this ritual.

In the course of time I have tried a large number of rituals from different parts of the world and found each one valuable. I will leave it to the reader to try the incomparable Apache girls' initiation (Farrer 1991), which my class of a hundred undergraduates performed in 1994 with startling success. There is now a smorgasbord of rituals for every taste, so that the coming generation should surely not lack a way to celebrate joining the adult world.

To conclude, to perform these and many other rituals, what is needed is a couple of hours, a knowledgeable leader and/or a good text, a willingness to have fun, and a capacity to lend oneself to alien ways of thinking and to allow a real intention to creep in. The fun aspect is very important. Anxiety for perfection is the ruination of ritual. One must be able to feel with the others, laugh, and then have a serious go at it. The results will be surprising.

REFERENCES

Farrer, Claire. 1987. Singing for life: The Mescalero Apache girls' puberty ceremony. In *Betwixt and Between: Patterns of Masculine and Feminine Initiation,* ed. Louise Mahdi. LaSalle, Ill.: Open Court.
———. 1991. *Living life's circle.* Albuquerque: University of New Mexico Press.

Goffman, Erving. 1974. *Frame analysis.* New York: Harper and Row.

Richards, Audrey. 1982 (1956). *Chisungu: A girl's initiation ceremony among the Bemba of Zambia.* London: Tavistock.

Turner, Victor. 1969. *The ritual process.* Chicago: Aldine.

———. 1979. Dramatic ritual/ritual drama: Performative and reflexive anthropology. *The Kenyon Review* 1, no. 3:80–93.

Turner, Victor and Edith Turner. 1982. Performing ethnography. *The Drama Review* 26, no. 2:33–50.

---

*Founded in New York in 1961 by Peter Schumann, the Bread and Puppet Theater actually changes people's lives and attitudes by its performances. Hidden under ground-length costumes, actors use poles to operate huge figures that have exceptional power because of their height. These figures are those of tragic oppression—victims of war, racism, etc.—symbolically arising and looming over us to raise our consciousness.

I'm very grateful to the Ndembu people in Zambia for lending us their rituals and to Sharron Brown Dorr for her excellent help with this manuscript.

Edith Sullwold

Dr. Edith Sullwold presents a new approach to training for mentors and others wanting to work with youth now. This approach also helps adults in their relationship to their own passages in both the past and the present, and could enable such persons to be better mentors.

Dr. Edith Sullwold has most recently been serving as consultant and therapist at the Amani Counselling and Training Center in Nairobi, Kenya over a period of four years. This is the first such training program in Kenya. Prior to this, she was founding director of the Hilda Kirsch Children's Center at the C. G. Jung Institute of Los Angeles. She teaches and supervises therapists in various parts of the United States and Europe, as well as at the C. G. Jung Institute of Zurich and also of Chicago.

Initiation rituals of adolescence reflect a process already occurring in the psyche. Adolescence calls for a movement out of the intimate family into the larger community. Although the psyche desires this movement and will energize the child toward it, the process needs the support and understanding of an adult collective, providing a container for this transition. Without this guidance and left to the adolescents themselves, the ritual forms that develop at this time often take on a distorted form, sometimes resulting, in the extreme, in suicide and violence.

The elders in traditional societies provided the ritual form as well as assistance in the incorporation of the newly emerging adult into this community. The adolescents of our time do not find such collective rituals. In the first place, our cultures are becoming more complex and full of choices. The teenager does not cross the threshold into a clearly defined form of adulthood with its prescribed beliefs, values, and required skills. But in addition, the older generation itself, not having gone through their own initiatory experiences at a conscious level, rarely thinks to assume its role in shaping rituals for the young.

For this reason, I decided some years ago to introduce the issues surrounding the loss of adolescent ritual to groups of adults, both in the theoretical and experiential way. I first ask the group members to share with each other their own adolescent experience in separate groups of men and women. Rarely in these groups has there been a sense of satisfactory preparation, instruction, and support for this passage from adolescence into the adult community.

In one such gathering the extreme contrasts of adolescent experience was shared. One woman described her first menstrual period as overwhelmingly frightening, and absolutely out of context with her life. She had been given no instruction by her mother or any other elders. One day, in the girls' bathroom in school, she began to hemorrhage. She screamed for her girlfriend who ran to her, but slipped on the blood and hit her head on the concrete floor. The girl not only thought she was dying but also that she had killed her friend. Outside, the boys and girls began calling out, wondering what was happening. The school nurse was called and administered help to the girl on the floor. The newly emerging woman had retreated into a toilet stall, shaking in silent fear.

In contrast, another woman told how her mother had sewn for her a special case with her name stitched on it containing what equipment she needed for her first period. Then she told her all she could about what it was to be a woman, physically, socially, and spiritually. The girl, who was nine years old at the time, would often take out the case, looking at it with anticipation and pride. The day the first blood appeared she ran to her mother in great excitement. They were both naked, having just come out of the shower. Her mother took her to the long mirror in the bedroom, and, looking at their bodies together, she told her how the girl's body would continue to grow and flower with a new life. At breakfast, the mother announced the happening to the father. He suggested a celebration that evening. They went to a restaurant she had not been to before, which had a dance floor. After a special meal, he danced with her for the first time, acknowledging her passage into the adult community. This simple, but sensitive preparation and ritual gave the girl confidence in herself as a woman.

Out of a longing to have had such a satisfactory experience themselves and with a sense of responsibility for the next generation, the group is then ready to begin to consider what ritual could be created that would be appropriate for our time.

I then share my belief that ritual form is shaped by a deep, natural understanding of the elements of initiation that are common to all cultures. It is what I call the backbone of rites of passage, seeing that each culture fleshes out this backbone and costumes it in the shape and form relevant to the context of the particular culture.

Briefly, there are a number of steps in ritual which make up this backbone: (1) At first the sacred space is prepared by the community, who purify it and invoke the larger energies of group and spirit. (2) Then the initiate is taken out of the old, the ordinary space, and (3) put into the care of the elders for a preliminary preparation and instruction. (4) The initiate enters a period of disorientation and isolation from the old orientation, going into a symbolic death state. (5) The initiates face severe tests and ordeals to prove their capacity to become adult men and women. (6) The deeper instruction is given by the elders into the mysteries of sexuality and spirituality and into the expected responsibilities to the social life of the community. (7) There is a reconstruction of the new being by a symbolic action, often reclothing. (8) All that has been accomplished is celebrated by a festive community event. (9) Thanksgiving is offered to the greater powers invoked, both of the group and of spirit. (10) The newly constructed initiate is returned to ordinary life and into the larger community as a responsible adult.

After these steps have been described and discussed, the group is asked to create a ritual of passage which uses this essential form. Usually, one person volunteers or is selected by the group as the initiate. The rest of the group provides the structure as initiatory elders or members of the larger community of supporters. I always remind them that this is not just an exercise, but an event which has the potential of satisfying the earlier loss of their own rites of passage. I have been amazed over the years by the incredible inventiveness that has emerged from these groups. Not only do they gain an understanding of ritual work, but they often are satisfied that they have had a true initiatory experience. Even though the focus is on one person as initiate, others seem to experience the event as though they too were being initiated. From the understanding and experience which is in contrast to their own adolescent experience, many participants in the groups have become involved in creating such rituals for adolescents, both privately and collectively.

I will share the experience of one young man in such a group. He had almost drowned in the ocean when he was eleven, trying to surf with older friends who taunted him by saying he couldn't take a "big wave." The experience had taken away his confidence in most physical activities.

The group prepared a space around a deep pool of water, created a sacred circle, and asked that he be given the courage he desired to pass the test successfully. He came forward in his swim trunks and entered the circle where a heavy terry-cloth robe was placed on him. The men took him to a private place in some woods where they instructed him about water, the pressures, the currents, how to relax into the water, allowing it to hold him, and how to emerge. When they felt he was prepared, he was thrown into the deep end of the pool. His task was to work his way out of the robe and emerge from the water at the other end of the pool. Ed came out successfully, enthusiastically. The oldest man in the group had brought a young palm tree for him to plant, signifying the new growth in his life. He dug a deep hole and planted it. Then he let out an amazing, spontaneous sound, akin to a baying coyote and said, "Now I have my body back."

He quietly dressed himself in fresh, new clothing and received gifts of fruit and flowers. Then, thanking the group and acknowledging his new strength, he made a public commitment to begin to work with the young boys at a nearby school. His intention was to begin creating meaningful rituals in the community and he asked the other men present to help him.

The ritual, although suited to the needs of this particular individual, touched a place universally alive but latent in everyone. The process was simple, powerful, and complete.

The reflection of this process is seen in many dreams. Recently I was given a dream by a man which was also initiatory, and had similar elements to the created water ritual. In the dream the man was asked by a group of men to go into a deep underwater cave to recover a treasure. He was given careful instruction about breathing underwater, then he courageously dove in and brought back the treasure of confidence in his body.

Relating the created ritual and the dream confirms my belief that the ritual process begins in the psyche and the body, which carries ancient knowledge that wants to be passed on to new generations, the generations now so desperately in need of this wisdom and collective concern.

The awareness of a true initiatory experience, necessary for the preparation of an elder, is reflected in the powerful poem that follows, "Almost Grown-Up," written by a participant in one of these groups.

ALMOST GROWN UP

Christine Mulvey

Christine Mulvey, from Dublin, participated in a workshop on adolescence by Edith Sullwold. In reexamining her process of becoming an adult, Christine Mulvey reexperienced some of the dynamics of her own private enactment of her passage. She is now training to be a Jungian analyst at the Jung Institute in Zurich, Switzerland.

ALMOST GROWN-UP

She knew the horses better than anyone, their little ways, their secret names
Yet they never let her drive the plough with them
'You're too small' they said 'to handle them' and 'besides you're just a girl.'

It was the morning after the ploughing championships
All the previous day she'd watched the men and boys compete
Then later celebrate the prizes won, commiserate the others lost.

She decided she was going to plough the bottom field
It took her ages to get the horses ready, everything seemed stiff and heavy
But at least no one disturbed her, they were sleeping late after the party.

It was still cool and morning fresh as she walked the horses down the lane
Their harness jangled, they were two well-matched Irish Draughts, gentle powerful giants.
She felt tiny and suddenly afraid of what she planned to do.

The plough handles, not intended for children anyway, were big and hard to grasp
There was little space left within the span of her fingers and thumb for the reins as well.
The ground was rough, the horses stepped out and she had to haul them back just to keep up.

It was the longest day of her life; she could smell the newly upturned earth,

Beneath her stumbling feet, weary soon in the summer heat and most of all she could feel
The blood on her hands when the reins first broke the flesh and then cut deeper and deeper.

It took her 'till dark to cut the last furrow, those who had come looking for her said nothing
As if they knew this is what she had to do, they brought strong tea and bread cut thick
Like they usually took to the men when they worked in the fields and they left her alone.

She was grateful for that, she didn't know herself if she could finish what she'd started
Time seemed endless and the shuddering in her body from the gyrating plough
Made her long to stop, give up, but something in her knew she couldn't, knew she wouldn't.

She finished, waiting for jokes about the crooked lines, the messy corners, they didn't come.
She tended the torn and bloody hands that looked like hers yet somehow didn't,
Now wounded, they seemed different, changed in a day to almost grown-up hands for she had put them to the plough and not turned back.

—Christine Mulvey, 1993

THIRTY THREE

DANCING JUST AS FAST AS I CAN

Lois Wiley

Lois Wiley, M.A., has taught elementary and junior high school for twenty-five years. She has received numerous teaching awards, grants, and fellowships including a National Endowment of Humanities Fellowship Award, and was featured in the *Washingtonian* magazine (December 1993) as an outstanding teacher and mentor of teenage girls.

Currently Ms. Wiley teaches both math and drama. She has also written and directed many plays; one of them, "Blue Black," was put into professional production in 1994 at the Pittsburgh New Works Theater.

I won't go back in the classroom, unless I get some help.

After nearly twenty-five years of teaching adolescents in D.C. schools, I can't take it anymore. I've had enough of children who are belligerent, rude, defiant, apathetic, and disrespectful.

I want to teach. But most of my students of late are out of control, and I no longer have the energy or the know-how to control them. I have tried every conceivable approach to motivate and maintain their interest in my fifty-minute math lesson. I have done the binomial butterfly dance and my area-of-a-triangle rap. I've used filmstrips, tapes, and computers—I've done everything short of dressing up like Janet Jackson and tap dancing on my desk.

Still, in the middle of my lesson, somebody will talk about somebody else's "mama" or something else unrelated to the lesson, and the show is on. The conversation continues until it evolves into a profane argument and sometimes a fight.

No one listens to my directions to stop. I reason, preach, speak in low tones and high tones, devise reward systems, confer with counselors, administrators, and parents about students' behavior. I try to be fair, and funny, and firm. But it goes to hell in a handbasket when the "joning" starts.

After school, five or ten or more of my students will show up in my classroom wanting to talk, share, laugh, and play with me, their teacher, the one they dis' (disrespect) during valuable class time. They are so wonderful after school—creative, funny, warm, profound. Some even apologize for their classroom behavior, but many have problems—serious, critical, even life-threatening problems—and they seek attention any way they can get it.

The students talk about how they are forced by their peers to save face once the insults start. They do not know how to show love or solve conflicts. They missed life's lesson on loving and respecting yourself and your neighbor.

I love my students, but I am not a miracle worker. I am not the mama or the social worker or the preacher or the conflict-resolution specialist. I am the teacher.

But I need help:

- Help from Superintendent Franklin Smith and the D.C. School Board. I need them to change their minds about cutting funds from the FY '95 budget for conflict resolution, peer mediation, and parent involvement. Almost every D.C. school needs the full-time services of a conflict-resolution specialist, social worker, psychologist, and counselor.

- Help from parents. I need them to make sure their children have the supplies needed for a successful day of learning—pencil, pen, notebook, textbooks, ruler, homework—and to talk to their children about the importance of respect, responsibility, and a positive attitude. I need them to meet with teachers, volunteer in the school, and go to PTA meetings. Students' grades and behavior improve when parents show up at school.

- Help from churches. I need them to follow the example of Shiloh Baptist Church and Seaton Elementary School and adopt a school. I need them to sponsor field trips and retreats, establish scholarship programs, and organize efforts to bring prayer back to school. Yes, I said it. Bring prayer back to school.

- Help from senior citizens. I need them to adopt a school-time grandchild, to tutor that child, to guide that child, to show they care.

- Help from business and government. I need small businesses to adopt just one student and do whatever is needed to help that child have a successful school year. I need federal agencies and private industry to adopt whole schools, providing scholarships, funding camps, and sponsoring mini-courses on useful and creative things of interest to the students.

If young people are going to become productive, contributing members of the society then we must all share in raising them. "It takes an entire village to raise a child," says the African proverb. Teachers can no longer be held solely accountable for teaching young people. The lessons must come from every aspect of the community.

It's now June, the end of the school year, and I am suffering from battle fatigue. Maybe after nine and one-half weeks of rest, I will be ready to suit up for the classroom again. With help, I can once again love teaching. But now, I've had enough.

© *The Washington Post*, 26 June 1994

Jerry Mander

In the book from which this chapter is taken,* Jerry Mander challenges the utopian promises of technological society and tracks its devastating impact. He observes the effects of TV on a remote Inuit tribe in northwestern Canada a few months after it was introduced there. TV affects more than levels of violence.

Jerry Mander was the President of the celebrated San Francisco ad agency of Freeman, Mander, and Gossage until the late 1960s, when he quit all commercial work to form the country's first nonprofit, public-interest ad agency, devoted solely to social, environmental, and political causes. Mander's ad campaigns for the Sierra Club, to save the Grand Canyon, and to establish a Redwood National Park, and his later campaigns for Friends of the Earth and other groups, led the *Wall Street Journal* to call him "the Ralph Nader of advertising." At present Mander is doing public-interest ad work as Senior Fellow of the nonprofit Public Media Center in San Francisco. He is also a Board Member of the ecological think tank, Elmwood Institute in Berkeley. He lives in San Francisco, California.

I traveled to Yellowknife in October. It's a three-hour plane ride due north from Edmonton, Alberta, including stops at two native communities along the way, Fort Smith and Hay River. The plane flew low over the terrain, which seemed an endless expanse of tiny lakes, granite boulders, and forests. There was already snow on the ground.

I was met at the Yellowknife airport by Cindy Gilday, the Dene woman who had contacted me on behalf of the Native Women's Association. I had met Gilday once before, in Washington D.C., at a conference concerned with creating a pan-Indian network of Western Hemisphere tribal peoples, to resist multinational corporate activity on Indian lands. Gilday had been one of about a dozen Dene and Inuit in attendance.

Gilday started telling me how she'd been enthusiastic at first about the arrival of television in the North. She explained that there was no effective, quick means of communication among Dene communities, which are often hundreds—and in a few cases more than a thousand—miles from each other. Except for the area directly surrounding Yellowknife, there aren't any roads into the bush; only airplanes, radio, and dog team. "Until recently," she said, "it didn't really matter. Most of those communities have been self-sufficient for centuries, but now that the government is out there changing everything so fast, people in the communities need to find out what's going on everywhere else."

Television seemed to be a logical way of easing the problem, but thus far it hasn't done so. In the communities that did accept television, 60 percent of the programs were from the United States, including "Dallas," "Edge of Night," "Happy Days," "The Six Million Dollar Man," and others, with the remainder coming from Ottawa and Toronto. "We're not getting any chance to deal with our own problems on TV," Gilday told me. "There's only one hour each week of locally produced programming in the Northwest Territories, and only occasionally does that include any Indians or Inuit, even though we are the majority population around here.

"Yellowknife, the capital and the most 'Canadian' of the cities in the north, was the first community to get TV. We can already see that it's had a devastating effect on the people here. Out in the Indian communities in the bush, where maybe it came only a year or two ago, it's even worse. People are sitting in their log houses, alongside frozen lakes with dog teams tied up outside, watching a bunch of white people in Dallas standing around their swimming pools, drinking martinis, and plotting to destroy each other or steal from each other, or to get their friends' wives into bed. Then after that they see a show that is about a man turning into a machine.

"The effect has been to glamorize behaviors and values that are poisonous to life up here. Our traditions have a lot to do with survival. Cooperation, sharing, and nonmaterialism are the only ways that people can live here," she told me. "TV always seems to present values opposite to those.

"I used to be a schoolteacher and when TV came to the villages I saw an immediate change. People lost interest in the native stories, legends, and languages, which are really important because they teach people how to live. And it's hurting the relationships between men and women too, and between the young and old. We used to honor our old people and listen to them," Gilday said, "but that's changing fast. TV makes it seem like the young people are all that's important and the old have nothing to say.

"And, you know, TV has been confusing the Indian people who've never seen anything like it before. For example, I heard of one old woman who prays every night for the people in the soap operas. She thinks they're *real*. We are all getting pretty scared, especially the women who have traditionally kept the family life together and made sure the culture was intact. But what really put the women over the edge about TV was the news that soon the Playboy Channel would be available in the north. The Native Women's Association became really active after that. Violence has increased here since the oil companies showed up and a lot of the men gave up trapping and hunting and started working for wages. They move into those work camps and start spending their money on alcohol and then when they get home they continue drinking and beating up on people. That sort of thing seldom happened before. The women expect things to get a lot worse with that Playboy Channel.

"You have to realize," Gilday continued, "that most people still live in extended families here. Ten people might live in a one- or two-room house. The TV is going all the time and the little kids and the old people and everyone are all sitting there together watching it. Now they'll all be seeing men beating up naked women. It's so crazy and so awful. Nobody ever told us that all this would be coming in with television. It's like some kind of invasion from outer space or something. First it was the government, then those oil companies, and now it's TV."

Gilday told me that while I was in Yellowknife I was to speak with two groups of native people. First, the Native Women's Association, and then, the next day, I would give a workshop at the offices of the Dene Nation. That would be for about fifty people who were responsible for various community programs: language preservation, community education, training in traditional skills, communications, alcohol and suicide prevention, and so on. In the days following, I would also be going to two outlying communities, Rae and Edzo, where I would speak with school kids.

The Native Women's Association met in the local hall of the Veterans of Foreign Wars. There were about seventy-five women in the room, most of them from outlying communities as far away as Tuktoyaktuk, about 1,500 miles north. The age spread was very even; about an equal number of young and old, and quite a few very old women. I discovered after my talk was over that many of the old women did not speak English. Immediately after my speech, these women gathered in a circle while one of the younger women gave a lengthy account of what had been said.

My intention with the speech was to create an agenda that could provide the basis for the series of workshops the Dene planned in the next few days, and for later workshops out in the communities. I raised a series of questions divided into a few categories, roughly as follows:

- **FAMILY LIFE:** Have Dene family and social relationships changed since the introduction of television? What sorts of traditional family and community activities are being sacrificed? Are people following the prior patterns of visiting, working together, gathering in groups, and talking? Are the changes good?

- **POLITICAL POWER:** How has television affected the Dene effort to wrest political power back from the Canadians? What are the political consequences of a one-way information flow, from Ottawa, New York, and Los Angeles, into the Mackenzie Valley? What bearing will this have on regional autonomy, and resistance to oil development?

- **DENE AND INUIT CULTURE:** Has television had an effect on native culture? If so, on which aspects? Respect for elders? Attitudes about property and land ownership? A sense of community? A sense of cultural worthiness? Does television leave the native people feeling better or worse about themselves?

- **VIEWS OF THE NATURAL WORLD:** How will television influence the native system of perception and values concerning animals, the land, and the human relationship to the environment? How will television affect attitudes that are crucial for survival in the North?

- **COMMERCIALISM:** How will the onslaught of commercials affect a culture that until very recently was not part of a money economy but was based on barter and sharing? Will the Indians be susceptible to the value systems in advertising?

- **LANGUAGE:** How will television affect the desire to learn the native languages, as well as the stories and myths that have guided northern culture? Will English seem more glamorous? Will the mythic heroes for the Indians become those created in Los Angeles?

- **IMAGES OF THE INDIAN:** How will Indians be shown on television? The urban drunk? The noble savage? Cowboys and Indians? How will the relative absence of Indians on television affect native viewers, and children in particular? How will this affect people's sense of self-worth?

- **EFFECTS ON LEARNING:** If TV is a useful educational instrument, what sort of education does it deliver? How does that mode of education affect Indian kids? What prior modes of learning are being lost? What is the trade-off?

I concluded with some comments about the manner in which television is usually introduced into cultures, and by whom. The people who introduce television, I said, are ordinarily the people who benefit: manufacturers, advertisers, and governments who understand that television is an opportunity to reach more minds much more efficiently. They don't say anything negative about it. They only praise its benefits. But once installed, TV is difficult to get rid of. In the United States, for example, television is barely one generation old and yet it is in virtually every home. Watching television has become the main thing Americans do with their lives. It has enveloped the culture, and yet it's only about forty years old. What is needed, I concluded, is the ability to understand the benefits and drawbacks of new technologies *before* they overtake us. In the North there is still time to engage in this discussion.

Before I had begun talking, Cindy Gilday had warned me not to expect much of an audience reaction. "Don't expect anyone to ask you questions or to make any comments today," she said. "They'll be too shy with a white speaker. But they'll think about it and tomorrow, in the workshop, they'll probably have a lot to say." That proved true. I had never given a speech met by such silence, though there was applause at the end.

The next day, things were different. The group was smaller and Cindy Gilday asked each person to give a brief report on their feelings and observations about television.

TESTIMONIES

Joanne Barnaby, communications department, Dene Nation:

> Some of the questions you raise have been raised already in the communities. For example, in Fort Good Hope, television came in six months ago. Every year before that the CBC [Canadian Broadcast Company] would come around to the village and say, "Well, you people want TV now?" and every year the people would say, "No." Six months later, the CBC would come around again and ask the same question. The reason people were against TV was that they heard from other communities how people weren't visiting each other anymore, and that the children were being influenced by it. It was hard to get the kids to do anything. The women weren't sewing anymore, either, and the woodpiles were too low. But last summer CBC showed up again at a meeting where there were only two or three people. One person said, "Well, okay, let's have TV," and another one said, "Okay" and right away, very fast, CBC installed the satellite dishes. The people were in an uproar because they felt they weren't really consulted. But CBC told them if they took down the facilities now, then Good Hope could never again get them back. It was real pressure. The people finally voted to leave it there, but only by a one-vote majority. You can already see the difference.

Dene language instructor:

> Nobody in Fort Franklin wanted TV either, but after a while people got in the habit of going over to the next village, Norman Wells, to watch the hockey games. That got it started. It's created a lot of problems. Franklin is a community where everyone speaks Slavey [one of twenty-two Dene languages] as a first language, and we were teaching English as a second language. But the English they're getting from TV is slang English, and they want to know why we don't teach them that. Another problem is that parents don't control the TV, so the kids stay up all night watching it and they're exhausted the next day. They keep falling asleep in school.

Barbara Smith, nutrition educator and writer:

> I've got four kids and we used to live on the land. When we first came into town, the kids didn't like TV. They were scared of it. They

wondered why that man on the TV was staring at them. But it didn't take them too long to get hooked on cartoons. I think if kids don't have TV in their childhood, then they're more creative later. But even my kids have been affected by it. A lot of the images they have in their heads now are TV images, like especially the people in "Fall Guy." I know a lot of kids who don't play at all anymore because they'd rather watch TV. It's easier than playing or reading. It's not enough to say that parents ought to turn the thing off because the kids can then watch at the neighbors' or in school. TV has more influence than parents do.

Mary Wilson (sixty-five years old), Slavey translator:

I was thinking how lucky I am that I brought up my children when there was no TV and no things to worry about, like sniffing glue and alcohol. I had a hard struggle to keep life together, but if I'd have had all these worries I don't know how I would have coped. At one time the women used to sit around all the time and talk about things and be sewing and competing to see whose husband was going to be the best dressed, but now they don't do that. The women are so involved in this soap opera thing. They even phone each other about what happened on the show.

Ethel Blondin, Department of Education, Government of the Northwest Territories (now a Member of Parliament):

I'm working with languages too, and I have mixed feelings about what you say. When we first got TV up at Tuktoyaktuk in the mid-1970s, I felt suddenly I had to be an entertainer to compete with it. I really couldn't compete with that kind of sexual image they put on TV. But I have a certain zest for life, which those TV characters don't have. I think the kids understood that. But one time I got to use TV to teach native languages. When I had control of it, I think it worked out okay. But it does affect family life. I know I have to supervise the way my kids use it. They have to turn it off when I say so. It all depends on the strength of the family unit, I think.

Cindy Gilday:

When TV first came to Rae, I was working there as a teacher. The social relationships of the people and the language and learning of the kids changed overnight. What they started learning best was all the stuff that's in those commercials from white society. But I would really like to know is what it is about TV that causes the addiction? I know something happens to me when I watch TV. I get glued to it, even if it's something like soap operas with those kinds of values. I wish I could figure out what keeps people watching because then maybe we could create a Dene soap opera. Could we ever get the kind of money they use on "Dallas" to put out our ideas of Dene life?

(The question of creating an Indian soap opera kept coming up. It was observed that the behaviors that create interest in the soaps were problem behaviors, such as adultery, emotional problems, lying, and scheming. To show Dene people engaged in those behaviors was not going to do the Dene any good. Also the rhythms of the soaps—a major crisis once or twice in every program—were different from the rhythms of life in the North, where events are very slow. "Would anyone want to watch a show about women sitting and sewing mukluks for hours, or hanging fish in the smokehouse?" one woman asked.)

Ernie Lennie, education coordinator, Dene Nation:

The type of learning we get in school and also on TV is the type of learning where we just sit and absorb. But in family life it's a different kind of learning. Children learn directly from their parents. That is the native way of teaching. Learning has to come from doing, not intellectualizing. A long time ago they only taught people by doing things, but now they just sit and watch TV. Taking away TV is like taking away a bottle of alcohol.

Barbara Smith:

There's an ancient native concept that words have power. So if you're putting a lot of energy into watching soaps, then you're concentrating your energy in a negative way. Pretty soon people who watch those shows start having problems like the people on the soaps. I know a lot of people who seem real negatively affected by TV.

Irene Bjornson, court reporter:

When I was living in southern Alberta, I used to watch TV so much. And because my town was in a later time zone, my friends used to call me to find out what happened on the shows before they were shown. I would buy food that was very easy so it wouldn't get in the way of watching TV. I learned a lot from TV and I learned a lot from white society too, but all that time I didn't learn anything about myself. I didn't like being a Dene. When I went to school I learned English and French and they told me it was stupid to speak Dene. Now, my husband is white and my husband's family doesn't like Indians. All they saw about Indians was those drunks they saw on TV and that's how they judged me. But now I really speak my mind and believe in myself. I hardly watch TV anymore. But I've got a six-year-old daughter who's going on sixteen because she watches so much TV.

Ethel Lamsthe, community development worker:

> Those stereotypes on TV really twist people. The way they show what a
> terrific thing it is to have a drink. Their lifestyles are so different. How
> does that make you feel about yourself? Every community now has got
> those VCRs. I try to get people to talk, but they don't want to anymore.
> They just sit and watch.

EFFECTS ON STORYTELLING

One of the most intense discussions of the day concerned TV's impact on traditional storytelling practices. For centuries it had been part of Dene family
life for the grandparents to tell tales to the kids for several hours each night
before bedtime. With television, storytelling has virtually stopped. Meanwhile, many storytellers are dying off without passing along their skills. One
suggestion was that perhaps TV could now be used to convey the stories.

Cindy Gilday:

> When I was a kid we were told the same stories over and over again, and
> then we'd ask for it to be told one more time. Every mother and grand-
> mother would be into it. And everyone would tell the story slightly dif-
> ferent. We wanted those stories so much we'd scheme so that maybe we
> could hear some story for the thousandth time.

Cindy's friend:

> Some of the old people were so good at storytelling. They had a breadth
> and level of language that my generation doesn't have anymore. When
> we talk about maintaining the legends we also have to talk about the
> level of language. If I was going to try to become a storyteller, I'd have
> to go back and live with the old people and eat and sleep with them and
> practice those stories over and over, because each time you hear those
> stories you hear something new in them.

Man from audience:

> It was such a refined art. They projected the stories in their bodies, not
> only in their words. There is both a conscious and a subconscious level
> in storytelling. Something will really be lost if we try to portray those
> stories on TV.

Barbara Smith:

> Legends are tools that help people grow in certain ways. A lot of what
> matters is the power and the feeling of the experience. It's like when
> you're tanning hides, it's not only important to learn how to do the
> scraping and the cutting. In the old way, the process was also a kind of

meditation, a prayer to help put power into it. There used to be prayers for how to grind the corn. It wasn't just grinding corn, it was also the feeling in it. But when you put something in a museum, or even on TV, you can see it all right, but you're really looking only at the shell.

I had been listening silently to most of the discussion up to this point, but I could not contain my desire to discourage the use of video for re-creating the legends and stories. It would not, I argued, be an adequate substitute. In the old way, when elders told stories to the young, the subtle dimensions were probably more important than the content of the stories. Sitting together on quiet, dark evenings, kids and grandparents huddled near a fire, the old people themselves became a kind of window through which to see thousands of years back into time, back to the sources of the Indian experience. Tremendous admiration, affection, respect, and love was mutually engendered by this tradition. Its continuation was critical to the Indian sense of self-respect and identity.

The stories also embodied a teaching system. The old transmit to the young their knowledge of how things are, in such a loving way that the children absorb it whole and request more. The death of the storytelling process will leave an absence of knowledge of Indian ways and thought, and of a sense of worth in Indian culture.

Another important factor is that the images woven by the storyteller are actually realized in the listeners' minds. The children create pictures in their heads, pictures that go far beyond the words of the storyteller, into the more elaborate, more fabulous world of the imagination. So the child is in some ways as creative as the teller of the tale, or put another way, the storyteller is only a stimulus for the imagination of the child. If the stories were conveyed by video, not only would the intimacy, love, and respect between young and old be lost, but the child's creative contributions would be lost as well. Finally, I said, video versions of the stories would be necessarily limited by the abilities and budget of the video makers. Even the most talented video makers would find it impossible to equal what the imagination does with a story told orally. So the net result of translating stories to television would be to confine, and actually lessen, their power, meaning, and beauty. Audio tape or radio would be far better.

I recalled an experience I'd had many years earlier while interviewing John Mohawk, a Seneca Indian who was then editor of *Akwesasne Notes,* the largest Indian newspaper in North America. I had spent several days with John and used a tape recorder to record his views on various Indian political and social matters. I had asked him about the stories that influenced him as a child, and he resisted telling me. One time, however, on a five-hour drive from northern New York State to Syracuse, he agreed to tell me some stories, but only if I switched off the tape recorder. When I asked him why, he said, "First of all I'm not supposed to be telling you this story at all. Secondly, if you have the machine going, or if you're taking notes, you won't understand the story. It depends on your listening with your heart. That won't come out on a machine."

Similarly, putting the stories on TV would reduce their evocative power, narrow their content, and destroy the interchange between the young and old. Kids who heard their stories in that way would have a "cold" memory of Indian stories. The warmth of feeling for the stories described by the Dene at the workshop would be lost, and with it an important piece of the culture's vitality.

In the Absence of the Sacred (San Francisco: Sierra Club Books, 1991).

PART FIVE INDIVIDUAL RITES OF PASSAGE

THIRTY FIVE · THE POWER OF WORDS: A PRISON EXPERIENCE

Nathan McCall

Nathan McCall, like Malcolm X before him, proved that advanced literacy changes lives. It gives a more developed vocabulary to identify and describe feelings. It expands one's world from the personal to the larger objective world. It provides a tool to give order to one's thoughts. It helps release the emotions through a written image rather than a battered body. And finally, it can give emotional distance to thoughts and feelings and leads to thoughtful choices rather than to thoughtless reactions.

Expanded literacy is not magic; it takes effort and persistence. But developing one's literary skills can work magic because framing thoughts and feelings in words rather than allowing them to explode in violence can change the world. As Nathan McCall says, "Words are power."

Following his release from prison, Nathan McCall graduated with honors from Norfolk State in journalism, landed a reporting job at the *Virginian-Pilot* and went on to work at the *Atlanta Journal-Constitution*. He came to *The Washington Post* in 1989.*

I developed through my encounter with Richard Wright a fascination with the power of words. It blew my mind to think that somebody could take words that described exactly how I felt and put them together in a story like that. Most of the books I'd been given in school were about white folks' experiences and feelings. But in *Native Son* I found a book written about a plain, everyday brother like myself. It inspired me to look for more books like that. Before long, I was reading every chance I got, trying to more fully understand why my life and the lives of friends had been so contained and predictable, and why prison—literally—had become a rite of passage for so many of us.

I was most attracted to black classics, such as Malcolm X's autobiography. Malcolm's tale helped me understand the devastating effects of self-hatred and introduced me to a universal principle: that if you change your self-perception, you can change your behavior. I concluded that if Malcolm X, who had also gone to prison, could pull his life out of the toilet, then maybe I could too.

Up to that point, I'd often wanted to think of myself as a baad nigger, and as a result, I'd tried to act like one. After reading about Malcolm X, I worked to get rid of that notion and replace it with a positive image of what I wanted to become. I walked around silently repeating to myself, "You are an intelligent-thinking human being; you are an intelligent-thinking human being . . . ," hoping that it would sink in and help me begin to change the way I viewed myself.

I spent most of my time reading, writing letters, and memorizing new words. After struggling through *Das Kapital* by Karl Marx, I realized that my limited vocabulary made me miss the full meaning of much that I read. I decided that whenever I came across an unfamiliar word, I'd stop reading, look it up in the dictionary, memorize it and use it in a sentence before I resumed reading. I then recorded the new words in a loose-leaf notebook and practiced using them in conversations. It took me months sometimes to get through a single book, but my speed and comprehension got better over time.

At some point in my reading, I ran across Rudyard Kipling's poem "If," which was so inspiring to me that I memorized and recited it as my mantra every day. It's ironic that I got so deep into something written by a person who is widely considered a racist. But the poem has no racist overtones. In fact, it has a universal appeal. That poem challenged me to reexamine self-imposed limitations and encouraged me to fight nagging fears that I had ruined my life beyond repair. I recited it to myself sometimes after visits from Liz [his girlfriend] and my son, Monroe. I recited it when I felt discouraged or blue. Later, when I got out of prison and went through other hard times working with white folks and trying to find my way, I recited it to help me keep perspective. One of my favorite sections in that poem said,

> If you can dream—and not make dreams your master:
> If you can think—and not make thoughts your aim:
> If you can meet with Triumph and Disaster
> And treat those two impostors just the same . . .

Frustrated and depressed [at one point during his prison term], I went to the prison canteen and bought a green loose-leaf tablet and started a journal, partly out of a need to capture my fears and feelings, and partly to practice using the new words I learned. I adopted a journal theme, a quote I ran across by Oliver Wendell Holmes—an encouragement to keep me pushing ahead:

> I find the great thing in this world is not so much where we stand as in what direction we are moving. To reach the port of heaven, we must sail, sometimes with the wind and sometimes against it—but we must sail, and not drift, nor lie at anchor.

It made me feel better sometimes to get something down on paper just like I felt it. It brought a kind of relief to be able to describe my pain. It was like, if I could describe it, it lost some of its power over me.

MENTORS

CHICAGO
We had meetings in the cellblock, and when Chicago spoke, everybody sat quietly. He talked about what was going right and wrong in the cellblock. He

talked with such authority, that you assumed he should be in charge. Everybody paid attention, from the hardest-nosed thugs to the most bombed-out junkies. I learned over time that he knew his stuff. He was well versed in philosophy, politics, and law. He knew how to organize against the system. I'd never seen a black man who could handle white people so well. He spoke to white jailers like he was their equal, like they weren't keeping him locked up so much as he was letting them detain him for a while. Chicago had real power in the jail.

Chicago also directed our daily therapy sessions. We also took time in those therapy sessions to talk about ourselves. The object was to get us to look within, to talk honestly about the personality problems and distorted views that landed us in jail.

MOSES BATTLE

The most popular old-head in there was a likable junkie in his early fifties who had been in and out of prison all his life. His name was Moses Battle. He was the elder statesman of the cellblock. Well-spoken and shrewd, Mo Battle was a born teacher who read a lot and loved to share his wisdom with younger guys like me. We spent long hours in the evenings, sitting on our bunks, talking. His favorite subject was philosophy. He saw philosophical meaning in everything. If two guys got into a rumble over food or cigarettes, Mo had a theory about why they'd bumped heads. He theorized a lot about jail guards, whom he hated. He said the difference between guards and inmates was so slight that if you took away the guards' uniforms you couldn't tell them apart.

The most important thing that Mo Battle taught me was that chess is a game of consequences. "Don't make a move without first weighing the potential consequences," he said, "because if you don't you have no control over the outcome."

JIM

A guy named Jim was the most respected inmate at Southampton. A Richmond native in his mid-thirties, Jim was on the tail end of a life sentence. He was admired partly because of the way he'd handled his time, but mostly because of his integrity and broad intellect. Unlike so many other dudes who became mentally passive after years in prison, Jim had somehow remained a free thinker who'd stayed focused on the world beyond that fence. Using his prison time to educate himself, he'd evolved into a self-assured, articulate brother with an unyielding commitment to what he called "black folks' struggle."

In his talks, Jim focused a lot on history. He said it was important to understand the past because it shapes our present perceptions about ourselves and the rest of the world.

Eventually, I figured out that the characteristics that made him so widely respected had little to do with how he looked; instead, it was his manly demeanor. Ever since I could recall, I and everybody else I knew had associated manhood with physical dominance and conquest of someone else. Watching Jim, I realized we'd gone about it all wrong. Jim didn't have to make a rep for himself as a thumper. He could whip a man with his sharp mind and choice words far more thoroughly than with his fists.

---

*The following passages are excerpted from "If You Can Dream," by Nathan McCall, *The Washington Post Magazine,* 30 Jan 1994; © 1995, *The Washington Post.* Reprinted with permission. This material was originally published in Nathan McCall's book, *Makes Me Wanna Holler: A Young Black Man in America* (New York: Random House, 1994).

THIRTY SIX   RITES OF INITIATION: A JOURNEY INWARD

Herb Martin

Herb Martin is Assistant Professor of Cross-Cultural Competency at California State University at Monterey Bay. His specialty is world mythologies and how to work with them in elementary school. He has won awards in teaching excellence at Louisiana State University in Baton Rouge as well as at California State University, Sacramento.

Professor Martin uses hero and heroine myths from various cultures to facilitate an experience of an inner Vision Quest in schools. His story of an inner experience at puberty stresses the need for inner direction.

Herb Martin uses myth as taught by Joseph Campbell and recommends this instruction in elementary grades so that the young person has a larger cultural context for understanding his or her own inner experiences.

INTRODUCTION

We see initiation, a social and cultural event of great, even paramount importance, as a means of tribal survival and self nurture. We also find here a pattern for understanding initiation as an individual and inner process of growth and individuation.

—LOUISE CARUS MAHDI, *BETWIXT AND BETWEEN*

In 1986, I wrote an article about rites of passage entitled "Running Wolf: Vision Quest and the Inner Life of the Middle-School Student." In this article (an adaptation of which follows these opening remarks) I wrote about a liminal experience of my own, which took place during my own puberty stage of life. The key point of that article, which was published in the *Holistic Education Review* (1986), was that the transition from childhood to adulthood, and indeed, any transformation, was accomplished by an inner journey. Any journey or set of events that carried the initiate to geographic locations, that are often a part of initiation rites, are secondary when compared to the inner geographic location, the human psyche.

I make this important geographic distinction because of the seeming confusion I have begun to note in some of the rites-of-passage programs that have begun springing up around the country. Many of them seem to concentrate, in some great detail, on certain specific geographic sites, with no attention to the fact that this is an *inner psychic transformation* that is being sought.

Along with this tendency, in some programs, to focus on the outer locales, is the equally misguided notion that the ones who conduct the rites-of-passage program can actually guide and direct a specific experience for initiates. This ignores a most important aspect of the initiatory experience: the inward journey to one's own spiritual terrain, without which little transformative or revelatory experience can take place.

A program for initiation that concentrates heavily on setting up ways to indoctrinate initiates from the outside, then, must be viewed with some concern. It is doubtful that the original purpose for initiation rites—the finding of one's personal life goals and self-identity—will be realized with such programs or were even the sought-after goals.

Additionally, while these same externally focused programs sometimes mention camping in the forest, the actual connection that nature plays in the liminal experience is totally missing. This is a crucial aspect that cannot go overlooked, if the connection with the Self is to take place. In Carl G. Jung's *Man and His Symbols* (1964), this point is driven home as he discusses the connection one makes with one's "bush soul" or totem creature or object. For example, Laine Thom, in his book *Becoming Brave: The Path to Native American Manhood*, refers to this bush or totem creature as a spiritual guardian. According to Thom, this guardian may assume many forms: bird, animal, tree, rock, water, dream, or vision. Certainly any of these, with the exception of the dream, may appear in physical form. However, without the accompanying synchronistic *inner* event, the meaning is lost. The guardian is expected to communicate with the initiate, in some manner, and reveal the powers it brings to the initiate's life.

This is the primary reason that so-called traditional societies, as Native Americans, Africans, and other indigenous peoples are referred to by anthropologists, have sent the young initiate off alone to fast, pray, and seek this vision, dream, or both in combination. Even if a physical event occurred, it had to be accompanied by the powerful inner psychic connection.

And so, it is difficult to understand how any rites-of-passage program can ignore the inner aspect of this transformation process. If the transformation is imposed from outside, how can individuation—the process of self-actualization—have a chance to occur? It would be wise, for those who intend to attempt rites-of-passage programs to help the youth of today with their "sacred passages," to remember that each individual initiate must journey *inward, alone,* to find the "treasure." Any attempts to manipulate or indoctrinate during this important process could actually prevent any type of inner transformation.

Finally, rites-of-passage programs which don't include or even seem to be aware of this important nature/unconscious connection should not be trusted at all. It is wonderful that the nation, in general, has caught on to rites of passage, vision quest, or initiation rites as important to today's youth, but we must exercise caution in the ways these programs interpret this idea.

RUNNING WOLF:
VISION QUEST AND THE INNER LIFE OF THE MIDDLE-
SCHOOL STUDENT

> *"Father, Oh father! I hear weeping. Is it my mother I leave in*
> *grief?" "Have Courage, my son . . . In your mother's womb you*
> *were conceived. From an individual human womb you were born*
> *to an individual human life. It was necessary, it was good. But*
> *individual human life is not sufficient to itself. It depends upon*
> *and is a part of life. So now another umbilical cord must be bro-*
> *ken—that which binds you to your mother's affections, that which*
> *binds you to the individual life she gave you. For twelve years you*
> *have belonged to your lesser mother. Now you belong to your*
> *greater mother. And you return to her womb to emerge once*
> *again, as a man who knows himself not as an individual but a unit*
> *of his tribe and a part of all life which ever surrounds him."*
>
> —Frank Waters, The Man Who Killed the Deer[1]

. . . The Boy heard the extra rustling of the yellow and brown autumn leaves—
a rustling that shouldn't have been there. But, he recognized it, nonetheless.
Turning to steal a glance over his shoulder, he saw them, as usual. They came
on in that ground-eating, tireless, lope of theirs. The Boy began to run, his
fright no less for the situation being so familiar. He ran with a kind of con-
trolled panic. His progress was agonizingly slow. He could feel the wolf pack
gaining with every bound. Long gray bodies, with a kind of beauty in the way
they moved, began easily to close the distance. Ahead of him, the Boy saw the
House. He could just reach it in time! Now if he could only get the door open
and closed before they engulfed him!

His hand closed over the door knob, threw open the door, and closed it
just in time. Then he looked at the door! The door, in fact, was only half a
door, having only the top portion down to the door knob. Just as he was notic-
ing this, the gray bodies of his pursuers came hurtling through the opening
that seemed made just for them! . . .

The Boy had this dream, on a recurring basis many times after his
eleventh year. He was in sixth grade in school. He became fascinated with
wolves. His teacher must have come to expect his never-ending series of
papers on wolves. He wrote poems, themes, limericks, and even term papers
on them. He became a child expert on the animal that simultaneously frightened, awed, and somehow *inspired* him. Gently, his teacher tried to suggest
other topics, but to no avail. This creature was numinous to him.

Then, in the middle of his twelfth or thirteenth year, he found The Book.
His teacher always gave his family all the old books that they wouldn't use
anymore, from primers to twelfth-grade readers. The Boy read them all hun-
grily. That is how he found the story that changed his life and gave it mean-

ing. The story appeared in a tenth or eleventh grade literature book. It was called "Running Wolf." It told the story, in beautiful fashion, of a Man from Michigan who went to Canada once a year for a solitary fishing expedition. His excuse was fishing, but he really went to this special, beautiful place for the sense of peace and serenity it gave him.

However, this year was different. When he settled down at night to cook his fresh catch, he had the disquieting feeling of being watched. He strained his eyes to see into the darkness surrounding his campfire. Finally, he was able to make out two burning eyes peering back at him. He was startled but figured that it was only some curious creature, like a raccoon, whose eyes were caught in the firelight. Soon the creature would lose interest and move away. Still the Man hardly slept that night. The next night was much the same, with a slight difference. His nocturnal visitor came earlier, at about twilight, and so was visible. The Man could now make out the ruggedly powerful frame of a huge timber wolf. It was the largest wolf the Man had ever seen! It must have weighed over 150 lbs! Its coat was coal black and its eyes glowed with an unearthly light. It came on and took up its position of the previous night to watch the Man.

Now, the Man was alarmed. The wolf seemed to know that he was unarmed, as it sat on its powerful haunches not twenty yards away, staring at him. The Man tried to frighten it away by yelling. The wolf didn't even blink. Nor did it make a threatening move, not even a snarl. The Man then grabbed a glowing faggot from the fire and hurled it at the Wolf. The wolf watched the firebrand placidly until it almost reached him, and then stepped gracefully aside, but moved closer to the fire and resumed his steady watching. The Man was astounded, but also strangely relieved.

He gave up trying to chase the wolf away and settled down to normal life. He came to expect the presence of his visitor each night and even addressed a few comical remarks in its direction. One alarming habit of the wolf was that occasionally it would seem to have appeared or disappeared suddenly. The Man accepted this as his imagination.

Finally, on the seventh or eighth night, the last night of the Man's fishing trip, the black wolf walked right up to the edge of the fire. In effect, he was actually sitting around the campfire with the Man. Strangely, now the Man was neither frightened nor surprised. A kind of rapport had been developed between the two. Even when the big wolf spoke, this all seemed to fit. The Man sat in awe and wonder as the wolf told a beautiful story. He spoke of the land on which the Man did his fishing. He said it was the sacred burial ground of his tribe. The wolf, in his former life, had been known as "Running Wolf" and had been an important member of his Indian tribe, a Medicine Chief. He spoke of the beauty of the land and many secret wonders of the Universe (which the Boy can no longer remember). *As the wolf spoke of all these things in such a sincere and loving way, the Man's sense of peace and respect for this place deepened, although he really couldn't be sure he wasn't just dreaming the whole thing. When the Man fell asleep that night, he slept soundly. He did not remember the wolf leaving or even himself going to sleep. In fact, when he awakened the next morning, he was sure he had dreamed the whole thing. He looked for paw prints around the fire and found none. This confirmed his suspicions about it being a dream, until he looked over by where the wolf had sat and found an old medicine bag. The beadwork on the side of the deerskin was a wolf in full flight!*

When the Boy finished this story, he was sobbing brokenly. Something inside him had been touched in such a way as he had never known. He would read this story over and over throughout his teen years and always, always, it was a source of inspiration. He also would *always* cry. So he had to go off alone to read it. In fact, the story represented the Boy's initiation into the Great Mystery that is Life. Finding this story at that time in his life was fortuitous. Eventually, he was to learn much more about Native American cultures, and many others, but he never forgot this story. He even adopted the wolf as his "totem" animal, giving *himself* the name, "Running Wolf." It is he who is the author of this paper.

This true account is the perfect lead-in to the topic of this paper—the middle-school student and his "Inner life." Grave difficulties have been noted nationwide with this age group (eleven to fourteen years of age). However, our curriculum developers have gone on their merry way in the social studies with approaches that mostly emphasize the physical attributes of culture—agricultural patterns, geography, the founding of civilizations, governments, and wars. This *outer* approach all but ignores the important *inner* stage or "threshold" that the middle-school student has just reached.

Along with the "normal" social studies offerings, a new and dynamic curriculum that pays attention to and even encourages this inner development, should be offered to all middle-school students.

At this crucial stage of their lives, very important questions about their lives are beginning to be asked. This is often a time of great inner turmoil, even when no outward sign seems to manifest itself, as happens sometimes when poor grades, apathy, or drug abuse point to a possible problem. Sometimes, without any previous warning, parents and teachers find out about a student's inner struggle too late—after he/she has committed suicide.

The suicide rate among youths aged ten to nineteen is alarming indeed. (Keep in mind that these figures do *not* factor in all the *attempted* suicides.) In a study done from 1954–1974 by child psychiatrist Leonard Magran, who was then Chairman of the Division of Child Development and Child Psychiatry at Albert Einstein Medical Center, Northern Division in Philadelphia, we find some numbing figures. In his study, Magran found that the number of suicides of youths aged ten to nineteen doubled—from eight thousand to sixteen thousand—between 1954 and 1974.[2] He estimated that by the end of

1984, this number would have tripled. Why were young humans barely having had a chance to enjoy life and seemingly with long futures ahead, taking their lives in such ever-increasing numbers?

Magran cited the breakup of the nuclear family, because of the divorce rate, as a main cause. He said that all this coming "at the moment when support is needed the most—during puberty, when the young person is beginning the process of psychological disengagement from the family" is the major reason for the alarming increase in teen suicides. There is a real "sense of loss," Magran noted, that is felt as the child sheds the trappings of childhood to begin the difficult "quest" that characterizes adolescence.

What Magran fails to point out, however, is that the middle-school-aged child (generally between the ages of eleven to fourteen) is especially susceptible to these pressures, even if the nuclear family is intact. In fact, in many traditional tribal cultures (and some even today), formal rituals existed for helping usher out one stage, such as childhood, and to initiate the person into the next. We seem to have once realized the psychic energy that is generated by the subject during this transitional phase, and built in a cultural vehicle to deal with the problem. However, as we have become more "civilized," many of these customs have been lost. Now such "exciting" milestones as getting a driver's license, getting a job, graduating from high school, turning eighteen (no longer a "minor"), etc. are about all that are left for today's youth to look forward to. Looking at the above list, suicide must look mighty attractive.

DEATH AND REBIRTH

But there is an even more profound reason for the concept of Death (suicide) to get mixed up in this transitional phase. Carl G. Jung (*Man and His Symbols,* 1964) has shown that the human psyche actually views such major transition periods (childhood-adolescence-adult) as Death and Rebirth—the symbolic death of the child and the symbolic rebirth of that child as an adolescent. Jung noted, in his studies of Australian Aborigines and in African tribes, the great care and importance that was attached to the initiation of the child as he stood at the threshold of manhood. The major problems are *inside,* and this was the area the initiation tried to reach. Therefore, when viewed from this Jungian point of view, it becomes easy to see why so many of our youth confuse this "symbolic" death urge with *natural* death. It also makes it quite clear to us, as educators, that we must teach students much more about what is actually meant by these strange tuggings and yearnings that have suddenly sprung up inside them. The struggles that are going on inside our youths today go largely unnoticed except for their *symptoms,* which we marvel at. We have forgotten how important what each person must face is, when it is confronted for the first time. Life, for *all* of us, is a Great Mystery. The Big questions like, What is the Universe? Where does it come from? Who *really* am I? What is my purpose?, are the questions we all come face to face with eventually. These questions seem to be of Universal or *archetypal* importance judging from the similarity of the themes of hero/heroine myths around the world. Joseph Campbell discussed the importance of the hero myth in initiation ceremonies on a global basis in *The Hero with a Thousand Faces* (1970). In *Myth and Reality,* Mircea Eliade discussed the concept of initiation as Rites of Passage.

But the most novel and interesting idea that comes out of this whole initiation theme is the concept of "Vision Quest." Hyemeyohsts Storm, the Cheyenne Indian author of *Seven Arrows* (1972) described this concept. On a mythical level, the Vision Quest is a story about a hero or heroine (in other words any one of *us*), who leaves everything behind, including the childhood home, and goes off alone to seek vision, insight, or meaning. Alone, fasting, in a state of expanded awareness, the hero/ine endures through a long, dark night, facing the monsters of childhood. At the darkest time of night, supernatural power or the Great Spirit confers a gift or a boon on the seeker. Often this spirit or helper may come in the form of an animal, such as this author's Wolf totem. The gift is of great use to the seeker or hero and to his community. The hero/heroine returns to the community and "demonstrates the vision on earth for the people to see."[3]

An actual example of this idea at work is Black Elk (Ogalala Sioux) born near Wounded Knee, South Dakota, about 1860. During his childhood, Black Elk had received a great vision, in which a great bay-horse had led him up to the Sky People where he was shown the future of his tribe and the important role he was to play in it. He thought that he had simply had a dream about visiting the Sky People, until he returned (he thought) in his dream and saw his Mother and Father and the tribal doctor kneeling over his own body in the teepee and suddenly exclaiming, "The boy is coming to; you had better give him some water."[4] Black Elk at the age of 9, had been sick almost unto death for *twelve days!* He did eventually demonstrate his vision on earth to help his people. He had many other visions besides his great one, always accompanied by a kind of sickness just before. The great and sad irony of his life was that he felt that he had not been able to save his people—which he felt was his purpose. His final plea to the Six Grandfathers on Harney Peak was "Let my people live." Perhaps, by reintroducing this idea into the human consciousness, we can help Black Elk carry out his vision. For his vision was a vision for all people.

There are actually a few high-school programs now that actually try to offer "graduating seniors" a Vision Quest course.

The problems, as stated earlier in this paper, beset our youth much earlier and *cannot* wait until they are ready to "graduate." If we try to wait, many of them won't be *around* to graduate. If not an actual *physical* Vision Quest, we can institute a kind of *mental* Vision Quest during the middle-school years. This can be done partially through the intensive study of hero/ine myths on a global basis (or as many cultures as possible). This will help the student to see that they are not "alone" in their struggles as many feel at this stage. Indeed, a kind of pride in their struggle can develop as they begin to compare the similarity of their plight with that of say, a young Arthur Pendragon (King Arthur), Moses, Siddhartha, or even Cinderella. Knowing the cultural meanings of these wonderful stories is important. This will help the students to translate this meaning into their own lives.

Besides the rich source of culture myths, there is also a rich, current crop of movies of this genre that can augment such a curriculum. The very best of these include, of course, *Karate Kid I* and *II*, *The Emerald Forest*, *Windwalker*, and *Legend*.

In addition to movies and myths, the world of art is full of the cult of the hero/ine and should be included in a good, dynamic, Vision Quest–oriented curriculum.

Finally, and very importantly, what the human psyche seems to crave at the middle-school age and into the late teens is an "other-worldly" experience. Turning to drugs, rebellion, and even suicide are all symptoms of this great need. Past cultures wisely dealt with this necessity by providing this otherworldly experience through rituals. As social-studies educators, we can at least simulate these rituals by allowing our students to study, in addition to the myriad offerings on the *physical* attributes of culture, the far more significant *inner* life of cultures at this important transitional stage. We may save many headaches for middle-school teachers, but more importantly, many *more* young lives.

NOTES

1. Frank Waters, *The Man Who Killed the Deer* (New York: Washington Square Press/Pocket Books, 1972), pp. 79–80.
2. Magran's study has not been published.
3. John G. Neihardt, *Black Elk Speaks* (1932) (New York: Washington Square Press/Pocket Books, 1972), p. 173.
4. Neihardt, p. 39.

REFERENCES

Brafford, C. J., and Laine Thom. 1992. *Dancing colors: Paths of Native American women.* San Francisco: Chronicle Books.
Brown, Joseph Epes. 1992. *Animals of the soul: Sacred animals of the Oglala Sioux.* Rockport, Mass.: Element, Inc.
Jung, Carl G. 1964. *Man and his symbols.* New York: Anchor Books, Doubleday.
Martin, Herbert L. Jr. 1986. Running wolf. *Holistic Education Review.*
Mahdi, Louise Carus, Steven Foster, and Meredith Little, eds. 1987. *Betwixt and*

between: Patterns of masculine and feminine initiation. La Salle, Ill.: Open Court.

Thom, Laine. 1992. *Becoming brave: The path to Native American manhood.* San Francisco: Chronicle Books.

THIRTY SEVEN — SACRED WORK IN MIDDLETOWN: GAY ADOLESCENTS

Alan Howard

"Sacred Work in Middletown" concerns an American experience of growing up that needs attention and more understanding. The author writes with insight about rites of passage of gay adolescents. He shares significant information about a world otherwise hidden from a large part of our population.

Alan Howard, a graduate of Yale University and UCLA Film School, is a writer and filmmaker living in Los Angeles where he also has a consultation practice.

Over thirty-five years ago, I attempted to come of age on the streets of Muncie, Indiana, then a small city of 75,000 which had been used as the subject for *Middletown* (1929) and *Middletown in Transition* (1937), classic sociological studies of typical American life by Robert and Helen Lynd.

Like my friends, I cruised the family car back and forth between drive-in restaurants, teen-age hang-outs at various ends of town. During these endless, numbing drives I became aware of a hidden world on the streets of downtown Muncie. With equal fascination and horror, I discovered that men and teenage boys made sexual connections while cruising in their cars.

By the time I was sixteen, I already knew that my sexual needs included boys as well as girls, and I had already secretly experimented with both. I was already in what felt like a dilemma with no solution. I was a popular, successful high-school student, president of the student council, and first in my class of eight hundred. But sexual feelings for boys my age and men in their early twenties arose naturally, like thunder showers, and I couldn't, try as I might, will them away. I had been at war with my father and older brother for years. They had been monitoring me to make sure I didn't turn into a sissy and were determined to toughen me up. There was an unacknowledged crisis in our home. I was growing up different, and my father was alarmed. I felt ashamed, rejected, and unloved.

Sometimes I experienced dark spasms of loneliness, melancholy, and confusion. Then I cruised the streets alone, drawn by the secret world, sensing that it held some kind of a solution to my terrible dilemma. My mother was in charge of books for the local university bookstore. One of her employees was a competitive diver named Chuck, who was twenty, athletic, and handsome. One night, while I was cruising alone, I saw Chuck walking with a flamboyant homosexual I'll call Bobby, who owned a flower shop in the center of town. Without thinking, I parked and literally chased after them, shouting Chuck's name before I came to my senses and turned back to the car. Chuck followed, leaving Bobby behind, thank God. Chuck revealed he was dropping out of college to move to Miami, to a freer, happier life. I was crushed. I had combed the streets of Muncie night after night for someone worthy. How could he be leaving? The next afternoon we met at his apartment which was already empty of furniture. We spent two hours together. I never saw him again.

Bobby, however, endured in my field of vision although I refused to acknowledge him as I drove the streets of Muncie. My attention turned to a classmate named Eddie, who was from the working-class south side of town and combed his hair like Elvis. Eddie used to lounge in darkened doorways and spotted me repeatedly circling the downtown blocks. Eddie confided that he and a few buddies were earning money for sex. I wanted to be tough like Eddie, so I let him show me the ropes. He helped me lure my only customer but I lost my nerve, gave back the money and made my customer promise not to tell Eddie, whom I never spoke to again.

When I was seventeen, I was chosen to lead the grand march of a high-school dance held in a downtown hotel. I gripped my date's hand as we ebulliently swept from the hotel ballroom outside to the streets, followed by hundreds of couples snaking behind us and blocking traffic. As Janie and I turned a corner, we ran dead into Bobby whose hair was piled in curls atop his head. Grinning, Bobby spoke to me by name. Janie giggled as I struggled to banish my panic and resolutely dodged around him to lead the march away. I did not sleep that night and vowed never to visit the streets again, a vow I broke within weeks to return to a secret world which I knew, in my hearts of hearts, was mine. The pull of the streets had a mystical power on me as if I were a celebrant in an ancient rite.

Soon I was leading two lives, a daytime life of high-school accomplishment and a nighttime life of secrecy, shame, and sexual experimentation. I couldn't figure out how to integrate the two parts of my being into a coherent identity. So, like millions of gay children in the early sixties, I froze at the edge of adolescence. I did not come of age. I did not fully mature. I became deceitful and learned to lie. I retreated into fantasy and turned grandiose, developing a lavishly delusional inner life which inflated my self-importance to make up for how horrible I felt about myself. Worst of all, I was alone. I had no one to talk to. No one.

At the end of my senior year, my solitude ended. A close friend I'll call David revealed that he was also having sex with other boys. David had a scathing, sarcastic sense of humor and appeared to be more temperate about our common dilemma. But when David went away to college, he drank heavily. At nineteen, he shot and killed himself. His suicide shocked and bewildered our circle of friends. I understood it completely.

There has been progress for gay adults since I drove the streets of Middletown thirty-five years ago. (I use the word "gay" as a convenience but

include gay males, lesbians, bisexuals, and transgenders in the definition.)
But life is still bitter for gay adolescents trying to come of age. Gay street
culture, an authentic substitute for traditional methods of coming of age, was
created by gay people in response to a homophobic power structure. But, with
the arrival of AIDS and hard drugs, gay street culture has become a crisis
zone.

At midnight, weekend traffic crawls on Santa Monica Boulevard in present day West Hollywood, California. Male prostitutes lope along in Levi's
like the boys from Muncie's south side. Here and there, another gender prevails as cross-dressing prostitutes saunter on spike heels like '50s movie god-
desses. Some are preoperative transsexuals.

Youth fetches a premium in this market. Many prostitutes are at the end
of their adolescence and have been working the streets to survive since their
homophobic parents cast them out upon discovering their sexual preference.
Some work to support drug habits. They dwell in a nighttime, shadowy realm
of danger. But, despite robbery, AIDS, arrest, beatings, rape, and murder, the
Boulevard on weekends at peak hours is defiantly bacchanalian.

In his introduction to *Gay Soul: Finding the Heart of Gay Spirit and
Nature,* Mark Thompson observes, "Most gay men are soul-wounded in early
life through rejection of their parents and peers." This rejection shatters the
adolescence of gay people and haunts their emergence into adulthood.

The soul-wounding of gay children begins years before puberty. In an
interview in *Gay Soul,* psychiatrist Richard A. Isay, author of the landmark
study *Being Homosexual: Gay Men and Their Development,* states, "Most
homosexual youngsters do not appear to be particularly feminine." Nevertheless, gay children make choices which violate traditional gender roles—a
male toddler demands to play with dolls or puts on his mother's make-up too
many times, a little girl insists on playing war games with little boys. Parents
and older siblings may panic, resorting to punishment and rejection to rein in
the child's natural impulses.

It's disturbing enough that few contemporary adolescents are offered
coming-of-age experiences. The gay child carries extra burdens: the terror of
discovery, the possibility of ostracism, ridicule, and physical attack. In short,
every adolescent's nightmare of not fitting in, of not belonging to the tribe.

The epidemic of teenage suicide is appalling to Americans. But there is a
secret horror within the acknowledged one. Many of the dead are gays. How
many? Who can say with precision? The facts of homosexuality are always
imprecise but there are estimates that more than 50 percent of teenage suicides are gay adolescents.

The religious right believes that efforts to assist gay teenagers to come of
age are, in fact, recruitment tactics practiced by evil, adult homosexuals on
innocent children. Is it any wonder that the terrible beauty I first experienced
on the streets of Muncie still exists not only on Santa Monica Boulevard but

across America? When gay adolescents creep onto the nightmare boulevards of our cities and towns, they arrive in a spiritual shambles.

The solution to the dilemma of the gay child may be the end of homophobia, but what can enlightened adults do in the meantime? The examples of two historical precedents—Native American culture and Athenian conscious- ness—are useful. Native Americans accepted a wide variety of gender behav- ior and acknowledged its sacred value to the community. Adult Athenians honored the moral and physical beauty of young males as a way to grow spir- itually and to enrich civic life.

When European warriors and missionaries invaded and conquered the New World, they were, according to surviving documents, horrified that Native American nations not only accepted but honored cross-dressing males who were called *berdaches. Berdaches* were thought to be sacred beings, with shamanic gifts, and were responsible for certain rituals and ceremonies only they were allowed to perform.

In his book *The Spirit and The Flesh: Sexual Diversity in American Indian Culture,* Walter L. Williams states,

> Berdaches serve a mediating function between women and men, precisely because their character is seen as distinct from either sex. They are not seen as men, yet they are not seen as women either. They occupy an alternative gender role that is a mixture of elements.

This startlingly mature acceptance of transgender behavior puts Native Amer- icans on the cutting edge of contemporary university gender studies which hasn't yet sorted out its meaning or value. In addition, homosexual relation- ships between two male-identified males were not thought abnormal in many Native American nations.

Because the history of homosexuality was hidden for thousands of years, gay and bisexual males had to rely on gossip and rumor to carry the memory of a glorious past in ancient Greece. But *Greek Homosexuality,* an exhaustive, scrupulous book by K. J. Dover, breaks down the Greek closet door forever. Greek men were partly, perhaps even mainly, gay or bisexual.

Over twenty-five hundred years ago in Athens, every fourth year, a sacred event—the Panathenea—was held to celebrate the birth of Athena, the patron goddess of the city. The Parthenon marbles, stolen from Greece and now displayed in the British Museum, include a massive frieze of a proces- sion which some scholars think may have been inspired by the Panathenaic festival. The frieze procession is led by a nude youth, perhaps seventeen or eighteen, who has the position of honor.

Ancient rumor has it that the model for the youth on the Parthenon frieze was the young Aeschylus who is said to have been the most accomplished and beautiful boy in Athens. Although there is no proof that this glowing marble lad is indeed Aeschylus—author of blood-spattered tragedies, including the Cresteia trilogy, a cornerstone of Western dramaturgy and thought—let's assume, for a moment, that the rumor is true.

And so, young Aeschylus is chosen to lead the Panathenaic parade because of his beauty, his athletic prowess, and his virtue. Marching nude, Aeschylus experiences a spectacular, public rite of passage, not only for himself but for the other young men of Athens he represents.

Both traditions—Native American and Athenian—valued the gay impulse as an expression of the sacred. Although the destruction of the sacred has been under way for centuries, the sacred organically reinvents itself in human consciousness, growing like a holy weed through urban concrete. Gay street culture can be perceived as the reemergence of sacred energy after centuries of suppression.

Nancy Qualls-Corbett, in her book *The Sacred Prostitute,* describes the erotic rite of the ancient temple prostitute with the stranger who approaches her. Both understand that their love act is consecrated by a deity which will renew them. "In this union—the union of masculine and feminine, spiritual and physical—the personal was transcended and the divine entered in."

In the dead of night, the transformative work of the sacred prostitute is being unconsciously attempted on the Santa Monica Boulevards of America. Denied the experience of coming of age, gay people are trying to complete a rite of passage and to link up with the divine. The mystery that propelled me to the streets of Middletown was a sacred one, an impulse directed towards the divine, expressing itself in the profane because there was no other avenue for it.

The possibility that a successful rite of passage can be accomplished in regions of infection, brutality, and death may seem unlikely. Nevertheless, until the human community stops wounding gay children, gay adolescents will continue to pursue this dance of death as a method of coming of age. I would like to suggest that what might be perceived as a travesty of sacred rites is, in fact, partly successful for gay American children who survive the street culture we have been forced to invent.

If the Boulevards are a descent into hell, daylight comes to those who weather the bacchanalia of Dionysus by arriving at the threshold of wisdom—at the doors of the gay community's vast and vibrant spiritual and political life. Twelve-step meetings which offer a spiritual solution to alcoholism and drug and sex addiction are packed throughout America's gay communities, which are also hotbeds of intense political activism with a national impact. Churches are full. Metaphysical teaching and study are valued. The rituals of death and dying are meticulously honored with AIDS caregiving and memorial services. Those who survive the ecstatic trip to Hades are renewed by the more mature sacred energy of contemporary gay adulthood, an energy which is, in some mysterious way, partly created by the sacred work on the Boulevards.

Compassionate adults can learn from the Native American example and help gay children pass into adolescence by acknowledging that homosexuality, bisexuality, and transgender behavior are part of the natural order, as natural as sea horses which change their sex or homosexual monkeys which bond with the same sex. Acknowledgment is the first step in the process of maturation of the gay child through adolescence into adulthood.

REFERENCES

Dover, K. J. 1994. *Greek homosexuality.* Indianapolis: Hackett Publishing Co., Inc.
Isay, Richard A. 1989. *Being homosexual: Gay men and their development.* New York: Farrar, Straus, and Giroux, Inc.
Lynd, Robert, and Helen Lynd. 1959. *Middletown.* Orlando, Fla.: Harcourt Brace and Co.
————. 1982. *Middletown in transition.* Orlando, Fla.: Harcourt Brace and Co.
Qualls-Corbett, Nancy. 1995. *Sacred prostitute.* Santa Rosa, Calif.: Atrium Publishing Group.
Thompson, Mark. 1994. *Gay soul: Finding the heart of gay spirit and nature.* San Francisco: Harper.
Williams, Walter L. 1992. *The spirit and the flesh: Sexual Diversity in American Indian Culture.* Boston: Beacon Press.

THIRTY

RIGOBERTA MENCHÚ: GROWING UP IN GUATEMALA

Rigoberta Menchú

I, Rigoberta Menchú: An Indian Woman in Guatemala (New York: Verso, 1984) tells the life story of Rigoberta Menchú, a Quiché Indian woman and a member of one of the largest of the twenty-two ethnic groups in Guatemala. She was born in the hamlet of Chimel, near San Miguel di Uspantan, which is the capital of the northwestern province of El Quiché.

This young Guatemalan peasant woman has become famous in her country as a national leader, but her life vividly reflects the experiences common to many Indians in Latin America. Faced with gross injustice and exploitation, she decided at an early age to learn Spanish and turned to catechist activity as an expression of social revolt as well as deep religious belief. After the coming to power of the Lucas Garcia regime in 1978, her brother, father, and mother were all killed in separate incidents of savagery on the part of the army.

Quietly, but proudly, she leads us into her own cultural world, a world in which the sacred and the profane constantly mingle, in which worship and domestic life are one and the same.

In this excerpt, Rigoberta tells about her experience of two important initiatory events on two birthdays at the ages of ten and twelve. Most striking is her family's expectation of commitment to the community at so young an age. And in encouraging their daughter to learn certain practical survival skills, they helped to ensure that she had self-confidence and a sense of self-sufficiency most of us find hard to attain well into our adult years.

The anthropologist Elisabeth Burgos-Debray, herself a Latin American woman, conducted the original interviews with Rigoberta Menchú and collected them for the book from which this selection is drawn. Rigoberta Menchú won the Nobel Peace Prize in 1992.

My tenth birthday was celebrated in the same way as all our people. I was up in the *Altiplano*. It might not have been the exact date of my birth because I was in the *finca* at the time, but when we went back up to the *Altiplano*, that was when we celebrated my birthday. My parents called me to them and explained what an adult's life is like. I didn't really need them to explain because it was the life I'd seen and lived with my mother; so it was really only a show of accepting what parents tell us.

My elder brothers were present and my sister who's now married. But my younger brothers were not. I'm the sixth in the family, with three brothers after me, but they weren't present because it's a ceremony in which my parents tell me about the new life I'm about to start. They told me I would have many ambitions but I wouldn't have the opportunity to realize them. They

said my life wouldn't change, it would go on the same—work, poverty, suffering. At the same time, my parents thanked me for the contribution I'd
made through my work, for having earned for all of us. Then they told me a
bit about being a woman; that I would soon have my period and that was
when a woman could start having children. They said that would happen one
day, and for that they asked me to become closer to my mother so I could ask
her everything. My mother would be by my side all this time in case I had
any doubts or felt alone. They talked about the experiences with my elder
brothers and sisters. My elder sister, who was already grown up (she'd be
about twenty-four, I think) told me about when she was young: when she was
ten, twelve, thirteen, fifteen. My father said that sometimes she didn't do
things as she should but that that wasn't right: we should not stop doing good
things but accept life as it is. We shouldn't become bitter or look for diver-
sions or escape outside the laws of our parents. All this helps you to be a girl
who is respected by the community. My father explained the importance of
our example and the example of every one of our neighbors' children. We
know that not just one pair of eyes is watching us, but the eyes of the whole
community are on us. It's not a case of giving things up. We have a lot of
freedom, but, at the same time, within that freedom we must respect ourselves.

Well, my mother, father, and all my brothers and sisters, gave me their
experiences. Suddenly they treated me like an adult. My father said, "You
have a lot of responsibility; you have many duties to fulfill in our community
as an adult. From now on you must contribute to the common good." Then
they made me repeat the promises my parents had made for me when I was
born; when I was accepted into the community; when they said I belonged to
the community and would have to serve it when I grew up. They said they'd
made these promises and now it was up to me to keep them, because now I
had to participate in the community as one more member of it. In those days,
there was already the mixture of our culture with the Catholic religion, let's
say Catholic customs. So my duty was to promise to serve the community
and I looked for ways in which I could work for the community. When you
reach the age of ten, your family and the whole community holds a meeting.
It's very important. There's a ceremony as if we were praying to God. The
discussion is very important because, as I said, it initiated me into adult life.
Not the life of a young girl but adult life with all its responsibilities. I'm no
longer a child. I become a woman. So in front of my parents, in front of my
brothers and sisters, I promised to do many things for the community. That's
when I started to take over some of my father's duties: that is, praying in our
neighbors' houses like my father does. Whenever there's a meeting, it's
always my father who speaks, and he coordinates a lot of things in the community. I felt responsible for many things and my mother let us into many
secrets, telling us to try and do things the way she had. It was then, I remember,

I became a catechist, and began working with the children both in the community and down in the *finca,* since, when some of the community go to the *finca,* others stay in the *Altiplano* looking after our animals, or whatever, so we don't have to take them with us to the coast.

There's another custom for our twelfth birthday. We're given a little pig, or a lamb, or one or two chickens. These little animals have to reproduce and that depends on each person, on the love we give our parents' present. I remember when I was twelve, my father gave me a little pig. I was also given two little chickens and a lamb. I love sheep very much. These animals are not to be touched or sold without my permission. The idea is for a child to start looking after his own needs. I intended my animals to reproduce but I also intended to love the animals belonging to my brothers and sisters and my parents. I felt really happy. It's one of the most wonderful things that can happen. I was very pleased with my little animals. They had a fiesta for me. We eat chicken whenever there is a fiesta. Years and years can go past without us eating beef. With us, eating a chicken is a big event.

It wasn't long before my little pig grew and had five little piglets. I had to feed them without neglecting my work for my parents. I had to find food for them myself. So what I used to do was, after work in the fields, I'd come back home at six or seven in the evening, do all my jobs in the house for the next morning, and then at about nine o'clock I'd start weaving. Sometimes I'd weave until ten. When we'd stop for our food out in the fields, I'd hang my weaving up on a branch and carry on weaving there. After about fifteen days, I'd have three or four pieces of cloth to sell, and I'd buy maize or other little things for my pigs to eat. That's how I looked after my little pigs. I also started preparing some ground with a hoe to sow a bit of maize for them. When my pigs were seven months old, I sold them and was able to sow a bit of maize for the mother pig so she could go on having piglets. I could also buy myself a *corte* and other things to put on, and enough thread to make or weave a blouse, a *huipil.* That's how you provide for your needs and, in the end, I had three grown up pigs, ready for me to sell. At the beginning it's difficult, I didn't know what to give them to eat. I'd collect plants in the fields to give my piglets and when I made the dogs' food, I used to take a bit for them too. By the time the first little animals are born, our parents can tell if our *nahual* gives us the qualities for getting on well with animals. I was one of those who loved animals, and they always turned out very well for me. Animals loved me too. Cows, for instance, were never awkward with me. My parents were very pleased with me.

_____

Leland Roloff

This is a discussion with South African psychologists in South Africa about some traditional rites of passage and their possible failure. For related information, please refer to chapter 27 by M. Vera Bührmann in *Betwixt and Between* concerning the South African Xhosa indigenous healers.

Lee Roloff is a Jungian analyst in private practice in Evanston, Illinois. He is a member of the Chicago Society of Jungian Analysts and an honorary member of the Southern African Association of Jungian Analysts. He is Professor Emeritus at Northwestern University.

The three of us were alone for a time, two black psychological professionals and myself. The day itself had been stirring and inspiring at the psychiatric hospital for black males—the manner in which I had been greeted, the openness and frankness of the staff regarding mental health of the patients. For all the maleness of the institution, the presence of a woman psychiatrist, women social workers, and women staff members had not made it possible to be alone with my black colleagues. At last we were. Over tea and biscuits, the conversation ranged over a variety of topics: life in the United States, the impending end of *apartheid,* depression amongst black males—a protean, thoroughly satisfying conversation by men committed to the growing intimacy and candor of the talk. Finally, a quiet pause occurred. We sat quietly, and out of that silence, I asked the question that I had been pondering for virtually the entire time I had been in South Africa. "Given the dispersal of tribal males throughout all metropolitan centers—Port Elizabeth, Cape Town, Johannesburg—are there male initiations at all? Do you carry on with older tribal customs under these difficult circumstances?"

There was an even longer pause now, and the two of them leaned over to me with an intensity of presence that was particularly marked by their penetrating eyes. The first who spoke did so with a voice practically a whisper, but yet filled with a low timbre and crisp articulation.

"Oh, yes, we carry on. While it is difficult given the nature of townships and all that, we carry on. We have to carry on. We cannot lose our identity, you see. Life itself is difficult enough just to make ends meet, but life is meaningless without our tribal consciousness, and life has no meaning if we forget our responsibility to the young men. Yes, it is difficult, but we do it."

The second man now spoke and with an insistence that I listen carefully.

"You whites do not initiate. You have various religious events—confirmations, I think you call them, and things like that. But you do not initiate

your boys, and that is why you have so many boy-men. That is your shame.
Do you understand?"

"Yes, I understand." I could feel a tremendous sense of loss, but I could
not say more than, "Yes, I understand." Another very long period of silence
filled with a quiet regard for the fullness of silence. "Given the difficulties,
how do you carry on these initiations?"

And the first man said, "Well, I will tell you this. We work hard to find
and identify our tribal families in the townships. We observe, you understand?
We watch the children, boys particularly. Then when we know (and do not
ask me *how we know,* we just know), we get into our trucks—oh, like your
pickup trucks, sometimes larger—and drive into the townships after midnight. We knock on doors, we say, 'We have come for your son.' The mother
begins her ceremonial wail, the boy is frightened, but there are others in the
truck with him. After we have gathered say six or seven, we drive into the
country to a remote place. Well, I cannot tell you where it is, but it is remote.
We give each boy a knife, matches, a blanket, and some water. We blindfold
him and take him into the land. We stop. We tell him he will be alone, he will
have to find food, he will be watched, and someone will come for him each
evening. What the boy does not know is that there is an older man watching
all the time. It is like a circle. The older man is in the center of a large circle.
At points on the outer rim of the circle, and separated from each other, each
boy has his place. The first night and day, of course, are the worst. At night
they are taught a number of things about manhood. About sexuality. About
how the mother is never to have power over them again. About being a man
and knowing what men must know to pass on—what our ancestors were like,
what our ancestors knew and want us to know, and how important it is to
keep in touch with the ancestors, to let them speak through you. This may last
three days, sometimes a week. But the men now are in charge. That is our
task, and we do our best."

Whatever is deeply intuitive in me knows that I must not ask questions.
But looking into these men's eyes, I simply ask, without thinking really, "And
then, how do you return?"

"Well, I will tell you," the second man said. "We have a final night
together in the country, and then in the very early morning hours we drive
back to the city and townships. We honk the horn, the boys are whistling and
shouting, and the families come out of their homes to greet the new men. It is
a very happy time, I assure you."

"You mean that all the boys return home as men?" I ask.

"Well, no. Not all. Some cannot . . . how do you say, 'take it.' They run
away from their site, and they are now lost, you see. They cannot return
home. They go away as far as possible. Some, very few, very few, take their
own lives. They are shamed, you see."

"How do you announce this to the parents?"

"Well, this is very difficult. Sometimes we throw their articles over the fence into the garden of their home. Sometimes, really more often, we toss the melon. You know these small melons about the size of a head? You see them being sold along the highway. Well, we toss the melon over the fence into the garden. It smashes, you see, and when the family comes out they see this broken melon and they know they have lost a son. This does not happen often. But it happens. The broken melon."

This conversation lasted perhaps an hour and fifteen minutes at the most and yet has stayed with me in such an unforgettable way. I know now why. The morning shivaree of triumphant return was powerful enough. It is the image of the *broken melon* that haunts.

FORTY

FATHER AND SON IN EGYPT

Chester Higgins, Jr.

Chester Higgins Jr. wrote this vignette about a ritual experience with his twenty-year-old son on their trip to Africa. It is a beautiful account of how a father and son developed their own ritual. Although this ritual occurred in Africa, there are naturally many possibilities closer at hand.

Chester Higgins Jr. is the author of the photo collections *Black Woman, Drums of Life,* and *Some Time Ago,* as well as the book from which the following chapter is taken, *Feeling the Spirit: Searching the World for the People of Africa* (New York: Bantam Books, 1994). A staff photographer for the *New York Times* since 1975, Mr. Higgins' photographs have appeared in *Look, Life, Time, Newsweek, Fortune, Ebony, Essence,* and *Black Enterprise.* His work is the topic of the PBS film, *An American Photographer: Chester Higgins Jr.,* and he is the recipient of grants from The Ford Foundation, the Rockefeller Foundation, the International Center of Photography, and the National Endowment for the Arts.

I took my son Damani to Africa for the first time when he was twenty. For three weeks we explored together the past and present of our people in Egypt and Ethiopia. I wanted him to see the land of his heritage; I wanted him to experience the intense ecstasy I felt on my first African visit when I, too, was in my twenties.

I asked my son to come along as my assistant to help photograph the planned reinterment of Emperor Haile Selassie I on what would have been His Majesty's one hundredth birthday on July 23, 1992. Twenty years before, I had photographed this most amazing ruler in his capital city of Addis Ababa. The memory of being in his presence has remained an inspiration in my personal life. Damani, who has locked his hair, shares my love of His Majesty and reggae, the music of the Rastafarians who worship Selassie. I decided to add a stopover in Egypt to our itinerary so that my son could also see the pyramids, temples, and tombs of our ancestors. Because my family has no memory from which ethnic group in Africa we are descended, I decided to reach back to the beginnings of all Africans.

About two weeks before we were to travel, the reinterment of Emperor Haile Selassie was postponed. We were both deeply disappointed, but neither of us considered canceling our trip, nor did the many thousands of Rastafarians who annually gather for Emperor Selassie's birthday. While we were in the highlands of Welo Province in Ethiopia, Damani in his locks blended into the population; his enthusiasm for this ancient African country warmed my heart. On a four-day trip to visit the sacred city of Lalibela, where in the twelfth century numerous churches were hewn out of the surrounding mountains, I had a dream. In my dream I saw two men, one older and one younger, facing each other against a background of ancient temples and pyramids. The father was speaking as he anointed the head of his son.

I became enamored with the possibility of enacting a ceremony with Damani in Africa. For the next six days I kept my ideas to myself, wondering what words to use in such a ceremony. By the time we arrived in Cairo I was ready. I told him I wanted to perform a ceremony with him in the tombs at Luxor, Egypt. His eyes shone with unexpected anticipation. But I wondered if he would still be receptive after my next statement. I remembered that in the dream the son, although appearing to be anointed, had remained dry. I took this to mean a powder rather than water was poured on his head, but what powder? I discounted ground herbs and flowers and finally settled on sand— naturally abundant in the Sahara. Sand represents and is the land; it also contains the remains of the people. That made metaphysical sense to me; but in the real world young adults, or almost anybody for that matter, are disinclined to have sand poured in their hair.

"I will need sand to anoint your head," I told my son.

"Sand?" he asked reluctantly. "How much?"

"Just a little; you can collect some in a film canister," I added hastily. We both knew a 35 mm film canister wouldn't hold much sand. "Take the canister and find sand you feel special about, and I'll use that."

In control of the amount of sand and where it would come from, he decided to take some from the desert in the shadow of the pyramids at Giza. Days later, when we reached Luxor, he collected more from around the remains of the Temple of Karnak—one of the largest and oldest stone temples in the world.

The next afternoon we sailed across the Nile River to Thebes and to the Valley of the Kings, a basin formed by towering mountains. From the heavenly perch of the ancient Egyptian deities, the valley resembles a huge bowl to which there is one narrow entrance flanked by more tall peaks. The tombs of the Pharaohs are hewn into the lower part of the mountains that form the basin. Inside each tomb twelve-foot-square passageways lead down several thousand feet into the solid rock. The scene that greets modern-day visitors to these sacred chambers is astonishing. Ornately painted walls reveal images of animals, people, and scenes that were part of the real and imaginary lives of Pharaonic Egyptians. It was here, inside one of the tombs of an Eighteenth Dynasty Pharaoh, that I chose to perform the ceremony revealed to me in my dream in Ethiopia.

In front of an enormous wall painting of Osiris, the god of resurrection, my son and I faced each other. I poured the sand he had collected into the palm of my left hand, and with my right I anointed the top of his head with this sand. Looking into his eyes, I said:

"I, your father, anoint the crown of your head with the soil of Africa. This piece of earth is a symbol of the lives of your ancestors. It is a bonding of their lives to yours. Like your father, you too are African. We are Africans not because we are born in Africa, but because Africa is born in us. Look around you and behold us in our greatness. Greatness is an African possibility; you can make it yours. Just as the great ones before you have by their deeds placed their names on history, so can you by your deeds place your name on tomorrow. You now have the rest of your life to benefit from this new awareness.

"Try your best to make your mark on life, or else you could very well die undeclared. The time will come when death will claim us all. For those of us in the Diaspora, our bodies will remain where we plant them but our souls will fly back to Africa. So here, in the company of those great ones who have waited patiently for your visit, you are loved, you are encouraged. Our faces shine toward yours. Go forward; may you live long, may you prosper and have health."

We hugged each other, feeling the spirit of the moment. Leaving him alone inside the tomb to meditate, I walked back toward the light and waited for him outside on the valley floor.

One year after my son and I journeyed to our African homeland, I found myself in Alabama standing at my mother's graveside looking across her coffin at my daughter Nataki, who was cradling her fourteen-month-old daughter Shaquila in her arms. Before my mother's coffin was sealed, my daughter and son had asked to put something from themselves inside it with their grandmother. Nataki placed a picture of Shaquila, a great-granddaughter never seen by her great-grandmother. Damani took off his bow tie and laid it beside his grandmother.

We all formed a triangle across the coffin, both my children and the baby on one side, with me on the other. I wanted us to enact the African rite of continuity I had learned about while photographing at the seventeenth-century African burial ground discovered in Manhattan in 1991. The youngest baby in the family is passed among surviving family back and forth over the body to signify the renewal of life.

We took turns handing Shaquila over my mother's body.

"The first pass is for our ancestors, those who came before us."

The second time we passed the baby, I said, "This time is for those of us left behind who are living, the survivors."

The third and final pass was for the future: "Those who will come after us."

We embraced for a moment, savoring the spirit among us of our mother, grandmother, and great-grandmother, and then we walked away so that the grave could claim her body, and her soul return to Africa.

Steven Foster

Steven Foster (Ph.D., Humanities) retired from San Francisco State University in 1971 to devote his time to the reintroduction of ancient passage rites into the mainstream of modern culture. To confirm this change of worlds, he lived alone in the Great Basin deserts for a year. In 1976, he married Meredith Little, a trainer of hotline volunteers at Marin Suicide and Crisis Intervention Center. Together they founded and codirected Rites of Passage, Inc., a school of wilderness transition rites, and have guided thousands of individuals through the initiatory steps of wilderness passage rites. Since the establishment of the School of Lost Borders in 1981, they have trained hundreds of persons from many fields and nationalities. They have a teenage daughter (in addition to Steven's two sons) and hold family life sacred. Much of their spare time is spent writing, exploring the desert mountains, and being with family. Steven coaches basketball at the local high school. They are not shamans, gurus, or sorcerers, but thoroughly human teachers in the Socratic tradition who respect and live close to the earth.

The fruits of their research, teaching, explorations of natural solitude, and apprenticeship to a variety of medicine teachers are set forth in several books: *The Book of the Vision Quest: Personal Transformation in the Wilderness* (1980, 1987, 1988), *The Trail Ahead: A Course Book for Graduating Seniors* (1983), *The Sacred Mountain: A Vision Fast Handbook for Adults* (1984), *The Roaring of the Sacred River: The Wilderness Quest for Vision and Healing* (1988), and *Betwixt and Between: Patterns of Masculine and Feminine Initiation,* edited with Louise Mahdi. *The Four Shields: A Psychology of Human Nature,* is forthcoming.

Foster unmincingly recounts the way in which high-school graduation is celebrated in his rural California hometown, on the Nevada border.

The children of the inner cities are not the only ones who need caring, conscious elders and their guidance. Foster's own work as a wilderness guide stands in stark relief against the background of one small community's indifference to—even support of—an adolescent ritual born out of our darker side.

When I was a child, I spake as a child, I understood as a child, I thought as a child; but when I became a man, I put away childish things.

—I CORINTHIANS 13:11

Bend City exists in one of the most beautiful places on earth. Travelers through these parts have often likened it to Nepal, Tibet, or the Andes.

Gargantuan mountains rise to heights two miles above sea level on both sides
of the valley. A few miles east of town, the tule-green Inyo River runs south
through big sage-rabbitbrush flats to the reservoir, where the valley narrows
to a few miles across, the Range of Light to the west, the Dwelling-Place-of-
the-Great-Spirit Mountains to the east. Green veins of trees line the river and
the numerous creeks that flow out of the mountains.

The region in and around Bend City offers unparallelled outdoor recreation, tourism, and "unconfined wilderness solitude." There's cross-country
skiing in the winter, trout fishing (rainbow, German brown, Eastern brook,
cutthroat, and golden) in the summer, hunting (elk, deer, game birds) in the
fall, backpacking, hiking, rock hounding, fossil hunting, four-wheeling,
mountain and rock climbing, hang gliding, photography, prospecting, nature
watching—all year round. Less than an hour away you can visit with bristle-
cone pines, the oldest living things on earth. Two hours away and you can
play in Funeral Valley, Termination Valley, Inconsolable Valley, Panamint Valley, Lost Valley, Deep Springs Valley, the Blanco Mountains . . . I could go
on.[1] With its unique combination of desert and alpine mountains, of lowest
and highest, hottest and coldest, the regions adjacent to Bend City are like no
others on the continent.

Since they are in such proximity to such beauty and wonder, you might
think the people of Bend City would be self-sufficient, independent, adventuresome noble savages, lovers and preservers of the wilderness. But that is
an urbanized notion. Anyone familiar with the rural American West knows
that there is little correlation between imagined romantic notions of the noble
savage living close to nature and the genuine article—the American "redneck." Not that all the citizens of Bend City are rednecks. If we could flush
all the citizens out of their holes we'd probably find a fairly wide variety of
cultural types, including many with convictions and values that run counter to
the prevailing redneck, small-town attitudes. But most of us with notions
opposite to the stampede usually prefer to keep a low profile. The rock standing too high in the middle of the rapids runs the risk of being overturned. Better for us opposition to practice guerilla warfare, and to pick our shots.

Bend City is "California redneck"—as opposed to "Arkansas redneck,"
"Idaho redneck," or "Southern redneck." And being as how it is only a little
over half a day from the Los Angeles area, Bend City contains a distinct sub-
species of "California redneck." *Redneckus Californium Bend Citii* is unique
in that it includes "redskin rednecks" (redneck Paiutes) as well as white ones.
To a certain extent, the two types overlap—that is, they are often seen
together, as in the little Bend City High School, with its student body of
eighty-three. After high school, redskin redneck and paleface redneck cultures seem to diverge, although many of the symbols and badges are still held
in common. It's often difficult to tell whose four-wheel drives, guns, and
clothes are whose.

The high school is the most advantageous place to study the Bend City redneck. The male and female adults have freshly hardened into their roles. In high school the most exaggerated tendencies of redneckism can be seen at their innocent, irrational best. Cars, sex, alcohol (the redneck drug of preference), firearms, parties, anti-intellectualism, racism, follow-like-sheep-to-the-right politics, and all kinds of "macho" poses are informal signs of redneck coming-of-age behavior. I'm reminded of the kid who came to the prom wearing the T-shirt that read, "Nuke 'Em Until They Glow." He was showing signs of being grown-up. He was taking a political stand.

These kids grow up surrounded by some of the most beautiful mountains on earth. Every morning they can get up with sunrise and see the radiant eastern face of the Range of Light. Every sunset they can watch the Dwelling-Place-of-the-Great-Spirit Mountains glow like the coals of a dying fire. Whatever horizon they peer into greets their eyes with beauty, vastness, sublimity. Shadowy distances beckon to be explored, wondered at, known. Peaks beg to be scaled, rivers and lakes to be fished, back country to be traveled, animals to be tracked, specimens to be taken. The challenge is there. Now bring on our adventuresome young to accept the challenge of the land.

The truth is, the vast majority of the kids in Bend City high school aren't interested in the land. Their preoccupations are primarily social. Girlfriends, boyfriends, gaining acceptance, doing the right things, wearing the right clothes, telling the right jokes, seeing the right movies, listening to the right music, partying with the right people (sound familiar?) are the aspects of life that concern them. The natural world (and school as well) is but a backdrop to the all-important social drama—or an enormous receptacle into which unwanted items can be dropped and forgotten. This lack of interest is evidenced by the comparative few who graduate and pursue college studies or skilled professions related to the care and preservation of the natural world. On the other hand, high-school graduates often wind up working for Water and Power, Caltrans, the county, the tourist industry, or a local mine or ranch.

To a certain extent, our redneck teenage culture is aware of the land, and the kids do venture out into it. Down to the river to tan and swim in the summer, four-wheeling it on (or off) outlying roads, fishing with a couple buddies, deer and dove hunting, partying all night up some dirt road above town, skiing up in Mammoth in the winter, parking and smooching along some country lane. Invariably, the motivation for getting into the land is social and recreational. Who wants to go hiking just to be hiking, or bird-watching, or tracking, backpacking, sleeping on the ground looking up at the stars? They do not go out there just to be going out there.

The infinite number of hiding places in the hills make for much outdoor drinking. One reason why there are such concentrations of beer cans and liquor bottles and other trash associated with drinking in outlying areas around town is because the high-school kids don't want to be caught drinking by the Sheriff. The best way to party freely is to drive to some semi-remote place seldom visited by the fuzz and drink there, making sure every bottle and can has been thrown from their car before they drive back to town. It would be very difficult indeed to persuade these kids to accept the challenge of their land. They have already voted. Their social-drinking rites of passage take precedence over pride and respect in the appearance of their incomparably precious home country.

One good reason why I've been interested in the local passage rites into adulthood is because my son Christian recently graduated from Bend City High School. I wanted to know what social mechanisms had been built into the redneck culture to bring him safe and sanely to manhood. Surely, I reasoned, any manhood passage rites, redneck or not, would have to include, or take place in, the natural environment. Surely it would include culture-wise teaching about the need to maintain, sustain, and protect, our natural resources, if only as a matter of survival. I'm not referring to all the informal, and often illegal, things the kids were doing in order to prove they were grown-up. I was interested in the formal means by which the Bend City culture effected the passage of boys into men—or if *any* means existed.

With the help of Chris, who was willing to be open with me, I kept abreast of what Bend City High School was doing to help him formally mark his passage into manhood. In his senior year there were various school dances, including Homecoming. There was participation in varsity athletics—basketball, football, and baseball. There was a series of classes on human sexuality. There was a "mock trial" contest, a spelling bee, an inter-school math competition, an Armed Services recruiting day, and a senior-class fundraiser (selling worms to fishermen on opening day). There was an ostentatiously expensive prom, an academic/athletic-achievement awards banquet, an SAT testing day, and a senior sneak. These manhood-marking events and services culminated in the passage rites of "Graduation," which included "commencement exercises" in the afternoon and a nonalcoholic all-night party later that night. Other than things the kids did on their own (like getting a job), this was the sum total of the formal rites of passage provided by Bend City, California. Note that they are not much different from those in most of the rural communities in America.

"Wait!" you say. "That's not enough. How can a boy become a man just by doing such paltry things?" Perhaps you are one of those who wonder, where's the risk? Where's the perilous passage that *proves* the boy has become the man? The more you think about it, the more ridiculous it seems. "Look," you say. "What about those mountains surrounding Bend City? What about that desert out there? What are you doing about that? Surely, a proper challenge could be found, one that truly tests the mettle of a young man and helps him to truly understand his place on and relationship to the Mother Earth."

I agree, and I don't want to disillusion you further, but there's more. There are also the "informal" rites which, by their occurrence through the years, have become secretly formal. I'm referring to certain clandestine activities such as playing hooky, mild acts of vandalism, secret stag parties with showings of X-rated videos, and the subject at hand: "bunny bashing."

What is bunny bashing? Perhaps we should take it as it came in the chronology of Chris' graduation day, sandwiched between the commencement exercise in the afternoon and the all-night party late that night. These three events roughly formed a tripartite sequence or process reminiscent of Arnold van Gennep's classic definition of the three phases of a rite of life-transition: severance, threshold, and incorporation.[2] Of course, Bend City school administrators never intended Graduation Day's events to be measured by an anthropological ruler. Largely ignorant of *rites de passage,* these dignitaries planned only two ceremonies. The middle or "threshold" ceremony, bunny bashing, was less legitimate and performed in semi-secrecy.

SEVERANCE

Traditional passage rites into adulthood begin with a kind of ending. The child is leaving home, school, and the haunts of innocence. He is saying goodbye to his parents, for henceforth he will live as a man among men. Because the cord attaching him to all he knows as security is being cut, the man-child is afraid. He faces an unknown ordeal, some kind of encounter with real or imagined death, at the conclusion of which the mantle of manhood will be placed upon him. But for now he is a trembling child, awed by the enormity of the challenge of the future:

> "Father, Oh father! I hear weeping. Is it my mother I leave in grief?" "Have courage, my son . . . In your mother's womb you were conceived. From an individual human womb you were born to an individual human life. It was necessary, it was good. But individual human life is not sufficient to itself. It depends upon and is a part of all life. So now another umbilical cord must be broken— that which binds you to your mother's affections, that which binds you to the individual human life she gave you. . . . Now you belong to your greater mother. And you return to her womb to emerge once again, as a man who knows himself not as an individual but a unit of his tribe and a part of all life which ever surrounds him."[3]

Nice sentiments, but hardly appropriate at the Bend City High School commencement ceremony. Mother may be weeping because Johnny's getting older, but she's certainly not saying goodbye to him. In fact, before she could let him go he had to promise that he would clean up his room tomorrow morning, and he had to stand there and listen to his father lecture about how not to abuse the family car. And if Johnny's afraid about anything, it has to do with whether or not the cummerbund is snug enough or the pants long enough to cover his sweat socks. Otherwise, he doesn't appear to be too apprehensive. The severest test of manhood he will face will be when he has to march in rhythm to "Pomp and Circumstance," take a precarious seat on the riser, and walk across the stage without tripping to receive the handshake and diploma.

The long-awaited June day arrived. But the weather refused to cooperate. Huge multi-layered clouds settled darkly into the valley, fueled by gale-force western winds. Scattered rain began to fall. It was as though Mother Nature was trying to say, "Look at me you fools! I mock your feeble ceremonies!" Plans to hold the shindig outside in the open air (surely in one of the most beautiful commencement settings on earth) were scuttled hastily. Chairs, risers, and props were moved inside the gymnasium, where the friends and relatives gathered to watch the graduates march down the aisle, robed in gowns of green and gold (the school colors).

Smirking self-consciously, tassels swaying awkwardly from mortarboards, the candidates took their places on the risers facing the audience. The school band played a number, a local reverend made an invocation, the valedictorian (Chris' ex-girlfriend) and the salutatorian (who happened to be Chris), gave nostalgic, inspiring speeches. I was proud of my son's speech, especially when he mentioned the need for humans to live in harmony with their environment, the only time during the entire proceedings when the subject was actually broached. Then the graduates of '89 were introduced to the audience. Great show was made of the switching of tassels, of mortarboards tossed in the air, of the graduates marching triumphantly back through the audience, bravely, innocently unaware of the enormity of the burdens of the adult world which they had just inherited.

Who was kidding whom? How could they be expected to understand that they had just formally severed from childhood? They weren't going anywhere, at least for a while. In the early hours of the next morning, exhausted and sleepless from the all-night party, they would straggle back to their homes, back into the womb of childhood, back into the routines of parent vs. adolescent, back to the same living situation they were supposed to leave, a situation that taunted them with the fear that they were neither strong, intelligent, nor resourceful enough to leave. They were, in fact, not expected to depart. They were to remain on the runway. They could rev up their engines and taxi around, but they couldn't take off. Full freedom wouldn't come until they were twenty-one, three years from then.

Despite the fact that the ceremony was one big empty promise, there was hardly a dry eye in the crowd. Though the commencement exercise had been almost completely devoid of experiential content that meaningfully formalized the act of severance, the audience, Indian and white, had been deeply moved anyway. It wouldn't have mattered if the graduates had run around in diapers. The tears would have flowed. Nostalgia and family pride would have brightened the air. I remember thinking how much more meaningful—in an unsentimental way—the ceremony would have been if it had been held out-side, in the full fury of the storm. No such luck.

I stood with Meredith and Selene and watched Chris and his classmates march out of the gym. I too felt the tugging of pride at my breast. At least the ceremony gave me a chance to feel that. Did this moment of fatherly pride make up for all the trauma, conflict, pain, and despair involved in the father-ing of this young man? Certainly not. Had the ceremony proved to me that my son was ready for manhood, that I'd done a good, or at least serviceable job, in fathering him? Certainly not. Had Chris been challenged by a rite of passage that had truly confirmed his mettle as a man? Certainly not. How well both Chris and I knew that his "commencement" had been incomplete, that the boy had been officially stamped "man" when, in fact, he'd done hardly anything to officially demonstrate his manhood. The speech—yes, that was important. And brave words were one thing. Deeds were another.

I stood and watched and wondered if I'd fathered him well enough. He'd had a difficult time growing through adolescence in this little redneck town. At age fourteen he'd left his mother, who was living in Santa Cruz, to come and live with me. Sub-species *Californium radicalis* mingled with *Bend City Redneckus,* but not without a few volatile reactions. He'd had to earn his place. His father's values had differed vastly from the values of his male peers, and from the values of many adult males whose professional task had been to instruct, coach, and otherwise prepare him to put on the Bend City redneck mantle of manhood. I had a seemingly endless anxiety list. Maybe I'd failed him in one way or another. I hadn't been accessible enough. I had-n't encouraged him enough. I hadn't been interested enough in his problems. I hadn't gone off with him on enough father-son trips. I hadn't been a good role model. . . . Any father is familiar with the routine.

Consequently, I was surprised and pleased when, after the hand-shaking and hugging were over, Chris came up and told me he was coming home. He'd decided not to go bunny bashing with his friends. He'd mess around at home for a few hours, then take off for the all-night party. "Chris is bugging out!" yelled Hank Williams, one of Chris' closest friends, from across the crowded commons. "I am not!" yelled Chris. "I'm tired. I've had about four hours of sleep in the last two days." Mark Talbot, a clean-cut kid headed for the Marines came running over. "O.K. then. If you're not going you owe me some money." Reluctantly, Chris handed over his share of the bunny bash. A lot of the guys were going. They'd been planning it for a long time.

BUNNY BASHING

In anthropological terms, bunny bashing is an informal, semi-taboo, puberty threshold rite performed in a "wild area" outside the security circle of the rural village. It carries the implied sanction of the Bend City male "elders." Although bunny bashing seems to be rooted in old Paiute rabbit hunting rituals, it is not exclusively Indian. A significant number of white adolescents willingly participate. The perennial celebration of the rite is insured by the fact that many of the young men who bunny bash never leave town or the reservation. A sizeable and growing number of bunny bashing initiates, going back some twenty years, guarantees that next year's crop of male graduates will also be bunny bashers. Bunny bashing exists because the adult male "elders" of Bend City are ignorant of any other way, and are secretly proud that the young guys are doin' it the way they did.

If, in Bend City High School graduation rites, the commencement exercise marks the severance phase, then the bunny bash marks the threshold, or liminal phase.[4] The boy-who-is-becoming-a-man leaves his mother and the maternal nest and ventures into the wild, unknown, sacred world of bunny bashing. He experiences what it means to be a male adult in Bend City.

> Sacred Symbols:
> —Booze (usually beer)
> —a dangerous firearm (preferably a shotgun)
> —four-wheel-drive pickup (if you can get one)
> —KC spotlights and good shocks
> Sacred Arena:
> —Alkali flats and sage-rabbitbrush fields east of town, down by the river
> Sacred Ritual:
> —Get drunk, pile into trucks, drive off-road into dark night, hop sagebrush, giggle and scream like maniacs, flush jackrabbit, freeze it in the lights, blaze away with guns, tear rabbit apart with gunfire. Bash not successful if corpse is recognizable as jackrabbit. Having murdered, return home, rest, dress up, and leave at ten for all-night party.

The entire rite is illegal, of course. Underage boys are drinking and driving and playing with firearms. In a more ethical sense, they are murdering Mother Nature's innocent creatures and transgressing the Law of Nature (killing for sport). Why, then, should such a meaningless, violent, repugnant, irresponsible ritual exist, especially at a time when graduating senior boys might be expected to exhibit signs of maturity?

The first and most obvious answer is that such a ceremony exists because it has the tacit approval of the small town, male-dominated culture and is assented to by the male-dominated women. "Boys will be boys. Hell, they ain't doin' anything I didn't do when I was a kid. No real harm done. A few flea-bitten rabbits, a few torn-up bushes. They're just havin' some innocent fun." Indeed, many of the bunny bashers borrow their fathers' guns.

But the fact that bunny bashing is nurtured by contemporary Bend City male values doesn't ultimately explain its existence. Given all the other possible alternatives open to them, considering the close proximity of a wilderness that can be truly dangerous, why this *particular* ceremony on this *particular* night? Why even think of doing such a thing? Why didn't they climb a mountain, swim a river, walk a mile blindfolded, or do something pseudo-dangerous, like hunting a mountain lion or capturing a live rattlesnake?

The Jungian psychologist might postulate that the boys' collective unconscious recognized the need for a liminal experience otherwise absent from the pomp and circumstance of graduation day, that the boys were acting out unconscious, ancestral urges to confront shadows and monsters and prove themselves as men. To that end, they went out into the darkness of night like Jason and the Argonauts into the unknown, to heroically flush out the terrible fire breathing dragon and do battle. So far so good. But now the allegory breaks down. The Bend City Argonauts possessed weapons and tools that were all-powerful, and their sacred quarry was not the terrible, fire-breathing dragon but the meek, shrub-nibbling jackrabbit whose only means of defense was to run away and hide.

For some reason, our young heros became the very fire-breathing dragon they sought, the very evil power they wanted to eliminate. Their quarry didn't stand a chance. And their story didn't turn out right. They didn't get very far before they turned back. They never honorably faced the monster. They never earned the golden fleece. Their odyssey into manhood was aborted. They prematurely shot their wad into the body of a completely helpless creature. The journey into manhood became anti-heroic and sadistic. Violence was committed against the heart of Nature. And the boys returned as boys.

The redneck male mentality finds nothing but humor in this story. "Hell, boys is boys. They were jest out on a lark. They gotta let off steam somehow. Jest be glad they took it out on a jackrabbit." The boys would agree. "We didn't mean no harm. We was havin' fun."

But one wonders, given the Bend City mentality, if something else besides "havin' fun" was going on in the psyches of these young men raised in the rain shadow of the Range of Light. "Boys is boys," yes. But when do they become men? And what makes a man? Is it possible that these boys were also attempting in some obscure way to prove themselves as men? That in a psychological sense they went into the darkness of themselves to hunt down the scared, confused, helpless rabbit (the little boy) of themselves? That they sacrificed the scared, innocent, helpless one so that the deadly, dangerous, all-powerful tool-wielding "man" could live?

If so, the folly of their actions is apparent. It's the folly of the "macho" psychology of the redneck male—to suppose that with a gun he can destroy the rabbit of fear within himself. Again and again the rabbit will reappear. Again and again the rabbit will have to be sacrificed in order for the man to maintain his image of himself as a man. The more this happens, the more he will look like an eternal adolescent trying to prove he is a man.

Although the Bend City senior boys are to be commended for wanting to add a threshold component to their rites of graduation, they were wide of the mark if they meant to confirm their manhood. If the proof of a man is his ability to endure certain trials, hardships, or states of consciousness, none of these are contained in bunny bashing. The all-important conditions of solitude and exposure to natural forces are missing. The boys did not go out alone, as did the traditional vision-questing Indian boy, to a fateful rendezvous with their greater Mother. Instead they hunted in a pack, giggling, egging each other on. It was all a big joke, and the biggest joke was on the jackrabbit. Peer pressure allowed little space for a single boy to develop a sense of who he was apart from the others. The constraint was to belong, to be accepted, to evade self-discovery.

Fasting, or "going without," an almost universal taboo in traditional rites of passage, was also missing from the bunny bash. The boys transgressed the ancient taboos of abstinence by filling themselves with beer. In this case the sacred drug, beer served as an anodyne to the exercise of personal conscience. They could forget such social strictures as "Thou shalt not kill," or "If you drink, don't drive." Beer, a social drug, also served to short-circuit any respect they might have had for nature as manifestation of "Spirit" or God. It was a drunken lark, and they got to play with men's toys—the trucks with the big engines, the dangerous guns, the still-forbidden (until the age of twenty-one) can of beer. The traditional solitude and empty belly of the vulnerable initiate instead had become a social lark, a "boys will be boys," an expression of savage glee culminating in a technologically aided murder.

"Murder?" yells the outraged Bend City father. "What do we have here, another one of them tree huggers? Those boys didn't murder anythin' but a dumb little jackrabbit." Well if it isn't the murder of a jackrabbit soul, what is it? Let's look at it from another perspective. Take the guns, spotlights, and big trucks away from the boys. What do they have left? Two good hands and feet. O.K.? Tell them if they want to eat they have to go out into the sagebrush flats down by the river, on a moonless night, and hunt a jackrabbit with their bare hands. Have each of them go alone. No flashlight, no lantern, no knife, no dogs. Bare hands. You think your boys would take you up on this? You don't even know how to do it. God knows what might be out there—rattlesnakes, mountain lions, jackrabbits with huge teeth and claws. Strip your boys down to their bare hands, and they'll be happy to stay home with mama. Put a steering wheel, a can of beer, and a shotgun in their hands and they'll bravely go into the night and murder a deadly leaf-chomper.

Murder? Yes. The traditional Indian vision-quest cry, "Have mercy on me that my people may live" has been changed to "Show no mercy to innocent creatures." The first cry comes from a young man who knows his place on the earth. The second cry comes from a boy who has no idea of his place on the earth, and who, with a gun in his hand, thinks he is God.

Informal rites such as bunny bashing will continue to exist and/or come into being wherever communities, institutions, families, and elders fail to provide adequate, meaningful rites of passage into adulthood. The boys (and the girls) will take it upon themselves to fashion their own rites. Because they lack the wisdom of true manhood, and have little idea of what actually makes a man (thanks to the inadequacy of cultural and media definitions), they will invent grotesque parodies, twisted psychodramas, dangerous and self-destructive scenarios (operating in packs or groups, like the Bend City boys), that sidestep or mock the major issues facing them as boys who are trying to be men in modern America.

THE ALL-NIGHT PARTY

First the ending, the severance from home and family—the commencement exercise. Next, the sacred threshold experience in a wilderness place, the trial of the boy to test his mettle as an adult—the bunny bash. Finally, the beginning of a new life, incorporation of the candidate into adulthood—the all-night party.

Traditionally, an incorporation ceremony might involve the elders, parents, and relatives—or at least the elders. They would sit in council as the candidate recounted how the story of the threshold hero reflected his "medicine power" or giftedness, and revealed the man and his life path. Then there would be a celebration, a party, a feast that honored the "graduate" and accorded him every right and privilege due a full grown man.

The Bend City "all-night party" bears little resemblance to the traditional incorporation ceremonies. Conceived mainly as an alternative to more potentially dangerous activities such as unchaperoned keggers (beer busts), tailgate parties, or other booze/dope fortified blasts, the all-nighter is mainly distinctive as a means of controlling a potentially dangerous situation. We don't want them to hurt themselves, do we? They're not truly men and women anyway. So let's get them all into one place and out of trouble. Let's keep them away from the dangerous adult world of alcohol, sex, cars, and freedom with responsibility. But we'll tease them a little. We'll let them have a party without a curfew.

By 9:30 that evening, the skies above the Inyo Valley had cleared. The moon rose into a crystal sky spangled with stars untold billions of years old. The Range of Light, still streaked with patches of snow at the higher elevations, glowed palely in the moonlight. Aspen Mountain, an old, old spirit, glowered down on our little town, and on the tiny ant-lights attached to cars headed north and south on the highway. Did Aspen Mountain care about human coming-of-age rituals in Bend City? Did Aspen Mountain care that the night was cool, but not cold, that the live music was good, the food was great, and the dancing was hot? Did Aspen Mountain care that the boys left the forbidden blood-lust of the bunny bash and presented themselves at the party, well-dressed, clean-cut, and drunk?

Old Aspen Mountain saw everything, heard everything, felt everything, probably knew everything. But I don't think he cared that the party was successful, that not a single teenager died that night, that by 4:00 that morning most of Bend City's newest "men" and "women" had gone home to their mamas and daddies. Human time must unfold incredibly fast before the eyes of Old Aspen Mountain. He hasn't had much time to develop any empathy for the ephemeral humans, who have been part of his awareness for less than an instant. By human time, the night passed hour by hour. By Aspen Mountain time, it was already over. The sun was already bathing the Range of Light with rose petals. Graduation day was history.

We didn't see Chris until 11:00 that morning. He shuffled into the living room looking worn and slightly hung over, mumbling a good morning. How'd the party go? "Uh, O.K." Did you have a good time? "Uh huh." Did you dance your ass off? "Uh, kind of." Who'd you dance with? "Uh, several girls." Well, welcome to the world of adulthood. "Thanks. Aren't the Lakers and the Pistons on T.V.?" The new graduate hardly seemed different from how he'd been hundreds of other mornings. We hadn't changed much either. Before the day was over, we'd probably get on him for not doing this or that, and he'd be mad at us for reminding him.

Nevertheless, Chris' chances for attaining manhood were better than for most of his ex-classmates. For one thing, he wasn't a bunny basher. His dragons were not jackrabbits. They'd scorched his hide a few times. He had a realistic idea of what he was up against. He'd never entirely bought the redneck macho line on what constitutes a man. He wanted to get out of town. He didn't want to fall into the Bend City going-nowhere alcoholic swamp that characterized much of young unmarried life in the valley. He'd had his fill of country-western music. He knew there had to be a cultural big-sky country out there somewhere. Two months later, he was gone. Now he's a student at Sonoma State University. We hardly hear from him anymore. He's groping his way toward manhood through jobs, girlfriends, examinations, cars, and the like.

Chris went off to find wider cultural horizons. He left behind the deep valley, the highest mountains. They couldn't hold him because Bend City couldn't hold him. He'd had enough of redneck ways, he said, "enough to last me the rest of my life." Funny, I used to get so upset with him because it seemed more important to him to be with his friends than to find out what was in the wild, beautiful, man-making desert kingdom called the Inyo-Mojave. I despaired that my fascination with the natural world would ever rub off on him. He seemed impervious to the call of the wild, a thoroughly domesticated couch potato. I was wrong. Within six months of leaving home, he'd found a place to live away from campus, out in the country. His house mates were laid back, organic, environmentalist types actively involved in a variety of earth-oriented causes.

And what happened to the bunny bashers? Graduation day came and went. Summer officially began. The boys had become men without the right to drink. What could they show as proof that they had attained the state of manhood? A high-school diploma? A class ring? A tassel hanging from the rearview mirror? A watch from Grandpa Earl? A new car from the folks? A few of the boys received scholarships—invaluable opportunities to sever—from the Armed Forces, lured by the promise of learning a trade and free college tuition, and wound up in Kuwait. A couple went to junior colleges. A couple more went into vocational training (truck-driving school and heavy-equipment repair). Most of the Indians and a fair number of the whites stayed right here, though employment opportunities were almost nil.

I see a few of Chris' old friends around town now and then. We wave at each other but rarely talk. I guess I always thought they were O.K., as small town kids go, though I might not choose to be super friendly just for Chris' and oldtime's sake. Some of them drive around town flaunting their official redneck badges: the cap, the gun rack, the Chevy pickup, the KC lights, the Warn hubs, the Desert Duelers, the Boom Box. I wonder what rites have these seemingly grown boys undergone recently to demonstrate, not only to the waiting world, but to themselves, that they are responsible, self-reliant, in control, able to go without, sexually balanced, spiritually aware, racially tolerant, humanitarian, and earth-mindful gentlemen of feeling, thought, emotion, and vision? What wilderness rites of passage could boys of this redneck mettle endure? How about three days and nights alone, without food, gun, ghetto blaster, dog, flashlight, or tent, on a bluff overlooking Baker Creek, where the cougar comes down every night to drink? Or how about a walking journey from Bend City all the way to Funeral Valley with a pack on the back, camping out, moving from spring to spring?

I feel like grabbing one of them, saying, "Hey Paul! How about a real wilderness challenge, a rite of passage worthy of a man? Let's go up on Black Mountain and I'll show you a couple things you can do to prove you have some of the real stuff."

But I know it wouldn't work. The essence of the redneck male is the little boy's fear of nature and her kind. If you take away that fear, you take away his reason to wield guns, bash cougars, and intimidate the environment. You take away his need to blast to smithereens the numbed, innocent jackrabbit hiding in the wasteland of himself. Paul's little boy's fears are too great. It would be too easy for him to relegate my challenge to the category marked REALLY WEIRD. Besides, he's a hometown boy, right? He grew up surrounded by the wilderness. He knows what's goin' on out there. He doesn't need to know more. He went to school: he dissected a frog; he graduated; he got his diploma; he danced at the all-night party. He passed the bunny-bashing test. Wasn't that proof enough that he was man?

NOTES

1. Place and personal names are generally fictitious.

2. Arnold van Gennep, *The Rites of Passage,* translated by Monika Vizedom and Gabrielle Caffee (Chicago: University of Chicago Press, 1960).

3. Frank Waters, *The Man Who Killed the Deer* (New York: Ballantine, 1972).

4. For explorations of the threshold rites of America and other cultures, see Victor Turner, *A Forest of Symbols* (Ithaca, N.Y.: Cornell University Press, 1967); Ray Raphael, *The Men from the Boys* (Lincoln: Nebraska University Press, 1988); and *Betwixt and Between: Patterns of Masculine and Feminine Initiation,* edited by Louise Mahdi with Steven Foster and Meredith Little (LaSalle, Ill.: Open Court, 1987).

FORTY TWO · A MODERN GIRL'S QUEST

Sarah Kilmer

In the absence of generally accepted rites of passage, it is the creative individual with support from his or her community who can help develop appropriate forms of rites of passage in our times. Sarah Kilmer, during a painful time at puberty, was supported by her mother's support group. Her personal experience of her transition shortly after her first menstruation is presented in some detail. Although not a group of peers, her mother's support group prepared her and then helped her go on a vision quest.

As a girl, Sarah Kilmer lived in the Midwest until 1985 when, at the age of eleven, she moved to Zurich, Switzerland, with her mother and brother. They traveled throughout Europe in the summer of 1985 and remained in Switzerland for two years. In 1988 they returned to the United States.

Ms. Kilmer is a college student who also works in geriatrics as a Certified Nurses' Aide.

A person's world can be turned all around in a mere moment, or in my case, one haunting, unforgettable night. My world and my life would have been unbearable if it had not been for my mother's women's support group. When I was eleven years old I was a foreigner in Switzerland. I was going to an English-speaking international school, and going through one of the most awkward and in many ways terrifying experiences of my life. I was the first to go through puberty in my class, and as nobody wanted to grow up, I was a target for the unleashing of many childish tortures. I don't know if it was hormones, or the anger and frustration of all of us being uprooted, but I was regarded by my peers as a freak of nature, a Frankenstein. For example, my breasts developed before anyone else's, and as far as I know, I was also the first to begin menstruating. At least, I was the first who would dare to admit it.

My mother was a student at the Jung Institute of Psychology in Kusnacht, Zurich, which was the reason we were there in the first place. Every week, a group of her fellow students and friends would meet at our apartment for support. Those were the times when I felt at home. I was in a world of lovable people, who treated me as an equal in their group. They were not afraid to open up their hearts in my presence, and they were not afraid of what was in mine when I spilled it out to them. They were open-minded, magical people who liked my ideas. They were the ones who prepared me for the onset of menstruation. Jyoti, not only a friend but my therapist, made arrangements for me to go on a vision quest.

On the day of my first period, I couldn't wait for school to dismiss so I could go home and tell my mother. She said that I could have any kind of party that I wanted, so I decided I wanted a chocolate party. So chocolate it was, for Switzerland is the one place on earth where chocolate is a euphoric experience. Everyone congratulated me and celebrated the new woman in the women's group. At first it was like a birthday party, but after the celebrating was over, much more was expected of me.

In preparation for my vision quest, I was required to fast for four days. On the fourth day, I was taken to the porch of an old, deserted cottage. It was the middle of winter, with a firm blanket of snow covering the surrounding wilderness. The cottage was locked: I was denied access to all but its front porch. I was being banished from human society. My company that night were the trees and the stars. I was even told to take off my watch and to tell time by the stars.

Alone and wide-eyed, I scoped out my terrain and watched the stars appear, one by one. The crisp night air and the clarity of my sharpened mind added to my feeling of alertness. This, plus the slight edge of fear, made it impossible for me to sleep, impossible to do anything but stay awake and wonder. Why am I doing this? What do they expect me to discover about myself? It was all a mystery, but I was completely in the element of my solitude. Many, many nights hence have I longed to be whisked away, back into that element, back on that mountain. It doesn't come at a moment's notice, but having been there once, the path is laid out.

My life was transformed that night. I faced my inner Satan, faced the fear of what I was and what I was becoming. I saw myself as a lamb chewing on a stick. Looking back, I can see myself as that sacrificial animal chewing on the bitterness of frustration, an unwholesome nourishment. Then, I proceeded to listen for my new name, what the gods would call me next. It was Jewel, and I realized, when I heard it, that that's what I was. I consider myself very fortunate for having the opportunity to experience that night of my vision quest. I was holding a vigil and making a truce with myself. I decided to be reborn as a more dignified woman, and that is exactly what happened.

My personal opinion is that my negative school experiences were due to the lack of just such initiations in society. My school class was confused by and in denial of the transition period between childhood and adulthood. I was a target because I was the first to go through the tunnel. I was the one who was teased and made fun of, but I am the one who had the most to be thankful for at that stage. If the other girls in my class, upon the onset of menstruation, had been greeted with the warmth and the ritual that I was, it would have made sense to them, too.

My mother says I went to Switzerland a little girl, and after two years, I left as a woman. I was proud when she said that. Now that I'm twenty, I even know how to let the little girl out to play, putting the adult role aside sometimes. That's the real trick, and don't forget it.

FORTY THREE · A NOTE ON THE VISION QUEST

Louise Carus Mahdi

Where there is no vision, the people perish.

—PROVERBS 29:18

There are many ways of discussing what has come to be known as the Native American "vision quest."[1] Best known is the Lakota term *hanblecheya,* which translates as "crying for a vision" or "lamenting for want of a vision." Around the world, there is a long tradition of spiritual leaders who used fasting and retreat to the desert or to the wilderness to connect with the greater power—Buddha, Moses, Christ, Mohammed, and others. What is important for us today is the use of a quest retreat by youth as well as by adults. This is where Native American culture and wisdom have contributed in great measure.

The visionary Black Elk (Oglala Sioux) had guiding dreams and visions at an early age. He reported that most people he knew in his early life were going on the quest for visions and dreams.[2] It is also known that many Christian saints received their guiding direction through images in dreams and visions in their youth.[3] In the temples of Aesculapius in ancient Greece, healing dreams of individuals were important, but I have not found references to youth.

Our understanding of "natural learning rhythms" of rites of passage for youth has been greatly enhanced by Josette and Sambhava Luvmour,[4] who build on the work of Maria Montessori, Rudolph Steiner, and Joseph Chilton Pearce. Inner experiences of dreams of initiation are a known phenomenon at puberty or at other transitions. Such dreams are part of natural learning rhythms and often appear at times of transition.

The reasons for focusing on the dream or vision quest are many. All people dream, even if they don't remember their dreams. We know from experience that deep and significant guiding dreams come to people whose intentions are sincere and focused, particularly at a time of transition. Fasting is a method used from time immemorial to enhance this intensity and to support the intent and the need for vision beyond that of ordinary, everyday consciousness.

Dreams and visions both have a common source in the unconscious of the individual. Specific consciousness of images of the greater power or guardian spirit can be experienced on the vision quest. The experience of moving into "sacred space" supports such experiences, although they can also happen spontaneously. The ego of the participant in such a quest is more open to the experience of powers greater than oneself. These can be guiding experiences, and need to be supported by one's community.

Solitude helps us listen to the inner voice and to be open to the images. Clearly, it is desirable to work with real mentors, guides and elders in the outer world, as well as the inner guide.

All of this leads the quester to focus on the greater Self within, by whatever name for the community, for the people. Most simply described, it is the inner *imago Dei*. This is the point where transpersonal energies and symbolic contents can be accessible and flow into personal life. I would like to suggest the work of Edward F. Edinger, specifically *Ego and Archetype* (published by Shambala in Boston, 1992). Although there is no single adequate psychology book dealing with the spirit and practice of the vision quest, Edinger shows how a person needs the larger Self.

Black Elk himself must have realized how important the quest for spirit and vision would become when he offered his own views on this for the book recorded by Joseph Epes Brown, *The Sacred Pipe: Black Elk's Account of the Seven Rites of the Oglala Sioux.*[5]

The rite of "Crying for a Vision" or lamenting for want of a vision as told by Black Elk is the major source on this subject. As Vine Deloria Jr. writes in his introduction to *Black Elk Speaks,* we have hardly begun to recognize the importance of Black Elk and what he has to teach us all.

I am very grateful for having had several interviews with Ben Black Elk, the son and interpreter, in the fall of 1970 on the Pine Ridge Reservation in South Dakota before he died. I have often thought about what he told me in his hospital room about the old ways of the Sioux women. He seemed to be preoccupied with his own passage and with the tradition of the Sioux women and their choice of where to give birth. It was their custom, he told me, to find a wide open place out on the prairie, where one could look out on the great hoop of the horizon and see in all directions. The mothers in giving birth felt the need to have a full view of the open horizon all around for these significant hours of giving birth. This is one of the great perspectives of the open plains where one can catch a glimpse of the great wholeness. Ben Black Elk was in a hospital room with only one window and longed for the open perspective, the larger view.

The purpose of the vision quest was to relate to the larger perspective for the sake of the community, for one's people.

NOTES

1. One of the first written references to "Vision Quest" in English is in *The Concept of the Guardian Spirit in North America* by Ruth Benedict, published in 1922. The different tribes had different terms for the fasting, which was in common use by

hunting tribes in the United States and Canada. This book was originally a Ph.D. thesis and is reprinted by the Kraus Reprint Corporation, 1964.

2. See John Neihardt, *Black Elk Speaks* (Lincoln: University of Nebraska Press, 1979). Also see Frank Linderman, *Plenty Coups, Chief of the Crow* (Lincoln: University of Nebraska Press, 1962).

3. See the classic, *Adolescence,* by G. Stanley Hall (New York: D. Appleton and Co., 1904).

4. Josette and Sambhava Luvmour, *Natural Learning Rhythms: How and When Children Learn* (Berkeley, Calif.: Celestial Arts, 1993).

5. Joseph Epes Brown, *The Sacred Pipe: Black Elk's Account of the Seven Rites of the Oglala Sioux* (Norman and London: University of Oklahoma Press, 1953.) Also on the youth quest, see A. Irving Hallowell's essay on "Ojibwa Ontology, Behavior and World View" in an anthology by Dennis Tedlock and Barbara Tedlock, *Teachings from the American Earth* (New York City: Liveright, 1992).

FORTY FOUR

AN OJIBWAY VISION QUEST

J. G. Kohl

Native American elders have long known and are still teaching us that turning-point dreams, including children's and adolescents' dreams, can be beacons.[1] The Native American quest for visions and dreams among both children and adults provides a wise perspective that is both natural and deeply human. Without something to inspire our sense of the unknown, a sense of a realm beyond ordinary perception, our lives are very limited. Since the early 1970s there has been a widespread revival of the quest for dreams and visions in the United States and Canada. Ojibway, Sioux, Crow, Winnebago, and other Indian autobiographical records of nineteenth-century vision quests give many significant details. There are also autobiographical reports of girls' vision quests, the best known of which was recorded by Mrs. Henry Schoolcraft in the mid-nineteenth century.[2]

The following passages are excerpted from a chapter by J. G. Kohl, and are left in their mid-nineteenth-century British English. Georg Kohl, of Bremen, Germany, was a widely read and traveled scientific author and librarian. His book, *Kitchi Gami,* has other fascinating chapters. It is kept in print by the Minnesota Historical Society in St. Paul, Minnesota.

I formed several peculiarly interesting acquaintances among the Indians, with whom I continued my conversations on several points affecting their countrymen. More especially I made deeper investigations into their great fasts and dreams of life.

I found this most remarkable; in fact, could it be possible to hear anything stranger or, I might say, more wonderful, than these stories of unheard-of castigations and torments, to which young boys of thirteen or fourteen subject themselves, merely for the sake of an idea, a dream, or the fulfillment of a religious duty, or to ask a question of fate? What courage! What self-control! What power of enduring privations does this presuppose!

I say such things would appear to me incredible, did I not hear them spoken of everywhere as ordinary occurrences. More surprising still is it when we remember that it is not merely some extraordinary youth who is capable of this, but that every Indian, without exception, displays such heroism.

Although, then, several had described to me their dreams of life, I was still desirous to hear more. Besides, much was still unclear and doubtful to me. Hence, when I made the acquaintance of old Agabe-gijik ("The Cloud") and had conversed for some time with him, I brought him to talk about these dreams. And this old man promised to tell me his dream of life, with all its accompanying details, if I would visit him at his hut where we could sit comfortably round the fire.

We started for his lodge one day after dinner. I had rarely seen so cleanly and carefully kept a wigwam as that of old Cloud. The flooring was raised above the damp earth, and we had to mount a couple of steps. Floor and walls, seats and beds, were covered with a quantity of fresh, gay-coloured mats, which gave the whole a very pleasing appearance. It was all so quiet around, as if the huts were uninhabited, that we were quite astounded, on entering, to see a number of persons collected in groups in the room. This stillness is usual in all Indian wigwams, when the fire-water has not made the denizens noisy. They never quarrel with each other, and cursing is a rarity among them. The old papa and grand-papa (a little, most intelligent-looking man, in spite of his bushy, uncombed hair) sat in the centre, smoking his pipe and awaiting us at the appointed hour. An old woman was sewing shirts and squatting near the windows or light-holes. Some grown-up sons or sons-in-law, with their squaws, sat at the places belonging to them, and seemed to be resting from their fatigue, or busy with their medicine-bags or hunting-sacks. Only very rarely did they exchange a few whispered words.

We went up to our old man, and sat down as quickly as possible on his mat, while laying a couple of packets of tobacco in his lap as greeting. According to Indian habits, it is not proper or polite to remain standing any length of time in their lodges. If you do not sit down soon, or if you walk about, the squaws will soon make some sharp remarks, or you will hear from all sides the exclamation, "Sit down! pray sit down!" Indian guests, when they enter a hut—even that of a stranger—hence sit down at once. If he be a perfect stranger, or has some favour to ask, he will take a seat very modestly near the door, and remain silent till the head of the family asks the cause of his visit. If, however, he has business with any person in the lodge, he walks straight up to his mat, and places himself at once under his protection by squatting down by his side.

The confined space in these wigwams, in which there is no room for walking about, causes this custom to appear founded on reason. As with every step you invade the territory of another family, and might see all sorts of things that a stranger ought not to see, respect demands that the guest should sit down directly, and fix his eyes on the ground. Indians, as a general rule, are not fond of restless people; little children and dogs have the sole privilege of disturbing the family, and in this hut swarms of both were crawling in and out.

"Well, then, Agabe-gijik, thou rememberest thy promise to us, yesterday, to tell us thy dream of life and thy great youth fast, with all the accompanying incidents. Wilt thou now keep thy promise?" So we spoke at once to our host, with whom we were as good as alone, for the rest of the company took no notice of us, but went on with their little amusements, as if living in so many different rooms.

"Ah!" The Cloud said, after a long silence and rumination. "Kitchi-Man-itou[3] sent us our Mides[4] from the east, and his prophets laid it down as a law that we should lead our children into the forest so soon as they approach man's estate, and show them how they must fast, and direct their thoughts to higher things; and in return it is promised us that a dream shall be then sent them as a revelation of their fate—a confirmation of their vocation—a conse-cration and devotion to Deity, and an eternal remembrance and good omen for their path of life.

"I remember that my grandfather took me on one side, and said to me, 'It is now high time that I should lead thee to the forest, and that thou shouldst fast, that thy mind may be confirmed, something be done for thy health, and that thou mayst learn thy future and thy calling.'

"The grandfather then took me by the hand, and led me deep into the forest. Here he selected a lofty tree, a red pine, and prepared a bed for me in the branches, on which I should lie down. We cut down the bushes and twined them through the pine branches. Then I plucked moss, with which I covered the trellis-work, threw a mat my mother had made for the occasion over it, and myself on top of it. I was also permitted to fasten a few branches together over my head, as a protection from wind and rain.

"Then my grandfather said to me that I must on no account take nourish-ment, neither eat nor drink, pluck no berries, nor even swallow the rain-water that might fall. Nor must I rise from my bed, but lie quite still day and night, keep by myself strictly, and await patiently the things that would then happen.

"I promised my grandfather this, but, unfortunately, I did not keep my promise. I saw the refreshing leaves of a little herb growing near the tree. I could not resist it, but plucked the leaves and ate them. And when I had eaten them my craving grew so great that I walked about the forest, sought all the edible sprigs, plants, mosses, and herbs I could find, and ate my fill. Then I crept home, and confessed all to my grandfather and father.

"They reproved me, and told me I had done wrong, at which I felt ashamed; and, as I had broken my fast it was all over with my dream, and I must try again next spring. I might now have been a man, but would remain for another year a useless fellow, which was a disgrace at my age.

"I may here add [a] parenthetical remark, that if the entire operation of the dreaming is interrupted by a nightmare, or any bad dream, it is rendered impossible during that spring. The boys are warned, so soon as a nightmare or a bad dream oppresses them, to give up the affair at once and return home, and try again and again till the right dream comes.

"When the spring of the next year was approaching, my grandfather told me that it was time for me to go out again to fast, and try my dream. As, how-ever, I was ashamed of my defeat in the last year, and had determined on car-rying out the affair now, I begged him to let me go alone, as I know what I had to do, and would not return till my right dream had come to me. I had already selected a place in the forest I knew, where I intended to make my bed. It was on a little island covered with trees, in the centre of a forest lake. I described the place to my friends, that they might come in search of me if anything happened to me, and set out."

I interrupted to ask The Cloud why he selected that precise spot.

"Because I knew that one of my relations and friends was lying on his dream-bed in the same locality," he replied.

So I inquired, "Didst thou intend, then, to communicate with thy friend during the period of dreaming and fasting?"

"Not so," he replied, "for he was some distance from me—two or three miles. But though I could not see or hear my friend, nor be allowed to speak with him, there seemed to me some consolation in knowing him near me and engaged in the same things to which I was going to devote myself.

"There was ice still on the little lake, and I reached my island across it. I prepared my bed, as on the first time, in a tall, red pine, and laid myself on the branches and moss.

"[At first] nothing appeared to me; all was quiet. But [then one] night I heard a rustling and waving in the branches. It was like a heavy bear or elk breaking through the shrubs and forest. I was greatly afraid. But the man who approached me, whoever he may have been, read my thoughts and saw my fear at a distance; so he came towards me more and more gently, and rested, quite noiselessly, on the branches over my head. Then he began to speak to me, and asked me, 'Art thou afraid, my son?' 'No,' I replied; 'I no longer fear.' 'Why art thou here?' 'To gain strength, and know my life.' 'That is good; for it agrees excellently with what is now being done for thee else-where, and with the message I bring thee. This very night a consultation has been held about thee and thy welfare; and I have come to tell thee that the decision was most favorable. I am ordered to invite thee to see and hear this for thyself. Follow me.'

"When he ordered me to follow him, I rose from my bed easily and of my own accord, like a spirit rising from the grave, and followed him through the air. The spirit floated on before me to the east, and, though we were mov-ing through the air, I stepped as firmly as if I were on the ground, and it seemed to me as if we were ascending a lofty mountain, ever higher and higher, eastward.

"When we reached the summit, after a long time, I found a wigwam built there, into which we entered. I saw four men sitting around a large white stone. They invited me to take a seat on the white stone in the midst of them. But I had hardly sat down than the stone began sinking into the earth. 'Stay!' one of the men said; 'wait a minute; we have forgotten the foundation.' Thus speaking, he fetched a white tanned deer-skin, and covered the stone with it; and when I sat down on it again, it was as firm as a tree, and I sat comfort-ably."

I interrupted The Cloud to ask him, "What is the meaning of this deer-skin: who was it that gave it to thee?"

"On that point I have remained in uncertainty," he said. "A man does not learn everything in these dreams. As I sat there and looked round me again, I noticed a multitude of other faces. The wigwam was very large, and filled with persons. It was an extraordinary council assembly. One of the four took the word, and ordered me to look down. When I did so, I saw the whole earth beneath me, spread out deep, deep, and wide, wide, before me.

"It had four corners. Immediately another of the four took the word, and bade me look up. I looked up, and saw the whole sky over me quite near. I gazed a long, long time, and almost forgot where I was, for it was a glorious sight. Then a third took the word, and spoke: 'Thou has gazed. Now say; whither wilt thou now—down below, whence thou camest, or up above? The choice is left thee.' 'Yes, yes,' I replied, 'I will go up.'

"The four men seemed pleased at my answer, and the fourth said to me, 'Ascend!' He pointed to the back of my stone seat, and I saw that it had grown, and went up an extraordinary height. There were holes cut in it, and I could climb up as if on a ladder. I climbed and clambered higher and higher, and at length came to a place where four white-haired old men were sitting, in the open air round the pillar. A dazzling cupola was arched above them. I felt so light that I wished to go higher, but the four old men shouted 'Stop!' all at once. 'Thou must not go higher. We have not permission to allow thee to pass. But enough that is good and great is already decreed for thee. Look around thee. Thou seest here around us all the good gifts of God—health, and strength, and long life, and all the creatures of nature. Look on our white hair: thine shall become the same. And that thou mayst avoid illness, receive this box with medicine. Use it in case of need; and whenever thou art in difficulty, think of us, and all thou seest with us. When thou prayest to us, we will help thee, and intercede for thee with the Master of Life. Look around thee once more. Look, and forget it not! We give thee all the birds, and eagles, and wild beasts, and all the other animals thou seest fluttering and running in our wig-wam. Thou shalt become a famous hunter, and shoot them all!'

"I gazed in amazement on the boundless abundance of game and birds which flocked together in this hall, and was quite lost at the sight. Then the four old men spoke to me. 'Thy time has expired, thou canst go no higher; so return.'

"I then quickly descended my long stone ladder. I was obliged to be careful, for I noticed it was beginning to disappear beneath my feet, and melted away like an icicle near the fire. When I got back to my white stone it returned to its former dimensions. The great council was still assembled, and the four men round the stone welcomed me, and said, 'It is good, Agabe-gijik. Thou hast done a brave deed, and hast gazed on what is beautiful and great. We will all testify for thee that thou didst perform the deed. Forget nothing of all that has been said to thee. And all who sit round here will remember thee, and pray for thee as thy guardian spirits.'

"After this I took my leave, and let myself down to my bed in the red pine. I opened my eyes and looked around me. I felt myself so weak that I could not stir. All at once I heard a voice, a whistle, and my name called. It was my grandfather, who had come to seek me.

"At home they prepared for me a soft bed of moss, on which I lay down like a patient. Three days later I was quite recovered, and strong. And from that time I was, and remained, a perfect man!"[5]

NOTES

1. John (Fire) Lame Deer and Richard Erdoes, *Lame Deer, Seeker of Visions* (New York: Washington Square Press, 1976). This book also includes a special bibliography. Lame Deer tells of his reckless youth, shotgun marriage and divorce, and tribal history and folklore. The first chapter focuses on his solitary quest for vision on a hilltop.

2. Basil Johnston, *Ojibway Heritage* (Lincoln: University of Nebraska Press, 1990). Recorded in detail in H. R. Schoolcraft, *Historical and Statistical Information Respecting the History, Condition, and Prospects of the Indian Tribes of the United States* (Philadelphia: Lippincott, 1850), pp. 390–94.

3. *Kitchi* means "great"; *Manitou* means "spirit."

4. This refers to sacred Ojibway ceremonies.

5. The original German text here reads "ein gemachter Mann." A better translation would be "a full man." The original German book goes back to 1859. The British translation was published in 1860. This would suggest that the Vision Dream Quest would have occurred around 1810 or 1820.

FORTY FIVE

THE VISION QUEST

Lame Deer

John Fire Lame Deer is a full-blood Lakota born in the late nineteenth century on the Rosebud Reservation in South Dakota. John Lame Deer is a medicine man, a vision seeker, a man who upholds the ancient ways of his people. He is a man of the earth. He has been many things in his time—a rodeo clown, a soldier, a sign painter, a spud-picker, a jail prisoner, a tribal policeman, a sheepherder, and a singer. But above all he is a *wicasa wakán,* a holy man of the Lakota.

John Lame Deer went to third grade for seven years because there was no higher grade in his school. He has taught and ordained eighteen other medicine men among the Sioux. He is one of the primary carriers of the philosophical and spiritual message of a resilient people. He has an unusual gift for anecdote and an acute awareness of the profound and poetic significance of Indian life—its rituals, its beliefs—and of the fierce and lonely pride of a defeated people that still today characterizes the Indians who live in their own land as strangers and wards of the state. Lame Deer is a man who has known and lived in the white world and made his decision to remain part of his own culture. He lives according to his great vision, which he received as a young man during a night's vigil on a lonely hilltop.

A man or woman seeking the way on the road of life, or trying to find the answer to a personal problem, may go on a vision quest for knowledge and enlightenment. This may mean staying on top of a hill or inside a vision pit, alone, without food or water, for as long as four days and nights. It is hard, but if the spirit voices reveal or confer a vision that shapes a person's life, then the quest is worth all the suffering.

The following tale, however, treats the vision quest with less than complete solemnity, with Sioux medicine man Lame Deer's characteristic quirks.

A young man wanted to go on a *hanblecheya,* or vision seeking, to try for a dream that would give him the power to be a great medicine man. Having a high opinion of himself, he felt sure that he had been created to become great among his people and that the only thing lacking was a vision.

The young man was daring and brave, eager to go up to the mountaintop. He had been brought up by good, honest people who were wise in the ancient ways and who prayed for him. All through the winter they were busy getting him ready, feeding him *wasna,* corn, and plenty of good meat to make him strong. At every meal they set aside something for the spirits so that they would help him to get a great vision. His relatives thought he had the power even before he went up, but that was putting the cart before the horse, or rather the travois before the horse, as this is an Indian legend.

When at last he started on his quest, it was a beautiful morning in late spring. The grass was up, the leaves were out, nature was at its best. Two medicine men accompanied him. They put up a sweat lodge to purify him in the hot, white breath of the sacred steam. They sanctified him with the incense of sweet grass, rubbing his body with sage, fanning it with an eagle's wing. They went to the hilltop with him to prepare the vision pit and make an offering of tobacco bundles. Then they told the young man to cry, to humble himself, to ask for holiness, to cry for power, for a sign from the Great Spirit, for a gift which would make him into a medicine man. After they had done all they could, they left him there.

He spent the first night in the hole the medicine men had dug for him, trembling and crying out loudly. Fear kept him awake, yet he was cocky, ready to wrestle with the spirits for the vision, the power he wanted. But no dreams came to ease his mind. Toward morning before the sun came up, he heard a voice in the swirling white mists of dawn. Speaking from no particular direction, as if it came from different places, it said: "See here, young man, there are other spots you could have picked; there are other hills around here. Why don't you go there to cry for a dream? You disturbed us all night, all us creatures, animals and birds; you even kept the trees awake. We couldn't sleep. Why should you cry here? You're a brash young man, not yet ready or worthy to receive a vision."

But the young man clenched his teeth, determined to stick it out, resolved to force that vision to come. He spent another day in the pit, begging for enlightenment which would not come, and then another night of fear and cold and hunger.

The young man cried out in terror. He was paralyzed with fear, unable to move. The boulder dwarfed everything in view; it towered over the vision pit. But just as it was an arm's length away and about to crush him, it stopped. Then, as the young man stared openmouthed, his hair standing up, his eyes starting out of his head, the boulder ROLLED UP THE MOUNTAIN, all the way to the top. He could hardly believe what he saw. He was still cowering motionless when he heard the roar and ramble again and saw that immense boulder coming down at him once more. This time he managed to jump out of his vision pit at the last moment. The boulder crushed it, obliterated it, grinding the young man's peace pipe and gourd rattle into dust.

Again the boulder rolled up the mountain, and again it came down. "I'm leaving, I'm leaving!" hollered the young man. Regaining his power of motion, he scrambled down the hill as fast as he could. This time the boulder actually leapfrogged over him, bouncing down the slope, crushing and pulverizing everything in its way. He ran unseeingly, stumbling, falling, getting up again. He did not even notice the boulder rolling up once more and coming down for the fourth time. On this last and most fearful descent, it flew through the air in a giant leap, landing right in front of him and embedding itself so deeply in the earth that only its top was visible. The ground shook itself like a wet dog coming out of a stream and flung the young man this way and that.

Gaunt, bruised, and shaken, he stumbled back to his village. To the medicine men he said: "I have received no vision and gained no knowledge." He returned to the pit, and when dawn arrived once more, he heard the voice again: "Stop disturbing us; go away!" The same thing happened on the third morning. By this time he was faint with hunger, thirst, and anxiety. Even the air seemed to oppress him, to fight him. He was panting. His stomach felt shriveled up, shrunk tight against his backbone. But he was determined to endure one more night, the fourth and last. Surely the vision would come. But again he cried for it out of the dark and loneliness until he was hoarse, and still he had no dream.

Just before daybreak he heard the same voice again, very angry: "Why are you still here?" He knew then that he had suffered in vain; now he would have to go back to his people and confess that he had gained no knowledge and no power. The only thing he could tell them was that he got bawled out every morning. Sad and cross, he replied: "I can't help myself; this is my last day, and I'm crying my eyes out. I know you told me to go home, but who are you to give me orders? I don't know you. I'm going to stay until my uncles come to fetch me, whether you like it or not."

All at once there was a rumble from a larger mountain that stood behind the hill. It became a mighty roar, and the whole hill trembled. The wind started to blow. The young man looked up and saw a boulder poised on the mountain's summit. He saw lightning hit it, saw it sway. Slowly the boulder moved. Slowly at first, then faster and faster, it came tumbling down the mountainside, churning up the earth, snapping huge trees as if they were little twigs. And the boulder WAS COMING RIGHT DOWN ON HIM! "I have made the spirits angry. It was all for nothing."

"Well, you did find out one thing," said the older of the two, who was his uncle. "You went after your vision like a hunter after buffalo, or a warrior after scalps. You were fighting the spirits. You thought they owed you a vision. Suffering alone brings no vision nor does courage, nor does sheer will power. A vision comes as a gift born of humility, of wisdom, and of patience. If from your vision quest you have learned nothing but this, then you have already learned much. Think about it."

From *American Indian Myths and Legends,* ed. Richard Erdoes and Alfonso Ortiz. © 1984 by Richard Erdoes and Alfonso Ortiz. Reprinted by permission of Pantheon Books, a division of Random House, Inc.

FILMING A MODERN WILDERNESS RITE OF PASSAGE FOR YOUTH

Steven Foster

For over twenty years our school in eastern California has offered a wilderness rite of passage for youth called the "vision fast." The core of this rite involves fasting and living alone in a wilderness place for three days and nights. The young people, usually between the ages of sixteen and twenty-one, commit themselves to the experience a year in advance. They write letters of intent stating why they want to participate—what they hope to learn from the experience. Their parents are also invited to participate in the latter stage of the rite, when their children return from their solo in the wilderness.

The vision fast is a "growing up" experience of great depth and magnitude, and is rarely forgotten, even years after, by those who participate. Based on the traditional three stages of a rite of passage (severance, threshold, and incorporation), the course is an "initiation" into values usually associated with adult maturity—patience, introspection, self-reliance, self-control, self-acceptance, self-discovery, and ecological insight. The young people sign up for various reasons, all of which are associated with the basic desire to become more mature, to stand on their own as adults with something of value to give their community.

Natural solitude, fasting, and exposure (with minimal but adequate gear) enhance the participants' intent. The loneliness of solitude engenders love for family, friends, and loved ones. The fasting (three days with water but no food) cleanses the toxins from their bodies and opens them up to a rich inner life that is suddenly free to express itself without the outside interference of others. Exposure to the wilderness without a home or parent to run to brings out the best in them, including a new reverence and understanding for the beauty and diversity of nature.

After the solo, the young people share their stories with a council that includes their teachers and parents. In this "elders' council" the adults respond to the stories and help the youth to understand the meaning of their experiences while alone and fasting. Significant gifts, strengths, abilities, attitudes, and personal symbols of value to the individual and the community at large are identified. The students are empowered to return to their lives with new understanding and hard-won maturity.*

We were not trying to avoid a filming. The right opportunity had simply never arisen. For years we had talked about how important a step it would be to reach a much wider audience with a message that would spark a revival of interest in the old ways of bringing up our young. We knew that if a rite of passage such as the vision fast were to be brought back into our culture, it would have a profound affect on the way we collectively handle those "difficult years" of adolescence. Not that we considered it to be the answer. But it was, without doubt, a piece of the answer.

When Kim Shelton of Two Shoe Productions (and a graduate of our training program) asked us if she could film a youth vision fast, we looked her in the eye. Did she really know what she was talking about? Yes, she thought she understood the difficulties, but she was ready to begin tackling them one by one, including funding. She had been through this process before. She had three award-winning documentary films under her belt already, and would probably make more. She wanted to know if we were willing to go ahead with the project. I looked at my partner, Meredith. She looked at me. It would be a rite of passage for us too.

We put it on the schedule for the summer of 1995. A ten-day vision fast for youth. Four days of intensive preparation, three days alone and fasting in the desert mountains, and three days of storytelling in the elders' council. Parents of the young candidates are invited to participate in the incorporation phase. ("By the way," we cautioned, "the entire rite of passage will be filmed. Don't come if you are not willing to face the camera.")

To be honest, we had our doubts. We had no idea how the presence of a camera and microphone might affect this ancient rite, which, to our knowledge, had never been filmed before. We wondered if the kids would feel inhibited, self-conscious, or reticent to talk about those matters that were closest to their hearts. We wondered what our own reaction might be, and if the filming schedule would upset the tempo and the timing of the rite.

We initiated a series of soul-searching discussions with Kim, who remained optimistic. She had no plans to interfere with the unfolding of events. She merely meant to be there with a cameraman and a sound man to record it all. "People get used to the camera," she said. "After the first day, nobody will notice." We weighed the possibility that the sacred rite might be profaned against the possibility that millions of kids might watch the vision fast on TV. Kim took the stance of the artist. "Real profanation," she said, "would be if we filmed and edited it badly." In the end, we had to agree. After all, we had given our life to the proposition that someday a meaningful rite of passage such as this would be an ordinary part of teenagers' lives.

In the meantime, young people began sending us letters of intent. Jeff (17), a tennis player from a broken home in Colorado. Alden (17), linebacker on the Longmont high school football team. Chad (19), a Portuguese-American Indian street brawler from the suburbs of Denver. Christina (16), a troubled Filipino-American girl from a small town in Iowa. Skye (19), a snowboarding honors student from Oregon. Kaya (16), an adventure-loving junior in high school from Montreal. Sean (16), a mystical, dreaming, home-schooled student from northern California. Before we knew it, we were one over our limit of six participants per course. We tried to hold the line, but two more popped up and we couldn't ignore them. One was John (17), a hometown boy who approached me one night at a high school basketball game and said he wanted to go on a vision fast because he knew it would be good for him. The other was Selene (17), the class valedictorian at Big Pine High School. We had to sign her up too. She was our daughter.

So we ended up with nine participants, six of whom were from broken homes. More than a handful. Fortunately, four trainees would be there to help us out: Pam, a therapist from Vermont who worked with young people; Sandra, a woman from New Zealand, credentials in the School of Hard Knocks, who wanted to work with abused adolescents; Flynn, a college teacher from New York who wanted to bring the vision fast into the curriculum; and Joya, a woman trained with the Bear Tribe, a friend of Christina's mother. In all, nine kids, four trainees, two teachers, three film people, and Win Phelps, a dear friend who leads people on vision fasts and directs commercial television. Seventeen people in all.

Meredith and I like to work with small groups. Rarely are we comfortable with a crowd. We looked forward to the youth vision fast with a certain amount of dread. When Kim arrived with Tim, the cameraman, and George, the sound man, two days early to check out our meeting place, we realized that their presence would not be as unobtrusive as we had thought. Our usual meeting place (a sunny glade beside the creek) would not be suitable for filming. It was too bright. The shadows would be too hard. The sound of the creek was too loud. We would have to meet further from the creek, in an area shaded by willows and birches. Unfortunately, the area they chose was quite small. How were we going to cram seventeen people plus camera and sound equipment into such a space?

SEVERANCE

The ceremony began a little late that first morning. Everybody was there but John, who hadn't showed despite his protestations the day before that he would be at the meeting. The kids were already accustomed to the camera. It had been there to greet them when they arrived the day before. It had followed them around as they set up their tents and ate dinner together that night. To our surprise, everybody fit into the new meeting place. It was a little tight, and we had to share it with thousands of ladybugs just emerging from hibernation in the grass on which we sat. As the meeting proceeded, the bugs crawled on our skin, hair, clothes, a legion of harbingers sent by the earth.

Everyone formally introduced themselves to the group and we got down to the business of outlining the day-by-day itinerary of the rite of passage. The camera watched like an independent head, its dark, glossy lens roving here and there, stopping wherever someone was speaking, then restlessly moving on. Not only did we quickly forget that it was there, but we learned not to see it even when it jumped up and stared us in the face.

That afternoon, we began the first of a series of interviews with the participants, including John, who had decided to rejoin the group. Each of these interviews went an hour and a half, and covered whatever the candidates wanted to talk about. We "tracked" them through the streets of their lives, going as deep as they wanted to go, sometimes gently probing to see if they were willing to go deeper. Usually, we tried to touch upon such topics as father, mother, school, friends, the neighborhood, self-image, dreams, fears, personal myths and values, love and sex, drugs, plans for the future, and whatever they might want to say goodbye to. Specifically, we concentrated on their intent. That is, what they were confirming by going out into the wilderness alone without food. We wanted their reason, their intent, to be crystal clear.

Thus began a series of "elders' councils," the elders in this case being the teachers, the apprenticed teachers, and the old friend/consultant Win. The youngest was in her early thirties, the oldest fifty-eight. The elders sat with each candidate in turn; they listened and asked questions. One of their functions was to "screen" the kids in terms of their ability to survive the rigors of the solo fast. The elders were there not to judge, but to help them realize their intent. From the beginning these councils were filled with the stuff of adolescent human nature: the rage of Christina at her father, the sadness of Jeff at the death of his older brother in an alcohol-related accident, the tears of Skye, weeping for no reason he could articulate, the quiet burning of Chad, who had been stabbed in the head at a party and by the skin of his teeth lived to tell the story, the pain of Selene, leaving parents and their narrow but comfortable small town and going off to college in New York, or the honesty of Sean, who confessed he had never cried, never "let go."

All the while, the camera and the wires and the pocket mikes were in attendance, unseen but for their concerns about who sits where and who gets wired. Our fear of the filming apparatus proved groundless. Spontaneity flourished. The kids showed no fear about getting at their deepest feelings, and sometimes went a lot deeper than they thought they could go. In terms of the film, they became actors in their own drama. They explored their own "character" and "played" themselves with consummate skill.

On the morning meeting of the second day, we presented Anglo-American Indian ("metis," "mix-blooded") medicine-wheel teachings relating to their "four shields": their bodies, psyches, minds, and spirits. These ancient teachings, a primitive form of "ecopsychology," balance childhood and maturity, self-consciousness and creativity, and are organically linked to nature. In the afternoon, the elders prepared the kids to live alone safely without food with minimum impact on the environment. The meeting, which covered equipment needs and the entire range of environmental and psychological hazards, took nearly four hours. At the break, the kids jumped into the creek. Energy was high. The group was beginning to cohere. Through it all, the camera watched. Already the regimen was taking its toll on the cameraman and sound man. Tim's back was killing him. George was having a hard time sleeping.

The morning meeting of the third day involved a study of ancient pan-cultural symbols, ceremonies, and ways associated with the vision fast: the death lodge, the purpose circle, the power place, the calling song, inter-species communication, the rattle and the drum, the all-night vigil, the meaning of vision, and the effects of fasting. In the afternoon, the elders reconvened for another interview-screening session. More tears, more laughter, more pathos. John was the last to be interviewed. He appeared restless, ill at ease, unsure of his place in the group. It looked as though he might be stoned on something, maybe speed. No doubt he was frightened of the prospect of fasting alone for three days and nights in the Inyo Mountains. He covered up his agitation with vows of commitment to the process. This would be his way of leaving childhood and his parents' divorce behind, he said, of getting ready to enter the Navy. In all, a gruelling interview. Some of the elders were concerned about his drug use. He admitted he took drugs, but said at the moment he was clean. We wondered if his somewhat manic behavior might not be related to his continual diet of candy bars and Twinkies.

By the end of the third day, the kids had become a vital group. They journeyed to a nearby hot springs, sans camera or microphone, and soaked and talked until late into the night. Although this part of the therapeutic process was not captured on film, this sharing of feelings and experiences was of vital importance to each of them. They were one, united in common purpose by their commitment to the process.

The fourth morning everybody, including film crew, packed up for the journey to the vision fast area in the Inyo Mountains. This logistical challenge was further complicated by the absence of John, who had not arrived by the time the vehicles were packed and ready to go. We cooled our heels for a half hour, wondering what had happened to him. Just when we had written him off as a no-show, he appeared, protesting that he had been detained by friends.

The drive to the vision fast area took an hour, the last several miles accomplished by four-wheel-drive vehicles. The site was spectacular. In a juniper-piñon pine forest at 8,000 feet, we looked west across the valley to the snow-streaked summits of the Sierra Nevada range, over 14,000 feet high. Today the kids would go out in pairs to find their fasting places, which were to be less than a mile from base camp. Each would stash two gallons of water at their place. On their way back, they would set up a stone pile where, each day of the fast, they would leave a note telling their buddy they were all right. Thunderclouds were building overhead. Rain seemed imminent. The mood suddenly quieted. For a long time, nobody said anything. Finally, Jeff and Alden shouldered their day packs and their water, and went out looking for their places. The others soon followed.

From the moment we arrived in base camp, Tim was active with the camera, watching faces, bodies, the approaching storm. George held the mike boom above our heads. With its wind protection fringes, it looked like a long-handled mop. By now, the film people had been sucked into the drama. They had become as much a part of our group as we were of theirs. They had taken it upon themselves to play their own parts within the elders' circle. One of the finest moments had come when Jeff was talking about his inability to let go with girls because of the "armor" that protected him. The headless body behind the camera suddenly spoke: "Armor is nice. But you can't make love with armor on."

That last night of the preparation phase the entire company formally met around the fire. Tomorrow their fasting alone time would begin. The candidates were asked to tell the elders what to pray for them while they were alone. The darkness closed in. The faces glowed like specters as they spoke quietly, earnestly. We sang together for an hour with rattles, drums, and sticks, inventing words and melody as we went. Then it was time to go to bed. Although the storm had not materialized, clouds still threatened. Thunder rumbled in the distance. We had erected a large tarp to show the kids how it was done (they were allowed tarps but not tents). That night, all nine kids slept beneath the tarp.

THRESHOLD

The morning of the threshold or "ordeal" phase dawned clear and hot. Packed and ready, the young people held hands with the elders, then one by one stepped into the threshold circle, where Meredith sent them off with the acrid-sweet blessing of sage incense. The camera and the mop were there, catching the expressions, the nuances of dress and conversation, the good-byes, hugs, and tears. Then out across the sagebrush flats the questers went in pairs of buddies (and one triad), traversing the high ridges, disappearing into the shadow-folds of the piñon-juniper woodlands.

The elders and the camera crew breathed a great sigh of relief. They had earned a little R and R time. But shortly after noon of that first day, the quiet routine of base camp was interrupted when first John and then Christina returned. This unexpected turn of events sent the film crew scrambling for their gear while we elders shifted back into compound low. Yes, we had known that it wouldn't be easy for Christina and John. We hadn't realized how quickly trouble would come. Christina was weeping copiously. How could she have known how painful some of her feelings would be? She was in a rage at her father. With her permission I played her father in a kind of psychodrama that helped her express these feelings *in extremis*. That night, she went to sleep exhausted, declaring she was still fasting, and that in the morning she would return to her fasting place.

John said he was done. He said he sat out there for a couple hours, tried to take a nap, then realized he "really had to come back." No, he wasn't scared. No, he wasn't lonely. No, he wasn't hungry. Even as he protested that he felt just fine about coming back, he looked like a recruit condemned to do latrine duty forever. His decision was accepted at face value by the elders, though they did their best to help John clarify exactly what was going on inside himself. Finally he came clean. He was hungry, he admitted; he missed his friends back in town. We wondered if his return to base camp actually had more to do with what was going on at home.

The second morning of the threshold phase, Christina went out again. We then convened a short meeting with John and asked him if he would be willing to go back out, this time with food. He jumped at the suggestion. Yes, he would like to try again. By the time John had headed out, Christina had returned. Her pack was lost. She'd put it down while she looked for a different place to sleep. She'd found the place, but now she couldn't find the pack. Win and I went out to look for it. Her pack was retrieved and she said goodbye to us for the third time.

That afternoon, the film crew went out looking for "the mirror of nature," i.e., the natural world in which the candidates were seeing themselves reflected. They found it everywhere, in the wind, in the shadows, in the lizards, the cactus flowers, the limbs of trees, the shapes of stones, the cipher of animal tracks in the sand. The camera, equipped with a magnificent zoom lens, roamed the ridges, identifying tiny patches of blue tarp a half mile distant. It zoomed in on the eastern crest of the Sierra Nevada, where Split and Birch Mountain and the Palisade glaciers beckoned like giant ice cream cones through heat waves rising from the meadow.

By evening, neither John nor Christina had returned. The trainees rested after a busy afternoon establishing the exact locations of fasting sites. The film crew climbed to a high promontory to capture a spectacular sunset. By the time they returned, it was dark. Poorwills called from the open meadows, and owls whispered softly in a spangled sky.

The third and final day brought the gnats, invisible bits of air that, according to local legend, "inject their victims with cobra venom." People had to cover up, or slaver on insect repellent. The wind quieted down. The morning was still and hot, the shrill of locusts echoing down the canyons. John reappeared just after breakfast. "I've come back to stay," he said. "Now, what's for breakfast?" We looked at him closely. What had come over John? Something about him had changed. What we saw was that, in his own eyes, he had finally done something significant. He had lived alone for one afternoon and one night. He had acted with great courage. He had succeeded at something that was important to him. He hugged everyone with gusto. He even swaggered a little. The sleek box with the glowing lights and the longhandled mop pressed in close to record it all.

Most of that last day the film crew was out in the field, poking into holes and crevasses. I drove back to town to bring up the parents of several of the kids, who were arriving that day. The plan was to get them to base camp, where they would stay the night and, in the morning, be there to greet the returning questers. I returned with the parents to the news that Chad had come in just before 6:00. I was surprised. Chad was strong and had certainly been keen on fasting. "Why did he come in?" I asked. "He just said he got what he came for. His time was up. He looks just fine." "What about Christina?" "She's still out there." "Did they catch Chad on film?" "Yes."

That night around the fire, the parents discussed their "children." There was pride in their voices—and an honoring. We suggested they acknowledge this shift in maturity by rewarding their son or daughter with some new privilege or responsibility, some lasting token or symbol of their individuation, a visible sign of their severance from childhood. For the next three days, the parents would sit with the rest of us in the incorporation, or storytelling circle. They would have the opportunity to respond to their children's stories.

Out in the darkness the kids were calling to each other. It was their last night of fasting and aloneness. Their voices sounded strong.

INCORPORATION

They came in two by two; walking slowly, carefully, burdened by their dusty packs. Their eyes were bright and brimming with tears. Before anyone could touch them, they had to cross the border of the sacred world and stand again in the same circle they left from. They walked into the hugs of fellow questers, parents, and elders. To anyone on the outside, it would have been a strange sight. On the back side of nowhere, twenty-seven people were milling around, embracing, laughing, clowning, in the midst of which could be seen a man with a great camera for a head and another man in a headset, holding aloft a black mop. Those of us in the crowd paid no heed to such incongruities. There was no film. All the questers had returned, and the sun was rising triumphantly in the eastern sky.

The group came back into itself like a quiet river pulled down through rapids. The simple break-fast was so brilliant with talk and good cheer that time seemed agitated, speeded up. In a nearby clearing we formed a large circle and each member of the group was given a chance to thank the earth for safely holding us. And then all too soon it was time to turn our backs on the mountains of vision and reenter the body of the world. The story telling council would convene the next morning. We packed up the vehicles and swept the area clean. In an hour we were at the river, four thousand feet below. We stopped there, for it is a natural incorporation boundary. All those who had fasted jumped into the slow current, to clean the dust of nostalgia from their pores, and to turn and face the body of the world which they had earned by virtue of their quest. The river was swollen with melting snow. Mosquitoes hung like bits of fluff above the flow. The sun shouted down with 100-degree heat. The kids whooped and hollered and paid the mosquitoes no mind. Meanwhile, the cameraman's helpless legs were attacked by a thousand needle pricks as he held steady, recording the flash and shout of movement and mood.

Returning to the campground, we set up again beside the roaring Big Pine Creek. Now the encampment included the tents of the parents and the children. Although the youngsters had been counselled to spend some time in solitude preparing their story for the councils of the following days, they could not bear to be apart. They socialized (high intensity) until it was evening and time for the traditional feast.

Six months later, as I review the videotape and audio transcript, I am most impressed by the three days of elders' councils when the candidates told their stories and the elders and parents responded.

No doubt, what we had here was a significant growth event in the lives of these adolescents, activated by their decision to test themselves in a wilderness rite of passage. What we also had here was a model for what could happen in a community or neighborhood. It could be any neighborhood, in any city. The youth could be the kids living down the block and the "elders" could be aunts and uncles and significant others who saw them every day. The "elders" had witnessed and found meaning in this real-life drama of maturity and self-discovery. The community would prosper from the contributions brought back from the lonely vigil in the wilderness.

I could talk about John's story, and about his father's tears of insight as he heard John tell of his tentative success in living alone, without his dad. I could talk about Christina's courage, her dream of running free in the wind, and her mother's response, so pure and true the heart trembles. I could talk about Chad's vision of the shadow of death, or Jeff's conversations with his dead brother, or Alden's calling to be a leader, or Skye's sadness for his mother and father, who sat before him, separated by divorce, but united in their pride. I could talk about the elders' responses to Selene's tale of inner struggle and frustration, and the blubberings of her mother and father, or I could talk about Sean's tale of the owl and the Ace of Wands and the medicine blanket given to him by his mother, a "medicine woman" in her own right. I could talk about the Kaya story, subtitled "What Is Beauty," and the corresponding beauty of her mother and her little sister, who for the occasion had decided to be a boy named Sam. I could talk about the painful ecstasy of letting go of children who are no longer children—or the dawning of maturity in the eyes of a hometown boy.

Only Alden claimed to have experienced an "easy" fast: "I wasn't hungry, I wasn't thirsty, I was just so happy, just being, simply being." His friend Jeff, on the other hand, had thought seriously about coming in every day. Chad had been haunted by flashbacks to his near death experience. He came to terms with it when he realized his shadow was death. And since he couldn't do anything about his shadow, he just had to let death be. Christina had wept and screamed until she felt too exhausted to walk. Still, she made it to the stonepile to check on her buddy. At one point, Skye had wept uncontrollably because he felt so lonely. John had actually started to walk back to town, a distance of some twenty miles (as the crow flies), until he saw the folly of his actions. Kaya had encountered a rattlesnake just after she'd taken off her clothes. Selene had struggled all night with the pain of leaving a happy childhood. As the sun rose on the last morning, she vomited bile. Sean had endured a gigantic boredom only to come to the conclusion that "Nothing was going to happen unless I made it happen." His realization is the very essence of the meaning of "vision."

Although the camera did not accompany the young people on their wilderness ordeal, it was present throughout most of the rite. Over fifty hours of videotape and a thousand pages of audio transcription contain the priceless record. On the other hand, the film does not depict the great exhaustion of the crew as the rite came to a close on the last day with a ceremonial "coming out" sauna for young people, elders, parents, and kids. It does not depict the painstaking manner in which Kim and her cohorts were able to create real and artificial "shade" for twenty-eight people, especially at high noon. It does not show the professional agony of standing, or squatting, or scuttling back and forth, or the monotony of incoming and outgoing tapes and batteries. Tim claimed it was the hardest and most rewarding shoot he'd ever been on. George, his nerves tried to the limit, had broken through into emotional areas he hadn't felt since childhood. Kim was haggard, tired to the bone, but animated by intimations of success. She had accomplished what she had set out to do. She had made her dream a reality.

The film, tentatively titled *Song of Myself*, will be unique in contemporary therapeutic circles. It will be a sound example of applied "eco-therapy." The methods and the teachings are ancient, and the emotions and the feelings are for all time. In this incipient work, human and nature combine to make art. The relevance of a wilderness rite of passage will be known in the twenty-first century.

---

*This introduction was written by the author.

PART SIX

CRUCIBLES FOR CHANGE

FORTY SEVEN

WHAT PARENTS CAN DO

William Kilpatrick

In his book, *Why Johnny Can't Tell Right from Wrong,* William Kilpatrick offers practical suggestions for what parents can do to help children make their transition or passage to young adulthood. He provides an inspiring challenge as well as a useful review of significant and stimulating ideas for parents. A concerned mother will choose between job offers and will do all she can to be home when her child gets home from school. A father wanting to parent his child(ren) will do all he can to foster an ongoing relationship and conversation with his offspring. The other valuable points Kilpatrick makes are much less obvious.

The community a child grows up in is in need of care, too, so that youth has a family beyond the nuclear household. Such a community is badly needed as puberty approaches.

William Kilpatrick is Professor of Education at Boston College. He is the author of three books of cultural criticism and is a frequent lecturer to university and parent audiences. He is a past recipient of a fellowship from the National Endowment for the Humanities.

An acquaintance of mine, a well-educated man from another country, told me that the most shocking aspect of the culture shock involved in moving to America was to discover how badly behaved American children are. He said that this was also the reaction of the other transplanted parents he knows. Since this man had moved not to some gang-ridden region of the inner city but to a wealthy suburb with a reputation for having one of the nation's best public-school systems, his observation merits some consideration. Moreover, since he happens to be a practicing psychiatrist with a thorough knowledge of child development, his judgment can hardly be dismissed as an example of outdated, Old World thinking.

His is not an uncommon experience. Even A. S. Neill, the founder of the English school Summerhill, and one of the world's foremost proponents of "natural education," was appalled at the behavior countenanced by his American disciples. He particularly didn't like the fact that children were allowed to continually interrupt adult conversations. Neill concluded that Americans didn't really understand what he meant by freedom.

One would expect that unpleasant behavior on the part of children might eventually provoke a hostile reaction on the part of adults. And indeed, this seems to be the case. There are mounting indications that Americans don't like children—at least, not nearly as much as they once did. One leading indication was the response to an Ann Landers column in the mid-seventies. She asked readers: If you had to do it over again, would you have children?

Seventy percent of the ten thousand respondents wrote that they would not. This revelation was followed by a number of books and articles devoted to the same theme. I remember one article with the title "Do Americans Like Kids?" The gist of these books and articles was that parents were too stressed to pay much attention to their children; either that, or they were too absorbed in the pursuit of their own individual fulfillment. According to these accounts, children were increasingly seen as an inconvenience. Some authors suggested that this antipathy was symbolically represented by a spate of Hollywood films that depicted children as demonic.

The situation seems no better now. The April 6, 1990, issue of the *Wall Street Journal* reported that on the average, American parents spend less than fifteen minutes a week in serious discussion with their children. For fathers the amount of intimate contact with their children is an average of seventeen seconds per day. And whereas strangers would once make favorable comments about children in the company of their parents, nowadays they are just as likely to glare unapprovingly or make disparaging remarks—at least, that is the testimony I have heard from a number of parents.

The simple explanation for this aversion is that children and adolescents are increasingly disrespectful and disobedient to adults. One reaction, especially toward older children, is the "to-hell-with-them" attitude expressed in the bumper sticker slogan "I'm spending my children's inheritance." The other reaction is to shun the company of children. The increasing number of children in day care may be one manifestation of this shunning. For many, of course, day care is an economic necessity, but for many others there is another motivation. As Mary Pride, the author of a book on child rearing, points out, "One of the biggest reasons that mothers today are so anxious to get a job is simply in order to get away from the children. If I had a dime for every mother with a child in day-care who went to work 'to get out of the house,' I could buy Wyoming." "Why are grown women incapable of bearing the society of their own children for more than a few hours a day?" asks Pride:

> The reason, of course, is that *the children are no fun to be around.* Misbehaving, bothersome children would wear anyone down. The prospect of facing all that hooting and hullaballooing alone for eighteen years is frightening.

What's the point of making these observations? I mention them because I think they help to bring perspective not only to our discussion of moral education but also to the discussion of child rearing in general. Child-rearing experts never cease to remind us that love is the central ingredient in raising children. And of course, they are right. But what also needs to be acknowledged by the experts is something they rarely say: it's easier to love children who are lovable. And all things considered, better-behaved children are more lovable than badly behaved children. Of course, we still love our children when they are nasty, whiny, disobedient, disrespectful, and selfish. But if that becomes their habitual behavior, the love of even the best parents begins to wear thin. By contrast, children who are obedient, respectful, and considerate have our love not only because it is our duty to love them but because it is a delight.

If parents are really serious about loving their children (and having others love them), the sensible course of action is to bring up lovable children. One of the most important things parents can do in this regard is to help their children acquire character. To do so has mutual benefits: it makes life easier for parents, but it also makes life easier for children. Well-behaved children are happier children, and they grow into a happier adulthood. Aristotle, who had a very practical cast of mind, recommended virtue not because it was a duty but because it was the surest route to happiness (which he considered the chief good and purpose of life). Many of the arguments in his *Nicomachean Ethics* (named after his son, Nicomachus) and *Politics* build the case that happiness and virtue are inextricable, and that true happiness cannot exist without virtue. For Aristotle a happiness based on virtue can never be taken away, whereas happiness based on other things (money, health, love) is always subject to the whim of fate.

Most parents want their children to be honest, reliable, fair, self-controlled, and respectful. They know these virtues are good in themselves, and also good for their children. What prevents them from taking strong action to encourage the development of such traits?

Part of the answer lies in the influence of powerful myths, some old and some new, which dominate our thinking about child raising:

- The myth of the "good bad boy." American literature and film loves to portray "bad" boys as essentially lovable and happy. Tom Sawyer and Buster Brown are examples from the past; the various lovable brats featured in film and television are contemporary examples. This strand in the American tradition has such a powerful hold on the imagination that the word "obedience" is very nearly a dirty word in the American vocabulary. The myth of the good bad boy is connected to . . .

- The myth of natural goodness. This is the Rousseauian idea that virtue will take care of itself if children are just allowed to grow in their own way. All that parents need to do is "love" their children—love, in this case, meaning noninterference.

- The myth of expert knowledge. In recent decades parents have deferred to professional authority in the matter of raising their children. Unfortunately, the vast majority of child-rearing experts subscribe to the myth of natural goodness mentioned above. So much emphasis has been placed on the unique, creative, and spontaneous nature of children that parents have come to feel that child rearing means adjusting themselves to their children, rather than having children learn to adjust to the requirements of family life.

- The myth that moral problems are psychological problems. This myth is connected to all of the above. In this view, behavior problems are seen as problems in self-esteem or as the result of unmet psychological needs. The old-fashioned idea that most behavior problems are the result of sheer "willfulness" on the part of children doesn't occur to the average child expert. If you look in the index of a typical child-rearing book, you will find that a great many pages are devoted to "self-esteem," but you are not likely to find the word "character" anywhere. It is not part of the vocabulary of most child professionals. For some historical perspective, it's worth noting that a study of child-rearing articles in *Ladies' Home Journal, Women's Home Companion,* and *Good Housekeeping* for the years 1890, 1900, and 1910 found that one third of them were about character development.

- The myth that parents don't have the right to instill their values in their children. Once again, the standard dogma here is that children must create their own values. But of course, children have precious little chance to do that, since the rest of the culture has no qualms about imposing values. Does it make sense for parents to remain neutral bystanders when everyone else—from scriptwriters, to entertainers, to advertisers, to sex educators—insists on selling their values to children?

This is not to suggest that the problem is simply one of sweeping away myths and illusions. Character formation is a difficult task even when we have a clear picture of what it entails. In addition, our society has a special structural problem that makes the job even more difficult. The problem is divorce—up 700 percent in this century, with most of the rise occurring in recent decades. Obviously, the advice that parents should stay together comes too late for many, but it needs to be stated anyway: the best setting for raising good children is in a two-parent family. We now have an unmistakably clear picture of the effects on children of parental absence. Raising children out of wedlock is a formula for disaster. So, very often, is divorce. There now exists a vast body of research on divorce and parental absence, and it all points in the same direction: children from single-parent homes are more at risk than other children for drug use, delinquency, emotional problems, and unwanted pregnancies.

They also appear to be more confused about right and wrong. Dr. Judith Wallerstein, a California psychologist who has been studying children of divorce since 1971, notes: "Children felt that their conscience had been weakened by their disenchantment with the parents' behavior, and with the departure of the very parent who had more often than not acted as their moral authority." Moreover, "the shaky family structure of the newly divorced family and the loosened discipline of the transition period combined with parental self-absorption or distress to diminish the available controls." On a more profound level divorce seems to shake the child's confidence in the existence of a morally ordered, meaningful world. Some psychologists have even concluded that the pain of parental divorce is more difficult for a child to overcome than the death of a parent.

One of the surest routes for bringing morality back to this society is to bring back marriage. As Mae West said, in a somewhat different context, "A man in the home is worth two in the street." He's worth a lot more than that in terms of raising disciplined and well-behaved children. His influence on his sons will be particularly marked. Boys whose fathers are present in the home are significantly less involved with drugs and delinquency, more self-controlled, more successful academically. Daughters too benefit when a father is present in the home. They have fewer emotional problems, are more immune to self-destructive behaviors, and are more likely to postpone sex. All this is widely documented. Also well documented is the fact that single mothers have extreme difficulty in controlling adolescent sons. This is not to detract from all that a mother does but to suggest how difficult it is to do the job alone.

However, just as the available research on the adverse effects of smoking was ignored for years, so was the large body of knowledge about the effects of single parenting. As Harvard psychiatrist Armand Nicholi, Jr., observes, "We refuse to accept findings that demand a radical change in our lifestyle." Even today one hears arguments that single-parent homes work as well as two-parent families. In a 1989 *Time* interview, Toni Morrison, the Pulitzer Prize–winning author, stated, "I don't think a female running a house is a problem, a broken family. . . . Two parents can't raise a child any more than one. . . . The little nuclear family is a paradigm that just doesn't work. It doesn't work for white people or for black people. Why we are hanging on to it, I don't know."

It is possible, as Morrison says, for a woman to raise a family on her own and to do a good job of it. Many women do—although most do it out of necessity rather than conviction. But it is one thing to recognize that something can be done, and another thing to recommend it. Many people are capable of working two eight-hour shifts each day, but it doesn't follow that this is a preferable alternative to holding one job. Women who are thinking of having children should think twice about Morrison's belief that "two parents can't raise a child any more than one." A better course of action for our society, one suggested by James Dobson and Gary Bauer in their book *Children at Risk,* is to restore the idea of the "good family man," the man who puts his family first and takes a hand in their moral education: "Fathers must be there to tame adolescent boys, to give a young son a sense of what it means to be a man, and to explain why honor and loyalty and fidelity are important. For daughters, a father is a source of love and comfort that can help her avoid surrendering her virtue in a fruitless search for love through premarital sex." What Dobson and Bauer recommend does not have the fashionable ring of Morrison's statement. Even so, it is their assessment, not Morrison's, that most closely fits the hard data about homes without fathers. One startling statistic which gives the lie to the notion that any family formation is as good as any other is the repeated finding that children are five to six times more likely to be sexually abused by a stepparent or boyfriend of the mother than by the natural father. A Canadian study published in the *Journal of Ethology and Sociobiology* reports that a preschool child living with a stepparent is *forty* times more likely to be abused than a child living with his or her biological father.

No matter what their marital situation, however, parents need to be working toward the creation of what Louis Sullivan, the secretary of health and human services, calls a "culture of character." As Sullivan says, "A new culture of character in America, nurtured by strengthened families and communities, would do much to alleviate the alienation, isolation, and despair that fuel teen pregnancy, violence, drug and alcohol abuse, and other social problems afflicting us." Sullivan points out that "study after study has shown that children who are raised in an environment of strong values tend to thrive in every sense."

But while working toward that goal, parents have to be realistic about the present situation. Parents cannot, as they once did, rely on the culture to reinforce home values. In fact, they can expect that many of the cultural forces influencing their children will be actively undermining those values. Sometimes, unfortunately, this even applies to the schools.

It doesn't make sense for parents to work at creating one type of moral environment at home, and then send their children to a school that teaches a different set of values. Families concerned to instruct their children in virtue and character cannot rely on schools to do likewise. As we have seen, many schools have adopted theories and methods that are inimical to family values. Indeed, some educational theorists seem to proceed on the assumption that parents and families hardly matter. John Dewey, still considered America's chief philosopher of education, conspicuously omitted any mention of home or family in his otherwise exhaustive *Democracy and Education.* Dewey's omission is now reflected in the classroom. Paul Vitz's 1983 study of elementary school textbooks concluded that "traditional family values have been systematically excluded from children's textbooks." Philosopher Michael Levin of New York University goes further by describing current public-school textbooks as having "a decided animus against motherhood and the family." The attitude of many educators is that parents are hopelessly out of date. Thus Princeton sociologist Norman Ryder approvingly observes that "education of the junior generation is a subversive influence," and identifies the public school as "the chief instrument for teaching citizenship, in a direct appeal to the children over the heads of their parents."

Enough has been said about public-school sex education programs, "lifestyle" curriculums, and Values Clarification courses to suggest that they reflect a commitment to moral relativism and a rejection of traditional values. Some public schools have rid themselves of such programs, and others are now beginning to institute programs in character education. Nevertheless, parents who are not interested in having their children learn the lifestyle-of-the-month cannot assume that their concerns are shared by the average public school. They will need to make some inquiries.

Often a visit to the school will be sufficiently instructive. The behavior of students in the classrooms and corridors is a good indication of a school's basic philosophy. When a school values order, discipline, and learning and expects students to value these qualities, the results are tangible. One does not have to be a trained sociologist to get an accurate impression of the school ethos.

But clean corridors, smiling students, and enthusiastic teachers do not always tell the whole story. It is wise to check further. For example, it is legitimate for parents to ask about curriculums in values, in sex education, in social studies, in home economics (not what it used to be), and in health science (units of which may turn out to be neither scientific nor healthy for your child). It is legitimate to ask to see classroom materials. As a parent you should realize that teachers and administrators are busy people, and you should be willing to work around their schedules. However, if you do that and still meet nothing but resistance and evasion, it's a sign that something is amiss. Parents should also be prepared to translate educational jargon. Educational language is designed to give comfort and reassurance, and is almost always upbeat. But parents need to understand what the terms actually mean. The repeated use of such code words as "values," "value-neutral," "holistic," "humanistic," "decision making," "awareness of their sexuality," and "responsible sex" is a good indication that the school has no real commitment to character formation. (Parents can also observe how teachers and principals react to words such as "character," "virtue," and "abstinence.")

Parents who aren't satisfied with what they find have one of two options. They can combine with other parents in an attempt to influence the school in the direction of character education, or they can look for another school. The first option is feasible in some situations: very often school personnel have the same reservations as parents about certain programs, and they will welcome information about better approaches. Parents should familiarize themselves with successful programs and be ready to provide sample materials as well as data on program effectiveness. Statistics can be persuasive. For example, a survey of schools using materials developed by the American Institute for Character Education found that 77 percent reported a decline in discipline problems, 64 percent a decrease in vandalism, and 68 percent an increase in school attendance.

In the case of a school or school system with a strong ideological commitment to "humanistic" or rational utopian education, however, the first option entails a long, difficult struggle. The second option is one that an increasing number of parents are pursuing. An article in the December 9, 1991, *U.S. News & World Report* entitled "The Flight from Public Schools" claims that "the nation's faith in its public schools is fading fast." Some families are abandoning public schools because they view them as educationally ineffective, some because they consider them dangerous, and some because they are seeking more traditional forms of moral or religious education.

What are the alternatives to public education?

- Private schools. The existence of private preparatory schools makes it possible for parents to choose a school with a philosophy and tradition in keeping with their own. In addition, some private schools offer another alternative which some parents may consider to be in the best interest of their children—the opportunity to attend a single-sex school. The private school option is, however, an expensive one and beyond the reach of most families.

- Religious schools. The number of private schools increased by nearly 30 percent during the 1980s, with most of the increase accounted for by Christian schools and academies. While many of these new schools are as yet untested, the results of Catholic religious education are well known. According to the *U.S. News* article, Catholic schools boast a rate of graduation of 95 percent versus 85 percent for public schools, and they send 83 percent of their graduates to college as opposed to 52 percent of public-school graduates. What accounts for the success of Catholic schools? Paul Hill of the Rand Corporation explains it this way: "If a school says, 'Here's what we are, what we stand for,' kids almost always respond to it by working hard. Catholic schools stand for something; public schools don't."

- School choice. The idea of parental choice and voucher plans that would allow parents to pick among public schools or receive public funds for private or parochial schools has been gaining steam in recent years. Such plans are already being put into effect in some states. For parents in search of schools with a commitment to character education, the school choice movement offers cause for optimism.

- Home school. The number of students schooled at home jumped from 10,000 in 1970 to 300,000 in 1990. Home schoolers take seriously the adage that "parents are their children's first and most important teachers." The advantage claimed by home schoolers is that parents can provide an education in keeping with their own religious and moral values, and at the same time supply more personal attention to their children's educational needs. Many good home-school curriculums are currently on the market, but before getting started, parents should check with a local home-school organization, since there are legal requirements for home schooling which vary from state to state.

Up until recent decades, schools were considered to be acting *in loco parentis*—in the place of the parent (this principle even prevailed in many colleges in the recent past). The idea that the parent is the first and foremost teacher was taken seriously: teachers acted for the parents as trustees of children's education. The culture of the school and the culture of the home reinforced each other; both had similar goals and values. It was, in short, a very sensible arrangement. It meant that children were not exposed to sharply conflicting moralities before they learned basic morality. Instead, moral lessons were doubly reinforced. It is still possible to find or create this kind of moral continuity between home and school. It simply requires a great deal of work and determination.

What else can parents do? Perhaps the most important thing is to realize that families, even more than schools, need to create a moral ethos. "A family is a group of people," according to the definition in one second-grade textbook cited in Professor Vitz's study of textbooks. But a family ought to be more than that. A family is part of the larger culture, but ideally, it is also a culture in itself. As the Puritan preacher William Gouge observed, "A family is a little church and a little commonwealth." We might add that it is also a little school and, hopefully, a school of goodness. There are practical methods for promoting character formation, but the most practical is to create a culture of the home.

The word "culture" comes from the word "cultivation." Both plants and people grow best when a good environment has been prepared for them. For the youngest and most tender plants the best environment is a greenhouse. It gives them a head start: upon being transplanted, such plants are larger, stronger, and more resilient to disease than other plants. Children need similar protection and nurturing for healthy moral development. "Then," as it says in the Psalms, "our sons in their youth will be like well-nurtured plants" (Psalms 144:12). The child brought up in a good home environment will be stronger, healthier, and more resistant to the various moral diseases circulating in the larger culture. This analogy, so plain to agricultural societies, is less obvious in industrial societies, where most people have little experience in growing things. We do, however, seem to retain some instinctive nostalgia for this "simpler" approach to child rearing. Perhaps this is the reason so many of our stories about wholesome family life are set on farms.

At a certain point, of course, the analogy between the gardener and the parent breaks down. The plant is passive; the child is active, a bundle of energy, intellect, and will. He needs to take an active role in his own development, and he needs to learn to set limits to his own behavior. Even so, children still need a lot of assistance; and the chief way for a parent to help is to encourage the development of good habits—habits that will someday turn into virtues.

The first way to develop good habits is through good discipline. When Jeane Westin, the author of *The Coming Parent Revolution,* asked parents of grown or nearly grown children what they would do differently, the most frequent response was "increased discipline." These parents felt themselves victims of parenting advice that put a premium on "understanding" children and "relating" to them. As a result of such advice, many of these mothers and fathers had "understood" themselves into immobility. Unable to set limits, they found themselves accepting their children's most outrageous demands and behaviors. They were acting on the assumption that discipline must come from within the child. The problem, as Westin points out, is that children never learn to discipline themselves unless parents start them on that road.

As uncomfortable as it is for our psychologized generation, parents who wish to raise well-behaved children must say no to actions that are harmful to their children. And getting his way when he shouldn't is considerably more harmful for a child than occasional frustrations of his desires. Christopher Lasch, author of *Haven in a Heartless World,* writes: "Without struggling with the ambivalent emotions aroused by the union of love and discipline in his parents, the child never masters his inner rage or his fear of authority. It is for that reason that children need parents, not professional nurses and courthouses." This view is corroborated by research into family patterns conducted by Dr. Diana Baumrind of the University of California in Berkeley. She found that the best-adjusted and most self-possessed children had parents who were loving, but also demanding, authoritative, and consistent in their discipline. By contrast, permissive parents, no matter how loving, produced children who lacked self-control, initiative, and resilience.

Setting limits and enforcing habits of good behavior is not easy in the short run, but it is the best policy for the long run. One paradoxical benefit for the child is more freedom when he grows older. Psychologist William Coulson observes of several friends, accomplished musicians who were made to practice their instruments as youngsters, that they "are able to do what they want today because they weren't free to do what they wanted when they were young." Some of this increased freedom will, of course, show up long before adulthood. A child who has learned discipline (the Latin root means "teaching") will, among other things, be much freer of the tyranny of the teenage peer group. Another paradoxical benefit is that good discipline improves the quality of the parent-child relationship. When authority is exercised with the proper combination of firmness and love, the effect is increased love and respect for the parent. Parents, in turn, find it easier to love well-behaved children. Finally, it should be noted that families are not the only beneficiaries of order and discipline. According to psychologist William Damon, respect for the parent who exercises proper authority leads to respect for legitimate social institutions, and to respect for law. In his book *The Moral Child,* Damon writes, "The child's respect for parental authority sets the direction for civilized participation in the social order when the child later begins assuming the rights and responsibilities of full citizenship." Damon calls this respect "the single most important moral legacy that comes out of the child's relations with the parent."

Another good habit for children to acquire is helping with household chores. According to a Harvard study, which followed the lives of 465 boys into middle age, boys who were given jobs or household chores grew up to become happier adults, had higher-paying jobs and greater job satisfaction, had better marriages and better relationships with their children and friends, and were physically healthier than adults who had not assumed similar responsibilities as children. Psychiatrist George E. Vaillant, who directed the study, has a simple explanation: "Boys who worked in the home or community gained competence and came to feel they were worthwhile members of society. And because they felt good about themselves, others felt good about them."

The point of chores is to give children a sense of contributing to the family. And this sense of contributing increases the sense of belonging. Moreover, by encouraging a child to help with the work of the household, parents develop the child's natural desire to imitate into a habit that will serve him or her well for a lifetime. This is not to say that the chores are entirely for the sake of the child. At a certain age a child can begin to make solid contributions to the work of the family. In addition to regular chores, family members can undertake common projects such as cleaning out a cellar, remodeling a room, or building a deck. Working together on difficult projects is an activity that goes a long way toward solidifying family bonds.

Parents should also encourage habits of helping outside the home. The fact that "charity begins at home" does not mean it should end there. Children can help with community drives, with environmental cleanups, with collecting money for worthy causes, with church work. However, the most important experiences are person to person: visiting a sick relative, helping elderly neighbors with chores, delivering groceries to a shut-in, babysitting without charge for a family experiencing an emergency. An article by Beverly Beckham in the *Boston Herald* suggests that the habit of caring for others has fallen into neglect. She tells of visiting an elderly acquaintance after many years and finding his house in a state of deterioration: "The grass was too high . . . the porch was shabby . . . the window box was empty." Beckham continues: "Leaving, I drove by children—11, 12, 13 years old—riding their bikes along the sidewalk and I thought: wouldn't it be nice if they rang this man's doorbell and offered to cut the grass for him, for free? Or volunteered to take care of his garden?" Her conclusion is not that the children were selfish, simply that they didn't know how: "Years ago, neighbors would have rallied around this man. Years ago, children would have automatically reached out. They would have learned *how* from their parents."

Habits, however, are not the whole story. Something else is necessary, something more basic. Parents need an organizing principle of family life if they hope to enforce good habits; and without such a principle, they will be hard-pressed to decide what constitutes a good habit in the first place. Earlier I indicated that a family is best thought of as a small culture, and that this cultural aspect is the key to character formation. Let me explain more fully by referring once again to Diana Baumrind's study of family discipline patterns. In addition to the three patterns—authoritarian, authoritative, and permissive—revealed by her research, there existed a small subset of "harmonious" families. William Damon, in commenting on Baumrind's work, notes: "In these families, the parent rarely needs to assert control, because the children anticipate the parent's directives and obey without command or discipline. Like children of authoritative parents, these children from 'harmonious' families turned out competent and socially responsible." Continues Damon, "Such family patterns may be far more common in Eastern cultures . . . indeed a sizable proportion of the few 'harmonious' families in Baumrind's own data base were Japanese-Americans."

I think Damon is correct in assuming that such patterns are more common in Eastern cultures. Eastern cultures have a strong sense of family and also of family ritual. In some senses family life itself is an object of religious devotion. Not much of this sense of tradition and ritual is left in American families. The only daily ritual practiced regularly in American households is the ritual of watching television. And family bonds have been weakened by the emergence of what social analyst Francis Fukuyama describes as a "social contract" model of the family: a model in which rational self-interest replaces absolute obligation. But as Fukuyama says, "families don't really work if they are based on liberal principles, that is, if their members regard them as they would a joint stock company, formed for their utility rather than being based on ties of duty and love. Raising children or making a marriage work through a lifetime requires personal sacrifices that are irrational, if looked at from a cost-benefit calculus."

Clearly, as Fukuyama implies, the family needs a stronger unifying principle than that of a voluntary association of self-interested individuals. Otherwise it cannot call forth the acts of self-denial on which its existence depends. To the extent American families are based on these individualistic principles, to that same extent family harmony will remain an elusive goal.

When I think of the American families I know that would fit under the category "harmonious," it strikes me that they all have a very strong sense of family and of ritual. I once asked the father of one such family what sort of rules he used to keep order among his eight well-behaved children. "We don't have any rules," he replied. I think that may have been a slight exaggeration, but I understood his point. The thing that seemed to make the rules quite secondary was a strong sense of family purpose and direction. What gave this particular family direction was a firm religious faith—Catholic, in this case. It was a family with a commitment, and the commitment was reflected in grace before meals, in nightly devotions, and in regular family liturgies which followed the Church's liturgical calendar. The other binding agent was what might loosely be called "the family business." The parents ran a small private school in their very large house, and as their own children grew older, they would lend a hand either with the teaching or with other attendant responsibilities. There existed a third commitment in this family—what can simply be described as a commitment to culture. Painting, music, sculpture, and drama were studied along with philosophy, history, and literature. One of the boys was an accomplished pianist, other family members painted or sculpted, all either played an instrument or sang; plays were staged twice a year; dances, sing-alongs, and concerts involving family friends (themselves members of large families) were a common occurrence.

Yes, it's beginning to sound like an American version of the Trapp family, and in this case the comparison would be apt. Obviously, this is an exceptional family—too exceptional to be offered as a model. Still, when we look at other successful families, we find similar elements at work. Probably the most important of these is the sense of family purpose or mission. Paul Hill's explanation of the success of parochial schools—"If a school says, 'Here's what we are, what we stand for,' kids almost always respond to it by working hard"—applies to families as well.

One group that has succeeded in raising loving and stable families is the Lubavitcher Hasidim. Although the Lubavitchers live in densely populated urban areas, their children are remarkably free of the plague of drugs, violence, and irresponsible sex from which other urban children suffer. For the Lubavitchers and other Orthodox Jews the center of religious life is the home. They regard the home as a sacred place, and their major priority is their children's moral and spiritual development. Lubavitchers place great emphasis on respect for parents and other elder relatives, such as grandparents. Close contact is maintained with relatives, and major Jewish holidays are occasions for convivial get-togethers.

Edward Hoffman, a clinical psychologist who has studied and written about the Lubavitchers, provides some revealing details of Lubavitcher life:

> Religious rituals like the weekly lighting of Sabbath candles on Friday evening are a focal point for the entire family; everyone is expected to be present and attentive. Similarly, all family members participate in singing the traditional thanksgiving prayers to God after each meal. In this way, youngsters are trained to develop the emotions of gratitude and reverence for something greater than their own ego's desires.

In addition,

> Far more than in mainstream America today, Lubavitcher children are
> taught to be compassionate and altruistic. Because charity is venerated as an act
> of piety, youngsters are expected to make a small contribution every Friday
> (before Sabbath) to the "charity box" that is prominently displayed in their
> home. In accordance with biblical precepts Lubavitcher parents are expected to
> tithe their income to charitable causes. In this way, too, family members learn to
> think in terms of mutual sharing rather than egoistic gratification.

If life among the Lubavitchers is more harmonious than in most families, part of the reason seems to lie in their orientation to a higher plan and
purpose than the merely secular. Hoffman writes, "Lubavitchers partly
attribute their vibrant family life to the fact that children do not 'take orders'
from parents. Rather, as one Hassidic rabbi explained to me, 'All family
members "take orders" from God, as we understand His commands in the
Bible and other sacred books.' In the Hassidic view, the presence of clear religious dicta delineating right versus wrong behavior makes the parental role
far easier—and less conflicted—than that faced by nonreligious parents in
America."

The Lubavitchers seem like a curiosity to most Americans. Yet we find a
similar orientation—to family and religion—among other groups who maintain thriving and cohesive families: other observant Jews, Greek Orthodox,
Black Muslims, Mormons, Amish, and Asian-Americans. From a historical
perspective, the greater curiosity is the current assumption that the family can
thrive as a purely secular entity. In Hebrew, Roman, and European civilizations of the past, and even in this country during the eighteenth and nineteenth centuries, the idea of the sanctity of the home was the rule, not the
exception. And as with the Lubavitchers, many religious rituals or scripture
readings took place in the home. Thus home life was linked to something
larger than itself, to a larger vision and purpose. This twin vision of the family as being sacred in itself and as set within a larger sacred framework gave
added authority to parents, and added strength to family bonds.

Is it possible to establish a secular equivalent of this sense of family
sanctity? Many families that are not religious do seem able to create a strong
sense of family mission and purpose. But as with religious families, this
seems to work best when there is a commitment to some larger goal or tradition or cause. Family life requires considerable sacrifice of individual wants,
and it helps if a child can be given a vision of something big enough and
good enough to make those sacrifices for. Families that have the loyalty of
their children manage to convey a sense that they are engaged in important
work: in carrying on a faith, a tradition, a craft, a philosophy, a vision of the
way things ought to be.

Unfortunately, many families today don't stand for anything. Neither
"little churches" nor "little commonwealths," they are more like "little hotels"

—places where one stays temporarily but with no particular sense of commitment. This is true not only of those children who regard the home merely as a way station on the road to autonomy but also of those parents who do not feel unconditionally bound to their offspring. What changed the family from a community to a collection of individuals each pursuing his or her own individual fulfillment? Certainly, modern psychology is one of the culprits. Its emphasis has never been on family or marriage but rather on separation and individuation. It is significant that Alfred Adler, who is considered the father of the optimistic American strand of psychology, called his theory "individual psychology." A second factor in the atomizing of family life is our Rousseau-like reliance on the strength of natural affections: we have forgotten that natural affections need to be cultivated if they are to grow. A third cause is the easy availability of divorce and the resulting view of marriage as an experiment rather than a sacrament or lifetime commitment.

But these destructive forces are not nearly as immediate and tangible as the fourth—the one that sits in nearly every living room. If there is a cultural vacuum in many homes, a large part of the reason is that television has become the organizing principle of family life. Television, as critic Kenneth Myers has observed, can no longer be considered simply a part of the culture; rather, as Myers puts it, "it *is* our culture." "Television," he goes on to say, "is . . . not simply the dominant medium of *popular* culture, it is the single most significant shared reality in our entire society. . . . In television we live and move and have our being."

More than any other medium or institution, television defines what is and is not important. It shapes our sense of reality. It confers significance on events by paying attention to them, or, by withholding attention, it denies them significance. It does not, for example, confer much significance on religion. Although religious faith still plays a significant part in the lives of real families, it is close to nonexistent in the lives of television families. As critic Ben Stein observes in the *Wall Street Journal,* almost never does a TV character go to church or temple, seek religious counsel, or pray for moral guidance. Another impression left by television is that sex underlies everything: that it is constantly on everyone's mind—or should be. At the same time, as content-analysis studies have shown, television sex rarely takes place within the context of marriage but almost exclusively outside it. If schools are sometimes working at cross-purposes to parental values, the dichotomy between television and traditional family values is even sharper. As one Lubavitcher father observes, "It opens up the home to become the receptacle for whatever somebody in Los Angeles, or wherever, wants to dump onto your living room floor and into your kids' minds." "Those who think that *their* children will remain immune are just kidding themselves," says another Lubavitcher father.

Perhaps the most profound effect of television watching, however, is its effect on family relationships. Regular television viewing deprives families of opportunities to interact with one another. There are just so many hours in the day, and, right now, for many families television takes up a disproportionate number of them. Watching TV is much easier than conversation, and it is certainly easier than confrontation—although confrontation is sometimes what is called for in family life. Because TV tends to pacify children, thus providing temporary harmony, many parents use it as a substitute for the hard work of establishing real discipline. As Marie Winn observes in *Children Without Childhood,* "Instead of having to establish rules and limits . . . instead of having to work at socializing children in order to make them more agreeable to live with, parents could solve all these problems by resorting to the television set. 'Go watch TV' were the magic words." Kenneth Myers makes a similar observation: "I do believe that addiction to television (as opposed to deliberate, measured viewing) makes sincere and deep relations with people and with reality more difficult to sustain."

One important step that any parent can take to restore family culture, to improve family relationships, and to take moral education out of the hands of "somebody in Los Angeles" is to revive the practice of family reading, once so common. There are many benefits. The close personal contact of sitting together as a family group, or just two, creates a bond of unity and a bond of mutual enthusiasm. And it is not an activity that needs to stop once children are old enough to read for themselves. At one time it was common practice for adults and children of all ages to take turns reading aloud from the works of Dickens, Twain, and Stevenson. Of course, the practice is not entirely extinct. One family I know describes "long evenings of absolute suspense" reading aloud from *The Lord of the Rings.* As with other pleasurable activities, part of the pleasure of reading good books is the pleasure of sharing them.

An added benefit is that reading together acts as a stimulus to conversation. And unlike the forced "therapeutic" discussions that take place in some modern households, it is a type of conversation that flows naturally. It often goes much deeper as well, allowing parents and children to share thoughts about questions that are at the center of human concern. In reading or listening to stories, moreover, children are learning to think and imagine more freely. Their emotional and intellectual response is their own, not the cued response generated by a television laugh track.

In addition, good stories can provide pictures of family life that act as an antidote to current shallow notions about the family. A good example is the *Odyssey,* several fine versions of which can be read by or to children. As Thomas Fleming, a writer and classics scholar, points out, "Even the plot is a paradigm of domestic fidelity":

> Odysseus, who had fought for ten years at Troy, is held captive by a beautiful goddess who wants to make him her immortal companion. Instead, the poor man pines for a sight of home—a rugged and worthless scrap of rock—and longs for his middle-aged wife and a son he hasn't seen for twenty years. Back

at home, his wife has been resorting to every sort of stratagem to keep a flock of noble suitors at arm's length, while her son spends his days brooding over his absent father. Odysseus' homecoming is for many readers the most dramatic and joyful moment in literature. After he slaughters his rivals and persuades his wife of his identity, the couple, after their joyous reunion, spends the night exactly as a modern couple would: they talk till the sun comes up.

On a cost-benefit calculus, the actions of Odysseus, Penelope, and Telemachus don't make any sense. But Homer paints on a larger canvas. He presents us with a conception of family life that far transcends such a limited calculus.

The most important benefit of reading is the positive effect on character. In reading to a child, you—not some distant scriptwriter—get to choose the models and morals that come into the home. Reading and listening to the right sort of stories creates a primitive emotional attachment to behavior that is good and worthy; it implants a love and desire for virtue in the child's heart and imagination; it helps to prevent moral blindness.

Finally, reading together puts you and your children in touch with one of the great civilizing traditions of the human race. All the great cultures of the past preferred to express their most serious thought through stories. The wonder of it is that we can share in many of those same stories today. They have survived because the truths they tell are timeless. Jim Trelease, author of *The Read-Aloud Handbook,* puts the matter well in explaining why he read to his children:

> I read because *my* father read to *me.* And because he'd read to me, when my time came I knew intuitively there is a torch that is supposed to be passed from one generation to the next. And through countless nights of reading I began to realize that when enough of the torchbearers—parents and teachers—stop passing the torches, a culture begins to die.

HIGHER EDUCATION AND RITES OF PASSAGE IN AMERICA

Miriam Dror and Flynn Johnson

Miriam Dror, M.A., is a psychotherapist and educator whose career is devoted to the study and practice of therapies that seek to integrate the domains of body, mind, emotions, and spirit. She is on the faculty of The Institute of Core Energetics in New York City and also conducts training programs in Vermont and England in that field.

Flynn Johnson, M.A., has a private practice as psychotherapist in southern Vermont where he also conducts vision quest wilderness programs for high school and college students.

INTRODUCTION

THE SAD TIME
Ain't no one I can talk to
There's no one who'll understand
What it's like to be living
in this social wasteland . . . (male/student)

    . . . I think it is sadly ironic that they attributed my decision to independence rather than disorientation. I didn't know which way was up . . . so I walked right into the lion's den . . . (female/student)

    I thought if I just had a voice, then things would be O.K. (female/student)

In the fall of 1995 we found ourselves sitting in a circle with nineteen college freshmen and sophomores hearing them softly describe their reasons for selecting to take our course. They had already been to our introductory class. Several had not returned out of concern that the class was too large. Nineteen was still large by Marlboro standards where classes are typically small (seven to ten) and much learning takes place in one-to-one tutorials with professors. As a Pilot Project, we had decided that all students who came would be accepted into the class, since among our many questions were "who would come?" and "why?"

Their answers now were brief. We came over the semester to recognize the hushed breathing and the bright yet shy eyes that accompanied the voices, their own voices daring to name a territory that throbbed within them yet was hardly spoken of and as yet to be named and shared. On the surface they said they came because they were curious about themselves, each other, and us. Two were suspicious and hostile to ideas that reeked of "New Age stuff" ("my mother has that inclination") and wanted to check this out. One woman protested she "hated adolescents" and wanted to know what they were about, thought she might find out in this class. She was eighteen. Some didn't seem to know why they were here . . . "something about the title of the course," they said.

I (Miriam) had been working at Marlboro College as a Psychological Counselor and Director of the Department for several years before a passion began to take shape in me. I think the passion was born of the voices of students that over a period of many hours and years became a chorus. Theirs were personal stories, all were compelling and unique, but there was also a universal and oft repeating theme. It told of the vitality of this age group, their energy and creativity unharnessed, untapped, and for the most part neglected, if not despised, by their elders. Theirs was a story of growing up in empty or often chaotic houses, falling into sex and drugs at astoundingly early ages. On the surface there may have been a sophistication, a daring, a skin that seemed hardened by more years than they numbered. Yet, again and again, in my office, with hardly any words passed between us, their eyes would brim with tears and their hearts would break into the sobs of loneliness, alienation, and a deep sense of their lack of importance to anyone and the seeming meaninglessness of their struggle.

To their amazing credit, and it was this upon which we built together, they knew that it could be different, that there was more to life than the dull hole into which they felt themselves gradually descending. There was many a day when I wished I could collect together the five or six students I had seen that day, so they could hear one another's stories. It seemed somehow odd that I should be the one privy to the universality of their longings and their struggles when they were the ones that could benefit the most from the sharing that might ultimately break down their walls of isolation and give meaning at last to their heroic efforts to sound a voice and claim direction in a vast wilderness that seemed theirs alone.

It may seem obvious that Counseling Groups was the way to go. I had had success with student groups in the eighties. Yet it now seemed that no matter what group we offered, no matter how we spiced the title or how tantalizing the content, no one or very few showed up. Educational programs, offered through the Health Center, were poorly attended.

We met with students to explore the reasons. Students were cynical and distrusting of one another. Also, they said, they had grown up in a culture of Support Groups with "Twelve Steps to anywhere that seemed to lead nowhere." They had seen parents in these groups and often felt a hostility toward them and their efforts. Clearly the present climate had rendered them more jaded about group work. They often felt they knew everything there was to learn about drugs and alcohol, birth control for sure—hadn't they been forced to attend those Health Classes in High School? So they weren't going to show up to educational sessions either!

Yet, it's not possible to sit with youth over any period of time and not become deeply troubled by the patterns of their behavior, in spite of this protested wealth of information. Certainly there were those who lacked the vital information and those whose wounds rendered them entirely too vulnerable to apply what they might know, and yet, something else was going on that called out for understanding; and this, no amount of factual education or one-to-one counseling hours seemed to penetrate.

The passion growing inside of me was in search of an understanding. The program herein outlined, while still in its infancy, is an evolving answer to our troubled observations. As such, the program and particularly the course sought to integrate an understanding of Youth and Culture, with inspired models of education and the use of "elders" as mentors, who would be sensitive, available, and grounding influences through crucial years of development.

The program is college based because that's where we were. But the more we reflected, the more we came to be inspired by the college years as being significant years of growth and development, particularly if the academic program is, or can be made to be, sensitive and inclusive of the developmental tasks of the students. However, we believe that this program, certainly the concepts that inspire its structure, can be translated to any number of academic settings that do not have academic teaching as their primary mission and vision.

YOUTH AND CULTURE

My parents didn't know what to do to help me find balance, and I wouldn't let them treat me like their child because I wasn't a child anymore. (female/student)

This was the worst part, feeling helpless. Something new and scary happened to me every day and the familiar landmarks of my life grew less and less, the spaces in between longer and longer. I thought many times that if only I could hold to a thought long enough to finish it I would have accomplished something. I didn't know how though. (female/student)

The years of adolescence and youth constitute a time of initiation. During this time one is meant to move from the innocence and immaturity of the child to the full responsibility and maturity of the adult. All parts of the self are brought into this transformative process—the physical, emotional, intellectual, and spiritual. Of necessity, this can only be a time of turmoil, when the inner upheaval spills to the outside; but perhaps more importantly, the sense of one's changing self needs to be expressed, tested, and measured in the external world in order to be known, grasped, and understood by oneself. This transformative process is a part of a natural calling from within, a part of the universal blueprint of development.

Traditional cultures responded to the welling up of this enormous and creative energy with some of the most elaborate rites and rituals of passage. These traditional Rites of Passage were the means to bring recognition and celebration to the lives of individuals within a collective, at crucial points in their development. They served to empower the individuals making the passage but also served the larger community in that its future, indeed its survival, depended on their young ones' sense of empowerment, belonging, and commitment to themselves and to the collective purpose. This assured the continuity of the collective vision.

Traditional cultures recognized the vital life energy embodied in their youth, the enormous potential for vision and passion, and created forms to acknowledge, guide, and enhance it. The elders in a traditional culture were instrumental in mirroring to youth the value of their search by providing them with mentor relationships. The collective of elders, which makes up a significant portion of any community, often also provided a mechanism to invite an individual journey utilizing one's own resources and energies that would answer to the "call" from within. Therefore, meaningful rites and rituals were provided for self-discovery and transformation. There was always risk and a symbolic death in the process. One had to face fear in order to lay claim to successful passage and in the end there was always a celebration and witnessing of the passage by the larger community.

Many of the choices of our young, that have become the recognizable trademarks of our "youth culture," appear to be motivated by this universal need to create rites of passage that symbolize power and belonging in a culture that has lost its sense of interconnectedness and fundamental appreciation of the value of the pieces that make up the whole. Youth culture does its best to express its universal need for growth and manifestation in a culture where the elders have at best abdicated responsibility and inspiration.

> I specifically pursued substances, because I wanted to separate myself from my past. (female/student)
>
> I guess I came back for the second semester because I thought that if I could survive the hell and heart-wrenching pain of the previous one, then life could only get better . . . It was at this point that I turned to alcohol and marijuana. I had experimented with both in the past, but until my second semester in college, I had never truly been stoned. When I was in the altered states these intoxicants provided, I felt like I could do or be anything I wanted . . . I loved being "messed up" . . . almost every night was spent either drunk or stoned or on occasion both. It got to the point where even the days seemed altered; I would consume so much at night that the next day would be spent in a haze . . . Some of my most important friendships seemed to crumble before my eyes. I wasn't really sure what was going to happen in my life.
>
> After separation (from home) I needed something new to combat the changes taking place in my life. The problem is that substances perpetuated the problem and that state of betwixt and between. (male/student)

The form that these youthful rituals and rites take in a culture with truncated relationships and discontinuous passages can be potentially destructive to the individuals and groups involved in them, but also, they may fail to achieve the actual goals of empowerment and the carving out of a meaningful place in the larger community. They sometimes even take the shape of "anti-passage," a refusal to "be" and "belong" which perhaps can feel like the only choice, if self-expression and becoming is experienced as unwelcome or if too many of the familial and cultural messages have already been experienced as shaming and defeating.

What we came to observe in our counseling offices was a cultural tragedy of undeniably large proportion. There was no doubt that the young people we were seeing had been through ordeals that had brought significant pain and turmoil to their lives. Many wore the physical and emotional scars to prove it. They had lost young friends to accidents and suicides in growing numbers. They arrived in our counseling offices battered, tired, defeated, and often already medicated by clinicians. They were embarking on an academic journey but, more often than not, were not sure why. They came to a place that inspired their curiosity and what was left of their spirit of adventure but became increasingly anxious when faced with the prospect of choice and commitment to an academic program, let alone the Plan of Concentration. The heart of the chooser seemed to have been lost in the battle of their adolescent years. *I was not willing to face my past and myself quite yet. I sought to escape through drugs and alcohol and spent most of the summer in an altered state of mind.* (female/student). Instead of going forward they seemed to be holding back. Instead of being empowered and centered on their path they were full of doubt. Instead of viewing their elders as inspiring mentors, steadying forces along their academic path, they feared them, shied away from seeking help, expected humiliation.

Some took solace in drugs that had been steady companions in their junior high and high school years, if not earlier. In fact, they used their new freedom from family and old peer groups to dive into new experimenting with more drugs, more sex, and altered eating and sleeping patterns. What was more disturbing perhaps than all of the behaviors, was the lack of fulfillment, the lack of a sense of meaning that was common to almost all. Even those that avoided the obvious and often dangerous behaviors seemed to live in a contraction of spirit, a dying in the midst of life.

YOUTH AND COLLEGE YEARS

While we might like to believe that young people arrive at college having completed the turmoil of their "adolescent" years, what we know, of course, is that though they've been through turmoil, this has not delivered them into adulthood. In fact, in our culture, the years of adolescence and youth span over an enormous period of time with few if any points of conclusion, let alone celebration of entry into a recognizable and welcoming community of adults.

The college years as a period of time, but, more importantly, as a vision and process of education, can serve as a means to create a passage that up until now has not been facilitated, let alone honored. We were fortunate to be staffing a Counseling Department at a small liberal arts college with an innovative vision of education. Students at Marlboro College are invited to design their own programs of study utilizing the rich array of offerings but also going beyond what is offered by engaging faculty in tutorials designed around their own personal and specific areas of interest. In the Junior and Senior years each student is involved in working on the design, development, and finally presentation of what is called one's Plan of Concentration. This presentation could involve large segments of the community, as in the directing and performing of a play, an art exhibit or lecture. No matter what elements go into this final plan, all students are eventually gathered into a two or more hour session with one or more "Plan Sponsors," the faculty that have been advising them through at least two years of their academic program, and an "Outside Examiner." The Outside Examiner is an expert from outside of the college in the field of the student's area or areas of concentration. It is not unusual in the last weeks of class for there to be a buzzing of anxious anticipation, that breaks into open celebration as friends, faculty, and staff greet students as they exit from this, their final ordeal, which is made up of the precious witnessing of their work.

In some ways there could be no finer a design for a Rite of Passage in an educational context if one had set out with the distinct intent to create one. But even our less innovative college programs have within them the intent to help broaden students' perspective and knowledge base so that ultimately they may clarify and define their own choice of direction. Couldn't this model be used as a foundation to facilitate a rite of passage?

ANSWERING THIS QUESTION

There was no one moment when the vision of our Human Development Education program took shape in our minds. Clearly it is still taking shape as we test the pieces, witness the outcomes, and try to remain humble stewards in the process of the evolution of the whole.

We began by envisioning a Mentor Program. Somehow the spirit of elder as mentor seemed the central ingredient consistently missing for youth in their efforts to traverse these years of their life. But also, there seemed available "elders" in the college community such as older students, faculty, staff, and work study supervisors. The importance of the relationships that these people were forging with students seemed not to be fully understood or appreciated for their power to inspire growth and transformation.

Mentor relationships clearly had the potential to honor the interdependence within the human community. These deep and supportive relationships are of the nature to benefit all in the circular process of give and take. For youth, they serve to inspire, awaken, and keep alive the quest to evolve and become more of oneself; the elder is renewed in their capacity as witness to

this energy and evolution but also affirmed in their own growth and the meaning of themselves and the importance of their example in a relationship with
another. We could envision circles overlapping and interrelating, that ultimately involved the entire community and finally embraced the mission and
vision of the educational program, which, after all, was what ultimately
joined all of us on this Vermont hilltop.

The problem with a large and all embracing vision, is where to start. We
had initiated, with growing enthusiasm, orientations for new faculty and
freshman advisors, participated in Plan Workshops—orienting Sophomores to
their entry into their years on Plan. We even developed a very successful
Gathering for Parents which took place at the time parents dropped off their
sons and daughters for Freshman Orientation. We trusted that students would
benefit, either directly or indirectly, from these efforts as their relationships
with parents and faculty became somewhat more including of the concepts
that we brought to these meetings. But what about the students? It was
becoming easier to talk about them, becoming easier to describe their trials to
others, yet something was clearly missing.

In the sequence of the development of our program, this point constituted a crisis of sorts. The "crisis" involved our own surrender to the
unknown, the wilderness of our own creative process. We became recommit-
ted to the spirit of adventure, our own, and learned to support one another
through our moments of doubt, when the strands of the fabric of our creation
seemed to all but vanish. We existed in this space of letting go for only a couple of weeks but it seemed like forever. What was born at the end, of what
seemed an interminably long and dark passage, was the title and design for a
course that would be offered for credit within the academic program. But perhaps, more important, we committed ourselves to embarking on this course as
a Pilot effort. We committed ourselves to a loose structure, design, and vision
that we hoped would enable us to test certain ideas and principles but leave
much scope for discovery. It was a vulnerable position to put ourselves in,
two Psychological Counselors in a rigorous and demanding academic community, but now the spirit of our adventure had the best of us, we had the support of the necessary faculty, there was no turning back.

"YOUTH CULTURE AND RITES OF PASSAGE IN CONTEMPORARY AMERICA"—A COLLEGE COURSE

As we embarked on both designing and implementing the course, there were
these strands to our exploration. Could a course, a class, be designed so as to
promote and bring to conscious awareness the feelings and struggles that lie
in the darkness of the unconscious, yet appeared in such large measure to be
the force and motivation behind the behaviors that youth became involved in?
If a class could invoke an understanding of that ancient archetype of

initiation, could the energy of this then help them see their lives more clearly and thereby affect positive change?

We defined "positive change" as a consciousness of oneself that allowed for self-reflection, understanding, and expression that led to an embracing of one's own life and that of the collective in new and inspired ways. Such change would therefore offer an individual more choices. In such change, the energy of actualization (Maslow) would be palpable.

We wanted to examine the role of mentors/elders in the lives of students and ask whether their presence or lack thereof appeared to have a significant impact on their development. Could this course inform us as to the necessary elements that should go into a program of education for peer and elder mentors?

Last, would such a course, as well as a peer/elder mentor program, bring renewed vitality and understanding to the academic journey, infusing it with the energy of a personal quest and adventure? As such, these (the course and program) might serve to clarify and affirm students' choices and therefore their motivation, increasing the likelihood that their studies would be more fulfilling to themselves and ultimately result in a more meaningful contribution to the communities into which they would eventually move.

COURSE DESIGN

The course was designed in the spirit of interdisciplinary education promoted by the college. As such, it sought to draw from the areas of Sociology, Psychology, Anthropology, Literature, and Mythology.

The focus of the course was on developmental passages that involved the type of change we called transformative, the adolescent and young adult years, of course, being one of the most outstanding and universally acknowledged examples of this, particularly in traditional cultures. A large portion of the course would focus on the elements that all significant developmental passages held in common. For instance, it was believed that the three states of traditional rites of passage—Separation, Threshold, and Incorporation—mirrored the inner psychological landscapes of youth. First, each young person feels the pull to separate psychologically from their parents in order to give shape to themselves as a separate person. Second, each young person finds themselves at the threshold of the adult world but still wandering through the dark woods of not-knowing, in search of their own independent identity—who they truly are and what is of value to them. Third, each young person longs to discover the gifts they have inside of them to bring back to their community.

We intended to look at traditional cultures and to contrast these with our American culture. We would examine the myths of our culture and how these impacted growth and development.

We wanted to create an environment for story telling through the use of folklore and mythology. Stories were used as the fire to evoke the students' imaginations. We hoped each story, whether a Russian Fairytale like the "Firebird" or the Hero's journey as contained within traditional rites of passage, would provide the imaginal juice necessary to allow the students to re-vision their lives and to discover their own passion and deepened sense of their own being and belonging. We hoped that within such an environment their own stories would find a way to emerge.

SPIRIT OF THE CLASS

The purpose of a Liberal Arts education is to help students to both clarify to themselves the areas of their own talents and passions and to open doors to new and unexplored territories. This class sought to meet people where they inevitably were in their lives, in the complex and stunning passage into adult-hood and to offer them a language of universal templates that would not only validate and give meaning to their experience but enable them to feel more deeply joined with themselves and others and therefore able to continue to reach toward life with more grounding, openness, creativity, and, of course, consciousness.

As a pilot project we purposely chose not to set the stage by invoking the behaviors and patterns that we were concerned about. Rather, we hoped that if these very behaviors, as we hypothesized, were somehow central to how "youth culture" makes a passage (indeed are their own rites of passage) in a culture that does not provide traditional/collective rites, that they would somehow emerge as such in the course of their discussions, writings, and journal reflections.

Our purpose was not to question the rightness or wrongness of any behavior but rather to somehow invoke a natural curiosity that could help them to give meaning to their past choices and open them to greater degrees of freedom and confidence for future choice making.

Students were told at the beginning of the course that by the third week of class they would need to focus their learning on a project of their own design. It was this project around which their learning, outside of the class, was meant to revolve for the remainder of the course. We offered to meet with students individually to help them to give form to this independent learning adventure. We offered them over twenty topics and invited them to create their own. It's from the classroom discussion, their final projects, their indi-vidual meetings with us, and their final course evaluations that we extract these observations and preliminary conclusions.

OBSERVATIONS AND PRELIMINARY CONCLUSIONS

THE PEER COLLECTIVE

The most important thing that I learned from this class is that there are peo-ple who have had similar experiences as I have . . . when I was growing up I felt alienated from other people . . . (student)

I think one of the most important things for me as far as this class goes has been having the chance to compare my background and initiation to adulthood to those of others, in history, mythology, and personal experiences . . . I came to understand more of others' developmental lives and some of the reasons why they were the way they were. I found it helpful to have the resources provided me that I did. Somehow with the perspective given me by comparisons of stories, things in my own experience became much more understandable. (student)

Students spoke quietly, hesitantly, and often reluctantly about their lives and about the material in general. We ourselves were impressed and moved again and again by what they offered and yet their reserve remained throughout. No one was pressured at any time to speak. In spite of the quiet, it was clear that students were engaged. Two responses appeared on nearly every evaluation. The size of the class was felt to be a detriment to in-depth exploration of the subject matter. Students felt threatened by the sheer numbers. This came as no surprise to us. What was somehow more of a surprise was that the single most valued aspect of the class, mentioned virtually on every single evaluation, was the opportunity to listen to one's peers speak. This, they said, made them feel "less alone." Somehow they had thought that they were the "only one"; the sharing seemed to relieve them of shame and guilt. It seemed a very meaningful bridge had been forged between them; an unspoken and unknown bond had been recognized. It was as if somehow they had been living under the illusion that their peers were doing fine in the midst of their own suffering. Because of their apparent shyness, we had failed to take to heart the significance of what they were hearing and what this meant to them.

We now also feel that in the future we will handle their silence with more grace, as we've come again and again to understand the necessary incubation and vulnerability as the trademarks of the "initiatory" process.

YOUTH CULTURE

I wanted to be different, so I became friends with the less popular people at school. I thought that the upper-classmen who dressed all in black and hung out in the back parking lot and smoked were really cool. That's why I became a "Death Rocker." I bought all of the right clothes, listened to the right music, dyed my hair black, and wore make-up that made me look pale. (female/student)

What I find most interesting about my adolescence is my overwhelming fear of depending on other people and clinging to others for strength. It took abusing myself and proving to myself that I could conquer even that alone, to bring me even to a minor level of stability. In other cultures community is emphasized, especially during adolescence, and in adolescence dependency is encouraged and seen as healthy. (female/student)

I became involved with this boy at a time when I was most insecure and uncertain about life. He was older and offered me acceptance and guidance through my troubled high school years . . . After our breakup I found myself at a total loss. The (name) that I had been for the past three years was so tied to my ex-boyfriend that I could not determine how to be, or act, or feel. We bonded at a

> time when my personality was still developing—much of who I had grown up to
> be was linked to who he wanted me to be, and who he was. I was even going to
> his college . . . In general, I questioned everything about myself and my life.
> (female/student)

Many behaviors indeed revealed themselves to be efforts on the part of adolescents to make passage. They attempted to serve the universal elements of transformation—a dying, a threshold, and a rebirthing. Youth would leave one peer group and join another in an effort to let the old "die" in order to embrace the "new." They would try on new behaviors. Drugs and sex often served as means of testing limits in an effort to lay claim to new territories internally, while being expressed externally. While youth seemed often to long for boundaries, mostly in the form of example, these were again and again rejected when offered by the family. Teachers could either serve as crucial forces of inspiration or terrible and disappointing examples of elders in a culture that they often perceived as intent on hating and destroying them. Many felt drawn tight into various groups while others withdrew into books, music, and dark basements. Throughout there was the background drone of loneliness and despair.

Interestingly, most placed great hope on their transition to college as a chance to bring about both an internal and external sense of difference if not change. Many, however, found themselves lonely for families from which they had previously felt alienated; longed for places that they had hardly noticed at the time. In their profound failure to make passage into the new to instill it with personal meaning and purpose, they found themselves looking back instead of forward, yet not knowing why. Clearly, life had moved them to this next station, and yet understandably, from our point of view, they felt they had left something behind.

> Unfortunately, when the last day at home came it didn't feel quite right. I
> didn't know why at the time, but I felt alone. My parents were in rather gloomy
> moods, my room was emptier than it had ever been, and I was going to a place
> where I knew absolutely no one. I kept stalling and making excuses to stay
> around. It really felt as if something or someone had died; I was sad and so alone
> . . . Although I had tried in the past to break away from my family . . . I continu-
> ally missed my old school, my friends, the road leading home; in short, I missed
> my life as it was . . . My life had been completely inverted. Everything that had
> been me was gone . . . (male/student)

Perhaps, therefore, it should come as no surprise that the favorite topic for a project was a personal myth of some sort. In each and every one of these projects, our students found the courage to go back to the center of their pain. The templates we had offered them seemed to work within them as they relived these times but now with an ability to give meaning to their struggles, direction and purpose to their quest. Never did they utter a word of regret or self-recrimination, nor should they have. Theirs, rather, was a taking back into the fold the essence of their being, the child of their future, to allow it to be celebrated for its heroic journey and to move on with it into maturity.

> I've shared this story with you because not only do I not regret it, but I am actually grateful to have experienced it. If I hadn't, I wouldn't be the person I am today: the REAL ME. (female/student)

YOUTH'S DEVELOPMENTAL TASK AND ACADEMIC VISION— CAN THEY BE PARTNERS?

> Waste your days caught up in a maze
> and you build your little dreams
> all those days are lost in a haze
> 'cause your mind split out at the seams.
> (male/student)

We learned that students placed great hope in embarking on their college experience. We learned that they very soon felt the wind taken out of their sails. The transition seemed impossible and there appeared to be little help. While advisors spoke of academic course loads their spirits were grieving the past and doubting the future. Here was yet another passage to be made with yet another wilderness, lonely and unacknowledged. While older students might certainly have served as mentors in this transition, ours had become a community of "sink or swim." And because of its smallness and its promise of intimacy, this could, and did, lead to a gaping sense of disillusionment for many.

So it seemed that many expectations were placed on the transition to college as somehow serving to cure the distress of the past. Rather than serving as such it was more likely to become yet another mountain to climb, again without a sense of one's own self, let alone the confidence to give expression to this self. In this context, the Plan of Concentration, or a Major, which on paper resonated with each student's true desire for the freedom in which to become oneself, now became the biggest threat of all. Who would name "the way," let alone provide "useful maps" for this challenge? Many students were thinking of leaving before they had even arrived. Others were aiming to "stick it out," seeing "the degree" as one more requirement demanded by that unreachable, unapproachable, and certainly unsupporting adult world.

Here clearly, within the context of a course, but also through the development of mindful and caring mentors, was a chance to turn this, for the most part, self-chosen academic opportunity into one of the most profound and meaningful "rites of passage." Through consciousness and appropriate education there was here a tantalizing opportunity to enlist the academic vision and journey as an integrated, while integrating, force in the natural developmental tasks of our students.

YOUTH AND MENTORS

> By this time I was so defensive that no one would come near me for fear of being pricked by my anger. I knew this, I could see it on the faces around me every day, but it only made me angrier because I knew it was empty rage. The breath from the kind word of a stranger would have blown it away . . . (female/student)

We have not as yet explored or elicited information regarding the significance of our presence and role in the class. Although we originally had not conceived of this, we no doubt modeled the role of the elder mentor. Our style, perhaps more because of our own nature than by design, was to validate, stretch imaginations, open curiosity, and most of all provide a safe atmosphere for learning.

As mentioned, the class was offered as a context in which to explore the meaning and availability of mentors in the development of our youth. The hunger for meaningful mentor relationships was evident universally in the sharings of our students. The necessary use of peer culture to replace elder modeling behaviors was clear.

Youth will always look for peer support in these years of development, but when elder mentors are lacking, the peer culture of necessity is forced to serve in this role. This can result in a kind of ingrowing of behavior patterns, rather than an expansion that ultimately reaches toward creative change. On the other hand, as mentioned, a common reported phenomenon among our students was for them to very suddenly abandon one peer group for another, we believe, in an effort to try on change and yet to assure at the same time their continuing sense of belonging.

We believe that the role of an elder mentor would be to invoke change, invite exploration, while not threatening this necessary sense of belonging and unity of the group. If this is offered from the outside, so to speak, by one whose position clearly is neither threatening nor threatened by the internal cohesiveness of the peer group bond, then it can be seen and understood, not to mention, be received, more readily.

It is this sort of inspiration, modeling, mentoring from without that appears all but lacking in this small sample of our youth culture. When it existed, clearly it was seen as the necessary ground to support one's very being. It is worth pointing out that it is not the function of the family, the parents, to fill this role in the life of the adolescent and young adult years, though clearly parents can either hinder or support with their own behavior and attitudes the development of the young person. The young adult is in a process of differentiation so deep that of necessity he or she must look beyond the scope of the family and what it has to offer at this time.

The typical positions for mentors to occur in were those of teachers, neighbors, a stepfather who had just come on the scene. For many there simply was nobody outside the peer group. These young people, and we have every reason to believe they were typical, demonstrated both a hunger for such relationships and a tremendous, while sometimes hidden, vulnerability within them.

> . . . the conversations . . . were my release, my reassurance that something was right with the world and somehow I had a place in it . . . they (conversations) taught me to understand who I was, why I was, and where I was. For the first time I began thinking about my potential as an individual . . . (female/student)

When there was a person that could function as an elder mentor, the attachment was very deep. Sometimes the boundaries of this relationship could become unclear. This, of course, was most damaging when the "elder's" boundaries were somehow not placed safely. It is clear that in a culture that often lacks a solid parental base and on the other hand offers few elder mentoring possibilities, that youth will bring a large set of expectations and needs to such relationships. This makes it even more compelling to provide a means for educating mentors or bringing a greater awareness to those who are already serving in such roles.

IN CONCLUSION

It seemed we came away with even more material and affirmations than we had bargained for. We had heard the story of our youth firsthand, in their own voices, and we now could translate this to others. We could use their stories as a basis for the development of effective programs because they had led us to the gaps that required bridging. We didn't need any further affirmation of their courage, their energy, creativity, vitality, and willingness to pick up again and again with the slightest offer of help or recognition, but their projects gave voice to this in the most stirring ways. Somehow miraculously, we had stumbled upon a way, within one of the simplest and best-known forms—the classroom—to demonstrate and give meaning to the true idea of education, which is to "draw forth."

In February of 1996, we had a reunion of the class; a chance for students interested in working with us on the development of the Mentor Program and others in the class, to reconvene. The students that joined us seemed bigger, brighter than how I remembered them. Could it be the room, I wondered . . . the fact that there were fewer? As we sat with them for the two hours reviewing the course, hearing them talk about the Marlboro Community and their lives within it, I knew for certain they had changed. Two had just been voted in as selectpeople (student leaders in the community), one as Head Selectperson. Both had been on the fringe of the community before taking the class. They all spoke with enthusiasm and vitality, a respect for one another, an ease in their agreed-upon views as well as in their search for differing perspectives.

Perhaps the most moving moments of all came when we turned to them for advice as to how to proceed, how and whether to bring the course more fully into the academic curriculum, what part they might want to play in a Mentor Program. I flashed back to that first class. Now, we were the ones hushed and overwhelmed by emotion. We were stilled by their profound understanding of what they had been through in the class and how it had served them and how well they were now able to speak of this. We were overwhelmed by their commitment to the class continuing and their generosity of spirit as they suggested they write letters to the Curriculum Committee and participate as peer mentors in the campus discussions we were about to initiate. Somehow we had come full circle and in the circle, that day, we came to recognize that the alienation of youth spelled the alienation of elders and that as one was heard and therefore met, so was the other; that the parts of a whole had come together in respect and celebration.

> . . . Live in the now
> It's all you ever had
> go ahead and choose
> ain't got much to lose.
> (male/student)
> Nothing can replace my struggle,
> my pain, my fear,
> I must nurture it, heal it,
> and let the child uplift my soul
> My journey will be a means to my end,
> but it is I who will navigate through the forest.
> (male/student)

BIBLIOGRAPHY

Bly, Robert. *Iron John: A Book about Men.* Reading, Massachusetts: Addison-Wesley, 1990.

Cajete, Gregory. *Look to the Mountain: An Ecology of Indigenous Education.* Durango, Colorado: Kivaki Press, 1994.

Campbell, Joseph. *The Hero with a Thousand Faces.* Princeton, New Jersey: Princeton University Press, 1973.

Corneau, Guy. *Absent Fathers, Lost Sons: The Search for Masculine Identity.* Trans., Larry Shouldice. Boston and London: Shambhala, 1991.

Eliade, Mircea. *Rites and Symbols of Initiation: The Mysteries of Birth and Rebirth.* Trans., Willard R. Trask. Dallas: Spring Publications, 1994.

Estes, Clarissa Pinkola. *Women Who Run with the Wolves: Myths and Stories of the Wild Woman Archetype.* New York: Ballantine Books, 1992.

Foster, Steven, and Meredith Little. *The Book of the Vision Quest: Personal Transformation in the Wilderness.* New York: Simon and Schuster, 1992.

Gennup, A. van. *The Rites of Passage.* Chicago: University of Chicago Press, 1960.

Mahdi, Louise Carus, Steven Foster, and Meredith Little, eds. *Betwixt and Between: Patterns of Masculine and Feminine Initiation.* La Salle, Illinois: Open Court, 1987.

Maslow, Abraham H. *Toward a Psychology of Being.* New York: D. Van Nostrand, 1968.

Meade, Michael. *Men and the Water of Life: Initiation and the Tempering of Men.* San Francisco: Harper, 1993.

Piper, Mary. *Reviving Ophelia: Saving the Selves of Adolescent Girls.* New York: Ballantine Books, 1994.

Raphael, Ray. *The Men from the Boys: Rites, of Passage in Male America.* Lincoln: University of Nebraska Press, 1988.

Turnbull, Colin M. *The Human Cycle.* New York: Simon and Schuster, Inc., 1983.

Turner, Victor. *The Ritual Process: Structure and Anti-Structure.* Ithaca, New York: Cornell University Press, 1969.

FORTY NINE

AFTERWORD: CRUCIBLES FOR CHANGE

Louise Carus Mahdi

rossroads approaches the study and practice of rites of passage for young people from as many perspectives as possible. These rites are vessels or crucibles for change.[1] They appear to have been practiced in most societies before modern industrial and postindustrial culture. Today there is what has been called a hunger for initiation. Both younger and older people miss not having rites of passage and initiation in their lives and create their own rites. This need has been appearing spontaneously at various times in the life cycle for several generations in the United States.[2]

Many rites-of-passage experiences are deeply imbedded in individual traditional cultures. However, the rites-of-passage experiences do have basic common elements around the world. These common elements have to do with the making of an adult, a real man or a real woman, as understood by a given culture. The whole person can live his/her vision; the half being is not fully awake or conscious.

As in the past, elders and mentors (see the chapters by Jean Houston and Edith Sullwold) are still needed to bring about constructive rites of passage. The problems go back to the writings of Homer and seem never-ending. With the collective loss of confidence in old-time values and virtues, we need a new type of leadership, of initiated mature men and women. We need to recognize the basic developmental (both biological and psychological) determinants which demand spiritual forms of experience, family integrity, stability, and continuity in relationships. We need concerned adults who are motivated by the higher Self, not by power or personal prestige motives, to develop and lead appropriate rites of passage for our times.

Like it or not, we are all involved in these problems, even if only as taxpayers paying for more and more prisons. These buildings are places of failed rites of passage for many—costly and unsuccessful, often counterproductive.

Traditional or so-called primitive societies were ahead of modern civilization in their dedication to functioning, effective human relationships at each stage of life. Because of this primal consciousness in such cultures and their focused rites of passage, each individual is a person of value and worth from birth to the day of death. And where does this conscious focus start? We need the groundwork in childhood, long before puberty. Let us learn from our large human history that has gone before us.

There is also an inner wisdom we can tap into. We know that adolescence is a tough time. There are many big unsolved questions of what to do with the unparented children. But there are natural rhythms of learning that include a natural sense of a need for rites of passage. The culture itself is in crisis. If each individual adult could take on just one child to help through the transition or passage into young adulthood we would be on our way to creating the village to raise our children. We know so much, but now we have to apply what we know.

Real change is inner change. If we want to range in new territory, we have to alter our relationship to "home," we have to be able to question, and not invent answers, but *listen* for answers, listen like Columbus on the deep sea for the new way. To be willing to be at sea. To be able to be seasick. You have to believe in the waves and the currents and the shores, you have to believe in law. Artists do not make the laws of revelation, they acknowledge them and work in league with them . . .

. . . We cannot be fulfilled as vessels of life without the fire. We know this as a wisdom, but we have to find our way into it as living experience. We have to discover what *fire* is—what *heat* is; if we want to change, we have to undertake it. We have to undergo the unknown. We cannot pull back and say No, I can't, I'm afraid. Of course we are afraid. But are we not afraid anyway—afraid of war, of the bomb, of death? . . .

Yet it is difficult to say what we are doing when we are doing this kind of work. We are trying to move into a new relation to The Power Who flows in us. People act as if nuclear power is all *out there* somewhere, stored in big bombs. They don't realize that we are all *walking stockpiles.* Every nucleus in our bodies is full of *that stuff. No wonder we can do so much damage and so much good to each other.* No wonder we are scared to death most of the time, and for good reason. No wonder we keep our legs crossed, our eyes veiled, and our step measured; we have to let out our line a little at a time, a little at a time, or we'll *explode.* Our unconscious inner controls know this, and the guy at the panel lets only as much juice through as he thinks we can handle. A power failure doesn't mean there isn't any power; it means *there's too much* for the available carriers. Now, what we've got to do . . . is have a care for ourselves as carriers of consciousness and the powerlines of interaction. They are the way things are. They are the form and structure of our plight. We can grow in our capacity to contain and handle them humanly. This is what it's all about, as far as I'm concerned. Again, it is not a matter of control and management. It is a matter of *awaking within The Source.* (From M.C. Richards, *The Crossing Point* [Middletown, Connecticut: Wesleyan University Press, 1966], pp. 21–22)

NOTES

1. See "Crucibles for Change" in *Common Boundary,* Washington, D.C., January 1996.

2. See *Inner World of Childhood* by Frances Wickes (1988; first edition 1927), *Symbolic Wounds* by Bruno Bettelheim (1954), *The Hero with a Thousand Faces* by Joseph Campbell (1949), *Thresholds of Initiation* by Joseph Henderson (1979), and *Archetypes* by Anthony Stevens (1982). Also see the books by Mircea Eliade.

SELECTED BIBLIOGRAPHY

(See annotated bibliography in Luvmour, Josette and Sambhava Luvmour. *Natural Learning Rhythms: How and When Children Learn.* Berkeley, Calif.: Celestial Arts, 1993.)

Arrien, Angeles. *The Four-Fold Way: Walking the Paths of the Warrior, Healer, Teacher, and Visionary.* San Francisco: HarperCollins, 1993.

———. *Signs of Life.* Sonoma, Calif.: Arcus, 1992.

Bacon, S. *The Use of Metaphor in Outward Bound.* Denver: Outward Bound School, 1983.

Benedict, Ruth. *Patterns of Culture.* New York: Houghton Mifflin, 1989.

Bettelheim, Bruno. *Symbolic Wounds: Puberty Rites and the Envious Male.* New York: Collier Books, 1962.

Blumenkrantz, David. *Fulfilling the Promise of Children's Services: Why Prevention Efforts Fail and How They Can Succeed.* San Francisco: Jossey-Bass Inc., 1992.

Bly, Robert. *Iron John: A Book About Men.* New York: Addison-Wesley, 1990.

Bosnak, Robert. *A Little Course in Dreams.* Translated from the Dutch by Michael H. Kohn. Boston: Shambhala Publications, 1993.

Brown, Joseph E. *The Sacred Pipe: Black Elk's Account of the Seven Rites of the Oglala Sioux.* New York: Penguin, 1971.

Campbell, Joseph, *The Hero with a Thousand Faces.* New York: Pantheon, 1949.

———. *Myths to Live By.* New York: The Viking Press, 1972.

———. *Transformations of Myth Through Time.* New York: Harper and Row, 1990.

Campbell, Joseph, and Bill Moyers. *The Power of Myth.* Edited by Betty Sue Flowers. New York: Doubleday, 1988.

Christopher, Nancy Geyer. *Right of Passage: The Heroic Journey to Adulthood.* Washington D.C.: Cornell Press, 1996.

Carnegie Task Force. *Starting Points: Meeting the Needs of Our Youngest Children.* New York: Carnegie Foundation of New York, 1994.

Cohen, David, ed. *The Circle of Life: Rituals from the Human Family Album.* San Francisco: Harper, 1991.

Csikszentmihalyi, Mihaly. *Flow: The Psychology of Optimal Experience. Steps toward Enhancing the Quality of Life.* New York: Harper and Row, 1990.

Deren, Maya. *Divine Horsemen: The Living Gods of Haiti.* Kingston, N.Y.: McPherson and Company, 1953.

Dover, K. J. *Greek Homosexuality.* Cambridge: Harvard University Press, 1978.

Eliade, Mircea. *The Encyclopedia of Religion.* Edited by Charles J. Adams, et al. New York: MacMillan, 1987.

———. *The Quest: History and Meaning in Religion.* Chicago: University of Chicago Press, 1969.

———. *Rites and Symbols of Initiation: The Mysteries of Birth and Rebirth.* Translated by Willard R. Trask. Woodstock, Conn.: Spring Publications, 1994.

———. *The Sacred and the Profane: The Nature of Religion.* Translated by Willard R. Trask. San Diego: Harcourt Brace Jovanovich, 1959.

———. *Shamanism: Archaic Techniques of Ecstasy.* New York: Penguin, 1989.

Erdoes, Richard, and Alfonso Ortiz. *American Indian Myths and Legends.* New York: Pantheon, 1984.

Erikson, Erik H. *Identity, Youth, and Crisis.* New York: W. W. Norton, 1968.

Farrer, Claire. *Living Life's Circle.* Albuquerque: University of New Mexico Press, 1991.

———. "Singing for Life: The Mescalero Apache Girls' Puberty Ceremony." In Louise Carus Mahdi et al., eds. *Betwixt and Between: Patterns of Masculine and Feminine Initiation.* LaSalle, Ill.: Open Court, 1987.

Foster, Steven. *The Book of the Vision Quest: Personal Transformation in the Wilderness.* New York: Prentice Hall Press, 1980.

Furst, Peter T., ed. *Flesh of the Gods: The Ritual Use of Hallucinogens.* New York: Praeger Publishers, 1972.

Gennep, Arnold van. *The Rites of Passage.* Translated by Monika B. Visedom and Gabrielle L. Caffee. Chicago: University of Chicago Press, 1960.

Gibbons, Maurice. *The Walkabout Papers: Challenging Students to Challenge Themselves.* Vancouver, British Columbia: EduServ, Inc., 1990.

Gilmore, David D. *Manhood in the Making: Cultural Concepts of Masculinity.* New Haven: Yale University Press, 1990.

Goffman, Erving. *Frame Analysis.* New York: Harper and Row, 1974.

Goleman, Daniel. *Emotional Intelligence.* New York: Bantam Books, 1995.

Graves, Robert, intro.; Richard Aldington and Delano Ames, trans. *New Larousse Encyclopedia of Mythology.* New York: Crescent Books, 1989.

Grof, Christina, *The Thirst for Wholeness: Attachment, Addiction, and the Spiritual Path.* San Francisco: HarperCollins, 1993.

Grof, Christina, and Stanislav Grof. *The Stormy Search for the Self.* Los Angeles: Jeremy P. Tarcher, Inc., 1990.

Grof, Stanislav, *The Adventure of Self-Discovery.* Albany: State University of New York Press, 1988.

Grof, Stanislav, ed. *Human Survival and Consciousness Evolution.* Albany: State University of New York Press, 1988.

Grof, Stanislav, and Christina Grof. *Beyond Death: The Gates of Consciousness.* London: Thames and Hudson, 1980.

————. *Spiritual Emergency: When Personal Transformation Becomes a Crisis.* Los Angeles: Jeremy P. Tarcher, Inc., 1990.

Hall, G. Stanley. *Adolescence. Its Psychology and Its Relations to Physiology, Anthropology, Sociology, Sex, Crime, Religion and Education.* 2 vols. New York: D. Appleton & Co., 1904.

Harner, Michael. *The Way of the Shaman: A Guide to Power and Healing.* San Francisco: Harper and Row, 1980.

Hart, Mickey. *Drumming at the Edge of Magic: A Journey into the Spirit of Percussion.* New York: HarperCollins, 1990.

Henderson, Joseph L. *Thresholds of Initiation.* Middletown, Conn.: Wesleyan University Press, 1967.

Hersey, John. *Hiroshima.* 1946. Reprint, New York: Bantam Books, 1975.

Higgins, Chester, Jr. *Feeling the Spirit: Searching the World for the People of Africa.* New York: Bantam Books, 1994.

Hollis, James. *Under Saturn's Shadow: The Wounding and Healing of Men.* Toronto: Inner City Books, 1994.

Jaffe, Aniela, ed. *C. G. Jung: Word and Image.* Princeton N.J.: Princeton University Press, 1979.

————. *Man and His Symbols.* New York: Doubleday, 1964.

————. *Memories, Dreams, Reflections.* Translated by Richard and Clara Winston. New York: Random House, 1989.

Keen, Sam. *Faces of the Enemy: Reflections of the Hostile Imagination.* San Francisco: Harper, 1986.

Kett, Joseph F. *Rites of Passage: Adolescence in America 1790 to the Present.* New York: Basic Books, 1977.

Kohl, Johann Georg. *Kitschigami: Life among the Lake Superior Ojibway.* London: 1860. Reprint, St. Paul: Minnesota Historical Society, 1985.

Kornfield, Jack. *A Path with Heart: A Guide Through the Perils and Promises of Spiritual Life.* New York: Bantam, 1993.

Kubler-Ross, Elisabeth. *On Death and Dying.* New York: Macmillan, 1970.

Lindbergh, Anne Morrow. *Gift from the Sea.* Reprint, New York: Random House, 1978.

Linderman, Frank. *Plenty Coups, Chief of the Crow.* Lincoln: University of Nebraska Press, 1962.

Lynd, Robert S., and Helen Merrell Lynd. *Middletown.* New York: Harcourt Brace and Company, 1929.

————. *Middletown in Transition.* New York: Harcourt Brace and Company, 1937.

McCall, Nathan. *Makes Me Wanna Holler: A Young Black Man in America.*

New York: Random House, 1994.

Mahdi, Louise Carus, Steven Foster, and Meredith Little, eds. *Betwixt and Between: Patterns of Masculine and Feminine Initiation.* LaSalle, Ill.: Open Court, 1987.

May, Rollo. *The Cry for Myth.* New York: W. W. Norton, 1991.

Meade, Michael. *Men and the Water of Life: Initiation and the Tempering of Men.* San Francisco: HarperCollins, 1993.

Mettrick, Sidney, and Renee Beck. *The Art of Ritual.* Berkeley, Calif.: Celestial Arts, 1990.

Moore, Robert, and Douglas Gillette. *King, Warrior, Magician, Lover: Rediscovering the Archetype of the Mature Masculine.* New York: Harper and Row, 1990.

Murdock, George Peter. *Africa: Its People and Their Culture History.* New York: McGraw-Hill, 1959.

Musick, Judith S. *Young, Poor, and Pregnant: The Psychology of Teenage Motherhood.* New Haven and London: Yale University Press, 1993.

Neihardt, John G. [Flaming Rainbow]. *Black Elk Speaks: Being the Life Story of a Holy Man of the Oglala Sioux.* Lincoln: University of Nebraska Press, 1961.

Oldman, Mark, and Samer Hamadeh. *The Princeton Review Student Access Guide to America's Top 100 Internships.* 1995 edition. New York: Villard Books, 1994.

Opler, Morris E. *Apache Odyssey: A Journey between Two Worlds.* Edited by George Spindler and Louise Spindler. New York: Holt, Rinehart and Winston, 1969.

Ortiz, Alfonso, and Richard Erdoes, eds. *American Indian Myths and Legends.* New York: Random House, 1984.

Post, Laurens van der, and John Taylor. *Testament to the Bushmen.* New York: Penguin Books, 1984.

Qualls-Corbett, Nancy. *The Sacred Prostitute.* Toronto: Inner City Books, 1988.

Raphael, Ray. *The Men from the Boys.* Lincoln: University of Nebraska Press, 1988.

Rebillot, Paul. *Entering the Mystery: Following the Path of the Hero.* New York: HarperCollins, forthcoming.

Richards, Audrey. *Chisungu: A Girl's Initiation Ceremony among the Bemba of Zambia.* 1956. Reprint, New York: Tavistock Publications, 1982.

Rilke, Rainer Maria. *The Selected Poetry of Rainer Maria Rilke.* Edited and translated by Stephen Mitchell. New York: Random House, 1989.

Roberts, W. O. *Initiation into Adulthood: Ancient Rite of Passage in Contemporary Form.* New York: Pilgrim Press, 1982.

Roth, Gabrielle. *Maps to Ecstasy: Teachings of an Urban Shaman.* San Rafael, Calif.: New World Library, 1989.

Saitoti, Tepilit Ole. *The Worlds of a Maasai Warrior, an Autobiography.* Los Angeles and Berkeley: University of California Press, 1986.

Sandner, Donald. *Navaho Symbols of Healing.* New York: Harcourt Brace Jovanovich, 1979.

Sarason, Seymour. *The Psychological Sense of Community: Prospects for a Community Psychology.* San Francisco: Jossey Bass, 1974.

Sheehy, Gail. *New Passages: Mapping Your Life across Time.* New York: Random House, 1995.

Siegel, Alan B. *Dreams That Can Change Your Life.* Los Angeles: Tarcher, 1990.

Steichen, Edward, ed. *The Family of Man.* Reprint, New York: Museum of Modern Art, 1986.

Stevens, Anthony. *Archetypes: A Natural History of the Self.* New York: William Morrow, 1982.

————. *On Jung.* New York: Routledge, 1990.

————. *The Two-Million-Year-Old Self.* College Station: Texas A & M University Press, 1993.

————. *Private Myths. Dreams and Dreaming.* London: Penguin, 1995.

Thompson, Mark. *Gay Soul: Finding the Heart of Gay Spirit and Nature.* San Francisco: Harper, 1994.

Turnbull, Colin M. *The Human Cycle.* New York: Simon and Schuster, 1983.

Turner, Edith, et al. *Experiencing Ritual: A New Interpretation of African Healing.* Philadelphia: University of Pennsylvania Press, 1992.

————. *The Spirit and the Drum.* Tucson: University of Arizona Press, 1987.

Turner, Victor. *The Anthropology of Performance.* New York: PAJ Pubs., 1986.

————. *Dramas, Fields, and Metaphors: Symbolic Action in Human Society.* Ithaca, N.Y.: Cornell University Press, 1974.

————. "Dramatic Ritual/Ritual Drama: Performative and Reflexive Anthropology." *The Kenyon Review* 1, no. 3 (1979): 80–93.

————. *The Drums of Affliction: A Study of Religious Processes among the Ndembu of Zambia.* Oxford: Clarendon Press, 1968.

————. *The Forest of Symbols: Aspects of Ndembu Ritual.* Ithaca, N.Y.: Cornell University Press, 1967.

————. *The Ritual Process.* Chicago: Aldine Publishing Company, 1969.

Turner, Victor, ed. *Celebration: Studies in Festivity and Ritual.* Washington, D.C.: Smithsonian Institution Press, 1982.

Turner, Victor, and Edith Turner. *Image and Pilgrimage in Christian Culture: Anthropological Perspectives.* New York: Columbia University Press, 1978.

————. "Performing Ethnography." *The Drama Review* 26, no. 2 (1982): 33–50.

Walker, Barbara G. *The Crone: Woman of Age, Wisdom, and Power.* San Francisco: Harper and Row, 1985.

————. *Women's Rituals: A Sourcebook.* San Francisco: Harper and Row, 1990.

Warfield-Coppock, Nsenga, and Aminifu R. Harvey. *A Rites of Passage Resource Manual.* New York: United Church of Christ, 105 Madison Ave., Suite 1101, N.Y. 10016, 1989.

Waters, Frank. *The Man Who Killed the Deer.* New York: Ballantine, 1972.

Weil, Andrew. *The Natural Mind.* Boston: Houghton Mifflin, 1972.

West, Cornel. *Race Matters.* Boston: Beacon Press, 1992.

Whitmont, Edward C. *The Symbolic Quest: Basic Concepts of Analytical Psychology.* Princeton, N.J.: Princeton University Press, 1978.

Whitmont, Edward C., and Sylvia B. Perera. *Dreams, a Portal to the Source: A Guide to Dream Interpretation.* New York: Routledge, 1992.

Wickes, Frances. *The Inner World of Childhood.* Boston: Sigo Press, 1988.

Williams, Walter L. *The Spirit and the Flesh: Sexual Diversity in American Indian Culture.* Boston: Beacon Press, 1986.

Wissler, Clark. "The Social Life of the Blackfoot Indians." *Anthropological Papers of the American Museum of Natural History 1,* part 1 (1911).

Woodman, Marion. *Addiction to Perfection: The Still Unravaged Bride.* Toronto: Inner City Books, 1982.

————. *Leaving My Father's House: A Journey to Conscious Femininity.* Boston: Shambala Publications, 1992.

————. *The Owl Was a Baker's Daughter: Obesity, Anorexia Nervosa, and the Repressed Feminine: A Psychological Study.* Toronto: Inner City Books, 1980.

————. *The Pregnant Virgin: A Process of Psychological Transformation.* Toronto: Inner City Books, 1985.

————. *The Ravaged Bridegroom: Masculinity in Women.* Toronto: Inner City Books, 1990.

LIST OF LEADERS AND ORGANIZATIONS

Blumenkrantz, David
RITES OF PASSAGE EXPERIENCE, ROPE
164 Farmstead Lane
Glastonbury, CT 06033
(203) 568-0181

Burton, Bob and Steve Rogers, Directors
VISIONQUEST, INC.
P.O. Box 12906
Tucson, AZ 85732-2906
(602) 881-3950

CARNEGIE CORPORATION OF NEW YORK
437 Madison Ave.
New York, NY 10022
(212) 371-3200

Eckert, Robert, Director
THE LEARNING INSTITUTE FOR FUNCTIONAL EDUCATION
Star Route, Box 34
Paul Smiths, NY 12970
(518) 327-3554

Foster, Steven and Meredith Little
SCHOOL OF LOST BORDERS
P.O. Box 55
Big Pine, CA 93513

Gibbons, Maurice
EDU SERV, INC.
1155 W. 8th Ave.
Vancouver, BC
Canada V6H 1C5

Grof, Christina, President
GROF TRANSPERSONAL TRAINING, INC.
20 Sunnyside, Suite A253
Mill Valley, CA 94941-1928
(415) 383-8779

Houston, Jean
FOUNDATION FOR MIND RESEARCH
P.O. Box 600
Pomona, NY 10970

COUNCIL ON FAMILIES IN AMERICA,
INSTITUTE FOR AMERICAN VALUES
1841 Broadway, Suite 211
New York, NY 10023
(212) 246-3942

Knudsen, Cynthia, Director, NORTHERN LIGHTS (Girls' Camp)
Knudsen, David, Director
TEMAGAMI EXPERIENCE
NORTHWATERS CAMPING PROGRAM VISION QUEST CAMPS
P.O. Box 477, St. Peters Village, PA 19470
(610) 469-4662

Luvmour, J. and S.
RITUAL RITES OF PASSAGE
P.O. Box 445
North San Juan, CA 95960
(916) 292-3858

Meade, Michael
MOSAIC MULTICULTURAL FOUNDATION
P.O. Box 364
Vashon, WA 98070
(206) 463-9387
Fax: (206) 463-9236

Oldfield, David, Director
MIDWAY CENTER FOR CREATIVE IMAGINATION
2112 F Street, Suite 404
Washington, D.C. 20037
(202) 296-2299

Sanyika, Dadisi
2110 W. 96th St.
Los Angeles, CA 90047
(213) 563-5823

Somé, Malidoma
2298 Cornell St.
Palo Alto, CA 94306
(415) 493-4073

Taylor, Artemus, Executive Director
AFRICAN AMERICAN MALE EDUCATION NETWORK (A-MEN)
9824 S. Western Ave., Suite 175
Evergreen Park, IL 60643
(708) 720-0235

UP WITH PEOPLE
International Headquarters
1 International Court
Broomfield, CO 80021
(303) 460-7100

Weissbourd, Bernice
FAMILY FOCUS
310 S. Peoria St., Suite 401
Chicago, IL 60607-3534
(312) 421-5200

Wooten, Ronnie
PROGRESSIVE LIFE CENTER
100 E. 23 St.
Baltimore, MD 21218
(410) 235-2800

INDEX

Also from Open Court

BETWIXT & BETWEEN
Patterns of Masculine and Feminine Initiation

Edited by Louise Carus Mahdi,
with Steven Foster and Meredith Little

This interdisciplinary approach to rites of passage comprises 31 essays by outstanding contributors, including Marie-Louise von Franz, Robert Bly, James Hall, Helen Luke, Victor Turner, and Marion Woodman.

Betwixt & Between is the first book of its kind, with new insights into the basic elements of initiations and rites of passage. The absence of these traditional supports creates problems in the lives of those who are caught in the void and lack definite expectations at various times of their lives.

*"Rites of initiation are indispensable if men and women are to have a sense of direction and achieve individuation within the community. The many aimless and isolated individuals in society witness to a loss of the sense of initiation. The surprising range of insightful articles in **Betwixt & Between** will help restore the discussion and practice of initiation and rites of passage for our times."*

ABBOT DAVID GERAETS
Benedictine Monastery, Pecos, New Mexico

*"Can a book sound an alarm that the failures of initiation are eating away the fabric of our existence? Can a book shake one from the lassitude of plenty, force one to see the accelerating failure of our culture? If any book can do this, it is **Betwixt & Between**. I ask you to read it. There is an initiatory experience for everyone somewhere in this book. **Betwixt & Between** is itself an entrance, and is food for the initiatory hunger of our time."*

RUSSELL LOCKHART
Jungian Analyst, Author of *The Word as Egg*

"a much-needed book . . . has a huge amount of valuable material to offer all kinds of helping professionals—those working with adolescents, families of the terminally ill, leaders of men's and women's groups, vision quest organizers, ministers, and family counselors of all persuasions."

ROGER WOOLGER
Author of *Goddess Within*

"A watershed book . . . an interdisciplinary array of essays highlights both the need for, and importance of, rights of passage to mark important transitions in our lives.'

THRESHOLDS

ISBN   0-8126-9048-6 (Paper)   ISBN   0-8126-9047-8 (Cloth)

TO ORDER, CALL 1-800-815-2280

Printed in the United States
720700002B